Management for Professionals

More information about this series at http://www.springernature.com/series/10101

Joseph Joy

Divestitures and Spin-Offs

Lessons Learned in the Trenches
of the World's Largest M&A Deals

 Springer

Joseph Joy
Deloitte Consulting LLP
San Jose, CA, USA

ISSN 2192-8096   ISSN 2192-810X   (electronic)
Management for Professionals
ISBN 978-1-4939-7661-4   ISBN 978-1-4939-7662-1   (eBook)
https://doi.org/10.1007/978-1-4939-7662-1

Library of Congress Control Number: 2017964262

Printed on acid-free paper

This Springer imprint is published by Springer Nature
The registered company is Springer Science+Business Media, LLC
The registered company address is: 233 Spring Street, New York, NY 10013, U.S.A.

This book is dedicated to my mother,
Annamma Joy, my constant pillar of support.

Acknowledgment

The world of M&A has always been complex and nuanced, and our clients have brought the toughest business problems to the table.

Divestiture and Spin-Offs: Lessons Learned in the Trenches of the World's Largest M&A Deals is a tribute to our clients who have trusted our brand to be part of their M&A journey and the lessons learned along the way of doing most complex M&A projects with them.

Being in the consulting business, we are accustomed to wearing an advisory hat. We advise our clients on the best practices—blended with our tried and tested methodologies. M&A is a different beast altogether. Separation and integration projects demand working in close coordination bringing clients and consultants together. The two-in-a-box model ensures that we are together as one team and is a true testament to the ingrained nature required for seamless execution.

This book is dedicated to some of the most amazing business leaders we've had the fortune to serve. It is a walk down memory lane with some of these tenacious, decisive business leaders we have worked with to help make those tough decisions and take command and control when required all while recognizing their people and trusting their teams. These leaders brought structure and calmness dealing with difficult situations, made personal sacrifices for getting the deal done, and did the right things even when no one noticed.

My immense gratitude goes to the following for the crazy ride (in no particular order): Christopher Paul Hsu, Scott Spradley, Swavek Bialkiewicz, Mike Dallas, Jim Murrin, Franklin Grosvenor, Sergio Letelier, Shane Wailes, Jonathan Faust, Michael Linford, Joseph Schulz, Adam Vazquez, Lalit Singh, Lisa Hicks, and Paul Raddon.

I would like to specially call out Christopher Paul Hsu for his leadership and guidance and for being the inspiration behind this book. I would like to thank my mentors – Ashish Goel, Matt Law, Edward Carey, Sam Balaji, Mark Walsh for their continued guidance over the years. I want to sincerely thank my leadership at Deloitte – Jeffery Weirens, Sandy Shirai, Trevear Thomas, Russell Thomson, Dave Couture and Anthony Stephan – for their support in this endeavor.

This book would not have been possible without their support, friendship, and collaborative effort throughout our careers in the M&A journey. This book is dedicated to all of our clients, for truly always being in the deepest of deep trenches with us.

Given the rapidly changing merger, acquisition, and divestiture environment, it was critical for the content in this book to be as timely and relevant as possible and also to represent the collective 200 plus years of experience. It would be nearly impossible to complete this work without support from below contributors who have played a critical role in compiling their years of experience (contributors in alphabetical order of the names):

- *Abhimanyu Basu, Consultant, Deloitte Consulting LLP;* Chapter 25, "Command Center: Setting Up Round-the-Clock Monitoring During Cutover"
- *Abhishek Mathur, Senior Manager, Deloitte Consulting LLP;* Chapter 27, "Transform as You Separate"
- *Abhishek Shanker, Manager, Deloitte Consulting LLP;* Chapter 27, "Transform as You Separate"
- *Ambar Patil, Senior Consultant, Deloitte Consulting LLP;* Chapter 20, "Managing the Application Separation Life Cycle"
- *Ankit Shanker, Specialist Master, Deloitte Consulting LLP;* Chapter 28, "Managing Data Separation and Migration During a Divestiture", Case Study 28
- *Asish Ramchandran, Principal, Deloitte Consulting LLP;* Chapter 35, "Separation Management Office: Leading Practices", Case Study 35
- *Barry Chen, Senior Manager, Deloitte Consulting LLP;* Case Study 15, Case Study 33
- *Bob Harman, Senior Manager, Deloitte Consulting LLP;* Case Study 24, Case Study 25
- *Brandon Bonzheim, Tax Senior Manager, Deloitte Tax LLP;* Chapter 17, "Legal and Tax Aspects of Divestitures"
- *Brian Pinto, Tax Partner, Deloitte Tax LLP;* Chapter 17, "Legal and Tax Aspects of Divestitures", Case Study 17
- *Carina Ruiz, Advisory Partner, Deloitte & Touche LLP*; Chapter 16, "Managing Banking and Treasury Implications During Divestiture", Case Study 16
- *Charlie Catino, Consultant, Deloitte Consulting LLP;* Chapter 19, "Managing Customer and Partner Transitions During a Separation"
- *David Andrew Oberst, Advisory Senior Manager, Deloitte Consulting LLP*; Chapter 8, "Clean Financial Separation", Case Study 7, Case Study 8
- *Don Miller, Consulting Managing Director, Deloitte Consulting LLP*; Chapter 13, "Managing the People Side of Divestiture: Retention and Motivation", Chapter 14, "Shaking Things Up: Reorganizing", Case Study 13, Case Study 14
- *Doug Mesthos, Manager, Deloitte Consulting LLP*; Chapter 9, "Building the Arsenal: Setting Up an Effective Separation Team and Governance"
- *Edward Carey, Management Principal, Deloitte Consulting LLP*; Case Study 27
- *Garima Dhasmana, Senior Manager, Deloitte Consulting LLP*; Case Study 12
- *Gaurav Dharmadhikari, Senior Manager, Deloitte Consulting LLP*; Chapter 15, "Legal Entity Operating Structure"

- *Gaurav Pandey, Senior Consultant, Deloitte Consulting LLP*; Chapter 32, "Expediting TSA Exits to Enable Strategic Transformation", Case Study 32
- *Miguel Angel Gomez Cuentas, Manager, Deloitte Consulting LLP*; Appendix A: Divestiture Playbook Overview
- *Habeeb Dihu, Principal, Deloitte Consulting LLP; Case Study 23*
- *Heiko Dorenwendt, Principal, Deloitte Consulting LLP*; Chapter 13, "Managing the People Side of Divestiture: Retention and Motivation", Case Study 13
- *Isha Tyagi, Consultant, Deloitte Consulting LLP*; Chapter 2, "Taming the Elephant: Introduction to Divestitures"
- *Ishan Bansal, Manager, Deloitte Consulting LLP*; Chapter 10, "Working Under the Tent: Confidentiality and Restricted Information Disclosure"
- *Jasneet Kanwar, Senior Consultant, Deloitte Consulting LLP*; Chapter 25, "Command Center: Setting Up Round-the-Clock Monitoring During Cutover"
- *Jayson Gasper, Manager, Deloitte Consulting LLP*; Case Study 24, Case Study 25
- *Jeffery Weirens, Principal, Deloitte Consulting LLP*; Chapter 9, "Building the Arsenal: Setting Up an Effective Separation Team and Governance"
- *Jeffry Sprengel, Specialist Leader, Deloitte Consulting LLP*; Chapter 21, "Simplifying IT Infrastructure Separation", Case Study 21
- *Jon Bowes, Partner, Deloitte Canada*; Case Study 30
- *Judith Onugu, Manager, Deloitte Consulting LLP*; Chapter 15, "Legal Entity Operating Structure"
- *Justyna Charytoniuk, Manager, Deloitte Consulting LLP*; Chapter 15, "Legal Entity Operating Structure"
- *Kapil Dixit, Advisory Senior Manager, Deloitte & Touche LLP*; Chapter 16, "Managing Banking and Treasury Implications During Divestiture"
- *Karima Jivani, Manager, Deloitte Consulting LLP*; Chapter 22, "Managing IT in Divestiture: Orchestration, Instrumentation, and Measurement", Case Study 22
- *Karina Rivera, Manager, Deloitte Consulting LLP*; Chapter 23, "Testing: Making the IT Separation Foolproof", Appendix A: Divestiture Playbook Overview
- *Kaushik Ramasubramaniam, Senior Manager, Deloitte Consulting LLP*; Case Study 27
- *Kavya Gollavilli, Senior Consultant, Deloitte Consulting LLP*; Chapter 6, "Slicing the Pie: Asset Allocation in Divestiture", Chapter 11, "Getting Ready for Announcement: Kickoff Planning", Case Study 6
- *Kenny Macdonald, Principal, Deloitte Consulting LLP*; Chapter 14, "Shaking Things Up: Reorganizing", Case Study 14
- *Kevin Laughridge, Principal, Deloitte Consulting LLP*; Case Study 12
- *Kristin Viger, Senior Manager, Deloitte Consulting LLP*; Chapter 13, "Managing the People Side of Divestiture: Retention and Motivation", Chapter 14, "Shaking Things Up: Reorganizing", Case Study 13, Case Study 14
- *Kunal Gupta, Manager, Deloitte Consulting LLP*; Chapter 18, "Accelerating Divestitures Through Minimal Rebranding"
- *Latngenhun Nongsiej, Senior Consultant, Deloitte Consulting LLP*; Chapter 24, "Cutover: Getting Ready for the Launch"

- *Manav Dange, Senior Manager, Deloitte Consulting LLP*; Case Study 11
- *Manish Laad, Consulting Managing Director, Deloitte Consulting LLP*; Chapter 10, "Working Under the Tent: Confidentiality and Restrained Information Disclosure", Chapter 11, "Getting Ready for Announcement: Kickoff Planning", Chapter 21, "Simplifying IT Infrastructure Separation", Chapter 26, "Protecting the Organization During Vulnerable Times", Case Study 10, Case Study 26
- *Manu Ishino, Consultant, Deloitte Consulting LLP*; Case Study 24, Case Study 25
- *Maulik Mehta, Manager, Deloitte Consulting LLP;* Chapter 4, "Upping the Ante: Enhancing Deal Value", Case Study 4
- *Mayank Gupta, Senior Manager, Deloitte Consulting LLP*; Chapter 23, "Testing: Making the IT Separation Foolproof", Chapter 30, "Transition Services Agreements (TSAs): Approach to De-risk Divestitures", Case Study 23
- *Michael Dziczkowski, Advisory Partner, Deloitte Consulting LLP*; Chapter 8, "Clean Financial Separation"
- *Michael von Rueden, Partner, Deloitte Germany*; Chapter 17, "Legal and Tax Aspects of Divestitures"
- *Monalisa Saha, Manager, Deloitte Consulting LLP*; Chapter 25, "Command Center: Setting Up Round-the-Clock Monitoring During Cutover"
- *Mushtaque Heera, Consulting Managing Director, Deloitte Consulting LLP*; Chapter 12, "Building the Execution Roadmap", Chapter 20, "Managing the Application Separation Lifecycle", Chapter 22, "Managing IT in Divestiture: Orchestration, Instrumentation, and Measurement", Chapter 29, "Real Estate and Site Separation", Case Study 20, Case Study 22, Case Study 29
- *Navneeth Srinivasan, Senior Consultant, Deloitte Consulting LLP*; Chapter 34, "Cost Reduction Through Outsourcing"
- *Nikhil Menon, Senior Manager, Deloitte Consulting LLP*; Chapter 4, "Upping the Ante: Enhancing Deal Value", Chapter 6, "Slicing the Pie: Asset Allocation in Divestiture", Chapter 18, "Accelerating Divestitures Through Minimal Rebranding", Chapter 33, "Managing Separation Costs, Stranded Costs, and Dis-synergies", Chapter 34, "Cost Reduction Through Outsourcing", Case Study 4, Case Study 6, Case Study 18, Case Study 34
- *Ninad Deshmukh, Manager, Deloitte Consulting LLP*; Chapter 31, "Contract Separation: Early Identification and Negotiations", Chapter 33, "Managing Separation Costs, Stranded Costs, and Dis-synergies", Chapter 34, "Cost Reduction Through Outsourcing", Case Study 34
- *Olivier May, Principal, Deloitte Consulting LLP*; Case Study 15, Case Study 33
- *Premal Parikh, Manager, Deloitte Consulting LLP*; Chapter 23, "Testing: Making the IT Separation Foolproof"
- *Rachael Chan, Consultant, Deloitte Consulting LLP*; Chapter 31, "Contract Separation: Early Identification and Negotiations"
- *Raed Masoud, Senior Manager, Deloitte Consulting LLP*; Chapter 7, "Financial Aspects of Carve-Out"
- *Rajesh Gupta, Manager, Deloitte Consulting LLP*; Chapter 32, "Expediting TSA Exits to Enable Strategic Transformation", Case Study 32

- *Rick Aviles, Senior Manager, Deloitte Consulting LLP*; Chapter 30, "Transition Services Agreements (TSAs): Approach to De-risk Divestitures"
- *Rochak Sethi, Senior Manager, Deloitte Consulting LLP*; Chapter 28, "Managing Data Separation and Migration During a Divestiture", Case Study 28
- *Rocio Melendez Bardales, Manager, Deloitte Consulting LLP*; Chapter 21, "Simplifying IT Infrastructure Separation"
- *Ryan Gordon, Senior Manager, Deloitte Consulting LLP*; Case Study 11, Case Study 12
- *Ryan Stecz, Tax Partner, Deloitte Tax LLP*; Chapter 8, "Clean Financial Separation", Chapter 17, "Legal and Tax Aspects of Divestitures"
- *Sameer Deshpande, Consultant, Deloitte Consulting LLP*; Chapter 10, "Working Under the Tent: Confidentiality and Restricted Information Disclosure"
- *Samir Singh, Senior Manager, Deloitte Consulting LLP*; Chapter 20, "Managing the Application Separation Life Cycle", Chapter 24, "Cutover: Getting Ready for the Launch", Chapter 25, "Command Center: Setting Up Round-the-Clock Monitoring During Cutover", Case Study 20
- *Sandeep Dasharath, Senior Manager, Deloitte Consulting LLP*; Chapter 21, "Simplifying IT Infrastructure Separation"
- *Sandy Shirai, Principal and US TMT Leader, Deloitte Consulting LLP*; Chapter 2, "Taming the Elephant: Introduction to Divestitures"
- *Sanjay Bhatnagar, Manager, Deloitte Consulting LLP;* Chapter 29, "Real Estate and Site Separation", Case Study 29
- *Saumya Lal, Senior Consultant, Deloitte Consulting LLP*; Chapter 24, "Cutover: Getting Ready for the Launch"
- *Saurabh Malhotra, Manager, Deloitte Consulting LLP*; Chapter 12, "Building the Execution Roadmap"
- *Sean Gross, Manager, Deloitte Consulting LLP; Case Study 11*
- *Sejal Gala, Principal, Deloitte Consulting LLP; Case Study 11*
- *Shalini Bhatia, Principal, Deloitte Consulting LLP;* Chapter 9, "Building the Arsenal: Setting Up an Effective Separation Team and Governance", Chapter 19, "Managing Customer and Partner Transitions During a Separation", Chapter 35, "Separation Management Office: Leading Practices", Case Study 19
- *Shweta Gupta, Manager, Deloitte Consulting LLP*; Chapter 35, "Separation Management Office: Leading Practices"
- *Simon Singh, Principal, Deloitte Consulting LLP;* Chapter 1, "Preface", Chapter 2, "Taming the Elephant: Introduction to Divestitures", Chapter 3, "Being a 'Prepared Seller' and Identifying the 'Right Buyer,'" Chapter 5, "Defining the Deal Timeline: Balancing Legal, HR, IT, and Finance"
- *Sreekanth Gopinathan, Senior Manager, Deloitte Consulting LLPI;* Chapter 31, "Contract Separation: Early Identification and Negotiations", Chapter 32, "Expediting TSA Exits to Enable Strategic Transformation", Chapter 33, "Managing Separation Costs, Stranded Costs, and Dis-synergies", Case Study 31, Case Study 32
- *Srivats Srinivasan, Principal, Deloitte Consulting LLP;* Chapter 27, "Transform as You Separate"

- *Stephen Michael Michalak, Tax Senior Manager, Deloitte Tax LLP;* Chapter 17, "Legal and Tax Aspects of Divestitures", Case Study 8
- *Subodh Kolla, Manager, Deloitte Consulting LLP*; Case Study 24, Case Study 25
- *Tim Altman, Manager, Deloitte Consulting LLP;* Chapter 15, "Legal Entity Operating Structure"
- *Titikshu Atoliya, Senior Consultant, Deloitte Consulting LLP;* Chapter 27, "Transform as You Separate"
- *Trevear Thomas, Principal, Deloitte Consulting LLP;* Chapter 7, "Financial Aspects of Carve-Out", Chapter 15, "Legal Entity Operating Structure"
- *Umang Handa, Senior Manager, Deloitte Canada;* Chapter 26, "Protecting the Organization During Vulnerable Times", Case Study 26
- *Utsav Dixit, Consultant, Deloitte Consulting LLP;* Chapter 20, "Managing the Application Separation Life Cycle"
- *Varun Joshi, Principal, Deloitte Consulting LLP;* Chapter 30, "Transition Services Agreements (TSAs): Approach to De-risk Divestitures"
- *Venkat Swaminathan, Consulting Managing Director, Deloitte Consulting LLP;* Chapter 9, "Building the Arsenal: Setting Up an Effective Separation Team and Governance", Chapter 19, "Managing Customer and Partner Transitions During a Separation", Chapter 35, "Separation Management Office: Leading Practices", Case Study 9, Case Study 19, Case Study 35
- *Vikram Latawa, Consulting Managing Director, Deloitte Consulting LLP;* Chapter 24, "Cutover: Getting Ready for the Launch", Appendix A: Divestiture Playbook Overview
- *Will Enright, Advisory Senior Manager, Deloitte & Touche LLP;* Chapter 16, "Managing Banking and Treasury Implications During Divestiture"
- *Zohaib Mahmood, Senior Consultant, Deloitte Consulting LLP;* Chapter 18, "Accelerating Divestitures Through Minimal Rebranding", Chapter 30, "Transition Services Agreements (TSAs): Approach to De-risk Divestitures"

Also, a big shout-out to the core team members without whom this book would not have seen the light of day. Thank you for your commitment and for burning the midnight oil to keep track of the content, for staying on top of things, and for spending untold hours reviewing and editing the book:

- Sreekanth Gopinathan, Anurag Bahal, Simon Singh, Gaurav Pandey, Kunal Gupta, Nikhil Wasnik, Abhimanyu Basu, and Vivekanand Saripalli for being "The Team" behind the book

A very special thanks to extended team for their continuous support:

- Tony Scoles, Deloitte Consulting LLP, who provided the legal guidance
- Lisa Iliff and Eric Zwygart, Deloitte Consulting LLP, who performed content review from quality and risk perspective
- Lisa Perez, Deloitte Consulting LLP, who performed detailed copy editing for content

I am also indebted to the amazing folks at Springer Science + Business Media LLC, including:

- Matthew Amboy, publishing editor
- Nicholas Philipson, editorial director
- William Curtis, president and managing director

Their ability to form the vision and guide the writing and editing of this book was beyond compare.

Contents

About the Author

Joseph Joy is a Deloitte Principal with more than 24 years of consulting experience and is a leader of Deloitte's Technology M&A practice. He has worked on more than 150 M&A deals and has extensive M&A due diligence, divestiture, integration, carve-out, and restructuring experience. He has led multiple large-scale, multibillion-dollar separation deals for several global clients, including some of the largest and most complex transactions.

He demonstrates strong skills in leadership and management with focus on risk analysis, quality control, framework development, methodologies, governance, and cost reduction. He is a thought leader in digital transformation and is passionate about helping clients create business value and undertake transformation journey.

Apart from client work, he has contributed to a multitude of M&A-related eminence activities including Wall Street Journal, and his work has also been published in leading books in the market.

Part I
Introduction

Chapter 1
Preface

1.1 What Is a Divestiture in M&A Realm?

While mergers and acquisitions (M&A) is a general term that refers to the consolidation of companies or assets, it also encompasses divestitures, which most commonly result from a management decision to cease operating a business unit because it is not part of a core competency. A divestiture, in its simplest form, is the disposition or sale of an asset by a company. Divestitures are a way for a company to manage its portfolio of assets. As companies grow, they may find that they are trying to focus on too many lines of business, and they must close some units to focus on more profitable lines.

Divestitures and acquisitions are similar in that they are often different sides of the same transaction, and they are both strategies that companies use to maximize shareholder value.

The act of selling a part of a business, whether you call it a spin-off, a demerger, or a divestiture, is fundamentally different from—but not quite opposite of—acquiring or merging with another business. The main difference is obviously that a business is being sold from the seller's perspective. Both acquisitions and divestitures are complex procedures, and companies often underestimate the capabilities that are required for a transformative business change of such magnitude.

Divestitures and separations have gained prominence, especially since the global recession of 2008, due to their ability to create value for both the buyer and seller companies. Yet, there is no single book on the market that covers the entire functional life cycle of executing a divestiture transaction.

In this book we will explain the divestiture related leading practices and pitfalls in detail. The key challenge in any divestiture is the ability to successfully execute across multiple dimensions within a compressed timeframe while maintaining business as usual.

Each chapter in this book can stand on its own as a resource on the topic it presents, but combined, these chapters offer an in-depth look into the various elements

© Deloitte Development LLC 2018
J. Joy, *Divestitures and Spin-Offs*, Management for Professionals,
https://doi.org/10.1007/978-1-4939-7662-1_1

needed to complete a successful transaction. All the critical phases of the divestiture process from initial due diligence to deal closure are covered in these chapters. The book also addresses key aspects of divestiture and separations by providing real-life examples and references, including key issues, risks, and possible mitigations.

1.2 What Makes Divestitures Important?

Divestment is driving positive corporate change by selling—rather than buying—assets, lines of business, or subsidiaries. The principle is simple: by staying laser focused on the core products or services driving the highest yield, and shedding assets that are less profitable or loss leaders, you can maximize performance.

Divesting or carving out a percentage of your organization's assets can accomplish a variety of goals—raise needed capital, increase management focus, realize untapped value, reduce debt, and position the business for a transformative change. Divestitures are beneficial for companies because they allow them to sell their noncore operations and improve business focus. Divestitures provide companies with funds, allow them to enhance stability, eliminate weak divisions, and realize value through transformations.

Companies often sell a division or business unit that does not constitute its core operations. By doing so, the company is able to shed noncore operations and focus on what it does best, since a multitude of businesses may prove to be a substantial distraction to the company's management.

Companies often divest their business units because these divisions do not perform according to management's expectations. Companies dispose of units through a sale to a third party or a closure and eliminate the need to further invest in these divisions.

A company may engage in divestiture because its breakup value is thought to be greater than that of a single company. For instance, a manufacturing company may possess a lot of real estate it does not utilize, and the company breaks into two companies, where one part focuses on manufacturing, while the other turns into a real estate investment trust. By doing so, the parent company can unlock value from its real estate holdings.

In order to add value, companies need to prepare for a divestiture and develop a strategy for continually evaluating those parts of the business that would make good acquisition targets. A divestiture has many moving parts to manage and organizational effects that need to be considered, analyzed, and weighed before you get to closing. A divestiture or carve-out is a complex transaction that typically takes months to complete once you have an interested party.

Planned divestitures may lead to creation of corporate value. However companies often divest in reaction to pressure from sustained losses, intolerable debt burden, analyst downgrades, or other market-driven forces that usually signal weakness and even failures.

For prepared sellers, divestitures may be an effective alternative to mergers and acquisitions for increasing capital, streamlining operations, and focusing an organization's efforts. By separation, both the parent company and the divested entity can add value and improve performance.

1.3   Typical Reasons that Companies Choose to Divest

- A business unit that is no longer in line with the seller company's main line of business. Companies may divest businesses that are not part of their core operations so that they can focus on their primary lines of business. Doing so can likely generate more value because cost of operations can be lowered and returns on core businesses can be increased.
- Capital gained from the sale that the seller company needs in order to purchase another entity that is more in line with its future business plans or to expand its operations in a new geography or invest in a new line of business.
- Companies engage in divestitures to eliminate subsidiaries or divisions that are underperforming and to comply with regulatory/antitrust requirements.
- Companies often divest to improve their bottom-line stability so that after divestiture, there is more predictability of earnings and their growth.
- A firm often breaks up into two or more companies to unlock value believed to be greater for separate entities than that of a consolidated company. This usually happens due to a combination of several factors that we will explore in greater detail.
- An impending bankruptcy of the seller company so the seller needs to sell anything that is not essential to the business in an attempt to stay afloat.
- A divestiture may provide an opportunity of keeping capabilities away from particularly strong competitors (which might mean turning down a deal that is favorable in other respects).

1.4   Key Terms and Players in a Divestiture

- RemainCo—RemainCo is the legal entity that remains after the divested entity is separated from the parent company.
- SellCo—SellCo (or the parent company) is the legal entity that is aggregate of the RemainCo and the divested business unit.
- Divested entity—Divested entity typically is the business unit that is up for sale or carve-out.
- Buy company—Buyer company typically is the legal entity that is purchasing the divested entity.
- Carve-out—The physical separation of the new company's infrastructure, applications, and data from the divesting company.

- Day 1—The day after the closing: the new company is the owner of the assets and operates independently. All interaction between the new company and RemainCo should be at arm's length and is considered business to business from this point forward.
- Divestiture—Legal transfer of ownership of assets to the new company at closing.
- Standup—The final separation of the divested business so that it operates independently and without parent company's support or transition services.
- Entanglement—The interdependencies between the RemainCo and the divested entities that make the divestiture intricate like provision of a shared HR service.

1.5   How to Ace Divestitures?

A divestiture is valuable if the planned outcomes for the divestitures are achieved in time. In our experience, successful divestures are characterized by:

- Divestitures that offer sellers an opportunity to focus on their core competence and that offer buyers an opportunity to gain from acquiring new capabilities through buying of the assets
- Alignment of the transaction's strategic and financial aspects of the deal upfront with an operational blueprint
- Execution of a familiar M&A process that engages key stakeholders at the right time and drives both accountability and "checks and balances"
- A financial competency to support divestiture execution, as well as robust financial synergy and cost tracking and monitoring
- Divestiture transactions that are executed with:

  - Speed to keep separation costs to a minimum
  - Rigor to help ensure a clean separation
  - Agility to quickly respond to the dynamics at play

In this book we will discuss practical approaches to help achieve the above outcomes, as well as illustrate these approaches with real-life examples.

1.6   What to Expect in This Book?

The book is a real-world guide for addressing the various complexities of divestitures and separations. It begins by providing a framework for divestiture deal planning, then delves deep into executing the divestiture, and then further into transforming the remaining company for sustainable value realization.

1.6.1 Planning for the Deal

A clear strategic vision for the deal is imperative, regardless of whether a company is looking to do just one transaction or multiple transactions at the same time.

- The due diligence process to identify the ideal buyer for a business unit
- Balancing timelines across different critical business functions like Tax, HR, IT, etc.

A team that recognizes the importance of good leadership and governance structure during the divestiture is essential to ensuring a successful deal. The first step is to set up a separation management office (SMO) that works under total confidentiality and secrecy before the deal announcement and expands into a more comprehensive team as required. Along with planning for the deal announcement, the SMO also takes responsibility for devising a strategy for post-announcement divestiture execution, as this is a decisive period for the deal. Planning for the deal must be comprehensive, including forecasting the budget and procuring the resources needed for execution.

1.6.2 Executing the Deal

Despite companies devising well-planned strategies and retaining able leadership, most divestitures encounter execution related hurdles due to the intrinsically complex challenges that materialize during the execution of the separation, many of which may not be apparent when formulating the separation strategy. In a 2016 Deloitte survey, titled "M&A Trends: Year-end report 2016," 84% of respondents said that at least some of their 2015 and 2016 deals did not generate the expected value or return on investment. With such a high rate of failure, execution becomes a deal breaker when deciding on a divestiture strategy.

Under executing the deal chapters, the author provides insights into the Day 1 implications for various functions, as well as the key components of execution. The book dives deep into key aspects of execution strategy and defines the tactical actions that are essential to execute a separation. These include functional aspects of separation such as human resources (HR), information technology (IT), finance, supply chain, tax, real estate, and legal. It goes into detail on topics, such as separating core infrastructure, applications, and cybersecurity. It also covers how to separate contracts with vendors and discusses transition service agreements (TSAs). Additionally, it explains often overlooked parallel activities that can be completed along with the separation, such as simplifying the future state, clean sheeting, and transforming the seller company. These parallel activities are essential to maximizing the value of the divestiture, as well as preparing for a clean separation post-Day 1.

The author also touches upon other important areas of a divestiture, such as vendor agreements, intellectual property issues, and real estate separation.

The separation of IT infrastructure is critical as it builds the core foundation for the separation of all other elements of the divested entity, and it should be complemented by a sound cybersecurity strategy to protect the company from any vulnerabilities arising out of the separation. This section takes a warlike approach to addressing this area—focusing on orchestration, instrumentation, and progress measurement. The author also discusses the agile and waterfall approaches to building, testing, and executing the separation of IT applications. Execution planning is done using a sequence of constant iterative improvements until an exact sequence is developed that can be followed to achieve an effective Day 1.

Finally, special emphasis is given to the cutover, which is the culmination of all the efforts that go into the separation. From their experiences in executing the most complex cutovers, the author defines a systematic approach to mitigate risks, including proper blackout planning and a command center approach to orchestrate effective execution.

Implementing TSAs and separating vendor and customer contracts are also critical activities that require significant effort and due diligence to help ensure limited post-separation liabilities.

1.6.3 Focusing on the Seller Company

A divestiture is not an end unto itself but rather a means to transform the seller company into a more agile, nimble, and efficient entity. To achieve this end, it is imperative for the seller company to visualize its future state and use that vision to dictate the unfolding of the divestiture process. Expediting TSAs can present a particular challenge, as the transformation process needs to be wary of multiple companies running on the same systems.

This section gives unique insight into cost-reduction techniques and new operating models for the seller company. Special emphasis is placed on the flexibilities and constraints chief information officers (CIOs) face in devising strategies to shape the future of the seller company.

Post-divestiture, the seller company is often in a state where it can implement a clean sheeting approach to transformation. The seller company's go-to-market strategy and operating model can be built from the ground up to align more directly with market dynamics. Clean sheeting is an effective approach to translate these refined business objectives into technology implementation strategies that help ensure a fast transition to end state(s).

1.7 Rest of the Book

To help the company maximize the return on a sale, while continuing to operate to its full potential, a strategic and well-executed divestment program is crucial. Transparency into data, business and IT assets, operational practices, and business processes—before, during, and after divestitures—empowers companies to be transparent about their own state of affairs as well as the end state they have in mind after the divestitures.

Whether a company is facing its first M&A transaction or it has executed several separations/combinations, our belief is that this book will enable its readers to mature their capabilities and realize incremental value from new divestitures. It contains the synthesis of experiences across a wide array of clients ranging in revenue from $500 million to more than $120 billion. The leading practices discussed in this book can help companies realize a valuable divestiture in the short run, as well as help them establish sustainable market-winning capabilities in the years to follow.

Chapter 2
Taming the Elephant: Introduction to Divestitures

A divestiture is the disposition or sale of an asset by a company, and it usually occurs when a business unit is somehow more valuable as a separate entity. A separation is when a large entity breaks up into two or more entities.

The decision to undergo a divestiture or separation is followed by the mammoth task of formulating and implementing the strategy to complete the transaction—a task as difficult as taming an elephant.

When a major deal announcement is covered widely in the news media, it generates interest beyond that of the immediate stakeholders. The challenge in a large divestiture comes primarily from the scale and complexity of assets that need to be separated. The involvement of third parties, such as partners, vendors, contractors, and suppliers, adds to this complexity. Teams need to discuss the most effective strategy to meet the transaction's tight deadlines, which often requires prioritizing speed of execution over everything else. The newly divested or separated entity must be stood up as a separate entity from the parent company on Day 1.

© Deloitte Development LLC 2018   11
J. Joy, *Divestitures and Spin-Offs*, Management for Professionals,
https://doi.org/10.1007/978-1-4939-7662-1_2

What makes taming the elephant difficult? Planning and executing a divestiture are difficult due to the complexity that arises from the fact that most organizations have shared services model where the support functions are shared across business units. To carve out a business and make it operational within stringent timelines become a daunting task. The complexity varies depending on the type of buyer:

- Financial buyer (e.g., private equities): The aim of financial buyer is to create stand-alone operational entity by Day 1.
- Strategic buyer (e.g., companies): The aim of strategic buyer is to eventually fully integrate the carved-out entity but in the interim accomplish Day 1 by logical separation.

As IT is central to all the shared services, IT function becomes the most complex function to separate in any given separation.

In this chapter we will be discussing in detail the objectives and the challenges related to a divestiture and separation. Further in following chapters, we discuss the strategy, tactics, and best practices to plan and execute a divestiture or separation.

2.1 Why Divest or Separate?

Companies undertake divestitures for a variety of reasons:

- *Refocus on core competency:* A company needs to be competitive in its main service or product offering. Refocusing on a core competency in light of competition is one of the biggest reasons for a divestiture or separation.
- *Raise capital:* Divesting a business unit generates capital that a company may use in areas where it can achieve higher returns.
- *Unlock value:* A business unit that may not be valuable at one company may perform much better under the umbrella of another company whose core competency aligns with that of the business unit targeted for divestiture.

> *A large enterprise hardware manufacturer divested its software businesses in 2017 because it wanted to focus on its core competency of enterprise hardware products. A divestiture seemed to be in the best interest of the company, and it would allow the to-be-divested business unit to find a new home at a company that specializes in software. The divestiture was mutually valuable to both the selling company and the buying company, and the deal went through with mutually agreeable terms.*

- *Meet antitrust requirements:* Due to antitrust laws, government regulators may require a company that operates in an industry without a lot of competition to divest or separate itself from a business unit in order to proceed with an M&A transaction that would further limit competition in the industry. The selling company must decide whether it is in the best interest of the company to divest or separate from the business unit or forgo the M&A transaction.

The ultimate goal of a divestiture or separation is to rebalance the parent company's business portfolio to enable the parent company for growth or reduce exposure to risks. Though it sounds straightforward, this task is an iterative, complicated, and critical activity. This task done efficiently sets us on the successful path of taming this elephant.

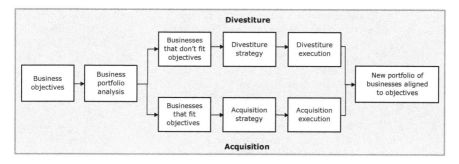

Fig. 2.1 Divestiture Rationale

2.2   Forms of Divestiture and Separation

Divestiture broadly encompasses those transactions which involves a buyer, whereas separation is a transaction which requires splitting of the business into two separate free-standing entities.

While nearly all divestitures and separations are driven by the need to maximize the returns on the investments made, they can take several forms, each with its own processing and timing implications and each with its own key challenges to tame:

Table 2.1 Forms of Divestitures

Type	Key characteristics	Challenges
Sell-off	• Divesting a division, unit, or asset to a buyer as a free-standing entity • Most common form of divestiture Example: Procter & Gamble's sale of Pringles to diamond foods[a]	• Splitting of shared overhead costs, common brands, and patents • Disentangling asset ownership • Change management
Spin-off	• Divesting a part of operations by replacing existing shares with classes of shares representing the new, independent operations Example: Breakup of AT&T[b]	• Ensuring the divested entity can function as a free-standing entity
Spin-merge	• A spin-off followed by a merger of the divested business with the buyer company Example: Formation of DXC technology from computer sciences corporation and enterprise services division of Hewlett Packard enterprise[c]	• Separating a business unit and merging it with a the buyer company • Understanding the buyer company's IT strategy
Asset trades	• Divesting via the bartering of similar assets, typically between companies in the same industry • Can occur as a result of antitrust laws Example: Swapping of coverage rights for different localities by TV broadcasting companies	• Separating a business unit while integrating bartered assets
Management buyout	• Divesting via ownership transfer to a buyer company whose management comprises all or part of the parent company's management • Typically involves entire company Example: Virgin megastores[d] (UK)	• Change management
Total liquidation	• Divesting all company assets for cash, typically by court order • Usually linked to a bankruptcy Example: Blockbuster video[e]	• Change management

[a]https://www.wsj.com/articles/SB10001424052748703806304576244460367967334
[b]http://www.investopedia.com/ask/answers/09/att-breakup-spinoff.asp
[c]https://www.forbes.com/sites/joecornell/2017/04/04/hewlett-packard-enterprise-completes-spin-merger-to-form-dxc-technology/#143639977058
[d]https://www.theguardian.com/business/2007/sep/18/media.retail
[e]http://www.ibtimes.com/sad-end-blockbuster-video-onetime-5-billion-company-being-liquidated-competition-1496962

2.3 Challenges in a Divestiture or Separation

A major deal announcement is covered widely in the news media and generates interest beyond that of the immediate stakeholders. However, the success of the deal depends on the execution strategy. It must be built up in a time-boxed manner which adds complexity to the already wild elephant. Key considerations are:

• *Scale and complexity:* The challenge in a large divestiture primarily comes from the scale and complexity of assets that need to be separated. The involvement of third parties, such as contractors and suppliers, adds to this complexity. The third parties must be on boarded to the divestiture project, and contracts for their services must be negotiated, before their services are rendered.

- *Speed of execution:* The divestiture team must discuss the most effective solution to meet the transaction's tight deadlines, which often requires prioritizing speed of execution over everything else. There is no opportunity to miss the Day 1 deadline when the divested unit needs to legally stand as a separate entity from the parent company.
- *Governance and resourcing related issues:* A company is in flux post-announcement and employees across different functions and business units need to work toward a common goal. A resource plan must be developed to identify and onboard functional team members for the divestiture process. Setting up a Divestiture Management Office (DMO)/ Separation Management Office (SMO) with effective leaders from across the company functions is a big challenge. Along with the DMO/SMO, a strong governance structure must be put in place to keep track of all the moving parts in a complex deal.
- *Business-as-usual activities:* During a divestiture or separation, the parent company must be able to continue with business-as-usual activities to serve its customers, despite any internal disruptions. The leadership team should discuss the intricacies of the cutover plan to ensure there is a minimal impact on the parent company's revenue goals.
- *Country planning:* Each country has rules and regulations that companies must follow, and the divestiture must be planned in compliance with these country-specific requirements.
- *Tax-free spin:* Divestiture deals are, in few cases, structured for minimal tax impact, which usually requires multiple waves of cutover activity.
- *Legal entity details:* To carve out or separate the assets, the most up-to-date legal entity data must be available, such as the company's name, tax ID, and banking information.
- *Financial close:* Parent and carved-out business units must be in a position to close their books during and post-divestiture or separation. Road maps developed for the transaction must take into account the timeframe required for financial close activities.
- *Organization design and employee selection:* The number and skill sets of employees who will transfer to the divested entity must be determined. Additionally, will

> *During separation planning for a large technology company, several legal and tax complications with the original timeline were discovered. Setting up legal entities in all the countries in which the to-be-divested business unit operates was proving difficult. The transaction was originally intended to be structured as a tax-free spin; thus, it was needed to split at least 90% of the legal entity, revenue, and assets by the Legal Day 1. Therefore, a major portion of the cutover and organization design and selection needed to be completed within 9 months, rather than the 12 months originally anticipated.*

the transfers be presented to the affected employees as optional or required for continued employment? Once the employees and management agree on the transfer terms, management should ensure their transition to the divested entity is seamless, particularly with regard to payroll and employment benefits.

- *Rebranding:* A global organization needs to undertake a major rebranding exercise across all of its physical locations and other assets to comply with the updated requirements post-divestiture or separation.
- *Financials and regulated filing for the divested company:* Divestiture of a division into a stand-alone entity requires filing of a Form 10-K for the newly created entity with the Securities and Exchange Commission (SEC). Also financial documents should be prepared under "Generally Accepted Accounting Principles in the United States" (US GAAP) or "International Financial Reporting Standards" (IFRS) for audit purposes.
- *International buyers:* In scenarios where the buyer is a foreign entity, the seller can face antitrust issues if the buyer does not have a presence in the market. Moreover, the Foreign Corrupt Practices Act (FCPA) demands extra due diligence efforts to uncover practices that could be considered problematic for the deal. An additional layer of complexity is added as regional agencies and regulations like financial position and prospects (FPP) procedures come into picture.
- *Real estate:* The parent company faces the challenge of defining and deciding the ownership that the divested/separated company has on the real estate.
- *One-time investment:* A lot of resources are invested to carry out a divestiture or separation. This poses a challenge to carry out business as usual. On average, the one-time IT separation cost is over 1% of the separated entity's revenue for Technology, Media, and Telecommunications (TMT) Industry.[1]

2.4   Assessing the Complexity of Divestiture

While planning a divestiture, one needs to understand the size of the elephant and be prepared with the wilderness. It is important to anticipate the potential issues and efforts required at each stage of the divestiture and be prepared for any eventualities. The divestiture complexity assessment framework (DCAF) can help the seller and the potential buyer estimate the complexity of the deal.

There are eight key factors which can help the buyer and seller to access the complexity and identify key areas requiring additional resources and effort. Each factor has some considerations which can be rated on a scale of low complexity, medium complexity, and high complexity. This will help the seller and buyer identify the factors, which can be potential issues while executing the deal, and channel their effort to resolve these problems as soon as possible.

---

[1] Deloitte Internal Benchmarking for IT M&A.

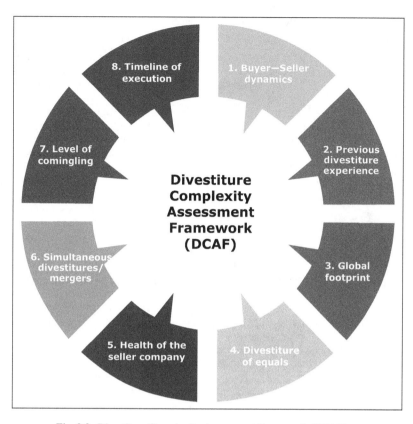

Fig. 2.2 Divestiture Complexity Assessment Framework (DCAF)

Table 2.2 DCAF Factors and Considerations

Assessment factor	Description/considerations
1. Buyer–seller dynamics	• Is the buyer a financial buyer or strategic buyer or a core competitor? • How is the culture of buying company and selling company similar? Will the employees of seller fit in with the culture of the buyer company?
2. Previous divestiture experience	• Does the seller have any previous experience of divestitures? • If yes, what was the scale in terms of revenue, headcount, and timeline? Have the experiences been documented? • If no, has the seller hired third-party consultants/advisors to assist with the deal?
3. Global footprint	• How many countries does the seller have a presence in? Does the buyer have a presence in all these countries? • How is the cultural fit between the seller and buyer in each of these countries?
4. Divestiture of equals	• What is the size (revenue, headcount, etc.) of the entity being divested and buyer company? Are they of the same size or is the buyer a larger entity or is the divested entity the larger entity?
5. Health of the seller company	• How is the health of the seller company? Will it be able to provide support to the buyer in form of TSAs post-divestiture? • Is there any dependency on the seller company post-divestiture?
6. Simultaneous divestitures/ mergers	• Is the company going through another divestiture or merger simultaneously? • Will additional external resources and investment be required to effect the transactions simultaneously?
7. Level of comingling	• How are the IT systems of the seller? What percentage of applications is shared by multiple business units of the seller company? • What is the level of sharing of IT assets (data centers, other IT infrastructure)? Can these assets be separated easily?
8. Timeline of execution	• What is the time period from deal announcement to day 1? • Is the quantum of additional resource and investments required for execution much higher than the available resources?

The buyer and seller can follow the "DCAF" and create a scorecard to assess complexity of each factor. This will help give them a sense of direction in estimating which factors need additional resources and efforts.

In the course of this book, we will focus on gaining insights in the methods and approaches which can help the seller tame this wild and big elephant successfully.

Questions
• What are the reasons a company decides to divest or separate?
• What are ways in which a company can divest or separate?
• What are the key challenges a company faces while divesting or separating?

Part II
Planning for the Deal

Chapter 3
Being a "Prepared Seller" and Identifying the "Right Buyer"

3.1 Introduction

Many organizations are wired to buy assets, not sell them, because most fail to develop an effective internal sell-side capability. An effective organization will focus on core businesses in order to maximize its return to shareholders, which means identifying underperforming business units for divestiture. An effective divestiture strategy requires establishing boundaries for unraveling businesses, selecting the optimal buyer after appropriate dili-

> *A Fortune 500 company successfully engaged in a major divestiture by adopting the 3 Ps—effective planning during buyer due diligence, correct positioning to the buyer, and portfolio realignment to enhance sell-side capability.*

gence, and developing a plan to meet the challenges of a divestiture. Divestitures require significant time and effort; hence, being a prepared seller helps identify risks and issues along with feasible solutions and mitigation steps. Ability to identify the pitfalls beforehand and being prepared to handle challenges are a testimony to the fact that seller has done the required due diligence and thought through the strategy to execute the deal to completion. This readiness of seller becomes a great confidence booster for the buyer company to go forward with the deal, eventually leading to maximization of the deal value.

3.1.1 Pitfalls of Not Being Prepared

A successful exit from a divestiture is the result of a long process that requires tremendous resources and commitment. An unprepared seller may end up underselling a business unit due to undervaluing its true potential or may not be able to sell the business unit at all due to overvaluing its potential. Another key pitfall of not

J. Joy, *Divestitures and Spin-Offs*, Management for Professionals,
https://doi.org/10.1007/978-1-4939-7662-1_3

being ready is the speed of execution. A potential buyer will start performing due diligence and request data from the seller early on. If the seller does not have this information ready to go, it may not only delay the transaction but may cause the buyer to hesitate, possibly undervalue the asset or even reject the deal. Also, inaccuracies and gaps in the data will likely raise doubts in the mind of the buyer about the true value of the business unit.

3.1.2 Advantages of Being Prepared

Becoming a prepared seller can help maximize shareholder value, reduce risk, bolster the sale price, lessen the execution burden, and create a more competitive parent company post-split. From a deal perspective, a prepared seller is beneficial for the buyer as well. A prepared seller can quickly close out a transaction and focus on core business operations. The prepared seller's assets are more valuable to a buyer since it will be able to quickly execute the transaction and focus on capturing synergies. To become a prepared seller, the entire divestiture process must be planned in advance of the transaction close date. Both transaction and separation readiness are key elements of a sale and must be executed in parallel.

- What does it mean to be a prepared seller?
- What are the key milestones on the journey to becoming a prepared seller?
- Prepared sellers anticipate the transaction, separation, and other key readiness factors.

3.2 Being a Prepared Seller

3.2.1 Transaction Readiness[1]

3.2.1.1 Define Separation or Carve-Out Strategy

First, identify the business unit to be divested. Next, develop a deal to drive the various aspects of the sale process. Then, create carve-out financial statements for the business unit as soon as possible. Also, a thorough impact analysis on key stakeholders—employees, customers, and vendors—should be evaluated alongside the carve-out financial statements. Lastly, any legal or regulatory constraints should be closely studied. After analyzing all of these moving parts, the prepared seller will have the perspective required to make an informed decision about moving forward with the divestiture.

---

[1] CFO Insights: Divestitures and Carve-outs: Becoming a Prepared Seller—A Deloitte Perspective.

3.2.1.2 Creating Offering Documents

Ideally, before the purchase, the buyer will want to closely evaluate the business unit targeted for divestiture. Toward this end, the buyer may ask pointed questions during deal negotiations or a follow-up interview. The buyer may also request a tour of the business unit's facilities, as well as additional data requests. A prepared seller will showcase the business unit's offerings and potential value through these negotiations, interviews, facility tours, and background documentation. A well-crafted response to the buyer's offer, accompanied by substantial documentation about the business unit, will enhance the seller's credibility and help the transaction close quickly. Much of the buyer's focus will be on the market the divested business participates in, product plans, and sales strategies—all traditional areas that someone will use to value and evaluate a business. This will drive the content in the offering memorandum. A carve-out, however, will also bring an additional layer of questions about the business, including a specific focus on how the business will be separated. Some of the commonly asked questions with respect to the separation of the business unit being sold are:

- Business strategy
  - What is the business horizon and road map for the business unit?
  - Which key initiatives are in progress?
  - How will the carved-out business operate separately from the parent? What process dependencies can be eliminated now vs. in the future?
  - What will be the cost of maintaining the dependencies between parent and carve-out entity?
- Operating model and organizational structure
  - What is the organizational structure, including the leadership hierarchy?
  - How many full-time employees (FTEs) will transfer with the business unit?
  - What is the FTE count split by role, location, and skill set?
  - How many of the FTEs are in-house versus outsourced?
- IT landscape
  - What is the current IT infrastructure landscape?
  - How many applications are present in the system?
  - What is the split of application based on criticality and number of active users?
  - What is the average downtime?
  - Is the IT infrastructure operated in-house or is it outsourced?
  - Have there been any major outages in the past 3 years?
- Third-party contracts
  - What external contracts support the business unit?
  - Who are the top vendors by cost?
  - What are the terms and conditions of the major contracts?
  - Is the contract transferrable? If no, what is the cost of renegotiation?

- Financials
  - What is the current profit and loss landscape?
  - Are the historical financial results reflective of the expected run-rate going forward?
  - What are the sources of future cash flow and business continuity?
  - Is there a valuation model to maximize value based on various scenarios?
  - Does the seller have any unrecorded tax exposures?
- Assets to be transferred in the deal
  - What assets/legal entities will be transferred as part of the deal?
  - How will asset allocation happen?
  - What will be the gain/(loss) on the transfer?
  - Will assets be transferred all at once or over a period of time?
  - What assets will not be transferred as a part of the deal?

3.2.1.3 Establishing Transition Services Agreements (TSAs)

Not all services will be completely transitioned to the buyer once the divestiture is complete. The seller will have to continue supporting the divested entity for a certain duration to help ensure smooth functioning of the entity. A prepared seller is clear from the outset regarding the services to be provided post-divestiture and the cost of those services.

3.2.2 Separation Readiness[2]

3.2.2.1 Establishing a Separation Blueprint

A prepared seller will document the degree of integration with the parent company and identify elements of the deal that are not negotiable. The seller will also develop functional carve-out strategies (i.e., business requirements and exit strategies) and reconcile the separation blueprint to the G&A and cost allocation analysis. A strong separation blueprint will help both the buyer and seller align on milestones, key deliverables, and interdependencies, as well as help identify key accelerators to ensure a smooth and speedy transition.

3.2.2.2 Eliminating Stranded Costs

After a divestiture, the parent company is often left with stranded costs incurred in serving the divested business unit. To reduce the parent company's run-rate, it is important to identify these stranded costs and devise a strategy to minimize them. A prepared seller will understand stranded cost implications and develop an overall reduction plan. A prepared seller will use the divestiture as an opportunity

---

[2] CFO Insights: Divestitures and Carve-outs: Becoming a Prepared Seller—A Deloitte Perspective.

to analyze the parent company's cost position and determine if the divestiture transaction can be a catalyst to reduce other costs and improve margins.

3.2.2.3 Establishing a Divestiture Management Office (DMO)

The values and benefits of a deal can be realized through seamless and rapid execution. The DMO is a stepping stone for driving seamless execution. A prepared seller will develop air-tight plans for a smooth execution process. The seller will clarify governance and decision rights, as well as anticipate and address challenges due to any conflict of interest. A prepared seller will also link transaction execution with functional separation requirements, as well as identify and manage interdependencies. A prepared seller will also create key deliverables, such as a divestiture playbook, and develop contingency plans to mitigate risks. A prepared seller will also ensure ongoing executive visibility and rapid issue resolution.

3.2.3 Other Readiness Factors

3.2.3.1 Delineating the Organizational Structure[3]

A tightly coupled business has clearly defined objectives and policies that are monitored by a regular inspection and feedback system. Employees work under close supervision, while business unit leaders make decisions that are in sync with the parent company's central strategy. This enables management to coordinate the functioning of various business units. For example, in terms of IT setup, this type of organizational structure translates into an integrated system, such as enterprise resource planning (ERP).

Such tight coupling, although a great advantage in normal business operations, poses specific challenges in the case of a divestiture, such as:

- Difficulties and incurred costs related to decoupling a business unit increase with the degree of integration
- Dependency of the divested business unit on the parent company, until it integrates into the buyer's IT system or develops its own IT system
- Risk of increased costs for the buyer to gather critical information, which happens because managers in a tightly coupled business typically focus on specific product lines, resulting in a lack of a single point of contact to represent the divestiture transaction

---

[3] CFO Insights: Divestitures and Carve-outs: Becoming a Prepared Seller—A Deloitte Perspective.

3.2.3.2 Managing Multiple Vested Entities and Their Interests

During a divestiture, the parent company, the business unit targeted for divestiture, and other interdependent entities may have different interests and ideas on how the divestiture will affect them. In the absence of a common goal, the seller may find it difficult to position the divestiture transaction in a favorable light to potential buyers, thereby casting shadows on the true value of the business unit up for sale.

3.2.3.3 Managing Business-as-Usual Activities Along with the Divestiture

An impending divestiture deal can often throw the selling entity into a state of distress as conflicts may arise between the day-to-day functioning of the parent organization and the to-be-divested business unit. This may affect the morale of employees who are already under pressure due to the deal announcement. A well-crafted Day 1 plan as well as a transition services schedule will go a long way in addressing employee concerns.

3.3 Interacting with Potential Buyers

The seller has engaged in multiple deliberations and analyses regarding the value of the business unit targeted for divestiture, including engaging external consultants and investment bankers. Finally, the seller has decided to divest the business unit, and the seller is ready to find a potential buyer. The seller may hire an investment banker to help find multiple potential buyers who will start their own due diligence before arriving at a decision.

The seller wants to identify a buyer who can offer a competitive price for the to-be-divested business unit, has a good track record with acquisitions, and is a strategic fit for the divested business. The seller should prepare for due diligence requests from the potential buyer.

3.3.1 Develop a Management Presentation for Buyers

The seller should prepare a management presentation, supporting separation documents, and other relevant deliverables about the value of the targeted business unit for potential buyers. These documents will provide an overview of the parent company, the to-be-divested business unit, assets that will be part of the deal, operational details for key functions, and the carve-out financial statements of the targeted business unit. The seller should also anticipate questions from buyers in advance and be prepared with responses.

Within the management presentation, the seller should consider the most useful financial metrics to frame the historical results. In most cases, these metrics include a "Management EBITDA" that includes adjustments to historical results for any nonrecurring, nonoperational, or out of period items. Careful consideration of this metric is crucial to the sales process, as it often is the starting point of a buyer's financial model and can significantly impact the buyer's bid.

However, the parent company should be careful to ensure it does not reveal critical competitive data during deal negotiations, since most buyers are also often competitors of the parent company and may misuse data if the deal is not finalized.

3.3.2 Develop Processes to Rapidly Respond to Buyer Requests

Once a business unit is put on the market for divestiture, it may become difficult to keep track of the requests coming in from potential buyers. The parent company must have a process in place and a dedicated team to respond to buyers' requests. Often, the investment bankers will take the lead in managing the buyers' requests and ensuring that they are addressed. However, the bankers will not be creating the data themselves; this is done by the seller and/or its external advisers. It is also essential to have subject matter experts (SMEs) for each function available to support buyer meetings. For example, an SME from IT can answer buyers' questions about the IT systems used by the targeted business unit. Providing credible data and facts will help reinforce to potential buyers that the seller is trustworthy and transparent about the value of the targeted business unit.

This process typically involves the creation of a virtual data room that allows secure access for buyers to the seller's information. Sellers should carefully review all information before posting it to the data room to ensure that no confidential information is provided. The legal team is typically involved in the process to confirm that all information is cleared before posting. Sellers also want to thoroughly review all financial information to ensure that it supports the prospectus and reconciles to the financial statements. This will help provide buyers' confidence in the seller's financial records and limit the amount of questions that arise during financial due diligence.

3.3.3 Support Due Diligence from Buyers

Buyers will conduct due diligence in a variety of areas including financial, tax, legal, operational, IT, and HR. This diligence will include analysis of documents made available in the virtual data room as well as on-site meetings with management. The seller should ensure that they are fully prepared for these meetings as buyers use the opportunity to not only learn more about the seller's operations but also to make preliminary judgments about the proficiency of seller management. It is customary to request a list of questions prior to the meeting to allow management to be fully prepared. It is also appropriate to limit the amount of information made available to buyers early in the diligence phase, reserving more in-depth analysis and information for a smaller number (or just one) more committed buyer.

3.3.4 Conduct Initial Diligence on Buyer

As the seller responds to buyers' requests, the parent company should also perform preliminary due diligence of potential buyers, including ensuring they are able to pay for the business, strategic fit with the entity being divested, and background checks.

Selection criteria to choose the right buyer:

- *Ability to offer the most competitive price*
- *Speed and certainty of deal closure*
- *Good fit with the business unit's current management and employees*
- *Ability to have an ongoing customer-supplier relationship*
- *The buyer is not a direct competitor*
- *Ease of post-divestiture integration and deal transition*

3.4 Conclusion

Prepared sellers generally succeed in maximizing the value of the business unit being divested and positioning the buyer with a clear corporate strategy that can result in a win-win for all the parties involved. Companies that eventually become divestiture-ready actively manage their portfolios, position a favorable divestiture strategy to buyers, and plan ahead, for pitfalls.

Case Study: 3

Background

A Fortune 50 technology giant (seller) was evaluating the divestiture of one of its businesses with revenue greater than $1B. The seller was in conversation with multiple buyers during the due diligence phase. The buyers included both strategic buyers and private equity players.

Challenges

The organization was under pressure to find a buyer quickly and close the deal. The divested business was also an attractive business drawing interest from multiple buyers in a short span of time. Given the amount of visibility in the market, the success of the deal was very critical to the seller.

Approach

The seller's IT organization was proactive and prepared for all requests that may come from buyers. Even before engagement with potential buyers, the seller started to assemble data packages consisting of details around IT strategy, assets, IT resources, application and infrastructure landscape, IT financials, key IT projects, and timelines.

As a result the seller was prepared with its version of IT Data Request Questionnaire and its answers. This helped the buyer in carrying out its due diligence quickly and effectively. It also helped built credibility for the seller.

The seller also established a Divestiture Management Office (DMO) early on to ensure effective planning, execution, and coordination among functions.

Impact/Results

This exercise ensured that the seller was prepared and it helped them in multiple ways:

- Identify the right buyer.
- Reduce the time taken for due diligence by the buyer.
- Better valuation of the deal.
- Reduced lead time to execution.
- Issue free Day-1 achievement.

Chapter 4
Upping the Ante: Enhancing Deal Value

4.1 Overview

Organizations decide to sell their business units for a variety of reasons, including:

- Turning strategic focus back to the core business
- Increasing shareholder value
- Generating funds for other priorities
- Reducing overall risk

Potential buyers generally evaluate deal value based on the strategic, operational, financial, and compliance strength of the business unit, as well as how their synergies can positively affect the targeted business unit across these dimensions.

The seller company will always strive to maximize the deal value of the business unit it plans to sell while aiming to minimize one-time costs and time required to complete the deal. One-time costs can be significant for carve-outs, especially for business units that are heavily commingled or integrated with the seller or parent company.

Factors that can increase deal value include:

- Structuring the deal creatively
- Executing the deal quickly
- Reducing the cost of the deal

Closing the deal fast helps ensure business continuity for both the buyer and seller companies and can result in significant value for the entities involved. The seller can increase the effective deal value by focusing on reducing the one-time costs and time required for the separation and sale of the business unit.

© Deloitte Development LLC 2018   31
J. Joy, *Divestitures and Spin-Offs*, Management for Professionals,
https://doi.org/10.1007/978-1-4939-7662-1_4

4.2 Approaches to Enhance Deal Value

4.2.1 Accelerating the Close of the Transaction

Closing the transaction in the shortest timeline possible after the announcement of the deal is typically one of the goals for the entities involved. Minimizing the time to close helps the seller company reduce one-time carve-out costs and focus on its core businesses while enabling the buyer company to begin executing its synergy revenue and cost road maps, which are developed preliminarily prior to the deal announcement.

The transaction close timeline is primarily driven by the time required to meet the following:

- *Legal and Regulatory Requirements:* The entities involved must submit financial and other documents regarding the sale to the regulatory entities for approval.
- *Operational Carve-Out Requirements:* Carving out the divested entity from the seller or parent company involves a complex series of activities that span project planning through separation execution.
- *Works Council Consultation Requirements:* Companies with business outside of the United States often must secure approval from works councils, which are similar to US labor unions, for mergers and acquisitions (M&A) transactions.

The seller or parent company can significantly reduce the operational carve-out timeline by implementing the following methods and practices:

- *Logical Separation:* Instead of cloning or standing up new applications for the divested entity's commingled or shared applications, the seller company can segregate shared applications into a logically separate instance, which can save time involved in procurement and system build.
- *Multitenancy of Directory Services:* Standing up separate directory services for the divested entity and migrating the information technology (IT) landscape to the new directory services require significant time. To accelerate deal close, the shared directory can be modified to enable multitenancy for a period of time.
- *Minimal Rebranding:* Completion of physical and system rebranding by deal close is difficult for business units with geographical spread and significant IT landscapes. Following a minimal rebranding approach in which only the high-impact, high-risk branding changes are completed prior to deal close will help shorten the deal close timeline. The remaining branding changes can be completed after deal close.
- *Risk Acceptance:* Completion of significant areas of the separation may not be possible in the timeline required to accelerate deal close. The seller company should consider accepting residual risks, including brand, data leakage, security, operational, financial, and regulatory risks, in order to accelerate deal close.

4.2.2   Reducing the Cost Envelope

Earnings before interest, taxes, depreciation, and amortization (EBITDA) of the divested entity is a driver of the valuation. The buyer company starts with reported earnings before interest, taxes, depreciation, and amortization (EBITDA) before making various normalizing adjustments (includes discretionary expenses) to arrive at adjusted EBITDA for the divested entity. Buyers then apply a multiple based on favorable or unfavorable industry market forces to this adjusted EBITDA figure to arrive at a valuation.

To improve EBITDA most companies try to consolidate shared functions such as IT, human resources (HR), and finance into a shared service function, which can lower costs. However, since these functions are often heavily commingled and interdependent, allocating individual costs to each function is challenging.

Thus, the seller or parent company can improve the EBITDA of the divested entity by setting a cap on shared service costs that will be transferred from the seller to the buyer. This cap provides the buyer clear view of the costs for global functions, which helps in modeling out the deal value, resulting in higher EBITDA. Cap on the global functions can be achieved by not transitioning any discretionary spend.

Thus, these approaches help in accurately estimating the EBITDA and understanding the costs of the divested entity. This clearer understanding in turn helps in driving the deal value.

4.2.3   Carving out the Business Unit Through Transformation

The seller or parent company generally adopts one of the following divestiture approaches to share its people, processes, and systems with the divested entity:

- *Clone or Replicate:* Replicate or clone the shared processes and systems to carve out the business unit.
- *Extract and Hand over:* Extract relevant and specific data, people, and processes from the seller or parent company and migrate them to the divested entity.
- *Logically Separate:* Separate shared processes and systems with security controls between the seller or parent company and the divested entity using transition service agreements (TSAs) until the buyer company can exit the shared landscape.
- *Concierge:* Set up business and IT resources in a concierge model in which the seller or parent company provides services to the divested entity until the buyer company is able to stand up or migrate the divested entity into its own landscape.

The approach chosen by the seller or parent company is primarily driven by such factors as the extent of comingling between functions, the deal close timeline, the buyer company's profile, and one-time costs required for separation.

If the seller company wants to maximize deal value, an alternate approach is to transform the divested entity's business processes and systems. However, in most cases, the business unit being sold is heavily commingled with the rest of the seller or parent company. Hence, cloning or replicating business processes and systems may not be the best solution.

Transforming the commingled landscape into fit-for-purpose business processes while bringing in out-of-the-box, cloud-based solutions is generally preferred over other approaches and results in:

- Stand-alone business processes and systems that the buyer can potentially use as an integration engine.
- Business processes are built in alignment with industry best practices, leading to improved customer, partner, and employee experiences.
- Reduced costs across business functions due to the clean balance sheet organization and cost analysis.
- Scalable and flexible processes and systems.

IT operational expenses are reduced by this streamlined IT architecture and application footprint, which drives significant top-line and bottom-line benefits for the divested entity, thereby increasing deal value for the buyer company. Meanwhile, the seller company can translate these benefits into a higher price for the business unit.

The approach, timeline, benefits, risks, and mitigations for transformation are detailed in Chapter 27, "Transform as You Separate."

4.2.4 IT Outsourcing

IT is a key shared function and the backbone of any company. IT applications and infrastructure are often shared by all business units in a company. When a business unit is divested, it requires support until it can be separated and operated as a stand-alone entity or completely integrated with the buyer company's IT landscape. Back-office or shared functions (e.g., IT, finance, accounting, HR) generally require support even after Day 1. Traditionally, both buyers and sellers use TSAs to provide this support.

As the companies involved in the deal start providing shared services, they face multiple challenges, including:

- *Lack of Focus on the Core Business:* The seller or parent company must extend significant amount of resources to draft and manage the TSAs, which limits its ability to focus on its core businesses post-separation.
- *Potentially Suboptimal Service Levels:* The services provided by the seller company may not meet existing industry standards, since the seller is not primarily into the business of providing such services.

- *Lack of Negotiating Power:* The seller may be required to obtain consents and additional licenses, as well as negotiate new, or renegotiate existing, service agreements. These activities may cost the seller company a lot, particularly considering the loss of scale provided by the divested entity.
- *Legal Risks:* Both the buyer and seller companies may be inadvertently exposed to the risk of legal non-compliance due to the commingled environment under TSAs.
- *Security:* It can be tough for the seller company to comply with various confidentiality obligations and privacy laws. The cost and complexity involved in protecting information can be prohibitive.

To overcome these challenges, a potential solution for the seller company is to outsource its IT activities to a third-party vendor who will be responsible not only for maintaining the IT systems but also optimizing costs. For a divestiture, the third-party vendor can continue to support both the seller or parent company and the divested entity after the separation.

Integrating the divested entity's IT systems with those of the buyer company is a mammoth task that requires a great amount of effort; thus, outsourcing the divested entity's IT systems can provide multiple benefits for the buyer, including:

- High-quality services during integration and separation at low costs
- Access to high capabilities aligned with industry standards through the third-party vendor
- Better risk management and risk-sharing methodologies that minimize business delivery risks by offloading the processes the buyer is less capable of executing
- Minimal retraining or knowledge transfer required as the same team can continue to provide services to the divested entity
- Ability to focus on core business activities rather than the outsourced service areas
- Flexibility to exit these services without stranded costs

Further, outsourcing provides the seller or parent company with the following potential benefits:

- *Higher Valuation:* Expected future cost savings and, hence, higher margins may increase the deal value.
- *Enhanced Capabilities:* Deal close can be expedited as the third-party vendor brings in additional resources and capabilities.
- *Lower Cost of Delivery:* Outsourcing, if done efficiently, delivers significant economic benefits due to labor arbitrage and economies of scale.
- *Quality of Service:* A third-party vendor can provide service levels comparable to leading industry practices. Generally, the same vendor provides services to the seller company, the divested entity, and the buyer or parent company.
- *Focus on Core Business:* The seller and the buyer can focus on its core capabilities.
- *Future M&A Transactions:* The effort required to separate and/or integrate the IT function as part of M&A transactions is reduced.

- *Reduced Separation Costs:* The costs and effort required to separate the IT function can significantly be reduced.
- *Flexibility and Scalability:* The seller company can scale its business more easily as a result of outsourcing.
- *Amortization:* Ability to create a financial architecture by spreading cost over 5 years to the outsourcer.

Selecting a third-party vendor can be a tedious process. Typically, companies choose vendors based on their past client service, delivery commitments, resource savings, and reliability.

Even after outsourcing all IT systems and services to the third-party vendor, both the seller and buyer companies should manage their relationships with the vendor in order to avoid implementation delays. Smoothing out the change management process for quick turnarounds and keeping an eye on the ROI with respect to the overall outsourcing agreement could prove useful for both the seller and buyer companies. Some possible roadblocks associated with the IT outsourcing model include:

- Time involved to gather requirements and analyze the value of the third-party vendor service agreement
- Overestimating and under-delivering on expectations set by the seller or buyer due to inadequate analysis of the third-party vendor's operating model
- Communication barriers between internal staff and the third-party vendor

The seller or parent company should review the scale of outsourced IT services against the needs of the divested entity to help ensure that outsourcing will be fruitful from a commercial perspective.

Despite multiple pitfalls and challenges associated with third-party vendors, outsourcing is a key to the effective transition of IT systems and services for both the buyer and seller companies.

4.3 Conclusion

In a nutshell, multiple approaches exist to reduce the cost and time needed to complete the deal. Consideration of any of the approaches listed in the chapter during an M&A transaction can help ensure a successful deal for both the buyer and seller companies.

Approaches discussed in the chapter are:

1. Accelerate closure of the transaction
2. Reduce the cost envelope
3. Carve out the business unit through transformation
4. IT outsourcing

These approaches while increasing the deal value can help the seller focus on the core business and enable the buyer to initiate execution of its synergy road maps.

But, these approaches should be evaluated critically due to various characteristics and nuances specific to M&A IT projects. To be most effective, the team should understand the deal's objectives and context, along with the seller's and buyer's IT landscape and IT organization.

Case Study: 4

Background

The executive team of a Fortune 50 technology company (the seller company) decided to divest one of its four business units. The seller company made a strategic decision to focus on its core businesses and, hence, sell the business unit.

Challenges

When the seller company's executives started finding potential buyers, they realized the multitude of problems driving down the valuation of the business unit up for sale. First, it was comingled with the seller company and, thus, had high one-time separation costs, as well as high run-rate costs post-separation. Additionally, the business unit's IT hardware was nearing obsolescence. Furthermore, discretionary expenses were not clearly accounted for resulting in high costs for shared services like HR, finance, and IT. What worried buyers most was the business unit's dependence on TSAs. Keeping the deal timeline in mind, buyers feared that the separation execution would be troublesome.

The chief operating officer (COO) formed a core team to identify potential options to transform the business and increase its valuation.

Approach

The core team understood companies were looking to buy a business unit that offered simplified business processes that could be easily integrated into their landscapes. The core team decided to adopt industry best practices in order to keep the customizations below 20% over an out-of-the-box, cloud-based solution. Since the customization of the solution was minimal, the run-rate costs were reduced drastically. The cloud-based solution ensured the business unit's systems were both scalable and flexible.

The next step was to reduce or set a ceiling for costs related to shared service like HR, finance, and IT. The company undertook a project to make its shared service function as efficient as possible with minimal interdependencies. The costs for shared services were divided into committed costs and discretionary expenses. A cap was set on discretionary expenses to ensure a higher EBIDTA to help improve the valuation of the business unit up for sale.

Dependence on TSAs was a primary reason for the low prices offered to acquire the business unit. The TSAs were planned for long durations, until the seller company's systems could be completely integrated with the buyer's systems. Buyers feared potential suboptimal services since the seller company would not have the expertise to provide such services. Another concern for buyers was the seller company's exposure to legal non-compliance risks. Furthermore, data security and adherence to confidentiality obligations and privacy laws required a high level of monitoring.

The core team decided that outsourcing the IT function could prove beneficial for both the buyer and seller companies. Outsourcing offered access to the higher capabilities provided by the third-party vendor, which were aligned with industry standards. Outsourcing would lower the cost of delivery due to labor arbitrage and economies of scale. Furthermore, the effort required to separate the business unit's IT functions was reduced, helping the seller company focus on its core business activities. The buyer company also benefitted from the outsourced IT services as they reduced the business unit's dependence on TSAs timeline.

Impact/Results

The multipronged approach to transforming the IT landscape, including capping shared services and discretionary spend and outsourcing IT, allowed the core team to significantly improve the value of the business unit up for sale. A majority of buyers' concerns were addressed, and the business unit appeared to add significant value for buyers. Some of the key achievements were:

- 70% reduction in shared app landscape
- Apps transformed onto the best of breed cloud SAAS solution
- 30% IT OpEx reduction
- Simplified business processes

A well-executed transformation plan for the business unit played a critical role in improving the valuation of the deal. All the execution plans, steps, and issues faced were well documented for future usage. Most importantly, the entire process provided the seller company with a template for further transformation exercises.

Chapter 5
Defining the Deal Timeline: Balancing Legal, HR, IT, and Finance

5.1 Introduction

The key to maximizing deal value is identifying an optimal deal timeline that is both aggressive and achievable. Faster time to close can typically result in a higher deal value while reducing costs at the same time.

While developing the deal timeline, it is important to consult with key stakeholders to determine the core functions affected by the deal, such as legal, HR, IT, and finance and their cross-functional dependencies. The legal, HR, and IT teams should interact and go through multiple iterations to identify the interdependencies. For example, the HR team which

Fig. 5.1 Balancing Interdependencies Between Legal, HR, IT, and Finance

handles the employee-related matters has to finalize the employee allocation and organization design structure to enable IT to test the access/authentication functionality. Similarly, unless legal sets up legal entities and bank accounts, IT will be unable to execute and test certain functionalities. Hence, it is imperative to avoid taking a functional approach when developing the timeline. Instead of planning how each individual function will be affected by the deal, we need to understand how various functions work together across the company. This understanding can then be used to develop an effective timeline that will work across the organization.

IT is typically the most complex function to separate given how IT supports the business in as a shared service across the enterprise. Changes to IT systems in support of a transaction can have impacts

> **Defining Deal Timelines: Step 1**
> *Identify core functions affected by the deal*

across multiple functions and process areas given most organizations reliance on IT to run critical business operations.

© Deloitte Development LLC 2018
J. Joy, *Divestitures and Spin-Offs*, Management for Professionals,
https://doi.org/10.1007/978-1-4939-7662-1_5

5.2 Key Functional Dependencies

Once the core functions have been identified, the deal or corporate strategy team must identify key stakeholders for each function and subsequently build teams to support each of these functions.

> **Defining Deal Timelines: Step 2**
> *Identify key stakeholders for core functions*

These functional teams will then work under confidentiality to help develop the timeline. The implementation of the core functions will be highly interdependent on IT. Hence, the IT function becomes the first function to define the first draft of critical path for the deal timeline. Then, the constraints related to other functions including legal, HR, and finance are accommodated to come up with a refined timeline.

Below is a set of key cross-functional dependencies that typically arise in the case of a divesture or spin-off.

5.2.1 Legal

Incorporating legal entities in each of the countries in which the divested business unit operates is a critical function performed by the legal team during deal execution. The legal team will scrutinize the operating model of the new organization, strategy for dissolving or creating new entities before incorporating legal entities. While the legal team determines the steps required to set up a legal entity, the IT team requires details about the new entities, such as company names, tax IDs, and banking information to design the plan for IT execution.

5.2.2 HR

Organizational design for impacted business units, selection of employees based on the new organization design, and consultation with labor organizations across several countries are the key HR activities that affect timelines of other functions.

As part of its organizational consultation process, HR must consult with labor organizations on the laws prevalent in the country where the newly created legal entities will operate. The HR team can then devise a strategy for transitioning of employees to the newly created legal entities in accordance with labor laws of the respective countries. Labor laws in certain countries like France[1] and Germany[2] may often impose strict rules against employee termination or disciplinary action

---

[1] Employment & labour law in France, Ming Henderson.
   http://www.lexology.com/library/detail.aspx?g=04707eaf-8286-4528-860c-b20c632b0ed0
[2] Germany's labor and employment laws, Celia M. Joseph.
   http://www.lexology.com/1052423/author/Celia_M_Joseph/

which prevail over the terms of an employment agreement. Depending on the stringency of labor laws, the transition process can take place from anytime between a few weeks up to 9 months.

In parallel, HR must analyze the organizational design of the parent company, including roles, hierarchies, and job descriptions, in order to identify and select employees who will transfer to the new legal entities. This process typically takes 2–6 months, depending on the number of employees involved and the outcome of consultations with labor organizations. This process directly affects the timelines of other functions.

The IT team in particular will have a huge dependency on the HR function. The outcome of analysis by the HR team will be a key input for creating Active Directory and HR information systems. This in turn impacts implementation of key IT features such as granting application access, authentication of credentials, access to emails, etc.

5.2.3   Finance and Tax

The finance team needs to set up bank accounts for all the newly created legal entities. This information is further used by the IT team as one of the inputs for developing their timeline.

The finance and tax functions can also develop carve-out financial statements for the to-be-divested entity, which can then be used to help secure the deal and create the timeline.

Carve-out financial statements refer to the separate financial statements of a business unit, which are derived from the financial statements of the parent company. The extent of the carve-out financial statements that are needed and, hence, the time required to create them depend on the nature of the transaction and government regulations. For instance, a public buyer in the United States may need a full set of audited carve-out financial statements for the to-be-divested entity for the three most recent fiscal years. Similarly, a spin-off of a division into a stand-alone entity will require filing a Form 10-K for the newly created entity with the Securities and Exchange Commission (SEC).

In addition to the time required to prepare the carve-out financial statements, Form 10-K, and other financial requisites, the finance and tax functions must keep in mind the lead time required by government regulators. For instance, carve-out financial statements filed for a public spin-off via Form 10-K must be available at least 60 days prior to execution of the spin-off.[3] Submission of Form 10-K with the SEC is essential to complete the spin-off. The statements must be created and submitted on time in order to avoid the risk of submitting dated or "stale" financials.

---

[3] "Carve-Out Financial Statements – Why such a fuss?," Matthew Himmelman, Brenda Mizer. http://deloitte.wsj.com/cfo/files/2012/06/DFPORH2012041600001.pdf

5.2.4   IT

In addition to cross-functional dependencies, there are certain intra-functional dependencies within IT that affect the timeline. Key IT dependencies include:

- *Infrastructure:* The IT infrastructure required at each phase (e.g., development, testing) should be implemented and available before that phase begins. Preordering infrastructure will optimize lead time and affect the overall timeline.
- *Data Center Network Segregation:* Logical networks should be separated to limit cross-business access.
- *Testing Close Process:* The duration of testing close process before Day 1 should be one of the key inputs while defining the deal timeline. This also includes accommodating for mock closures testing which is very important to ensure successful financial close

Once each function identifies their key activities and interdependencies, the deal team conducts multiple cross-functional dependency alignment sessions to discuss each dependency and functional constraint.

> **Defining Deal Timelines: Step 3**
> *Conduct cross-functional alignment sessions*

5.3   Defining Deal Timelines

Based on the outcomes of cross-functional alignment sessions, the deal timeline or road map is developed that takes into account key milestones and cross-functional dependencies. It is essential to ensure all functions are aligned and in agreement with this timeline.

> **Defining Deal Timelines: Step 4**
> *Define deal timeline and obtain agreement from key functions*

An additional nuance to defining the deal timeline is the concept of executing the deal in "waves." Typically, the time required for activities like legal entity setup, works council negotiation, and IT readiness varies across countries. Hence the deal execution may be split in multiple waves grouping countries based on their readiness. This helps ensure continuous progress in deal execution without being constrained by external dependencies, hence de-risking the transaction.

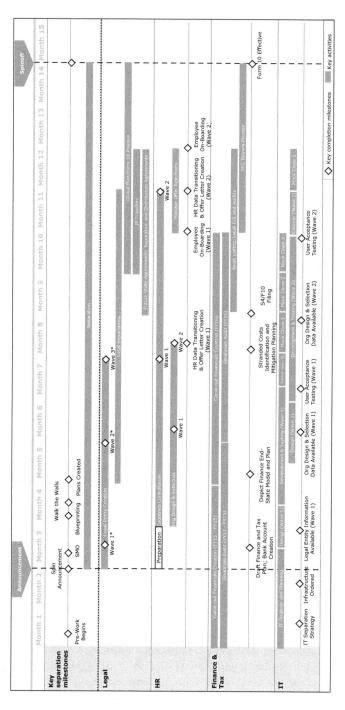

Fig. 5.2 Sample Spin-Off Timeline

Defining Deal Timeline: Leading Practices
   Identify core functional teams that understand the organization and can quickly identify key steps and interdependencies.

1. *Ensure all functional teams adhere to a predecided and Agreed upon timeline with timely escalation in case of any concerns or issues.*
2. *Engage subject matter experts and external consultants early on, if necessary, to get an unbiased view of the feasibility of the timeline.*
3. *Conduct multiple cross-functional alignment sessions to ensure all functional interdependencies are considered in the timeline.*
4. *Define a clear road map, including key milestones and interdependencies between functions.*
5. *Obtain agreement from all functions on the final timeline and road map, since their time and effort will be required for successful deal execution.*

5.4   Conclusion

Apart from maximizing deal value and potentially reducing costs, defining the deal timeline also helps the functional teams to focus on a common end goal. The final timeline acts as an anchor upon which functional teams can then build out their own detailed plans. It also ensures all functions are aware of their critical interdependencies and understand the effort required for deal execution.

Case Study: 5

Background

After months of preparation, the executive committee of a technology company had finally announced its decision to divest one of its business units. Considering the aggressive deal timeline, the corporate strategy team quickly huddled up to identify with an overall timeline for execution of the deal. Among the attendees were the heads of various functions such as IT, finance and tax, legal, and HR along with external consultants having expertise in execution of divestitures.

What were the processes followed by the team to design the timeline? What were the challenges? Were they successful in adhering to the timeline considering the fast approaching Day 1?

Challenges

Finalizing the deal timeline was a challenge considering the high and complex interdependency between functions. It required coordination between each of the functions and multiple iterations before arriving at an agreeable, optimal, and achievable timeline. Working in silos would have increased the implementation timeline and cost, resulted in rework to accommodate interdependencies. A faster close time on the other hand could result in a higher deal value!

So how did this corporate strategy team successfully execute the process of defining the deal timeline?

Approach

The corporate strategy team first identified the core functions affected by the deal—IT, legal, HR, and finance and tax. Based on internal discussions and third-party consultants' experience, it was agreed upon that IT would be the most complicated to separate considering its intricate interdependencies with other core functions.

It was agreed upon that the IT team will design the first draft of the timeline based on its key milestones. The legal, HR, and finance and tax teams would then provide their inputs on key constraints to further refine the timeline. The external consultants would provide oversight and an unbiased view on the feasibility of the refined deal timeline.

First Draft of Deal Timeline

The IT team created a high-level timeline consisting of IT strategy and planning, design, development, testing, mock cutover, and go-live dates. While defining the timeline, the IT team had to consider intra-functional dependencies such as:

- *Infrastructure:* Availability and timely delivery of preordered infrastructure impacting development and testing timeline
- *Data Center Network Segregation:* Separation of logical networks to limit cross-business access
- *Testing Close Process:* Closing testing process for defining go-live dates

Identifying Interdependencies

Once the first draft was created, the IT team conducted multiple sessions with other functions to understand the interdependency between IT and other functions. Based on the meetings, the following key interdependencies were identified:

Legal: The legal team was responsible for setting up legal entities in countries of operation of the divested entity. The IT team would require details of new legal entities, company names, company codes, tax IDs, etc. before the beginning of development phase.

Human Resources (HR): The HR team will be responsible for creating a new organization design and structure (OD&S) and strategy for transitioning employees to the divested entity. The first step toward creating the transition strategy would be addressing the intra-dependency of consultation with labor organizations on the laws in the country where the new entity will operate. The next step would be analyzing the existing organization structure. Once the intra-dependencies are addressed, the HR team will be in a position to provide the IT team information on the new organization design and selection (OD&S) structure. Additional details on roles, hierarchies, and job description will be required to test some key features such as payroll, performance management, and authentication/access function. Information from the HR team will be required before the beginning of testing phase.

Finance and Tax: The finance and tax team will provide information on the bank accounts set up for newly created legal entities to the IT team. This information will act as an input for the design phase. Additionally, the finance and tax team will have to address the requirements of preparing the carve-out financial statements of the entity to be divested and complying with regulatory requirements. IT timelines will have to be designed in a manner to ensure compliance requirements are satisfied without delays.

Finalizing the Deal Timeline

After multiple iterations and arriving at a consensus on the dates for key milestones, the corporate strategy team sets out to create a final version of the timeline. The road map was redefined with inclusion of key milestones and highlighting interdependencies between core functions. The third-party consultants provided their inputs and verified the feasibility of the plan. Guidelines were established for escalation of concerns and issues to ensure steps are taken for timely resolution of issues.

Impact/Results

The approach of involving stakeholders from all core functions for establishing the deal timeline proved to be beneficial for everyone. Each stakeholder had a clear view of the milestones and interdependencies and could plan their time and effort in a better manner. Detailed road maps for each team were built with the goal of achieving the overall deal timeline. It eventually helped in optimizing the carve-out timeline, reduce execution costs, and further maximize the deal value.

Chapter 6
Slicing the Pie: Asset Allocation in Divestiture

6.1 Overview

One of the key activities during a separation or divestiture is the assignment of assets between the entities being separated. This involves allocating the ownership of the physical assets and then creating pro forma balance sheets (projected future-state balance sheets of both companies post-separation) based on the asset allocation. In most separations and divestitures, the allocation of shared assets can be a tricky and contentious process.

A separation or divestiture affects the entire balance sheets of the companies involved, including tangible and intangible assets. Tangible assets include, but are not limited to, cash, account receivables, inventory, software, and hardware. Intangible assets include, but are not limited to, patents, trademarks, copyrights, and goodwill. The complexity of the separation or divestiture depends on the level of asset sharing between the entities being separated. The asset allocation method will be unique for each carved-out asset. Equitable and fair allocation of assets between the separated entities is essential in order to set them up for success.

Information technology (IT) assets are a significant portion of a company's fixed assets and often, the most difficult to separate because they are highly comingled with each other (e.g., all business units of a company may be using the same ERP software including shared licenses and infrastructure); thus, this chapter will focus on IT asset allocation.

© Deloitte Development LLC 2018
J. Joy, *Divestitures and Spin-Offs*, Management for Professionals,
https://doi.org/10.1007/978-1-4939-7662-1_6

6.2   IT Asset Allocation in a Separation or Divestiture

IT asset allocation in a separation or divestiture is important for the following reasons:

- It has a direct impact on the overall balance sheet and valuation of each entity involved in the separation.
- Pro forma balance sheets must be created that take into account the asset base for each entity and how it will operate going forward.
- Proper separation of IT assets may result in lower business risk, stranded costs, and operating costs in the future.
- The timing of asset allocation decisions is critical since the timing will affect application disposition and the infrastructure activities needed for separation.
- Pro forma balance sheets related to asset allocation must be completed early in the separation process as these are required for regulatory filings such as Form 10 (a filing with the Securities and Exchange Commission (SEC) to register securities for trading on US exchanges. Information on SEC Form 10 includes the type and amount of security being issued and financial information of issuer).

For these reasons, asset allocation is a top-of-mind aspect that most chief executive officers (CEOs), chief financial officers (CFOs), and chief information officers (CIOs) want to handle effectively.

6.3   Key Considerations for Asset Allocation

Key considerations to prepare for asset allocation problem include:

IT Asset Landscape: Identify the baseline inventory of assets in the IT landscape, particularly the fixed assets.

Nature of Transaction: Whether the transaction is a split or sale to a buyer, the nature of the business and the type of IT assets required by the business, customers, products, and regions are critical and must be considered in the asset allocation strategy.

Usage of Assets: The extent to which each entity involved in the transaction will use the assets drives the asset separation strategy. Various drivers determine the usage, including the number of users and licenses.

Overall Asset Allocation Strategy: IT asset allocation should be in sync with the asset allocation strategy across the seller. Both the seller and the entity being separated should be set up for success, and asset allocation should support the business processes critical to each entity. The asset allocation strategy should not be executed in silos but in tandem with the Day 1 and future-state strategies for applications, infrastructure, and other areas within IT.

6.4   Developing an Effective Asset Allocation Strategy

Once the key considerations are reviewed, the following approach may be used to develop an effective asset allocation strategy.

1. *Create Asset Inventory*: Work with IT Finance to create an inventory of assets tagged to IT cost centers. Key data to be captured includes location, current usage, and ownership. Utilization of existing tools within the organization such as asset register, software license inventory, etc. can expedite this process. Determine the book values of both dedicated and shared assets.
2. *Categorize Assets*: Categorize the assets in the asset inventory based on IT areas such as application software, data center assets, site-related assets, and end-user assets. Each of these categories has a unique allocation method. Additionally, assess the guidelines for potential asset write-offs.

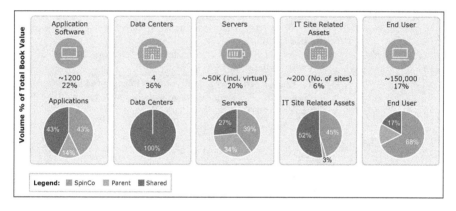

Fig. 6.1 Sample Asset Inventory

3. *Allocate Assets*: Once the asset inventory has been categorized, the next step is to allocate assets to the entities that are being separated as illustrated in Fig. 6.1.

   (a) Assets that are being used only by one entity, also called dedicated assets, are directly allocated to the corresponding entities.
   (b) Shared assets required by only one entity can also be directly allocated to the corresponding entity.
   (c) Shared assets required by neither entity can typically be allocated equally or written off, but companies should consider the application of generally accepted accounting principles (GAAP).

Allocate the assets based on the following criteria:

Table 6.1 Allocation Criteria

Area	Allocation considerations
Application software	• *Dedicated assets*: Assets used by only one entity can be allocated directly • *Shared assets*: Various drivers determine the allocation of shared assets, including business unit consumption, number of users, revenue, and headcount
Data center and servers	• Data centers can distribute assets between the separated entities based on usage • One entity can retain existing data centers, while the other entity stands up its own data centers • Data center services can also be transitioned to a third-party service provider • All underlying hardware, software, and telecommunication assets should be allocated based on data center disposition to minimize separation risks and costs
Site related	• This is typically tied to real estate site disposition done by the real estate function • Site-related assets usually transfer to the entity operating at the related site
End user	• Allocation of end-user assets is aligned to employee separation; in other words, the assets will move with the employees who use them (i.e., end users)

Table 6.2 Sample Asset Allocation

IT asset category	Description	Book value to be allocated ($M)	Asset disposition criteria	SpinCo allocated book value ($M)	Parent allocated book value ($M)	Allocation percentage
1. Application software	Application software assets such as Oracle, SAP and R&D applications	$200	Allocated using metrics such as number of users, hosted location, database consumption, BU revenue	$80	$120	SpinCo: 40% Parent: 60%
2. Data center and server	Data center facilities, hardware (e.g. servers, storage), software (e.g. monitoring) and security operations center (SOC)	$500	Allocated 2 datacenters to SpinCo Allocated 2 datacenters to Parent	$300	$200	SpinCo: 60% Parent: 40%
3. Site related	Site related network and infrastructure (e.g. WAN, site security, routers)	$50	Allocated based on Day 1 site dispositions (using housed headcounts)	$45	$5	SpinCo: 90% Parent: 10%
4. End user	Desktops, laptops, user specific software (e.g. antivirus)	$150	Based on employee counts SpinCo: 80% Parent: 20%	$120	$30	SpinCo: 80% Parent: 20%
Total		**$900**		**$545**	**$335**	SpinCo:60% Parent:40%

4. *Adjust Balance*: Next, to ensure fairness, make adjustments as needed to the overall cash and liquid asset distribution between the separated entities. Transition service agreements (TSAs), TSA schedules, and other documents must be updated as needed.
5. *Continue to Refine*: IT asset allocation is a continuous process during separation. While the initial point of view on allocation of assets is developed during the early stages of separation planning, the IT and finance functions at the separated entities should refine the allocations to correspond with organizational design, application dispositions, data center separation, and contract separation and assignments.

6.5   Setting Up Entities for Success Through IT Asset Allocation

IT asset allocation affects many other aspects of separation:

- *Transition Service Agreements (TSA)*: IT asset allocation determines which entity will be the provider of TSA services, which affects TSA documentation, costs, and exit strategies.
- *Organization Design and Selection*: IT asset allocation affects the allocation of IT employees and roles across the two separated entities. The entity receiving the assets will also receive the employees required to run and maintain those assets.

> *In a recent separation of equals in the technology industry, IT asset allocation was a key input into future-state infrastructure strategy decisions.*
>
> *Instead of burdening either entity with over $500 M of data center assets that will limit flexibility and increase costs, a decision was made to transition data center assets and operations to a third-party service provider.*

- *Future-State IT Operating Expenses*: Allocation of IT assets will directly affect the IT costs for the separated entities as they will need to depreciate and absorb other operating expenses for the assets such as maintenance, contract costs, and licensing fees.
- *Future-State IT Decisions*: Asset allocation can affect future-state IT decisions for the separated entities, including application dispositions and infrastructure strategy.

A skewed asset allocation between separated entities can negatively affect the future operations and financial outlook of both entities.

Consider the example of the three-way spin-off of Life Sciences ParentCo from Fig. 6.2 (impact of asset allocation on future operations and financial outlook). If the allocation of assets was equitable, all of the three spun-off entities should have been in the top-left quadrant (lower stranded costs and higher flexibility to transform). As a result of inequitable allocation, only two of the three spun-off entities (Life Sciences SpinCo A and Life Sciences SpinCo C) are set up for success while Life Sciences SpinCo B is not.

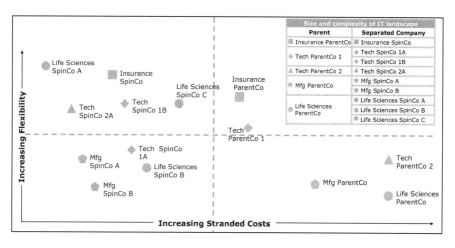

Fig. 6.2 Typical Asset Distribution

Table 6.3 Asset Allocation

Allocating more assets than required	• A large asset base will drive higher operating expenses, making it difficult to achieve cost targets
	• The entity will have to mitigate higher stranded costs for assets it does not use, including operating and disposal costs
	• Typically, an entity uses a separation or divestiture to transform the IT landscape by upgrading technologies and reducing costs, but a large number of legacy assets will reduce the entity's flexibility to engage in this transformation
Allocating lesser assets than required	• The entity may appear to have a weak asset inventory when the pro forma balance sheets are created and published
	• The entity will have high one-time costs to acquire the new assets it needs to operate or replace services that were provided by the other entity

Based on the above reasons, an equitable allocation of assets is essential to help ensure that the separated entities are set up for success.

6.6 Conclusion

The shared nature of IT assets makes asset allocation complicated. Since finalizing the separation of the balance sheet is critical to completing the separation activities, IT asset allocation must be initiated early in the separation process. Also, since asset allocation affects the financial outlook of the entities involved in the transaction, optimizing the allocation of IT assets is critical to the success of the transaction and the separated entities.

Similar approach needs to be leveraged for all the different asset categories in the balance sheet to define the separated balance sheet for each of the entities. Each asset category across should be analyzed and allocated between the separated entities. While nuances and approaches will differ across asset categories, asset allocation will still leverage the principles of utilization and equitable allocation to help ensure both entities are set up for future success.

Case Study: 6

Background
A Silicon Valley-based technology giant was separated into two entities. Assets had to be allocated between both of these entities and were key to successful separation. The separated entities would have a 50:50 split of revenue and an 80:20 split of employees.

Challenges
The entity with the smaller number of employees was pushing to take around 20 percent of the assets. The entity with the larger number of employees was opposed to this idea. This entity was of the opinion that it may be allocated a disproportionately large asset base resulting in higher stranded costs and lower flexibility.

Approach
The seller engaged an independent third-party consultant to critically evaluate the asset inventory and identify an equitable allocation between the two separated entities. Working with the IT finance team, the third party identified the list of assets, categorized them appropriately, and allocated them between the two entities based on relevant criteria. The seller's IT finance team then refined the initial view proposed by the third-party consultant.

Impact/Results
An optimal asset allocation of approximately 60–40 percent was determined, by using an independent approach, which gave both separated entities a strong starting point for their future operations and transformation efforts.

Chapter 7
Financial Aspects of Carve-Out

7.1 Carving Out Finance Is Not Trivial

Separations, by their very nature, are risky and complex. They require functions such as finance, information technology (IT), and human resources (HR) to be fully operational on Day 1 (i.e., transaction close), whereas integrations typically allow for the deferment of activities post-transaction close.

For the finance function, a divestiture requires fully separating the financial close, reporting, planning, and back-office processes of the divested entity and the seller or parent company. On Day 1, the entities involved in the transaction should also have:

- A completely staffed finance organization
- An independent service delivery model
- A separate and functional technology architecture
- Validated targeted operating costs

Many organizations find it difficult to stand up a fully independent and operational finance function for the divested entity by Day 1 and, therefore, use transition service agreements (TSAs) to aid in the stand-up. TSAs are signed agreements between the entities that allow one entity (typically, the seller or parent company) to continue providing agreed-upon services to the other entity (typically, the divested entity) for a specific period of time post-transaction close to prevent the disruption of critical functions (e.g., month-end close). Primarily, the services under TSAs flow from the seller or parent company to the divested entity; however, reverse TSAs may be used when the divested entity possesses capabilities essential to mitigate the disruption of the seller or parent company's operations. Table 7.1 highlights potential complexities that finance functions may encounter during a separation.

J. Joy, *Divestitures and Spin-Offs*, Management for Professionals,
https://doi.org/10.1007/978-1-4939-7662-1_7

Table 7.1 Separation Complexities

	Expanding global footprints	As companies continue to expand their presence in the global marketplace the Finance organization should build capabilities to manage the increased economic and geopolitical risks
	Complex technology platforms	Finance organizations should ensure they are leveraging available technology to appropriately support new or additional required capabilities and business needs
	Unwieldy legal entity structures	Entity structures becoming increasingly complex as organizations merge and it is important for Finance to understand the value of an optimized legal entity structure strategy
	Timing and realization of synergies	The timing of synergies and the cost of realizing them, should be considered as important as synergy identification
	Organizational structure and business models	Finance should certify that their operating and service delivery models are correctly aligned to the targeted operating model defined for the newly combined organization
	Differing cultures and environments	It is vital for Finance organizations to manage integration to ensure limited business interruption and seamless operational effectiveness post Day 1

More often than not, the technology architecture separation strategy, whether a "clone, cleanse, and go," a "logical separation," and/or a transformation, is the "long pole in the tent." It can drive the establishment of the transaction close date. Pursuing a tax-free separation for an organization with a sophisticated, global legal entity structure may, similarly, drive the establishment of the transaction close date. The more entities, the more Tax Legal Step Plans (TLSPs), and the more complicated the TLSPs, the more time is needed to close.

Separating the finance function is more than reassigning headcount from one organization to another. It's more than setting up a chart of accounts and a general ledger. It's more than making sure the finance applications and IT systems are up and running. Separating the finance function is a synchronized combination of operational and deal/transaction interdependent milestones and activities as well as cross-functional dependencies (e.g., HR, IT, and supply chain). These milestones and activities need to come together in a robust separation plan tightly managed with disciplined and mature program management processes. A dedicated finance workstream operates in close coordination and collaboration with a central Divestiture Management Office (DMO).

7.2 Understanding the Complexities

The primary drivers of operational complexity when separating finance functions for a divestiture include:

- Expanding global footprints
- Expansive technology platforms

- Highly sophisticated legal entity structures
- Global organization structures and business models
- Different cultures and environments
- Aggressive timelines for operating within target cost envelopes
- In-parallel transaction milestones and activities

As companies continue to expand their presence in the global marketplace, the finance organization is tasked with building capabilities to manage the increase in economic and geopolitical risk. In a separation, it is critical to duplicate those capabilities, especially if the divested entity will continue to operate in the same countries. Statutory and local compliance requirements then add to the scope of execution activities and must be incorporated into the overall finance function separation plan. It is also important to note that, as the steps of the TLSPs are executed, the business impacts in the countries may result in change requests that may alter the overall separation plan.

Expansive technology platforms with a large number of IT assets, business assets, interfaces, and multiple instances are a reality for global Fortune 50 companies. For example, the technology platform for a global Fortune 50 hybrid IT solutions and services company is comprised of 15 different order management systems and more than 700 IT applications and interfaces. Separating the technology platform was certainly a challenge. Attempting simplification of the technology platform during the separation would have increased the transaction risk profile to unpalatable. The resulting execution risks, inclusive of systems cutover failures, Day 1 delays, separation cost overruns, and penalties paid to the seller pushed the company to defer simplification. Mitigating execution risks necessitates the development of detailed systems and process cutover/transition plans, systems testing plans, systems testing cases, and disaster recovery, in the event of catastrophic failures, contingency plans.

Highly sophisticated legal entity structures can deliver tangible value that may lead to a material reduction in the effective tax rate. Enabling these structures are value chains in compliance with detailed transfer pricing policies and controls. The decision to simplify legal entity structures may loom large, but it is not an easy one to make.

Companies may choose to defer simplification because they expend significant effort and resources in developing the TLSPs that drive the separations. It is also possible to execute tax-free separations, assuming the TLSPs comply with regulatory tax rulings and requirements. Tax-free separations may require the divested entity to retain its original legal entity structure during legal entity formation for transaction close. Consequently, legal entity simplification for the seller or parent company is deferred to post-transaction close.

The pace at which legal entities are formed (i.e., the pace of the divestiture) is directly correlated to the simplicity of the seller's legal entity structure. The less simple, the longer the duration; the more intricate the legal entity structure, the longer the duration. The pace of the separation is also affected by funding requirements for the transaction and the capital needs of the entities involved. A company may issue debt to secure the funds to capitalize the entities. Sophisticated entity structures involve a large number of legal entities, which increase the complexity of moving capital through from the seller's legal entity structure to the newly created legal entity structure of the divested entity. Moving the capital occurs prior to Day 1, and the legal entity structure for the divested entity must be completely formed, operational, and legally registered to facilitate the process of moving the capital. Funding the entities takes time. Legal, tax, and treasury work jointly to determine the time required for capital to flow from the seller's legal entity structure to the divested entity's structure. The more complex the legal entity structure, the longer it takes to move the capital to fund the entities. Working backwards from Day 1, they define Operational Day 1 (OD1). This is a period in which the divested entity is operationally separate while still part of the seller or parent company. OD1 may be anywhere from 4 to 12 weeks prior to Day 1. The same Fortune 50 company, mentioned earlier, required approximately 8–10 weeks to move capital through its entity structure; OD1 was set for 12 weeks prior to Day 1. An OD1 may not be required if the divested entity's structure is simple and the capital can move in a single day.

Legal entity formation is a cross-functional effort. Finance, a key stakeholder, should be responsible for delivering opening balance sheets in alignment with tax-driven entity valuations and capital requirements. The tax function should work diligently to set up direct and indirect tax identifications for each of the newly created divested entities. The legal department should file the forms to complete legal entity registration with the authorities. Treasury, usually a separate function in large organizations, should work closely with finance to open bank accounts for customer payments, vendor payments, payroll, and capital flow needs. The finance function is also responsible for ensuring that financial master data accurately reflects the operational nature of the divested entity (e.g., sales entity, holding company).

The HR function, typically, takes full control of the employee notification and transfer process. HR works, jointly, with all functions, to facilitate the process. Employees targeted for transfer to the divested entity are notified of the intent to transfer and have the option of accepting the offer. Employees are transferred to the newly formed entities, and systems should be enabled to support transactions on OD1. Divested entity customers and vendors should be set up in the divested entity's systems. Applicable contracts, where customers and vendors are buying and selling to the divested entity, should be transferred. These contracts govern the commercial terms between the divested entity and its future customers and vendors. The contracts are transferred between OD1 and Day 1. Delay in the transfer of the contracts may result in stranded contracts. Stranded contracts may not be of value to the seller and would be willing to facilitate the servicing of these contracts if the divested entity and the seller agree to a TSA.

Operational readiness prior to transaction close puts a lot of pressure on the functions, especially finance. Every single finance process must be fully functional on Day 1. Any processes at risk of not being fully functional may be facilitated through a TSA between the seller and the divested entity. Finance does not get a pat on the back for simply separating the function; instead, finance is expected to generate and drive value through the separation. Some of the required activities and value drivers include:

• Defining the finance operating model in alignment with the target cost envelope to help the function meet operating cost targets

- Delivering the carve-out financials for the seller and the divested entity and filing the required regulatory forms with ample time for review by regulatory agencies, if applicable, such as the Securities and Exchange Commission (SEC) to help mitigate the risk of potential transaction close delays
- Developing opening balance sheets for the divested entity, in alignment with the carve-out assumptions and valuations, to help mitigate the need for significant reconciliation post cutover
- Establishing the cash management strategy and providing clarity on the transaction funding approach to help capitalize the entities
- Understanding the go-to-market strategy to help finance understand the potential effects of changes in pricing, transfer pricing, currency translation, and other finance activities (e.g., invoicing, credit, collections)

It is critical to establish the go-forward financial cycles (i.e., close and planning) and key performance indicators (KPIs) needed to support any external reporting requirements, statutory and local compliance, and business operations. Clarity on reporting standards (e.g., accounting principles generally accepted in the United States of America (US GAAP) and International Financial Reporting Standards (IFRS)) should define the conversion, if applicable and relevant to the facts and circumstances of the divestiture, from US GAAP to IFRS, enablement strategy for the divested entity. Conversion may include accounting entry adjustments and tools to enable the execution of the adjustments. A playbook outlining the required accounting entry adjustments can facilitate the process. Developing the internal controls environment in alignment with the disposition of finance applications is also critical to maintaining the integrity of the financial statements. Table 7.2 offers some questions finance should consider as it drives the separation of the function.

Table 7.2 Separation Priorities

Maintaining the tax advantage	Create an acquisition structure that *optimizes post-acquisition cash circulation* and *align* tax structure, global capital requirements, IP ownership, and transfer pricing with *integrated business model* /supply chains.
Bridging the finance systems	What is *the near term strategy* for bridging the finance systems? How does it align to *QCOM's strategy for shifting to cloud platform?* How does the strategy align to the *reporting standards?* What is the *functional currency?*
Defining the finance operating model	What is the strategy for the *operating model* on Day 1? What is the *end state strategy* and *in-country footprint?* Does the strategy align with the *financial envelope?* What is the strategy for *shared services centers?*
Establishing financial envelope and expected synergies	How will finance achieve its *synergy targets* and enable the rest of the functions to achieve theirs? What role will finance play in *synergy tracking and capture?* What is the *target envelope* for NewCo and what is the
Executing on filings and conditions to close	What is the *timing for filing the S4* and delivering *proforma financials?* What is the *approach for confirming IP, patent, and assets valuations?* What *process/tool* will be used for valuations needed to push asset values and goodwill down to appropriate legal entities? What will be the *IFRS to US GAAP* conversion process? What role does finance play in program managing the *conditions to close?*
Establishing working capital and cash management strategy	What are the *working capital targets?* What is the *cash management strategy?* What is the approach to *cash repatriation?* How can we *fund the transaction?* What are the *existing liabilities and off balance sheet obligations?*
Aligning to go to market strategy	How will *product and customer strategy* and *pricing decisions* impact Finance support, transfer pricing, currency translation and other finance operations?
Aligning on the close and rhythm of the business	What is the *new fiscal calendar?* What is the *new close cadence?* How will the *stub period reporting* be developed? What level of *combined budget, reporting and forecasting* can be in place immediately? What are the *near term and end state KPIs?* What is the *investor relations strategy?*
Defining reporting standards	Will *multiple reporting standards be required?* What is the *conversion enablement strategy* given the different IT platforms? What is the *shareholder equity ownership* and *assets split* across QCOM and NXP?
Mitigating risk, governance, and controls	Will *segment reporting* change? Will *tax strategies and synergies* drive *a new legal entity reporting structure?* What are the differences between *controls environments?* What *standard* will be applied to NewCo?

Defining the divested entity's finance operating model is critical to the success of the separation. It helps align the finance function's resources across the portfolio of finance services and subfunctions (e.g., revenue accounting, payroll, revenue forecasts). It defines the service delivery model and drives clarity on the geographic footprint of the finance function. It also establishes a center of excellence (COE), shared services, and managed services strategy. A COE, typically, enables the centralization of a high-value process (e.g., analytics). COEs can operate in lower-cost locations if the talent is available. Shared services centers, typically, own the processing of back-office transactions and operate in low-cost locations, creating labor arbitrage. Managed services are processes transitioned to a third party and are subject to service-level agreements that govern processing efficiency and quality. In developing the service delivery model, finance should consider:

- Statutory and local compliance requirements
- Required in-country footprint (e.g., China)
- Legal entity simplification and country presence
- Automation and master data cleanup
- Potential process simplifications and improvements
- Potential capability enhancements
- The governance and talent model

Figure 7.1 provides an example of a service delivery model.

Fig. 7.1 Illustrative Service Delivery Model

Even when the strategy for driving the separation is lift and shift, it is inevitable for the finance function and the entire organization to experience significant change. Lift and shift means that the legal entity structure, finance processes, and finance systems are not changing. Lift and shift can be an effective and risk-mitigating strategy when timeline pressures are high and when executing the transaction is highly complex.

It is vital to craft and execute a management of change strategy that can retain top talent, prevent the divested entity's employees from feeling disconnected, and effectively communicate progress and updates across the function. This effort should go beyond training and training material development and recognize that the risk for attrition is high during a separation and that some of the very people leading and driving the execution team may, themselves, be affected by the separation.

It is important to align the management of change strategy with the overarching and, typically, HR-led management of change approach and strategy. All tools and mechanisms should be on the table, including:

- Podcasts
- Webcasts
- Town halls
- Conference calls
- Newsletters
- Team outings
- Coffee chats

Top finance talent is hard to find and even harder to replace when it walks out the door.

7.3   Is it Possible to Deliver a Successful Finance Separation?

Yes, it is possible and has been achieved by many organizations in the past. Almost all successful separations generally have three common ingredients:

- A well-defined separation strategy
- A robust approach that turns that strategy into detailed, executable Day 1 plans
- A committed team empowered by the leadership to manage and execute those plans

Just like building a house, the journey to stand up a fully functional finance organization starts with the development of detailed process blueprints. The blueprints serve as a foundation on top of which the Day 1 separation plans and TSAs can be built. The Day 1 separation plans should document all key activities the finance team must perform in order to operationalize the separation strategy, and hence, the plans must be as detailed and accurate as possible, capturing all critical milestones and dependencies. Together, the plans provide the most comprehensive view into separation activities for the finance leadership, providing the necessary level of visibility into separation progress and potential issues. Once the plans have been

developed, periodic tracking and reporting are essential to assess the finance function's readiness for Day 1. Figure 7.2 provides a sample road map to Day 1, breaking down the separation strategy into planning and execution steps.

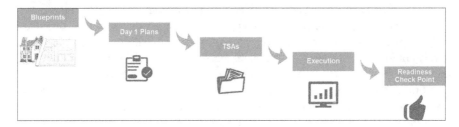

Fig. 7.2   Planning and Execution Roadmap

Blueprints: The Day 1 blueprints take the separation strategy and translate it to the
process, systems, and people level. The blueprints identify and document the processes,
systems, and resources (people) that are critical for Day 1. In essence, the blueprints
become the source of truth throughout the life cycle of the separation, including outlining current processes, defining the Day 1 (and future state, if applicable) strategy for
each process, and the anticipated system and resource requirements.

Day 1 Plans: The Day 1 plans are the logical next step after blueprinting and created
to manage the operationalization of the Day 1 separation strategy. Overall, the Day 1
plans are typically managed globally. At the subfunctional or process area level, the
plans are organized by projects, which can be linked to separation costs and resource
needs. The plans capture critical milestones, due dates, cross-functional and cross-
project dependencies, and planning assumptions. For companies with significant global
footprints, refining the global Day 1 plans into country/local Day 1 plans is essential.
The country/local Day 1 plans should document additional country-specific activities
(e.g., setting up local legal entities for local finance functions and tax filings).

TSAs: As mentioned earlier, TSAs are signed agreements between the seller or
parent company and the divested entity (or vice versa in the case of reverse TSAs)
that allow one entity (typically, the seller or parent company) to continue providing
agreed-upon services to the other entity (typically, the divested entity) for a specific
period of time post-transaction close to prevent the disruption of critical functions
(e.g., month-end close). To minimize potential disruptions on Day 1 and help ensure
operational continuity, it is essential to identify any infrastructure, process, or
resource gaps upfront and plan for the specific TSAs that will be needed to address
these gaps. In general, TSAs comprise two key components:

- Legal agreements
- Schedules

While the legal agreements are the responsibility of the legal team, the schedules
are drafted by the finance function that is the recipient of the services. These schedules

help ensure a clear understanding of what services are to be provided, by whom, and for how long. The schedules typically contain the following key information:

- Service name and description
- Service provider and recipient
- Service period
- Pricing of services
- Service managers
- Exit plans

Execution: Exhaustive Day 1 plans alone will not guarantee a successful separation. The chances of success increase significantly when such plans are complemented by meticulous execution and supported by tested program management tools and templates. Equally important is the active engagement of finance leadership in tracking the progress of separation activities against the separation timeline and monitoring and resolving critical issues, risks, and dependencies in a timely manner.

The tools and templates used are outlined below.

Workstream Status Template:

- Weekly status reporting template, focusing on major developments, issues, and risks to be *submitted on a periodic basis by project leads.*
- Discuss readiness for major planning milestones.

Project Matrix:

- A project tracking tool that identifies Day 1 project owners and status; it also supports cross-finance function coordination (i.e., coordination with tax, treasury, and internal audit).

Cross-functional RAID Log:

- Cross-functional log to track risks, actions, issues, and decisions.
- These items are identified by project leads and communicated, escalated (as needed), and driven to resolution across functions and the program management office.

Readiness Checkpoint: One of the typical strategies employed to assess separation progress and readiness for Day 1 is a readiness checkpoint (RCP). The RCP is a 1 or 2 day workshop, for all finance function leaders and key stakeholders (including Day 1 project leaders), focused on the need to confirm the operational readiness of the financial close process, the payroll process, the accounts payable process to mitigate disruption of payments to vendors vital to product supply procurement, and cash application and collections processes. It also confirms that critical deal close conditions (i.e., Form 10 filing) are on track for successful completion. Ultimately, the RCP gives finance leadership the confidence that Day 1 will be executed successfully with minimal impact to month-end, quarter-end, and year-end close processes. The outcome of the RCP yields a finance go/no-go decision for Day 1.

Case Study: 7

Background

A Fortune 500 technology company recently completed a significant acquisition funded by a substantial amount of debt. In order to pay down the debt, the company decided to sell certain of its noncore businesses. The company wanted to market these noncore businesses as stand-alone product lines, as well as a combined business.

Challenges

No historical financial statements existed for these noncore businesses and, therefore, needed to be created for the sales process. The management, sales, and distribution of the different product lines overlapped significantly. Furthermore, the different product lines did not manage balance sheets on a stand-alone basis, and the majority of fixed assets were shared across the different product lines. Gross margin was tracked by product line, but no other operating expense information was managed on a stand-alone product basis. Additionally, certain portions of the business that historically were included with these noncore assets were not going to be included in the transaction.

Approach

In order to develop financial information for each product line, it was important to first identify all information that could systematically be tracked by product. This formed the starting point of the product line financial statements. Below is the approach that was followed:

- Each financial statement line item was assessed to determine how information was recorded historically at the ledger and sub-ledger level.
- Specific attributes were determined that could be used to assign information to a specific product line.
- Finally, for areas with no reasonable data-driven method for attribution, a reasonable allocation approach was developed for the purposes of the financial statements.
- Once a methodology was developed for each financial statement line item, quality of earnings and working capital analysis reports were created for each product line, as well as for the combined business.

Impact/Results

The above approach allowed the seller to frame historical results in the most positive light for buyers and adjust historical results for items considered to be nonrecurring, nonoperating, or out of period. Additionally, the creation of these reports allowed management to prepare for diligence meetings and develop an understanding of the key deal issues that would arise in due diligence.

Finally, a working capital analysis was performed that provided management with the information it needed to successfully negotiate a working capital peg in the purchase agreement that protected the company from cash leakage.

Although the creation of product line financial information required more time and effort than simply creating one set of combined financial statements, it gave the company flexibility in marketing and allowed it to receive more competing bids for the businesses. Ultimately, the businesses were sold on a combined basis; however, the ability to market the businesses in different ways gave the company leverage in negotiations and helped it to realize a higher sales price than if it had simply marketed the business as a whole.

Chapter 8
Clean Financial Separation

8.1 Overview

The need for carve-out financial statements is driven by a company's decision to separate a part of its operations either through a sale to a third party, a spin-off to its current shareholders in a taxable or tax-free transaction, or a divestiture. Each of these types of transactions has unique financial statement requirements. In general, the financial statements will include a balance sheet, an income statement, a cash flow statement, and a statement of equity for a certain number of years based on how and by whom the financial statements will be used. This chapter will focus on the creation of carve-out financial statements used in connection with a spin-off that are compliant with regulations from the Securities and Exchange Commission (SEC) as well as accounting principles generally accepted in the United States (GAAP); however, we will also discuss considerations when full carve-out financial statements are not required.

8.2 Identification of the Business

The first step in preparing carve-out financial statements is to determine the definition of the business being separated. The carve-out entity may consist of all or part of an individual subsidiary, multiple subsidiaries, or even one or more business units.

Carve-out financial statements should present information about all parts of the carve-out entity's historical results, but not information related to knowledge of future business decisions. Keep in mind there could be instances in which the carve-out financial statements include assets or operations that will not be part of the final carve-out transaction. Occasionally, an entity may also provide pro forma financial

© Deloitte Development LLC 2018
J. Joy, *Divestitures and Spin-Offs*, Management for Professionals,
https://doi.org/10.1007/978-1-4939-7662-1_8

information to adjust the historical carve-out financial statements to reflect only the net assets and operations being carved out.

The business being separated can either be viewed as a legal entity, management view, or product carve-out. For a legal entity carve-out, the parts of the business being divested are accounted for as separate and distinct legal entities. There is either no or limited comingling of products or businesses in the legal entities, and all the operational accounts and balance sheet accounts of each legal entity can easily be identified and rolled up to get to the starting point for the combined carve-out financial statements.

More often, the legal entity structure is established for tax purposes and therefore may contain complete product lines or business units, or portions thereof that may not align with the entity being divested. In this scenario, a segment or business unit with defined financial results may be a good starting point for identifying the carve-out entity. Often, however, only a portion of a segment or business unit is being divested, increasing the difficulty of identifying the assets and liabilities related to the carve-out entity. These management view or product carve-outs are typically more complicated than legal entity carve-outs, and management must have a good understanding of the assets and liabilities related to the carve-out entity.

In a speech at the 2001 American Institute of Certified Public Accountants (AICPA) National Conference on Current SEC Developments, SEC staff member Leslie Overton indicated that if the carve-out entity is an SEC registrant or will undergo an initial public offering (IPO), the carve-out financial statements "should include all relevant activities that have been a part of the history of the business and that can be expected to repeat as the business continues in the future."

The remainder of this chapter focuses on the process required to establish a product carve-out.

8.3   Getting the Team Together

When assembling a project team to prepare carve-out financial statements, avoid the temptation to simply look at the process as an accounting and reporting exercise. The ideal project team will likely comprise a mixture of controllership, accounting, external reporting, and business and operations personnel from the sales, R&D, supply chain, and IT organizations etc. who possess the knowledge of the divesting company's operations, as well as specific knowledge of the part of the business that is being separated.

8.3.1   Controllership, Accounting, and Reporting

The controllership, accounting, and reporting functions will be primarily responsible for the preparation of the carve-out financial statements. A staff member from the controllership function tends to take responsibility for managing the project, including assigning tasks and workstreams to the various functions involved in creating the carve-out financial statements.

As noted later in this chapter, a good understanding of the general ledger system, including how transactions are recorded in the system and how that data is rolled up into the financial statements, is critical to deconstructing the data for purposes of carve-out financial statements. The controllership and the external reporting function typically have the best line of sight to such information. In addition, the groups responsible for compiling subledgers for property, plant, and equipment, accounts receivable, and accounts payable are integral to the carve-out process. Data within these accounts will need to be specifically identified for purposes of the carve-out financial statements.

8.3.2   *Information Technology (IT) and Other Operational Functions*

Engage the IT department early in the carve-out process. Due to the need to extract data from IT systems in ways that may be different than the current reporting structure, the IT group may need to perform a significant amount of work throughout the carve-out process. In addition to creating the code to extract the data, the IT group may need to create additional controls for the new reports being generated specifically for the carve-out financial statements. The required controls must be identified and tested before auditing the carve-out financial statements.

Certain corporate costs and costs specifically related to the entity being divested must be understood so the required policies around expense allocation can be documented and followed. It is for this reason that business and operational people must be involved in the production of the carve-out financial statements. Their participation occurs at different points throughout the process, but particularly in the planning and data collection phases.

The investor relations group must also be involved throughout the process. Given the time it takes to create a set of carve-out financial statements for a divestiture or spin-off, the divesting company will likely need to report the status externally to its shareholders. From the initial deal announcement through the creation of the carve-out financial statements, shareholders will ask many questions regarding the progress of the carve-out process. Investor relations primarily deals with shareholder-related issues; thus, involving investor relations throughout the carve-out process is essential. The Divestiture Management Office (DMO) and investor relations should coordinate any public statements made regarding the carve-out process, especially as the process gets closer to its final execution and the distribution of shares of the divested entity to existing shareholders.

8.3.3 Role of the External Auditor

The external auditor plays a unique role in the preparation of carve-out financial statements. The external auditor will need to understand the overall basis of presentation and accounting methodologies used in the carve-out financial statements. Engaging the external auditor early in the carve-out preparation process will help avoid the necessity of reworking the carve-out financial statements.

The time required for the external auditor to complete the audit of the carve-out financial statements and provide a signed audit opinion letter confirming the sufficiency of the carve-out financial statements for their intended purpose should be layered into the overall divestiture plan. Engaging the external auditor to perform much of its work on a parallel track with the carve-out work will help shorten the timing of the divestiture plan. If the audit work is performed only after completion of the carve-out financial statements, significant time will likely need to be added to the overall divestiture plan, which may jeopardize the timing of the overall transaction.

8.4 Identification of the Data: How Separate Is Separate?

Often, during initial conversations about a carve-out, management will insist the carve-out process should be easy because the underlying financial data of the entity being divested is either already separated or easy to separate. But this is typically not the case. Management often receives reports in which accounts such as revenue and cost of sales are broken down in a similar way to those required for the carve-out financial statements; thus, management thinks the process will be easy. But usually not all financial accounts are broken out this way. The accounts on the balance sheet are almost never broken out this way. Therefore, identifying which financial data can be specifically identified to the carve-out entity and which financial data cannot be specifically identified will require some other method of allocation in order to be included in the financial accounts of the carve-out entity and can be difficult. Creating the carve-out financial statements requires analyzing each account in the consolidated trial balance of the divesting entity. The more the divesting company's operations are integrated, the more difficult and time-consuming it will be to create carve-out financial statements.

8.4.1 Data Collection and Data Repository

Once the financial data for the carve-out entity has been identified, management of the divesting company must determine where to house the information while creating the trial balance upon which the carve-out financial statements will be built. The speed at which the company must create the carve-out financial statements, the complexity of its current reporting system, and the availability of appropriate personnel to complete the carve-out process will be integral to determining what data repository to use.

Use the Current Enterprise Resource Planning (ERP) System: Using the divesting company's ERP system can be complicated, given the complexity of the ERP system and the need for IT staff to recode it for this purpose. Essentially, IT should set up a dummy company code in the divesting company's general ledger through which all accounts specifically identified for the carve-out entity can be mapped. Additionally, carve-out journal entries would also be processed through this dummy company. The benefit of using the divesting company's current ERP system is that relevant company personnel are already familiar with the processes in place to book journal entries and combine the information for the trial balance. By using these same journal entry and reporting processes, there are a limited number of incremental financial and operational controls that will need to be put in place specific to the carve-out financial statements to satisfy the company's SOX control requirements.

Use an External Tool: When a company hires external consultants to assist with the carve-out financial statements, they often bring their own external tool that creates an offline repository for the carve-out financial data. The benefit of this approach is that it tends to be quick and easy to set up. Typically, this tool is capable of pulling trial balance information at the legal entity level from the company's ledger system. After reconciling the totals to the latest audited period, the consultant usually removes items that are specifically identifiable to the divesting company, leaving a baseline trial balance for the carve-out entity. From there, the consultant continues to use this external tool to gather information related to all of the carve-out adjustments and stores it in the offline repository. This can also speed up the efficiency of the audit process since all of the adjustments are stored in one central repository specific to the carve-out. Using this external tool also makes it easier for the tax department of the divesting company to create the required "as-if" tax provision since the carve-out adjustments can be tagged to individual legal entities or, at a minimum, country codes, so that the appropriate effective tax rate can be applied.

8.5   How to Manage Heavy Operational and Financial Integration

Many companies expand over time by acquiring other businesses, and they often integrate the acquired businesses into their overall business model. The level of integration may differ for each acquisition based on strategy or the size of the acquired business. In a carve-out, the data collection effort often crosses over this entire spectrum of prior acquisitions, thereby magnifying the difficulty of compiling even the most fundamental baseline financial information before any carve-out adjustments. The level of integration can also affect a company's ability to collect the information necessary to identify and allocate costs.

8.6 Planning for the Work Ahead

An important piece of the puzzle to keep the carve-out heading in the right direction is developing a good project plan for the financial statement carve-out process. The project planners must understand the business being carved out well enough to identify areas that will require more intense focus and effort. In many ways, the project plan should mirror the financial statements, with each line item of the statement of cash flows corresponding to a workstream. Information for straightforward workstreams, such as the payment of dividends, will be easy to collect in a short timeframe, whereas more complicated workstreams, such as corporate expenses and intercompany transactions, may take several weeks to complete. Make particular note of areas with overlapping data, as well as areas that are prerequisites for data collection in other areas, and use this information to identify appropriate due dates and review cycles to help ensure the timely and quality production of carve-out financial statements.

8.7 Materiality

Materiality is another item to consider when developing carve-out financial statements. For instance, if the carve-out entity is small in relation to the divesting company, amounts previously considered immaterial to the divesting company may become material for the carve-out entity's operations. Because of these new materiality thresholds, management may need to examine audit adjustments that had historically been passed in a particular audit to determine if such items need to be accounted for in the carve-out entity's financial statements. In addition, the external auditor will examine the materiality of various accounts and balances to determine if additional testing needs to be performed on these components to meet audit requirements.

8.8 Allocation of Costs

It is important to keep the end in mind when planning carve-out financial statements and understand the documentation and deliverables required to support the audit, particularly since the audit procedures may be different than typical year-end procedures. For instance, the allocation of costs in relation to the carve-out entity is especially detailed and often requires heavy documentation. Start by defining the rules of the road for accounting position papers and other deliverables to help establish a framework by which the carve-out financial statements will be created. It is important to get agreement from the external auditor on this framework early in process to reduce the risk of rework later in the process. Next, define the bucket of costs from which the allocation will be based. This will help the external auditor determine the incremental audit procedures that need to be performed on the detail supporting those costs. Lastly, reach agreement among relevant stakeholders and the external auditor on the allocation drivers that will be used to calculate the allocation of comingled costs, such as percentage revenue or headcount.

8.9 Execution

Once the appropriate personnel are engaged to create the carve-out financial statements and an effective plan has been developed to tackle the project, execution becomes the all-encompassing objective. During this effort, make sure to build an auditable file to support the underlying carve-out financial statements. What follows is a discussion of some of the issues that may be encountered during execution.

8.9.1 Balance Sheet

The balance sheet is typically the area that requires the most judgment when creating carve-out financial statements. Most companies do not usually track separate balance sheet accounts for their business units. The ability to simply push a button and produce a stand-alone balance sheet simply does not exist. Rather, those involved in the carve-out process must understand the assets and liabilities that will be used by the carve-out entity and the underlying legal agreements that will be affected by the separation.

8.9.2 Working Capital

Most companies have corporate cash management functions that maintain sweep accounts, as well as centralized cash collection and bill payment centers. Specific accounting guidance exists that can help the preparer of carve-out financial statements understand what to include as cash and cash equivalents on the face of the balance sheet. Often, the carve-out entity and the divesting company share the same customers and vendors, which makes it difficult to specifically identify receivables and payables for the carve-out entity. Thus, management should develop a solution early in the carve-out process to address this issue, such as using individual stock keeping units (SKUs) to allocate shipping and tax charges appropriately across the two entities.

8.9.3   Property, Plant, and Equipment (PP&E)

When a facility is comingled between the carve-out entity and the divesting company, it can be difficult to separate hard assets, such as buildings and equipment, in the carve-out financial statements. In such cases, management of the divesting entity must analyze the percentage of use of the asset by each entity, as well as any underlying contractual agreements regarding use of the facility, before determining which entity, the carve-out entity or the divesting entity, will retain the facility in the separation. Typically, the separation of PP&E closely represents the opening balance of the carve-out entity.

8.9.4   Goodwill

When preparing carve-out financial statements, management must consider any goodwill amounts the divesting company will contribute to the carve-out entity. Because the intent of the carve-out financial statements is to segregate transactions within the divesting company's financial statements that are specifically related to the carve-out entity, any historical goodwill amounts attributed to the carve-out entity should be included and disclosed in the carve-out financial statements.

Usually, the carve-out entity's operating segments and business units differ from those of the divesting company. A decision needs to be taken to identify the chief operating decision maker (CODM) of the carve-out entity. Additionally, an analysis should be performed to determine whether the characteristics exist to conclude that the carve-out entity may have more than one segment for their business. If so, discrete financial information is required for each operating segment identified.

An analysis should also be performed to determine whether goodwill impairment testing is required at the time of the separation due to the new segments identified.

8.9.5   Accrued Liabilities

Accrued liabilities are often difficult to identify due to the lack of underlying data captured during the initial recording of the transaction. Certain accounts, such as environmental liabilities, can either be specifically identified with the carve-out entity or allocated based on terms negotiated during the separation.

8.9.6   Debt

Many companies must determine whether the divesting company's debt, which had not historically been pushed down to the financial records of their subsidiaries, should be reflected in the carve-out financial statements. The answer depends on whether the divesting company's debt includes transaction-related debt for the carve-out entity. Specific accounting guidance, such as Staff Accounting Bulletin (SAB) Topic 5.J, New Basis of Accounting Required in Certain Circumstances, exists concerning how to record pushdown debt in the carve-out financial statements. Additionally, there are several SEC interpretations available regarding whether debt first entered into by the divesting company should be recorded on the books of the carve-out entity.

8.9.7 Pension Liabilities

In some cases, employees of the carve-out entity participate in a defined benefit plan sponsored by the divesting company. While no specific accounting guidance exists on how to record such plans in the carve-out financial statements, there are two acceptable methods:

- A multiemployer approach
- An allocation approach

Under either approach, the carve-out entity's income statement should reflect an allocated portion of the net periodic benefit cost of the plan. The factor that differentiates the allocation approach from the multiemployer approach is that under the allocation approach, portions of the benefit obligation, assets, and accumulated other comprehensive income (AOCI) for the plan are also included in the carve-out entity's balance sheet.

8.9.8 Deferred Compensation

Deferred employee compensation is also typically allocated in the carve-out financial statements. Generally, the deferred compensation should follow the employees who intend to move to the carve-out entity. Because amounts may have been allocated in the historical financial accounts of the divesting company, management should consider utilizing similar allocation methodologies for the carve-out financial statements.

8.9.9 Derivatives and Hedging

Derivative instruments are another area with limited accounting guidance related to the carve-out financial statements. Regardless of whether the derivatives are designated as hedging relationships, there should be an evaluation of all derivative contracts to determine whether any are specifically identifiable to the carve-out entity.

Generally, if a derivative instrument hedges an item that has been allocated to the carve-out financial statements, that derivative instrument should also be included in the carve-out financial statements. The identification of derivative instrument hedges can be difficult due to hedging strategies in effect at the corporate level. Because of the blending of assets and liabilities the derivative instrument is meant to hedge, it is sometimes difficult to identify the derivative associated with a specific asset or liability included in the carve-out financial statements. In such cases, a decision must be taken to determine whether the positions taken as a result of the derivative instrument hedges should be included in the carve-out financial statements.

The accounting for derivative instruments included in the carve-out financial statements should generally mirror the accounting historically applied by the divesting company. As with other aspects of the carve-out financial statements, the accounting for derivative instruments should give users of the carve-out financial statements an appropriate understanding of the historical activity of the carve-out entity.

8.10   Income Statements

8.10.1   Direct and Indirect Expenses and Allocation Methods

In general, the carve-out income statement is typically easier to create than the carve-out balance sheet because companies usually do a better job of tracking revenue by product or business segment, as well as the margins associated with that revenue. The SEC generally views expenses in two categories:

• Expenses directly related to revenue-producing activities
• Indirect expenses, such as corporate overhead and interest

Expenses associated with revenue-producing activities are generally easy to identify, whereas indirect expenses require more analysis as they may be subject to allocation methodologies that need to be identified during the planning process as described in Sect. 8.6: Planning for the work ahead. Typical drivers used to allocate indirect expenses include percentage of revenue, number of employees, or square footage.

There is limited accounting guidance on how to perform allocations; however, many companies use by analogy SEC SAB Topic 1.B, *Allocation of Expenses and Related Disclosures in Financial Statements of Subsidiaries, Divisions, or Lesser Business Components of Another Entity*. The SEC believes that all costs of doing business, including both direct and indirect expenses, should be reflected in the historical carve-out financial statements. For indirect expenses not specifically identifiable, the SEC encourages companies to develop a reasonable allocation method to attribute the indirect expenses to the carve-out entity. Management must disclose details related to the method used for all expense allocations, as well as an explanation regarding why the method chosen is reasonable. In addition to this general statement, the SEC also generally provides interpretive responses to several questions surrounding this topic.

When disposing of a segment, a company may have already allocated certain corporate expenses, including executive management, IT, accounting, legal, and treasury costs, as part of its historical financial statement presentation. While a similar method of allocation may be appropriate for the carve-out financial statements, management should review the allocation methodology used in the historical presentation to determine whether any changes need to be made to the underlying allocation drivers. It should be noted that the process of allocating historical corporate costs may not reflect the actual expenses that would have been incurred had the carve-out entity operated as a separate stand-alone company for the periods presented.

8.10.2 Intercompany Transactions

Because the intent of the carve-out financial statements is to show the historical financial results of the carve-out entity, a review of all intercompany transactions must take place to determine the appropriate presentation of those intercompany transactions within the carve-out financial statements. Management must decide whether these transactions, which in the past were likely eliminated as part of an intercompany process, need to be reflected as intracompany transactions with a related party. Transactions deemed to be intercompany transactions within the context of the carve-out entity will still be eliminated for purposes on the combined carve-out financial statements.

8.10.3 Share-Based Payment Awards

Carve-out financial statements should reflect all stock compensation expenses attributable to the carve-out entity. These expenses may be specifically identifiable to a stock compensation plan; if not, then an allocation of such expenses is required. Often, stock compensation information is available at the individual employee level, thereby making the expense allocation fairly straightforward. However, there are situations in which the stock compensation is tracked at a higher level, thereby requiring an allocation similar to other corporate overhead charges.

8.10.4 Transaction Costs

Entities that incur transaction costs, including accounting and tax fees, legal fees, and investment banking fees, in connection with carve-out transactions must consider which of those costs to include in the carve-out financial statements. For example, the cost of auditing the carve-out financial statements is a specifically identifiable cost of the carve-out entity and, therefore, should be included in the carve-out financial statements. Determining how to include shared costs may be more challenging as such costs must be allocated in a manner consistent with the principles outlined in SEC SAB Topic 1.B. This is an area of varied application and should be discussed with the external auditor early in the process.

8.10.5   *Income Taxes*

Income taxes involve a significant workstream in any carve-out process because management will need to prepare the calculation for income tax expense and associated tax payable on an as-if stand-alone tax basis. This means the tax expense and payable reflected in the carve-out financial statements could differ from the amounts reflected in the divesting company's historical financial statements. In addition, the appropriate deferred tax positions need to be calculated as well. This requires an understanding of the legal entity structure that makes up the carve-out entity. As mentioned in the beginning, some carve-outs follow a legal entity path and other follow a product path. If the carve-out follows a product path, the company must still be able to associate the underlying assets and liabilities of the carve-out entity to specific legal entities so the associated deferred tax positions can be determined.

In addition to its inherent complexity, the calculation of taxes is made more difficult because it requires a set of pretax carve-out financial statements to be completed before the work can begin. Therefore, close coordination in the project planning phase is required, as well as communication of any subsequent changes to the underlying carve-out financial data after tax work has begun.

8.11   Cash Flows

Cash flows are one of the most difficult financial statements to carve out. While most of the captions in the carve-out statement of cash flows, and the classification of transactions included therein, will be similar to those in the divesting company's historical cash flow statement, certain classifications of transactions will require more attention from management. These items relate primarily to the presentation of intercompany transactions in the carve-out cash flow statement, including deemed dividends, noncash transfers between the divesting company and the carve-out subsidiary, or intercompany sales or other types of cash transfers that should be evaluated by management. It is important to understand how such transactions were settled historically and, therefore, how they will be reflected in the carve-out statement of cash flows. There is limited accounting guidance on how to properly classify items within a carve-out statement of cash flows and, therefore, it is important to maintain a well-documented file to support decisions taken by management.

8.12   Financial Statement Notes

Preparing the notes to the carve-out financial statements requires answering the following questions:

- How are the financial statements going to be used?
- What guidance dictates what needs to be included?

If the carve-out financial statements are going to be used for a registration of securities utilizing either a Form 10 or S-1, then they need to comply with all of the rules and regulations prescribed by the SEC. If the financial statements are going to be used for purposes of a sale (see Sect. 8.13 below), then there may be more leniency as to the form and content of the notes. In the case of carve-out financial statement used in connection with a sale, the requirements for those financial statements can be negotiated between the divesting entity and the buying entity and may not include all of the financial statement footnotes required under a public filing.

In the end, creating the footnotes to the carve-out financial statements requires understanding where the financial data is located and how easily it is to separate that data using the same methodologies employed to create the carve-out statement of income and carve-out balance sheet. As the divesting company establishes the overall divestiture plan for the carve-out financial statements, consideration should be given to the data requirements for the footnotes and ensuring that the necessary information is available. Capturing the information will not add significant time to the project plan.

There are situations in which certain footnotes will need to be created specifically for the carve-out financial statements. This can occur when the information underlying the notes is deemed immaterial for purposes of the divesting company's historical financial statements, but the information is significant enough to justify separate footnote disclosures for the carve-out entity. Segment information is another example of new financial data that may be required in a note. As previously discussed, it may be determined that different or additional segments are required for the carve-out financial statements. As a result, a plan for such a change must be created, a determination made if the financial information required for the new segment presentation is available in the system, and a structure to capture the new information is created. Making this decision early in the process will allow the data collection to occur simultaneous to the creation of other carve-out financial statement support.

8.13 "Deal" Financial Statements

In certain scenarios, full carve-out financial statements as discussed above may not be required for the purposes of a divestiture. These situations typically fall into two categories: situations where the buyer has received a waiver to provide the SEC abbreviated financial statements in lieu of full carve-out statements and situations where the buyer has no financial reporting obligations.

Abbreviated Financial Statements

In situations where the entity to be divested is being carved out of a much larger entity, buyers can request a waiver from the SEC to provide abbreviated financial statements in lieu of full carve-out financial statements. This waiver is generally given by the SEC when the following criteria are met:

- The entity to be divested is not accounted for as a separate entity, subsidiary, or division of the seller's business.

- Seller does not manage the business to be divested on a stand-alone basis.
- Stand-alone financial statements of the business to be divested have never previously been prepared.
- Seller does not have sufficient financial information about the business to be divested. The carve-out entity's manufacturing, purchasing, sales, and distribution functions are all shared with other portions of the seller's business, and such costs have not been historically managed, or allocated, on a product-line basis. Seller has never allocated corporate overhead expenses.

Abbreviated financial statements are comprised of a Statement of Revenues over Direct Expenses, a Statement of Assets Acquired and Liabilities Assumed, and related footnotes. The Statement of Revenues over Direct Expenses includes all direct expenses incurred by the seller in running the business, including an allocation of costs where certain functions are shared (such as sales/distribution/customer support); however, they do not need to include an allocation of corporate overhead. The Statement of Assets Acquired and Liabilities assumed should be based on the purchase agreement agreed to with the sale. This statement would only include the specific assets and liabilities that are being transferred in a deal. These financial statements generally cannot be produced until a purchase agreement has been signed as the balances to be included in the financial statements are driven by the purchase agreement. Although these financial statements are still required to be audited by an independent audit firm, the time and cost incurred to complete the audit is generally significantly less than that of full carve-out financial statements. In situations where the seller thinks that the buyer may qualify for the SEC waiver, it is strongly suggested that they apply as it will result in significant time and cost savings for the seller.

Buyer Has No Financial Reporting Obligations

If the entity to be disposed of is immaterial relative to the buyer, the buyer may not have any obligation to provide historical audited financial statements to the SEC. Even in these cases, however, they will likely request historical financial statements as a part of the due diligence process. The most common financial information requested includes a management P&L (generally totaling to operating income or Management EBITDA) and a working capital schedule. In a carve-out situation, sellers have significant latitude in determining how these financial statements are compiled as there is no clear guidance. Sellers should consider the carve-out leading practices discussed above in compiling the financial information and, however, should also consider additional factors such as:

1. Are there any significant nonoperational, nonrecurring, out-of-period items, or significant acquisitions/dispositions in the historical P&L that should be adjusted for in determining Management EBITDA?
2. Is the P&L fully burdened for the use of the seller's shared service functions (such as accounting, finance, HR, etc.) from which it benefits?
3. Are there any significant nonoperational, nonrecurring, out-of-period items, or significant acquisitions/dispositions in the historical working capital that should

be adjusted for in determining the estimated working capital balances required to operate the business on a stand-alone basis?
4. Are the assets/liabilities in the working capital analysis indicative of the actual assets/liabilities that would be required to operate the business on a stand-alone basis? If not, is there a reasonable method to estimate these amounts?

Every carve-out scenario is unique, but the goal of this financial information is to provide buyers a view of what the business to be disposed of would look like on a stand-alone basis. This may require an analysis to estimate the stand-alone costs of services currently being provided by the seller. When compiling these financial statements, it is important to clearly document the assumptions that were used in their creation. While buyers may not always agree with the assumptions a seller makes, clear documentation allows them to better understand the financial information as presented and to adjust for their own assumptions (to the extent necessary).

Case Study: 8

Background

In an effort to ensure the appropriate amount of focus on its diverse product-line portfolio, the client, a Fortune 500 global healthcare company, had recently completed a spin-off of one of its significant lines of businesses ("Controlled").

"Controlled" comprised approximately 40 percent of the client's revenue in the year immediately preceding the announcement of the spin-off and had operations in over 60 countries. In order to effectuate the spin-off, the client was required to file Form 10 financial statements with the Securities and Exchange Commission ("SEC").

Furthermore, Company management stated that it wanted the spin-off to be completed within 12 months of the decision.

Challenges

- Although "Controlled" was a separate business within the client company, its operations and financial results were not separately tracked within the Company's internal financial accounting systems.
- Further, most of "Controlled's" operations were contained in mixed legal entities (i.e., the legal entities contained operations of Controlled and other Company businesses), and "Controlled's" financial results therefore could not be queried simply based on legal entity reporting.

As a result, the client was faced with preparing and filing SEC compliant financial statements for a business for which underlying financial and transactional detail was not readily available.

Hence, a detailed analysis of historical financial records was required to identify and separate "Controlled's" results on a global basis.

Approach

Given the challenges to prepare SEC compliant financial statements, the client worked with its advisors and auditors at the outset of the project, to identify an approach to prepare and audit the financial statements within management's time-frame for the spin-off.

The Company concluded that it would employ a "tiered" approach to assess materiality of "Controlled's" operations on a jurisdiction-by-jurisdiction basis. This tiered analysis revealed that more than 90% of "Controlled's" operations (i.e., pre-tax book income) were confined to approximately ten key countries, which allowed the team to focus the overall carve-out efforts on the most impactful jurisdictions.

Abbreviated carve-out procedures were performed in other less material jurisdictions, which allowed the client to appropriately focus its internal and external resources to achieve management's timeline for the spin-off.

Impact/Results

The client was successful in preparing financial statements for "Controlled" and also has auditors complete their audit, to file SEC compliant financial statements within management's timeline and complete spin-off of Controlled to the Company's shareholders.

Time spent on up-front planning, including the tiered analysis, put the Company in a position to timely address other issues and complexities that arose throughout the year-long process. Without this up-front consideration, the aggressive timeline put forth by management may not have been met.

Chapter 9
Building the Arsenal: Setting Up an Effective Separation Team and Governance

9.1 Introduction

Companies are increasingly turning to divestitures to shed noncore assets, generate cash, and satisfy investor demand to be nimble and focused.[1] In a recent Deloitte survey, over 70% of executives said they expected to sell units or assets in 2017. The trend toward divestitures has been increasing, and research indicates they are likely to continue to be important to a company's overall business and M&A strategy. Many companies have faced pressure to grow aggressively, which has made their operations more complex and may have stunted their ability to respond to dynamic market needs. As a result, executives are choosing to divest one or more business units, leading to an increase in parallel or serial divestiture deals over the past few years.[2] Additionally, to succeed in a competitive marketplace, some companies are using divestitures as transformational catalysts to shed inefficient operations and optimize remaining business functions during deal execution.

Divestitures are challenging as they require precise execution against a rigid timeline, balancing one-time costs, run-rate trends, and organizational and operational risks.[3] Intertwined international operations, multiple divestitures running in parallel, and programs to transform the seller company's[4] operations are some of the unique challenges facing businesses looking to divest in today's marketplace. Some companies considering a divestiture should also consider the extensive planning, change management, and communication programs required to execute the

---

[1] "M&A Trends: Year End Report," Deloitte Consulting LLC, December 1, 2016; "Spin Cycle: The rise of technology sector de-mergers," Deloitte Consulting LLP, July 7, 2015; "Building a nimble workforce to drive technology innovation," Lake, McCree, CIO from IDG, November 1, 2016.

[2] "Five ways to master serial divestitures," Deloitte Consulting LLP, April 1, 2016.

[3] "Divestiture M&A News: 2016 Q1 recap: Global divestiture market experienced a slower start to 2016," Deloitte Consulting LLC, May 2016.

[4] "Seller company" is a placeholder for the business units remaining post-deal until a new name is publicly announced.

© Deloitte Development LLC 2018
J. Joy, *Divestitures and Spin-Offs*, Management for Professionals,
https://doi.org/10.1007/978-1-4939-7662-1_9

divestiture in a timely manner without affecting employee morale or attrition. Such programs can put a strain on key talent who suddenly need to wear multiple hats, fulfilling both their day-to-day jobs as well as driving divestiture-related activities to a successful closure.

Global business operations add significant complexity to divestitures. Teams must disentangle legal entities in multiple legal jurisdictions and navigate compliance within multiple regulatory environments, an issue compounded by cross-border M&A transactions. Between January and May of 2017, US companies were the most popular target of foreign companies, which translated to over 4400 deals worth approximately $530 billion.[5] The complications of international laws, cultural differences, and interdependencies within global business units complicate every step of the divestiture process in a cross-border transaction, from identifying potential buyers to operationally separating the business units. As a result, divestitures are starting to resemble complex military deployments.

More than 40% executives believe their companies will pursue divestitures in 2017 compared to those surveyed in 2015.[6] As large companies with cross-border divisions begin divesting noncore functions, increasingly complex deals will likely become the norm rather than the exception, and organizations looking to become more nimble need to be prepared.

For companies to successfully pull off these "complex military deployments," it is important that they build the necessary arsenal. Successful divestitures require capable teams driving the separation activities, ample leadership support, regular engagement with the buying company, strong governance structures, and clear guiding principles.

9.2   How Do You Identify Effective Leaders for the Divestiture?

It is important to choose strong leaders to manage and guide a divestiture. From the lead divestiture executive to cross-functional workstream managers, leaders play critical roles in directing separation teams and driving activities to completion. In particular, strong separation leaders must be able to:

- Establish the appropriate team structure and cadence
- Drive divestiture planning and execution
- Facilitate communication among teams
- Escalate key issues to appropriate executive leadership
- Make key decisions

Regardless of the size of the entity to be separated, strong leaders typically possess a combination of the following characteristics.

---

[5] Thomson Reuters Data, May 2017.

[6] Divestiture Survey Report 2013: Sharpening Your Strategy," Deloitte Consulting LLP, January 1, 2013. Accessed February 8, 2017.

9.2.1   Connection to Business Units

Leaders with close ties to a business unit are effective in guiding a divestiture because:

- They are familiar with the business unit's staff and can scope and resource team members who will be assets to the separation effort.
- They bring insights into potential separation challenges faced by the business unit and how to resolve them successfully.

Divestitures are cross-functional in nature, and each function likely has a unique work style, culture, and communication style. Leaders with strong connections to business units can use their understanding of these nuances to effectively communicate across different functional teams, as well as bring foresight to address conflicts and challenges before they arise.

9.2.2   Deal Experience

In the fast-paced environment of a divestiture with many interdependencies, stringent business requirements, and aggressive deadlines, prior divestiture experience is critical. Even before the deal announcement, project leaders are often expected to hit the ground running, with little time for a learning curve.

Although the program management challenges are similar to those encountered in any large-scale initiative, the manners in which they manifest and are resolved are unique and require experience and seasoned judgment. A common example is scope creep. In a divestiture, it is common for various groups to siphon resources for initiatives unrelated to the core divestiture effort. Recognizing what is critical to the divestiture and what is a nice bonus or even worse, a distraction, is a critical skill gained through experience.

9.2.3   Leadership Support

Active support and commitment from senior management (e.g., business unit leads, functional leads) are critical to achieving a successful divestiture. Visible involvement from senior leadership can help drive deadlines and recruit key talent, in addition to infusing the divestiture support teams with confidence, urgency, and purpose. Drawing support from senior management can be critical in escalating an important decision to executives, recruiting a resource, or communicating an important message to affected employees. Keep in mind that communication goes both ways. Remaining connected to senior management helps ensure that functional teams have visibility into the broader picture and are strongly connected to the corporate strategic vision and direction.

9.3   Setting Up an Effective Governance Organization

Setting up a robust governance organization is one of the most important steps in the separation process because it establishes the structure under which the teams involved in separation activities will function and make decisions.

9.3.1   Governance Structure

Establishing an effective governance structure is key to a successful deal. While the appropriate structure will depend on the companies involved in the deal, the governance structure should allow for appropriate interaction between teams and business units involved in the separation effort while also ensuring that issues are escalated to the appropriate person quickly. A leading practice is to establish an executive steering committee, a separation management office (SMO), and functional and cross-functional team support. The executive steering committee should consist of business unit leaders, functional leaders, and relevant seller company executives. Representatives from the seller company and the divested business unit should be included on the separation teams.

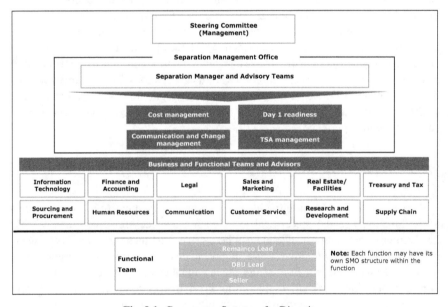

Fig. 9.1 Governance Structure for Divestiture

The SMO, often referred to as the project management office (PMO) or Divestiture Management Office (DMO), acts as the central nerve center for the separation effort, gathering updates on the status of separation activities, identifying functional and workstream issues, evaluating the impact of issues on the overall divestiture program, and escalating issues, when necessary, to the executive steering committee. The SMO also focuses on establishing reporting cadence and determining critical divestiture milestones.

The executive steering committee serves as the decision-making body for critical issues. It often includes the chief financial officer, the chief operations officer, the chief information officer, and leaders of the remaining and divested business units. In order to help ensure this body is appropriately enabled to make decisions, select a combination of executive leadership that is properly enabled to make difficult decisions quickly in order to resolve red flags in a short period of time.

Establishing strong, well-resourced functional teams is also critical. Functions should utilize divestiture-focused, dedicated support to plan and execute their activities and complete milestones. It is a leading practice to have strong, dedicated functional support for the following workstreams:

- Finance (i.e., treasury, tax)
- Human resources (HR) (i.e., organizational design, employee carve-out)
- Information technology (IT) (i.e., systems, apps)

Certain core business workstreams should have additional dedicated support. For example, if a business unit up for divestiture is attractive to buyers because it has a strong research and development (R&D) arm, a dedicated R&D workstream should be formed to help ensure a successful carve-out. Functional teams are a key to divestiture success because they identify key milestones, raise issues, and support execution of the separation effort.

Functional workstreams should comprise equal representation from the seller company and the divested entity. A leading practice is to follow a "two-in-the-box" approach in which the separation team for each workstream contains two leaders— one from the divested entity and one from the seller company. It minimizes risks for both entities and supports better collaboration. Companies divesting business units with the intent to sell should consider potential buyer priorities when developing separation plans to make the divested business unit more attractive to buyers.

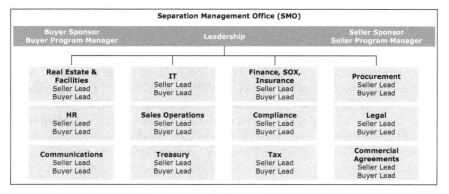

Fig. 9.2 Sample SMO Structure

Some critical programs and processes require regular support from multiple functions; in these instances, utilizing cross-functional teams to complete separation activities is a leading practice. For example, executing a transaction may require continuous input from the legal, treasury, and tax functions as new tax registrations are submitted, new legal entities are formed, and new bank accounts are set up to support the divested entity. It may be necessary to build a transaction execution team, a team focused on legal, tax, and treasury, to coordinate the activities of the functions, thwart last-minute legal surprises, and help ensure deal success. Operationally, an order-to-cash team consisting of representatives from finance, the supply chain, order management, and sales operations can help maintain business momentum. Additionally, important separation-related, cross-functional processes, such as developing transition service agreements (TSAs) or managing stranded costs, should have their own dedicated support to ensure proper coordination and drive cost savings.

Regardless of whether or not a specific cross-functional team is developed, different functions should meet with each other on a regular basis to discuss their milestones, progress, and issues in order to maintain alignment on the overall plan and scope of the divestiture. The SMO should establish the cadence for these cross-functional meetings. The functional teams should be empowered to form ad hoc teams to quickly resolve cross-functional issues uncovered during these weekly meetings.

Finally, the size of the deal is important when setting up the governance structure. Often with small buyers or small division spin-offs, functional teams have less appetite, need, and resources necessary for creating extensive divestiture plans. Smaller, less complex operations generally don't require extensive teams and planning to execute. In smaller deals, where executives may be less involved, the separation team should be lean and empowered to break rules or work outside of the typical divestiture playbook to quickly solve issues and make key decisions. Given the size and complexity of larger deals, there is often more negotiation and coordination with the buyer and its Integration Management Office (IMO), the team responsible for managing integration activities.

9.3.2   Meeting Cadence

The governance structure can only be effective when workstream expectations and meeting cadence are established by the SMO. Individual separation teams for different workstreams should meet with the SMO regularly on a weekly or biweekly basis to present standardized status reports or raise issues. The SMO is then responsible for escalating issues to executives, ideally during the regularly scheduled executive steering committee meetings, or assembling cross-functional teams to solve the issues, if required. Ad hoc or infrequent meetings between the SMO and the executive steering committee can be detrimental to program success, as it may result in only large, program-wide issues being addressed and leave small issues to grow out of control, significantly threatening the execution of the deal. Figure 9.3 provides a sample meeting cadence.

In addition to coordinating meetings, it is important for the SMO to take an active role to manage these meetings. The SMO team must hold separation teams for different workstreams accountable to their timelines while trying to identify and resolve threats. Issues and threats should, ideally, be resolved within a 24 h period. Effective SMOs also establish consistent reporting standards across all separation teams and receive regular updates to gauge progress. Overall, effective SMOs can identify and resolve issues fast, execute deals fast, and drive more deal value.

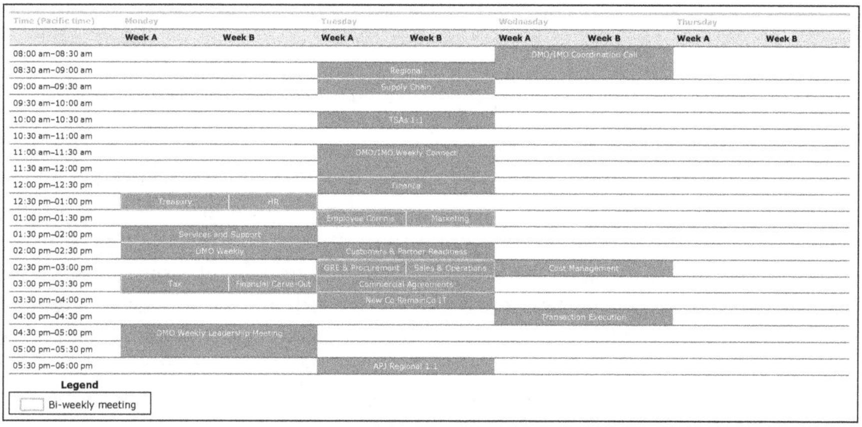

Fig. 9.3 Sample Meeting Cadence

Where and how should the PMO play?	
Passive role ⟷	**Active role**
Accountability for separation success	◆
• Provide limited functional assistance	• Direct functional SMO activities
Governance	◆
• Offer sample processes and tools	• Drive cross-company/functional coordination • Apply tools across company/functions
Workplan design and management	◆
• Monitor programs at a high-level	• Drive workplan optimization and management • Manage firm-wide resource pool
Issue and risk management	◆
• Manage program-level issue resolution only	• Complete detailed Day 1 readiness reviews • Conduct proactive contingency planning • Aggressively facilitate rapid decisioning
Communications and management reporting	◆
• Consolidate functional status reports	• Mandate consistent reporting standards • Lead program-wide communications
Cost model development and implementation	◆
• Consolidate functional tracking reports	• Drive savings identification and capture; set clear targets • Proactively track costs/benefits

Fig. 9.4 DMO Roles

9.4   Layering the Buyer into the Process

Preparation for a divestiture must include careful consideration of the buyer's motivation, capabilities, and integration strategy. Incorporating the buyer's perspective into the approach to separation will help increase transaction value and reduce time to close. Demanding buyers can force tough negotiations on issues and coordination items. Contrastingly, when a seller identifies gaps in the separation process for the buyer and, consequently, integration requirements, it builds the seller's credibility and reduces uncertainties. The seller is enabled to scope its separation efforts and plan the divestiture accordingly. The following are a few guiding principles to help the buyer and seller prepare for the divestiture and meet timelines to close.

9.4.1   Principle 1: Determine Joint Governance and Cadence

Especially on large deals, the seller's SMO and the buyer's IMO must collaborate and support each other's needs in order to achieve milestones and goals within the agreed-upon timelines. In order to establish accountability and ownership on both sides of the deal, the seller's SMO, when building a relationship with the buyer's IMO, should adopt the same structure it uses to manage separation teams, including utilizing the "two-in-the-box" approach and meeting weekly to identify and resolve issues. Additionally, monthly joint executive steering committee meetings can help provide guidance and strategic direction for the divestiture effort.

9.4.2   Principle 2: Establish Clear Data Sharing Guidelines

Until Day 1, both the seller and buyer must ensure compliance with federal laws and legal restrictions related to sensitive and highly confidential data. Following Day 1, the seller must be careful when separating and sharing data with the divested entity. To facilitate information sharing between the two entities, a legal team composed of internal legal counsel, outside legal counsel, and/or consultants should establish rules of engagement to coordinate all matters related to restricted information requests. This legal team must communicate clear guidelines to all relevant stakeholders on how to share data, which ideally should be done using a standardized form or process that generates a clear paper trail for data sharing requests. If all data sharing activities flow through this standardized form or process, then the legal team can attest to compliance with legal and regulatory requirements related to sensitive and highly confidential data leading up to and after Day 1. The legal team's primary activities to manage compliance include:

- Managing the flow of data, presentations, and meetings between both parties
- Fulfill legal requests and maintain compliance throughout separation
- Inform divestiture or integration planning

9.4.3 Principle 3: Coordinate Needs, Escalation, and Resolution

Coordination between the buyer and seller must be solidified at the start of divestiture planning so both entities can be socialized with relevant stakeholders from the opposing company to facilitate early resolution of issues. Developing a comprehensive list of joint milestones and coordination items up front is critical. With diverging agendas, open-ended aspects built into the agreements, and potential communication issues, executive alignment is needed to facilitate the resolution of issues before they escalate into contentious or legal battles. Effective communication and regular meeting cadence can help facilitate this alignment.

As a first step, coordination needs should be discussed at the workstream level. Separation teams for both the buyer and seller should identify and coordinate separation milestones and Day 1 requirements. Regular touchpoint meetings, held between the workstreams and the SMO, once or twice a week can help both entities stay coordinated for Day 1 readiness. About 70% of all issues are usually resolved at the workstream level.

Unresolved issues at the workstream level should be escalated to the SMO and IMO teams, which then escalate the issues to executive leadership for intervention and resolution. Depending on the size of the deal, regular (weekly) buyer coordination meetings (i.e., regular meeting between the buyer and seller) should be held to reach consensus on key separation decisions that may impact the integration or deal. Cross-functional issues that must be addressed include employee-related matters (e.g., payroll, benefits), cutover readiness concerns, outside counsel involvement (e.g., negotiations with works councils and labor unions), and incremental budget requirements (e.g., funding for additional workstream support). Divestiture project managers resolve issues between separation teams, including project resourcing, timing, and financing issues. The SMO team, the IMO team, and divestiture project managers resolve approximately 10–15% of issues, as noted in Fig. 9.5.

Usually 5% of issues in every deal are escalated to the executive steering committee for a final decision. Some of the issues escalated to the executive steering committee involve problems that affect the divestiture budget, cause Day 1 timeline delays, or require amendments to deal terms, commercial agreements, or filings with the Securities and Exchange Commission (SEC) or other government regulators.

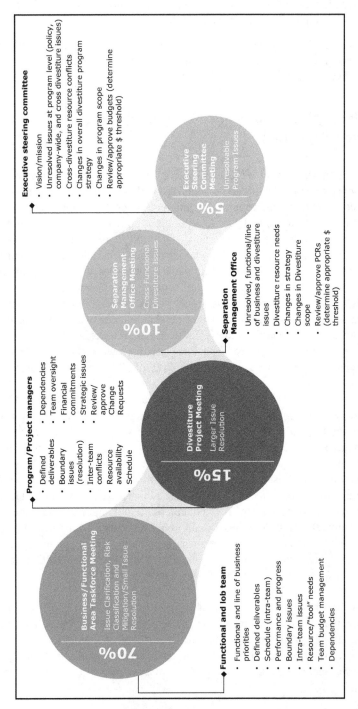

Fig. 9.5 Issue Resolution and Decision Management Process

9.5 Guiding Principles for a Successful Transaction

Every separation comes with its own set of challenges, but an effective separation team and an appropriate set of guiding principles can help resolve them quickly. The following guiding principles are considered leading practices for divestitures of all sizes.

9.5.1 Principle 1: Start with the End in Mind

Before assembling a team to execute the divestiture, executive leadership should clearly communicate the end-state vision for the deal to all internal and external stakeholders. Clearly communicating the end state at the start of the deal will help all teams work toward the same goal. Some questions for consideration include:

- How will the seller's go-to-market strategy be transformed by the deal?
- How aggressive of an execution timeline is appropriate?
- How will the divestiture affect the overall business strategy?
- To what extent should TSAs be utilized to expedite Day 1?

9.5.2 Principle 2: Maintain Business Momentum

One of the keys to an effective divestiture is for the entities involved to stay focused on running their day-to-day businesses. For the seller company, this means not letting the divestiture become a distraction for the company's other business units, as well as helping the divested business unit maintain separation execution momentum throughout the transition. This can be achieved by fencing separation activities, from regular business activities, thereby enabling minimal disruption.

9.5.3 Principle 3: Prioritize a Seamless Day 1

All teams involved in separation activities should bear in mind that Day 1 should be considered fixed and that any movement to Day 1 would likely result in significant and negative ramifications (e.g., financial, regulatory, brand). The Day 1 date should be agreed upon by the buyer and seller and should take into account the timelines to complete all of the major separation activities. Setting a firm Day 1 up front is critical to helping teams prioritize activities and resolve issues.

9.5.4   *Principle 4: Foster a Partnership*

A divestiture presents an opportunity to foster a long-term partnership with the potential to drive revenue growth between the buyer and seller. This can be achieved through buyer considerate separation planning, execution, and support. The post-close partnership centers around commercial agreements and TSAs that flow through extension, stabilization, and exit phases. To that end, the companies involved in the deal must be transparent with each other and decide on how to resolve issues as quickly as possible.

9.5.5   *Principle 5: Balance Talent Decisions*

Functional leaders must ask certain talent resources if they can move to the divested business unit in order to balance the separation and create two viable organizations. Establishing ground rules between the buyer and seller is vital to this effort. For example, under no circumstances should the poaching of talent, by the buyer or seller, be tolerated as this will inevitably undermine cross-functional operations. Instead, companies should rely on HR to facilitate employee transitions across the buyer and seller business units, if necessary.

9.5.6   *Principle 6: Command and Control Ops*

Orchestrating an effective divestiture relies on an effective command and control program structure. An active divestiture program can play a critical role in not only driving the divestiture but also in shaping go forward operations. It must establish common goals for workstreams and provide direction for delivering the transaction value. With effective command and control, one can maintain a single source of status (limited debate) and drive divestiture activities. Activities will include driving cross-company/cross-functional coordination, applying tools across company/functions, conducting proactive contingency planning, rapid decisioning, mandating consistent reporting standards, leading program-wide communications, driving savings identification and capture, setting clear targets, and proactively tracking costs and simplifying benefits.

Case Study: 9

Background

A technology company with more than $33 billion in annual revenue engaged in two simultaneous and critical separations of its noncore asset businesses, of a total transaction value of ~$16B ($8.8B + $8.5B). Spin-off announcements for both businesses were 3 months apart, and the businesses were being sold to buyers in different countries. This resulted in extreme resource and time crunch for the organization, because each deal had multiple separation nuances (legal and financial) and tight, but fixed, timelines to accomplish Day 1.

Challenges

The divested business units were deeply intertwined with the seller company's operations (e.g., common go-to-market model, joint services and support, mixed contracts), creating issues around the processes and systems that would be used by the divested entities, as well as their relationship not only with customers and suppliers but also with one each other. Products and services, which were historically provided by one business unit to another, at cost, had to be transitioned to value-generating commercial agreements.

Approach

A strong governance structure was established to oversee both deals, which enabled fast decision-making and issue resolution. Kickoff for both programs was held within 2 weeks of announcement, with planning, blueprinting, and work plan completion within the first 1 month. Both deals involved legal entities spanning more than 100 countries. The company managed the divestitures in parallel and transferred learnings from one deal to the other in real time. This proved valuable in anticipating and resolving issues.

Impact/Results

Building the arsenal means ensuring there is an effective governance structure in place to execute the deal, including appropriate leaders, and that the buyer is engaged throughout the divestiture and separation process.

Chapter 10
Working Under the Tent: Confidentiality and Restricted Information Disclosure

10.1 Introduction

The year 2016 ended with announcement of mergers and acquisitions (M&A) deals worth $3.2 trillion.[1] Multiple studies put the failure rate of M&A transactions at 70–90%,[2] which is remarkably high. This failure can be in the form of falling short of the initial financial expectations of the combined entity, not producing benefits in terms of shareholder value, etc. The divestiture, which is one of the M&A transactions, of a company or business unit involves the change in structure of the company including restructuring of the workforce, information technology (IT) systems, and potentially the business strategy. Now consider a divestiture in terms of distinct personalities and behaviors of thousands of employees spread across multiple countries with different laws and regulations. When an M&A deal is viewed in light of these complexities, the failure rate appears to be not so surprising.

Mere speculation of a divestiture or carve-out affects both the buyer and seller in the transaction. Depending on the entities involved, market momentum, past history, and the impact on the industry, a divestiture can sometimes erode the market value of the companies engaged in the proceedings or, alternatively, improve their stock prices. In the case of a divestiture, the seller is arguably more affected until a potential buyer is identified. Carve-outs and spin-offs can be equally complicated. A myriad of legal, regulatory, and reporting requirements combined with the tight integration of systems and processes throughout modern organizations ensures that

---

[1] Dealing with the Future, Deloitte M&A Index – Outlook for 2017, https://www2.deloitte.com/uk/en/pages/financial-advisory/articles/deloitte-m-and-a-index.html.

[2] "The Big Idea: The New M&A Playbook," Clayton M. Christensen, Richard Alton, Curtis Rising, and Andrew Waldeck, Harvard Business Review, March 2011, https://hbr.org/2011/03/the-big-idea-the-new-ma-playbook.

© Deloitte Development LLC 2018
J. Joy, *Divestitures and Spin-Offs*, Management for Professionals,
https://doi.org/10.1007/978-1-4939-7662-1_10

divesting or carving out a business is no easy task.[3] The uncertainty and chaos accompanying a divestiture or carve-out can prove to be very taxing on all the stakeholders. Employees, customers, vendors, shareholders, and competitors face an uncertain future due to market speculation. Employees are the most affected due to the sheer amount of work involved, coupled with the anxiety surrounding possible job loss and other imminent changes. These challenges can take a toll on employee morale and productivity. Considering the high stakes involved, maintaining the confidentiality of the deal is also critical to a successful separation.

The divesting company and the acquiring company must continue to operate as independent competitors until regulatory approval is granted and the final deal is approved by both entities. Divestitures can happen for a variety of reasons, including streamlining operations or acquiring cash to fund other projects. However, restriction on access to data, including, but not limited to, customer information, proprietary algorithms, and vendor data, can impede planning and decision-making post-Day 1.

Why is deal confidentiality so important? What are the implications of information leakage? How do successful companies deal with confidentiality at every stage of the long journey? When can organizations reveal specific information to stakeholders? Let us start by looking at the stages of the divestiture life cycle (see Fig. 10.1), which have varying degrees of confidentiality requirements and stakeholder involvement.

Stages of the divestiture life cycle:

- Due diligence phase—This stage where entities involved in the transaction complete due diligence on the deal, and it occurs before the deal is announced to stakeholders.
- Deal announcement to Day 1 phase—This is when the divestiture is executed.
- Post-Day 1 phase—The entities separated in the transaction begin to function as separate companies.

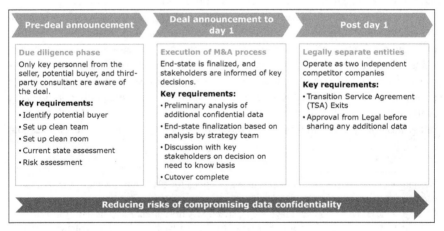

Fig. 10.1 Stages of Divestiture Lifecycle

[3] "A closer look at carve-outs," Robert Coury, Andrew Wilson, and Jeffery M. Weirens, 2009, www2.deloitte.com/content/dam/Deloitte/jp/Documents/finance/rs/jp-rs-carveouts-separation-survey.pdf.

So what happens in each of these stages? How do companies control the flow of information? At what point can different information be disclosed? Which parties should have access to particular information? These queries are addressed in the following sections.

10.2   Due Diligence Phase: Before the Deal Is Announced

10.2.1   The Confidentiality Agreement

This is the most critical phase for confidentiality. Very few key personnel in the seller company will have knowledge of the company's intention to sell.

The due diligence phase begins with scouting for potential buyers. But even before deal discussions can start, the potential buyer and seller must enter into a confidentiality or nondisclosure agreement (NDA). Typically, during the divestiture process, IT, financial, customer, supplier, and vendor data, as well as intellectual property (IP) and company secrets may be shared between key stakeholders involved in the transaction. Leakage of this information without a binding agreement in place can have disastrous consequences to all parties, potentially affecting the future of both companies.

The confidentiality agreement requires a degree of professionalism and legal obligation from the potential buyer to protect the data. It can also prevent poaching of employees from the seller.[4]

Insider trading is a real threat in any divestiture deal. According to a recent study by professors at the New York University Stern School of Business and McGill University,[5] about 25% of all M&A transactions involving publicly traded companies were associated with questionable trading before deal announcement pointing toward some form of insider trading. Strict laws have been enacted to prevent such occurrences, including provisions for huge monetary fines and possible prison sentences for offenders. Not only is the personal integrity of the deal makers at stake but also the future of the company and its shareholders. Hence, maintaining the confidentiality of the deal is critical to the success of the transaction.

Typically, during due diligence, the buyer will seek information from the seller on various topics, such as confidential information on run-rate costs and their components, the number of full-time employees (FTEs), infrastructure and application

---

[4] "M&A Confidential: The Role of Nondisclosure Agreements," Lawrence M. Braun and Justin S. Yslas, Los Angeles Daily Journal, September 15, 2008, http://www.sheppardmullin.com/media/article/593_MandA%20Confidential%20-%20The%20Role%20of%20Nondisclosure%20Agreements.pdf.

[5] "Information Options Trading prior to M&A Announcements: Insider Trading?" Patrick Augustin, Menachem Brenner, and Marti G. Subrahmanyam, New York University Stern School of Business and McGill University, May 2014, http://irrcinstitute.org/wp-content/uploads/2015/09/Informed-Options-Trading_June-12-20141.pdf.

landscape details, and information about major ongoing projects. Generally, the seller engages a legal advisor to identify the data that can be shared. A third party, such as an advisory or consulting firm, is also usually retained to obtain and share this data with the potential buyer and limit the number of employees on the seller's side who are aware of the deal. Before discussing or even possibly hinting about the potential deal, a "clean room agreement" is signed with the third-party company who will be privy to this information. This agreement is generally a subset of the NDA with additional restrictions including antitrust legal review and addresses concerns relating to handling and sharing of competitively sensitive information. A few key trustworthy employees other than the senior executives from the seller side may also be aware of the deal. These employees are aware of critical aspects of their business units like process flows, financials, architecture, etc. and can provide crucial inputs during data analysis. Even after signing the clean room agreement, in most cases, only information necessary for the employee to complete his/her task is provided. These third parties (advisors of seller and buyers) may connect with the key employees of the seller side for gathering data to be shared with potential buyers. Inclusion of third parties who do not have a stake in the buying or selling entity helps provide objectivity. All such third parties are required to work under the provisions of the NDA as representatives of the buyer or seller thereby maintaining confidentiality during the process.

The due diligence team including third-party consultants involved in the analysis of sensitive and confidential information is called the "clean team." A number of firms employ a clean team during the due diligence process to analyze data, quantify potential synergies, and prepare a preliminary plan to realize the targets. The clean team may be created from the moment a potential buyer is identified and continue to function until Day 1 of the merger.

10.2.2   What Is a Clean Team?

A clean team[6] is a group of individuals who serve as independent entities to companies planning M&A transactions. The team may include recent retirees, consultants, and/or select current employees. Multiple consultants may be involved in the due diligence phase based on their area of expertise. For instance, one consulting firm may be employed for financial due diligence and a second consulting firm for IT due diligence. Data is shared with each employee or sub-team based on the clean room protocols and need-to-know basis only. The clean team receives strategic information from both the selling company and the potential buyer, analyzes the information, and makes recommendations to the management only after obtaining legal approval from the antitrust counsel designated and agreed to by the parties in

---

[6]"Integration Playbook Deliverable," Sangeeta Chandra, Deloitte, September 2014, www.km. deloitteresources.com/sites/live/consulting/_layouts/DTTS.DR.KAMDocumentForms/ KAMDisplay.aspx?List=513ae4d5-443f-4bc1-9f25-8f68dc5aa0c0&ID=337269.

the clean room agreement. The clean team's working environment must be separate and secure from both the buyer and seller. Typically, the parties request advisors to acknowledge the clean room protocols or NDA individually or at an entity level to ensure that a controlled data environment and confidentiality is maintained.

In the event the deal is not consummated, the clean team must destroy all data and analysis, sharing nothing with the buyer and seller in accordance with the clean room protocols.

Since the data being analyzed is highly confidential and has wide ramifications, there is strict control on sharing and the flow of that data. For this purpose, a separate and secure environment called a "clean room" is set up.

> *A Fortune 50 company set up a clean team consisting of the COO and five external consultants, including investment bankers and corporate strategy experts to maintain data confidentiality not only from external entities but also internal stakeholders within the company.*

10.2.3   What Is a Clean Room?

A clean room is an exclusive raw data repository used by clean teams to gather data for analysis. Data is shared by the seller, buyer, and third-party advisors in the clean room, and access is strictly limited and controlled. Additionally, external dedicated servers may be employed for data storage with password protection to ensure data integrity. Almost all deals involving due diligence use clean rooms, which may have dedicated folders for due diligence of various functions, such as IT, finance, and human resources (HR), or separate clean rooms set up exclusively for each function. In most cases, for confidentiality purposes, the data is destroyed after a certain period .

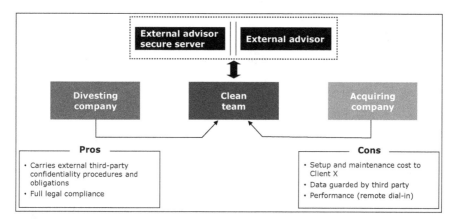

Fig. 10.2 Clean Room

10.2.4   Components of a Clean Team

Staffing

- Recent retirees, external consultants, and select few key employees may form the clean team.
- Members of the divestiture management office (DMO) cannot be part of clean team.
- New company executives cannot be part of the clean team.

Data Requests

- Functional teams provide data requests to the DMO.
- DMO leads confirm the data analysis needs for the divestiture and decide if clean team needs to be involved in data analysis.
- The legal department verifies whether information is indeed highly confidential.
- Executive sponsors confirm the data analysis needs.

Requests for Additional Information

- Clean team leaders or clean team administration cannot communicate directly with the functional teams.
- Approval from both, the legal department and DMO leader, is required for any information requests.

Result Communications

- Legal approval from the antitrust counsel designated and agreed to by the parties in the clean room agreement is required before the clean team leaders or clean team administration communicate with management of buyer and seller companies.

10.2.5   Components of a Clean Room

Electronic Information Storage

- Electronic information is stored in a repository in the clean room using third-party infrastructure.
- Electronic information is inaccessible outside of the physical clean room.

Electronic Information Processing

- Clean team members can work only on their laptops or desktops for data analysis
- At the end of every day, electronic information is uploaded back to the clean room repository, and local copies get deleted.

Sometimes, the clean team focuses on balancing efficiency with confidentiality. In such cases, there is room for change in the clean team and clean room components.

For example, for electronic information processing, if the focus is on confidentiality, then the clean team is working on dedicated laptops or computers without exceptions.

10.2.6 Announcement of the Divestiture

After due diligence is completed and the go ahead is received from all key stake-holders, the divestiture is announced and made public. The entities now focus on ensuring synergies are realized as close as possible to Day 1. It may take a few months and in certain cases up to a year to receive regulatory approval for a deal. During that time, information is gradually shared with all key stakeholders—employees, customers, suppliers, and shareholders. So what happens when the deal is announced? How does the seller company share data while still maintaining confidentiality? All these questions are analyzed in the next section.

10.3 Deal Announcement to Day 1

There may be a lot of chaos and unanswered questions when the deal is announced. Stakeholders will try to analyze the impact of the divestiture on themselves and will have a lot of questions, but no information will be forthcoming. Depending on the announcement, the reaction from stakeholders may or may not be positive. Therefore, the deal announcement is a critical juncture, and both the buyer and seller must ensure unified communications to all stakeholders, as well as the media. The most affected stakeholders are the employees of both entities. Not all information can be shared with all employees at the same time. Many employees will have questions about their future in the organization. Will they be retained? Will they move to the buyer company? Or will they need to look for opportunities elsewhere? Employee buy-in is vital to the success of the divestiture. Hence, management should tread carefully while addressing employee questions.

However, much analysis must be conducted before arriving at decisions related to employees, infrastructure, and transformation plans.

10.3.1 Role of Corporate Strategy and Divestiture Team in the Deal Announcement to Day 1 Process[7]

Part of the challenge in a divestiture is simultaneously addressing the requirements of corporate functions and the various departments within those functions, which may span across geographical regions. Clearly, this challenge is in addition to the existing workload. Moreover, in a divestiture project, corporate functions will

---

[7] "IT Merger & Acquisition Playbook," Eugene Lukac, Bill Eager, Nikhil Menon, and Rex Morey, July 2016, www.km.deloitteresources.com/sites/live/_layouts/dtts.dr.kamdocumentforms/displayformredirect.aspx?id=kmip-569919.

have to work within the constraints (e.g., approach, communications, finances, etc.) imposed by the buyer company.

All functions must work as part of the larger organization to achieve the end state for a successful divestiture effort. Based on the activities involved, the confidentiality of data under analysis, and the results of the analysis, the effort is typically divided between two teams:

- Corporate strategy team
- Divestiture team

The next section reviews the scope and details about each team.

10.3.2   Characteristics and Confidentiality Requirements for the Corporate Strategy Team of the Seller

The objective of the corporate strategy team is to decide the strategy for the seller company post-Day 1 of the divestiture. The team will analyze data, come up with what-if scenarios, and provide data points to the leadership to help decide the future state of the organization. The team will generally be very small, comprising key personnel from the office of the COO, and will have access to the most confidential information. The team may potentially decide the future of the seller company's strategy. A few examples of analysis performed by the corporate strategy team and the types of confidential data used for decision-making follow:

Run-Rate Costs: The corporate strategy team is tasked with planning the seller company's annual budget to meet the revised operating expense (OpEx) targets of the remaining company post-divestiture. The team analyzes various components of costs, including costs going away as part of the deal and costs retained by the remaining company. A realizable plan is then devised to help the remaining company of the seller to achieve this target run-rate.

Confidential information, including FTE costs, vendor contracts, and infrastructure details, are analyzed. This confidential information must be handled with supreme caution to prevent any data leaks.

Future-State Organization: The corporate strategy team analyzes the future-state FTE requirements while keeping in mind the financial targets set for the remaining company. The team decides the organizational structure of the remaining company and estimates the number of FTEs required to sustain it. The team analyzes and estimates the number of FTEs to retain or transfer, as well as the number of roles to eliminate. Confidential employee information is reviewed, including roles within the organization, FTE salaries, and performance appraisals. Employee names and personal information may be masked for data confidentiality and employee security purposes.

Special care must be taken to ensure this information is kept confidential. This information will be limited to remaining company, and, hence, a multiparty clean room is not required. However, a data room similar to clean room can prove to be useful in maintaining confidentiality. Data leaks will only add to the existing turbulence and may affect employee morale.

Infrastructure Strategy: The corporate strategy team will conduct a thorough analysis of the existing infrastructure at the remaining company, including real estate, telecommunications, computers, and data centers. Based on the financial target to be achieved, the team will devise scenarios to analyze the impact of retaining or outsourcing various infrastructure elements. A number of suppliers and vendors will be affected by this decision.

The strategy team will analyze existing contracts with vendors and service providers and analyze the costs of premature termination. Since the size of the remaining company will change, contract prices will need to be renegotiated. If the entire infrastructure is outsourced, then the organization will have to look for new vendors with minimal implementation costs. This decision may have a large impact on existing vendors and pricing of services provided. Any data leaks can potentially increase vendors' bargaining power in a negotiation, or vendors may try to influence key decision-makers before negotiations.

Contract Management: The corporate strategy team will analyze all contracts related to corporate functions, including finance, HR, transportation, and IT (e.g., software and services contracts). These contracts must be thoroughly reviewed since they include clauses related to license transfers, discounts based on headcount, and usage-based discounts. Most contracts will be renegotiated, and the corporate strategy team will analyze scenarios involving variations in discounts offered by vendors.

The data being analyzed will be confidential since the contracts are sacrosanct and unique to each vendor. This information may not be shared with the buying company since doing so can breach the vendor contracts. This analysis also has a direct impact on the balance of trade; for instance, assume vendor A is providing services to client X who is divesting. There is a possibility that client X is also a service provider for vendor A. Negotiations will impact the relationship between client X and vendor A based on the approach followed. Hence, it is very important to ensure data confidentiality when analyzing contracts for renegotiation.

10.3.3   Characteristics and Confidentiality Requirements for the Divestiture Team

Separate divestiture teams are set up to execute and monitor the progress of the divestiture. These teams generally comprise employees from each of the seller company's functions, a contractor workforce, and third-party advisors. The team analyzes the current situation and potential issues in the divestiture process and then proposes alternative solutions along with a cost-benefit analysis. Data confidentiality is important in this phase for the following reasons:

- Employees may be concerned about their roles if a new strategy is implemented. Their skill sets may not be relevant going forward, which may cause discontent and chaos even before the end state is agreed upon. For example, if an organization is moving from providing custom IT solutions to providing automated IT solutions, developers may be concerned about their future.

- A timeline for execution and implementation is also identified. Based on the phase of execution, more employees will be aware of the impending changes to the organization. A high-level timeline can be shared with relevant stakeholders; however, specifics such as the function retirement date and downsizing timeline must remain confidential as these may tip off employees on the future of their function and affect employee retention.
- Vendors may be tipped off about possible changes, which may impact future negotiations.
- Financial data, such as run-rate costs and the separation budget, are provided to the team for analysis.

10.4 Post-Day 1

Post-Day 1, the two entities are legally separated. Even though utmost care has been taken to complete the separation and the transfer of confidential data, there may be obstacles to the smooth running of the two entities. For instance, the buyer company may have data requests (e.g., past records for employees) that may have been missed during the divestiture. Any query that involves confidential data should be strictly routed to the legal team. Post-Day 1, the seller company and the buyer company along with the acquired entity continue to operate as two independent competitors.

10.5 Key Learnings

- Mere speculation of a divestiture deal can have wide-ranging ramifications on all key stakeholders. Hence, deal confidentiality is critical until it is announced to a wider audience.
- To avoid information leakage and insider trading, as well as obtain an unbiased view, it is important to carefully manage confidential information. To do so, parties could form a clean team and clean room for analysis:

  ○ A clean team is a group of individuals who serve as independent parties to a divestiture deal. It generally consists of external consultants, investment bankers, the legal team, and key members of the organization.
  ○ A clean room is an exclusive raw data repository used to gather data for analysis in a single place with strict access controls.

- Until the announcement of the deal, only the clean team and select few executives/employees from the buyer and seller companies will have knowledge of the potential divestiture.
- Handling of competitively sensitive confidential information vary across different stages of the divestiture:

  ○ Due diligence phase—Entities involved in the transaction complete due diligence on the deal, and it occurs before the deal is announced to stakeholders.

- Deal announcement to Day 1 phase—The divestiture is executed.
- Post-Day 1 phase—The entities separated in the transaction begin to function as separate companies.

- During the due diligence phase, clean teams from both sides work together in a clean room away from the influence of the buyer or seller.
- Data in the clean room is typically completely destroyed after a certain point of time to maintain confidentiality and prevent misuse in case the deal fails to materialize.
- The corporate strategy team analyzes confidential information such as number of FTEs, compensation rates, and run-rate costs. This analysis is used to devise what-if scenarios for the future state of the remaining company.
- The DMO governs the separation process and reveals information to stakeholders as and when required on a need-to-know basis.
- Post-Day 1, the seller tries to exit TSAs as soon as possible. Any requests for additional confidential data are strictly routed to the legal team before the information is shared.

Case Study: 10

Background

The executive team of a Fortune 50 technology company decided to divest one of its four business units. Decision-making, the easy part of the divestiture, was done. Now came the complex part—executing the divestiture. The team had to identify potential buyers for the business unit, while maintaining confidentiality and protecting the company from adverse reactions to the decision. So how did the team go about it? What were the challenges? Was the team able to successfully execute the deal?

Challenges

The business unit to be divested accounted for nearly 30 percent of the company's total revenue. The divestiture was part of the company's vision to focus on core offerings and diversify into other emerging technology areas. The success of the remaining company hinged on the success of the divestiture, since the entity to be divested was heavily comingled with the remaining company.

The team was worried about ensuring the confidentiality of information while searching for potential buyers. Any information leak would have wide ramifications. Stock markets could react negatively and significantly impact the valuation of the company. Competitors would take notice and react sharply, further causing trouble for the company.

The CEO entrusted the job of successfully executing the deal to the COO, who had successfully led divestitures before. However, the COO was still concerned about the support he would receive from internal stakeholders. For the employees, jobs were at stake and emotions were already running high. But the divestiture had to be successfully executed to ensure a better future for the company.

So how did this Fortune 50 company successfully execute the divestiture while ensuring confidentiality?

Approach

The COO reached out to an external consultant and an investment banker. After all, the executive team did not want anyone within the company to know about the potential deal. Before these third parties could meet the COO, they had to sign a nondisclosure agreement (NDA). The COO had clear requests for the consultant and the banker. He asked the consultant to provide an unbiased view and analysis of the divestiture, while he asked the investment banker to identify potential buyers.

The consultant and investment banker quickly assembled an additional ten-member clean team that included two external consultants, one corporate strategy expert, one investment banker, two legal team members, and one key member from each of the four business units within the organization. Every individual on the clean team had to sign an NDA before onboarding.

Things moved rapidly once a potential buyer was found. The team began due diligence—analyzing and estimating the benefits of the deal. The buyer also assembled its own clean team to work with the seller's clean team to ensure the fairness of the due diligence process.

A separate clean room was set up for the buyer's clean team within the seller's office. Each team member was provided with an identity card to gain access to the clean room and a desktop computer for data analysis. Entry was strictly restricted and monitored. No material could be taken out of the clean room for any purpose. A third-party setup separate servers to host the data shared by the seller and the buyer, and data was exchanged by uploading files to a SharePoint site hosted on the third party's server. No emails or printing were allowed. Any communication between the clean team and management of buyer or seller company was monitored by the seller's legal team. Requests for additional data passed through the legal team to ensure confidential information were not passed on to the buyer.

After intense data analysis lasting approximately 1 month, the potential buyer agreed to acquire the entity up for divestiture. The COO and clean team had successfully executed the entire process without any information leakage. Everything went smoothly over the next few weeks, and finally, the deal was announced to the media.

As expected, there was a lot of chaos after the announcement. The stock price for both the buyer and seller companies increased by about 10%. The mood in both camps was upbeat. Executing the deal and ensuring a successful divestiture were the next big tasks at hand.

Deal Announcement to Day 1

After reaching the first milestone of finalizing the deal, the COO had his goal set for an uneventful and successful Day 1. To accomplish this goal, he formed two teams—the corporate strategy team and the divestiture management team (also known as the DMO).

The corporate strategy team had access to the most confidential data, including the number of FTEs, compensation rates, and run-rate costs. To ensure only a few employees were aware of the finer details of the deal, the team was comprised of clean team members. The corporate strategy team analyzed all the data and came up with various what-if scenarios, which were presented to other key stakeholders in the organization, and the end-state of the organization was finalized.

Meanwhile, the DMO came up with a road map to execute the divesture plan. Phasing and execution of the plan was run by the DMO office, and any potential issues were escalated to the COO and CEO in a timely manner. The DMO was also responsible for all communication with internal and external stakeholders.

Conclusion

The entire process lasted about 9 months post-deal announcement. The COO could finally manage a smile. Months of negotiations and analysis had borne fruit, and the divestiture was a success. None of this would have been possible if confidential information had leaked at any stage. Not even the top executives of the divested entity were informed of the deal to prevent potential conflicts of interest. The legal team ensured that only the data that was absolutely necessary for analysis was shared between the buyer and seller companies. The COO appreciated the efforts and analysis by third-party consultants who provided an unbiased view and took a firm stance whenever necessary.

Impact/Results

A well-crafted strategy to maintain confidentiality at every stage of the divestiture life cycle played a crucial role in the successful execution of the deal. Failure to maintain confidentiality at any point of time during the deal would have jeopardized the smooth functioning of both the seller and buyer company. Every process, shortcoming, and issue was documented right from the day the decision to divest the business unit was made until the completion of Day 1. This experience provided the company with a readymade template for further divestitures.

Chapter 11
Getting Ready for Announcement: Kickoff Planning

11.1 Introduction

The first few weeks of planning after the announcement of a divestiture or spin-off are very critical to successful execution of the transaction. Before defining separation plans and starting execution, it is essential to identify budget and resource needs and onboard stakeholders and execution teams. These are keys in setting up the Separation Management Office (SMO) or Divestiture Management Office (DMO) that will guide, track, and oversee separation or divestiture activities. Planning for this phase helps ensure quick ramp-up of resources, reduced time to start execution, and accelerated time to complete execution.

A Fortune 50 company planning multiple serial divestitures had just announced another divestiture.

Execution of the divestiture was against a very aggressive timeline and involved the separation of a highly entangled business with multiple global functions.

The parent company, "RemainCo," based on prior experience, immediately launched proactive planning exercises even before the deal was publicly announced, by identifying a small core group of people, putting them under a nondisclosure agreement, and getting a jumpstart on the planning process.

RemainCo was able to reduce planning effort from 3 months in a prior transaction to less than 3 weeks in subsequent transactions. RemainCo was also able to leverage the methodologies, tools, and templates to achieve aggressive deal timelines and complete the initial program kickoff 30 min after the deal was announced publicly to the Street.

© Deloitte Development LLC 2018
J. Joy, *Divestitures and Spin-Offs*, Management for Professionals,
https://doi.org/10.1007/978-1-4939-7662-1_11

11.2   Budgeting

One of the key components of the kickoff and starting execution is to have a clear understanding of one-time costs for the execution. It is important to determine and understand budget requirements for end-to-end execution of the transaction. While the detailed bottom-up one-time costs would be ideal to understand, it is typically not possible to have a bottom-up view early in the transaction cycle due to the lack of adequate inputs and people required to provide such input. A top-down function or business unit level cost is used as a starting point and then adjusted post-announcement once the detailed separation strategies are outlined and evaluated. A top-down budget by function or business unit is estimated based on benchmarks or prior experience with similar deals and with some assumptions of the separation strategy.

There are typically two major components of cost required for separation: labor and non-labor. The Labor component includes internal labor as well as external labor such as consultants and contractors. Non-labor expenses include travel, training, hardware, software, etc.

Costs play an important role in determining the separation strategy and vice versa. For example, if "shorter time to execution" is a critical business requirement of the separation strategy, the separation team may resort to solutions that are faster but might be more expensive and not necessarily very elegant.

While overall separation strategy is defined by time and cost constraints, teams should adhere to the deal guideline principles and assumptions while coming up with bottoms-up cost estimations.

11.2.1   Top-Down Budget Estimation

In some cases, that execution teams may not have the flexibility to decide the budget they require and would be "handed" a budget by the central Separation/Divestiture Management Office. In such cases, it is still essential that the separation team identify the budget they actually need and document the reasoning for the estimation. This is because this team may sometimes have better insight into actual effort required and the budget provided may be over- or underestimated.

Top-down costs are estimated based on benchmarks, past experience or through detailed analysis of requirements. For example, typical IT separation costs range from 0.75 to 1.25 times the annual IT operating expense of the entity that is being separated. This may, however, vary based on complexity of the IT landscape and amount of entanglement between the entities being separated.

Once the budget funding is approved, the next step for the DMO would be to allocate these funds to different functions and workstreams based on criticality and separation complexity of the underlying projects under each of the functions or business units.

11.2.2 Bottom-Up Budget Estimation

As we will see in a subsequent section of this chapter, the organization running the separation execution is typically divided into further workstreams. In a bottom-up scenario, every workstream identifies their individual budget requirements based on the separation work that they would have to undertake. Inputs from every team are then rolled up to provide an overall view of the separation one-time budget. It is common practice to clearly document assumptions and build in contingencies into the bottom-up budget since the detailed separation plans have not been constructed yet.

11.2.3 Tracking Budgets

Although budgets are allocated at the function or workstream level, separation workstreams still have to eventually identify projects, resource requirements against each, and thus cost for each project in the sub-workstream. These details are typically entered into a Project Portfolio Management tool such as Microsoft Project. The DMO then analyzes this against overall budget to ensure costs are on track. The Project Portfolio Management tool is updated with actual cost spent on a regular basis including any changes in forecasted future spend.

Note: The below numbers are illustrative only. Actual figures depend on size of the company, nature and size of transaction, and number of employees involved in the transaction.

Work-stream	Labor Cost ($M)				Non-Labor Cost ($M)					Total ($M)
	Internal Labor (IT)	Internal Labor (Business)	Contractors	Total Labor	Hardware	Software Licenses	Travel	Other Non-Labor	Total Non-Labor	Total
Finance	$3.0	$4.0	$2.0	$9.0	$1.0	$0.0	$1.0	$0.5	$2.5	$11.5
HR	$2.0	$2.5	$3.0	$7.5	$2.0	$0.5	$1.0	$0.2	$3.7	$11.2
Supply Chain	$1.5	$2.0	$1.5	$5.0	$1.0	$1.0	$1.0	$0.2	$3.2	$8.2
Sales	$1.0	$2.5	$2.0	$5.5	$1.0	$0.5	$1.0	$0.4	$2.9	$8.4
Shared Execution	$0.5	$0.5	$1.0	$2.0	$0.0	$0.0	$1.0	$0.2	$1.2	$3.2
DMO	$0.5	$0.5	$1.0	$2.0	$0.0	$0.5	$1.0	$0.5	$2.0	$4.0
Total	$8.5	$12.0	$10.5	$31.0	$5.0	$2.5	$6.0	$2.0	$15.5	$46.5

Fig. 11.1 Sample Budget Dashboard

11.3 Resourcing

One of the most important requirements for successful execution of the separation or divestiture is to have the right team running it. The resources running the program typically have a huge impact on the pace and timely completion of the transaction.

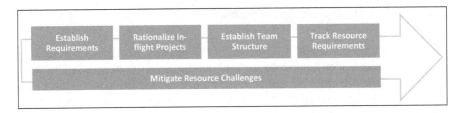

Fig. 11.2 Steps in Resourcing

Effective resourcing may require the following steps:

1. Establish resource requirements for separation or divestiture.
2. Rationalize or re-prioritize in-flight projects to free up key resources required for program execution.
3. Establish an effective team to deliver the program successfully.
4. Track resourcing requirements through the use of tools and dashboards.
5. Identify and mitigate potential challenges.

11.3.1 Establish Requirements

Similar to budget, establishing resource requirements also follows both a top-down and bottom-up approach. The DMO identifies high-level resource requirements by workstream based on industry benchmarks (if available) and based on prior experience of executing such transactions.

In parallel, execution teams also identify their resource requirements in terms of internal and external FTEs. These are then consolidated to identify the true requirement by workstream. The requirements and eventual allotment of FTEs are managed via a project or resource management tool.

11.3.2 Rationalize In-Flight Projects

When a transaction is announced, the parent company typically has planned in-flight projects as a part of their normal business operations. Some of these projects might be capital and resource intensive and may not allow for enough resources and funds to execute the separation. The separation DMO will need to put an immediate emphasis on identifying which of these in-flight projects or planned projects will be either stalled, canceled entirely, canceled partially, or continue unbated. This exercise is done on the basis of criticality to the business in light of the transaction execution. In some cases, it may be essential to free up resources who have key subject matter expertise necessary for transaction execution. It is critical to identify relative priority of separation projects vs in-flight projects quickly and expedite the disposition of the in-flight and planned projects.

11.3.3 Establish Team Structure

As resources are being freed up, it is important to identify the right organization structure to run the program successfully. This is typically referred to as the governance structure. An effective governance structure facilitates top-down decision-making and accelerate divestiture execution. It enables cross-functional coordination, ease of escalation, and clearer interdependencies.

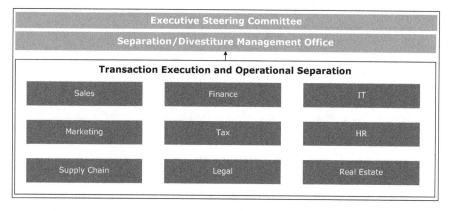

Fig. 11.3 Sample Governance Structure

The governance structure is designed in a manner aligned to the current organization, critical areas for the separation, business requirements, etc.

Governance Structure Design: Best Practices

1. *Align SMO governance model to current organization in order to enable more seamless experience for teams.*
2. *Ensure that areas critical to separation have high focus rather than be embedded in other workstreams.*
3. *Determine if the size and scope of each workstream is appropriate. Workstreams that are too large to handle may be divided further in order to ensure better visibility and focus.*
4. *Be mindful of existing relationships, conflicts, and other soft aspects that are unique to the organization.*
5. *Clearly define roles and responsibilities of each lead. Use frameworks such as RACI (responsible, accountable, consulted, informed) in order to objectively determine responsibilities and ownership.*

Following design of the governance structure, leads for every function and workstream are identified based on (a) past experience in running such programs, (b) subject matter expertise in the relevant area, and (c) business continuity requirements.

> In a recent transaction, a Fortune 50 technology company divested one of its businesses (DivestCo).
>
> The divestiture had to be executed against an aggressive timeline, with the remainder of the business (RemainCo) continuing to function as usual.
>
> The RemainCo leadership designed a governance structure which ensured that key resources from RemainCo had minimal involvement in separation.
>
> Since the RemainCo team continued to focus on business as usual, the company was able to maintain continuity and avoid disruption to RemainCo business while executing the DivestCo divestiture successfully.

Function and workstream leads then identify their core teams, including program/project managers, architects, and analysts. In this process, it may be ascertained that the internal resources may not be enough for the estimated effort. In such cases, external contractors with the relevant skill sets are brought in as required.

11.3.4 Track Resource Requirement

Resource requirements entered in the resource management tool are tracked periodically by the DMO to understand current allocations and future forecasts. Any gap to forecast may be filled in by hiring contractors with the required skill set. The DMO may also create dashboards to understand and critically analyze requirements across different workstreams.

Note: The below numbers are illustrative only. Actual figures depend on size of the company, nature and size of transaction, and number of employees involved in the transaction.

Workstream/Area	Forecasted FTEs				Allocated FTEs			
	Internal FTEs		External FTEs		Internal FTEs		External FTEs	
	Quarter 1	Quarter 2	Quarter 1	Quarter 2	Quarter 1	Quarter 2	Quarter 1	Quarter 2
Finance	360	850	40	90	324	765	36	81
HR	60	450	10	50	54	405	9	45
Supply Chain	40	500	5	50	36	450	5	45
Sales	210	500	20	50	189	450	18	45
Shared Execution Functions	70	170	10	20	63	153	9	18
DMO	20	30	10	20	18	27	9	18
Total	**760**	**2500**	**95**	**280**	**684**	**2250**	**86**	**252**

Fig. 11.4 Sample Resourcing Dashboard

11.3.5 Mitigate Resourcing Challenges

Below are some challenges that companies may face in the process of managing key resources:

1. *Key resource liability*: Employees may be moving to the new company as part of the divestiture or spin-off. In such situations, it is essential to identify these employees early on and ensure that they continue to focus on successful execution of the divestiture. It is also important that they transfer any critical knowledge about parent company's processes and systems to employees who will remain with the parent company.
2. *Retention and morale*: Separation teams may be overburdened with divestiture activities in addition to business-as-usual activities. Increased workload and pressure to meet deadlines may lower employee morale. It is thus essential to take up initiatives and mechanisms to help improve employee morale and offer retention packages to key employees and leaders.

11.4 Kickoff Planning

Often, key functional leaders are "brought under the tent" before the announcement of a transaction. This team begins planning for a post-announcement kickoff meeting where leaders from the rest of the organization are briefed about the nature of the deal, separation strategy, key decision points, and expectations from teams.

Planning for a Kickoff Meeting: Leading Practices

1. *Ensure timing is as close to announcement as possible, preferably within a few hours after announcement. This may cause less confusion about what is expected of teams and also helps teams quickly pivot to separation or divestiture activities.*
2. *Plan for a physical meeting instead of a virtual meeting. Having all key leaders in the same room helps ensure they get the right message to share with their teams as well as quick decision-making.*
3. *Prepare material to be shared well in advance and review to ensure the right message is being conveyed. Be mindful of confidentiality of such material.*
4. *Think of key outcomes to be achieved from the meeting, especially given the availability and focus of all leaders at the same time.*
5. *Plan for breakout sessions where leaders can discuss and make decisions in smaller groups and get a jumpstart on the separation planning. Logistics to be considered include meeting rooms, scribes, and templates to capture outcomes.*

Below are some key considerations for planning a kickoff meeting:

Area	Considerations
Audience	• Identify the key stakeholders who will be executing the divestiture • This typically includes leadership and decision-makers from all key functions
Logistics	• Ensure meeting invites are sent out to invitees well in advance • Identify speakers for the kickoff meeting as well as venue that provides the right amount of privacy given the underlying confidentiality • Appoint scribes to capture key decisions and action items
Content	• Focus on setting the context and aligning stakeholders on objectives, guiding principles, and confidentiality guidelines so that all teams have a consistent understanding of expectations • Develop content covering timeline, inter-functional dependencies, and separation strategy for key functions • Ensure details such as governance structure, meeting schedules, processes, and tools are also covered

Breakout sessions	• Plan for breakout sessions with the right teams to solve critical problems with program-wide impact. Sample topics include:
	  ◦ Identifying key dependencies between functions
	  ◦ Validating governance structure and identifying key team members for each workstream
	  ◦ Identifying areas where inputs are needed from buyer in case of a divestiture

11.5 Immediate Next Steps

Below is a list of immediate next steps that typically proceed the kickoff meeting and initial planning effort:

- Schedule follow-up meetings for pending action items from kickoff meetings.
- Establish overall as well as functional program management offices.
- Identify and onboard execution teams.
- Establish and operationalize program working and reporting cadence.
- Establish clear roles, include decision-makers.
- Define mechanisms to escalate and resolve risks/issues, etc.
- Create 30/60/90-day plans for execution.
- Establish tools, templates, and processes that will be used during the program.
- Understand current state landscape and refine separation strategy.
- Create functional blueprints.
- Conduct joint IT/business wave interlock sessions and identify critical path.
- Finalize Day 1 project plans.

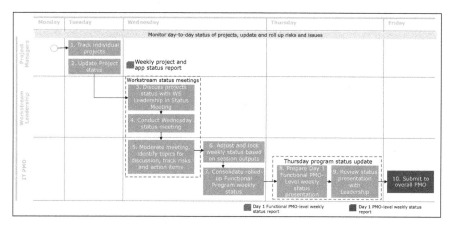

Fig. 11.5 Sample Weekly Reporting Cadence

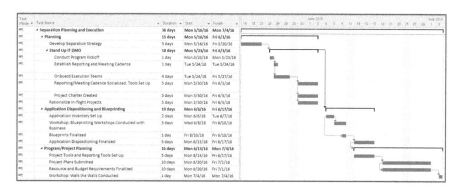

Fig. 11.6 Sample 30-Day Roadmap

11.6   Next Steps

The initial planning effort is valuable only when it is treated as the beginning of the program execution rather than a silo'd event. It sets the stage for the complex set of activities that teams would undertake in the upcoming months and provides clear guidance around how the program should be executed. It establishes prework in order to enable teams to ramp up and for leadership to set the right expectations with teams.

As the planning effort sets the foundation for the program execution, teams should look to get tactical in terms of immediate accomplishments as well as long-term success of the program.

Case Study 11

Background

Client is a Fortune 100 global payments processor, who divested one of its largest noncore businesses to a financial sponsor as part of a long-term corporate restructuring initiative. For this divestiture, the client opted to execute multiple preclose cutovers of business-critical systems and processes to ensure the operational success of the transaction. The client had to execute against a very aggressive timeline, across multiple global functions (corporate development, technology, finance, legal, tax, human resources, shared services) to separate the highly entangled business.

Challenges

The divestiture was one of the largest in this industry, and preannouncement and preclose challenges compounded due to the complexity of the deal:

- Tight preannouncement and sign-to-close timeline coupled with changing requirements
- High level of complexity and functional interdependencies both internally and externally with the buyer
- Global nature of the legal entity structures (30+ countries)
- Increased regulatory reporting requirements
- Buyer readiness for separation varied significantly between functions
- Divestiture execution with competing organizational priorities to grow core businesses organically
- Significant number of external dependencies including operating licenses, vendor contracts, works councils

Approach

Preannouncement through preclose, the client established six critical pillars to set the stage for a successful divestiture:

- *Program management and resourcing* – Developed and implemented an enterprise-wide M&A approach and program governance structure with localized execution.
  - Designed a program structure that aligned transaction-specific deal teams with organizational functions and other stakeholders (1,000+ member separation team).
  - Performed program governance, reporting, and issue management.
  - Developed separation budget approach, quarterly forecasting, and process to manage ongoing spend.
  - Developed and implemented a tailored M&A process built around the "issues lifecycle" and robust cross-functional problem identification and resolution focused on PMO cadence, guiding principles, checklists, playbooks, tools, and templates to aid in planning and execution.

- *Divestiture planning and execution* – Established planning and execution processes to execute divestiture and carve-out program across multiple global functions.
  - Performed workstream governance, reporting, and issue management.
  - Facilitated development of detailed separation work plan and identified and managed project and cross-project dependencies.
  - Interfaced with deal team and key stakeholders and provided function-specific advisory in order to develop strategy and de-risk the execution process in order to minimize service interruptions.
- *Legal entity restructuring* – Designed and executed program to restructure legal entities in 30+ countries.
- *TSAs stand-up and management* – Structured 1000+ TSAs for across divestitures, defined TSA administration model, and advised on TSA exit planning and execution strategy.
- *Separation budget management* – Instituted rigorous separation cost budget analysis and forecasting cadence to ensure alignment with overall separation strategy and provide leadership visibility into stand-up and separation cost and resourcing projections and timeline.
- *Stranded cost management* – Designed stranded cost program to manage and mitigate costs as TSA's exit.

Impact/Results

As the client readied for announcement, disciplined separation strategy planning (including legal entity restructuring planning) led to a reduced sign to close timeline and issue-free Legal Day 1. Methodologies, tools, and templates implemented positioned the client to execute future parallel divestiture programs across 3+ major deals and multiple product and service businesses against aggressive deal timelines.

Chapter 12
Building the Execution Roadmap

12.1 Introduction

The first 30 days after the announcement of a separation or divestiture are extremely critical. The seller company must build out a detailed execution plan, mobilize the entire organization, and engage a buyer. Even before a mergers and acquisitions (M&A) deal is made public, a significant portion of preparatory work should already be completed, including outlining the overall separation strategy, identifying the separation leader, setting up the governance structure, developing a top-down estimate of one-time costs and resource requirements, and drafting an execution plan. The first 30 days are critical to align the larger leadership team and engage subject matter advisors (SMAs) to help refine the execution plan and jump-start the implementation. At the end of 30 days, there should be one plan, one goal, and one team marching toward the single aim of a successful Day 1.

Typical activities completed in first 30 days include:

- Setting up the Divestiture Management Office (DMO)/Separation Management Office (SMO) and onboarding the leadership team
- Setting up reporting tools and meeting schedules
- Finalizing the budget for the separation or divestiture
- Rationalizing in-flight projects
- Engaging a buyer for joint planning
- Finalizing the separation timeline with well-defined functional interdependencies
- Building detailed execution plans and allocating resources

© Deloitte Development LLC 2018

J. Joy, *Divestitures and Spin-Offs*, Management for Professionals,
https://doi.org/10.1007/978-1-4939-7662-1_12

12.2 Setting Up the DMO/SMO and Onboarding the Leadership Team

The governance structure of the DMO/SMO should be in place before the deal announcement but made operational following the kickoff meeting. To keep track of all moving parts in a complex deal, the DMO/SMO should include a comprehensive mix of functional leaders from across the company. The DMO/SMO leadership serves as a critical decision-making body that provides strategic directions and resolves conflicts. Roles and responsibilities must also be clearly defined and understood by all the leaders. A responsible, accountable, consulted, and informed (RACI) matrix can be helpful in objectively determining responsibilities and ownership.

Although key functional leaders may be brought under the tent before the deal announcement, a larger team of workstream leaders and SMAs should be onboarded soon after the deal is announced. Typically, an in-person kickoff meeting is conducted in which the separation leader briefs the identified workstream leaders about the nature of the transaction, its alignment with business strategy, the transaction approach and timeline, and expectations.

As part of the kickoff meeting, detailed working sessions may also be conducted with the workstream leaders to identify key interdependencies between business units that will affect separation activities. For example, due to the need for a company code, tax IDs, and banking information for the new entity, the finance department IT team may be dependent on the set up of legal entity status for the spun off or separated entity in order to complete the system design. The plan for the next 30 days is also discussed in these working sessions, including how to handle in-flight projects, engage a buyer for joint planning, finalize the separation timeline with well-defined functional interdependencies, build the detailed execution plan, and allocate resources

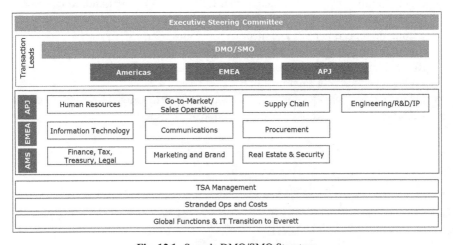

Fig. 12.1 Sample DMO/SMO Structure

12.3   Setting Up Reporting Tools and Meeting Schedules

Real-time visibility into progress on key milestones and risks related to the divestiture or separation will help the DMO/SMO leadership take proactive action to correct any issues before they affect the viability of the deal or disrupt the execution timeline. To this end, setting up meeting schedules and reporting dashboards within the first 30 days to track the execution of divestiture or separation activities is critical.

12.4   Finalizing the Budget for the Separation or Divestiture

One of the biggest hurdles to tackle within the first 30 days is finalizing the budget for the separation or divestiture. Typically, before the deal is announced, a top-down cost estimate, which is expressed as a percentage of the current operating budget, is created based on benchmarks from comparable transactions. After the deal announcement, functional leaders must build a bottom-up cost estimate which is a detailed budget for individual functions that is needed for the separation or divestiture. The top-down and bottom-up cost estimates, along with a clear set of documented assumptions, are then used by the leadership team to determine the final best/worst case cost estimate.

It is important to include a buffer of between 5% and 15% of the final cost estimate for unexpected expenses that may emerge during execution of the deal.

The major cost components in a separation or divestiture are labor and non-labor costs

Labor costs include costs for internal labor at the seller company, as well as external labor outside the seller company, such as consultants and contractors.

Non-labor costs include travel, training, hardware, and software costs.

It is critical to get accurate one-time cost estimates, since the budget for the separation or divestiture is based on these estimates. Executives should manage one-time costs for alignment with these preliminary estimates for the duration of the transaction.

12.5   Rationalizing In-Flight Projects

An M&A deal is a strategic growth vehicle, and it requires the focus of top executives (CEO, COO, and the board) and critical resources at both the seller and buyer companies. This poses a challenge as not all of a company's key personnel can devote their time exclusively to the deal; instead, they must also focus on the company's ongoing in-flight projects and deliver on business priorities. Likewise, not all of a company's capital can be invested in the deal, since the RemainCo business must not only continue to operate but potentially grow throughout deal execution.

In order to free up critical resources and funding for divestiture or separation activities, a careful analysis of in-flight and upcoming projects is needed. The project rationalization framework outlined in Fig. 12.2 helps identify capital-intensive and non-strategic projects that can be suspended to release key resources and funding necessary to help effective deal execution.

For example, in a recent transaction, where a Fortune 50 technology company divested one of its businesses, a reduction of 40–50% was achieved through rationalization of in-flight IT projects.

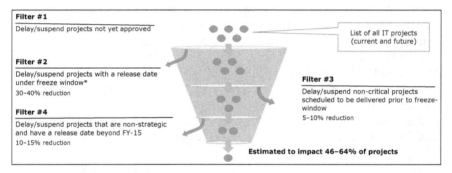

Fig. 12.2 Project Rationalization Framework

12.6   Engaging a Buyer for Joint Planning

A divestiture requires the buyer's alignment on some separation decisions and activities; thus joint planning by both the buyer and seller companies is necessary. Similar to the seller, the buyer also typically assembles teams tasked with ensuring the transaction is a success. A working relationship should be established between the seller and the buyer teams working on the transaction, along with a common framework and terminology to reduce miscommunication, speed up the execution, and meet the timeline. The teams need to align on the divestiture timeline and particularly on critical activities for Day 1.

In terms of assets, in order to run the new business effectively, the buyer company needs to know the assets it is acquiring as part of the deal. Hence, alignment between the buyer and seller companies on the disposition of applications on Day 1 is necessary, along with an approach to IT infrastructure security during the transition of such applications from the seller company to the buyer company.

The buyer and seller companies must also agree on a list of projects they will need to jointly run, including the tracking of separation activities. The buyer and seller should work on these joint projects together to help ensure the transaction runs smoothly. Any issues and risks related to these joint projects and activities must be addressed and mitigated by both companies.

#	Example
1	*Active directory services*—Project carried out by buyer and seller to distinguish users in active directory and to support the build of global address list for messaging
2	*Sharepoint and other common sites*—Joint project scope is to identify buyer/seller only sites and clone the sites and to remove access of users (two-way)
3	*Data center data networks*—Joint project scope is to provide connectivity between data centers (if needed) for the agreed duration between buyer and seller

12.7 Finalizing the Separation Timeline with Well-Defined Functional Interdependencies

A critical objective within the first 30 days is to finalize one single, end-to-end road map for deal execution, with key milestones and functional interdependencies integrated within it.

Fig. 12.3 Walk-the-Wall™

The following multistep process can be used to build an effective deal execution road map:

1. Create an inventory of all the assets that will be separated within each business unit.
2. Define the preliminary separation strategy (Day 1 disposition) for each asset.
3. Define Day 1 projects to be carried out to achieve the separation strategy.
4. Develop the execution timeline to implement these projects.
5. Call out interdependencies between business units in the execution timeline.
6. Conduct "Walk-the-Wall™" sessions to bring all the business units together, address the interdependencies, and finalize the road map.

Typically, as part of the pre-deal announcement preparatory work, most business unit leaders complete steps 1–5 in the road map process, including developing draft execution road maps for their business units. After the deal announcement, these road maps are refined based on SME input, and all the business units are brought together to conduct step 6 to refine the interdependencies and finalize the integrated road map.

The final step (step 6) in preparing a separation timeline is to conduct a session to bring all business units and workstreams together in one room with a visual representation of the timeline, as depicted in Fig. 12.3.

In this session, each business unit leader discusses critical milestones and interdependencies with the whole team involved in separation activities. The output of this session includes a plan for the disposition of applications on Day 1, along with the overall divestiture or separation road map, which serves as the timetable for separation activities.

12.8 Building Detailed Execution Plans and Allocating Resources

Creating detailed execution plans should also be done in the first 30 days. The DMO/SMO will develop processes and templates for the execution, and all teams must adhere to the structure and broad timelines specified in the execution plan template. In addition to global plans, country-level plans are also created that take into account country-specific activities and requirements.

A centralized repository should be built to track all execution plans. Reporting teams should be assembled to build out dashboards that help DMO/SMO leaders keep track of critical milestones, risks, issues, project status (i.e., complete, active, on hold), and a RAG (red, amber, green) status, along with a rationale for that status.

Execution plans are typically made available through a tool already in use by the company (e.g., company website), and the plans should be accessible to all team members involved in the separation.

12.9   Conclusion

The first 30 days after the deal announcement are critical. Planning activities for the separation process must be completed, including devising a road map, budgeting, and resource allocation. Reporting pathways should be set up, including real-time dashboards to monitor the progress of separation activities. These dashboards will enable the DMO/SMO leadership to take proactive action to correct issues before they affect the viability of the deal or disrupt the execution timeline.

Case Study: 12

Background
A leading global bank acquired a multibillion dollar commercial lending portfolio from a large global financial services organization. Successful separation and TSA exit were dependent upon rapid delivery of technology activities across 30+ workstreams. Separation road map activities included required LD1 separation, as well as end-state separation and TSA exit.

Challenges
To plan for separation, the bank established a separation governance structure and road map which enabled the business to run while also planning for TSA exit and end-state separation activities:

- Speed was critical due to short time period between deal announcement and LD1.
- Large cross-functional complexity required coordinated efforts to define the execution road map, including key milestones and interdependencies between functions.
- Divested business operated with support of shared service groups that were co-mingled with other businesses, requiring extensive TSAs to support the buyer post-close.
- Coordination of cross-functional teams (IT, operations, line of business, and corporate) created additional complexity and challenged program timelines and priorities.
- Limited technology staff were included in the deal, requiring buyer to learn acquired business' systems with minimal knowledge transfer while moving at fast pace to maintain customer experience.
- High product complexity compared to buyer's bank portfolio required system changes/ enhancements in buyer's applications.

Approach
The overall transaction governance and technology and operations SMO teams were established to define the separation road map. At deal announcement, a separation road map was developed to drive to a successful Legal Day 1 (LD1), establish

joint transition services agreements (TSAs), and develop exit plans for separation activities across 30+ technology and operations workstreams. Post-close critical road map activities delivered among all cross-functional teams (IT, operations, line of business, and corporate) for the governing bodies were as follows:

- Established program governance to centrally manage 100+ projects in support of execution road map.
- Conducted multiple cross-functional alignment workshops to ensure all technology and other functional interdependencies were considered in road map.
- Organized executive review toll-gate meetings to ensure alignment across technology, lines of business, and other enabling functions.

Impact/Results

Critical separation road map success factors for the achievement of Legal Day 1 success and stabilization of the separation/buyer integration process included defining end-state architecture, driving cross-functional planning, and coordinating delivery of TSA transition plans and dependencies:

- Mobilized program governance for deal close in an expedited manner, delivered comprehensive Day 1 and Day 100+ plans, established TSA schedules and structure, and defined TSA exit plans.
- Road map oversaw execution of LD1 and command center leading to an issue-free LD1 with no customer impact.
- Drove completion of efficient data separation and data feed cutover activities for LD1 and post-close separations.
- Facilitated cross-functional communication and stakeholder engagement to promote employee buy-in.

Part III
Executing the Deal

Chapter 13
Managing the People Side of Divestiture: Retention and Motivation

Leveraging Retention Tools to Nurture the Development of a High-Performing, Stand-Alone Organization

Divestiture activity is increasing as companies evaluate and optimize their product portfolios and service lines. In general, divestitures bring tremendous change and an extended period of uncertainty—beginning with the pre-deal announcement phase, throughout the divestiture planning phase (deal announcement to Day 1), and continuing post-Day 1, when the transformative activities peak.

During this period of change and uncertainty, protecting business continuity is critical, including:

- Maintaining customer, vendor, and alliance relationships
- Sustaining momentum on business-as-usual projects, product releases, and other initiatives of strategic imperative
- Accomplishing separation activities with limited resources (e.g., financial, human capital, time)
- Mitigating productivity losses stemming from employees' uncertainty about their future at the company
- Discouraging critical talent from leaving the company to join competitors that are currently not going through a "state of change"

Maintaining employee engagement and talent retention are critical to achieving overall transaction success. Furthermore, effective talent retention planning is seldom one dimensional or follows a one-size-fits-all approach. Rather, the most effective talent retention strategies use a balanced, multipronged approach to retain and motivate employees. This approach involves both financial and nonfinancial retention efforts, as well as a strategic communications campaign.

In the early stages of divestiture planning, the talent retention strategy should be developed hand in hand with the overall talent strategy and workforce plan. The responsibility for a successful retention strategy and execution is the joint responsibility of senior leadership, managers, and HR. All play a critical role in defining the talent retention strategy and driving through execution.

Answering a small number of critical questions will help guide the company toward retaining the talent essential to the success of the remaining entity.

© Deloitte Development LLC 2018

J. Joy, *Divestitures and Spin-Offs*, Management for Professionals,
https://doi.org/10.1007/978-1-4939-7662-1_13

A divesting company should think about leader and employee retention early on in the divestiture planning process. To define an effective retention strategy that drives the success of both the divestiture and the remaining entity, HR leaders should follow these *five critical steps*:

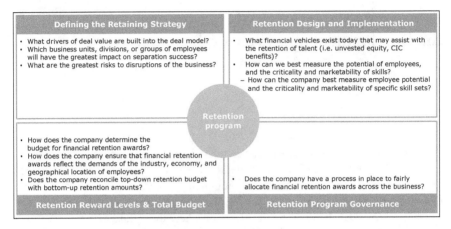

Fig. 13.1 Factors in Retention Programs

1. Define and segment the target population.
2. Determine retention award eligibility.
3. Determine the appropriate retention awards for key employees.
4. Execute retention via effective change communications.
5. Establish an ongoing governance structure.

While the development of a retention strategy typically takes place in the preannouncement phase of a divestiture, the execution of the strategy can take place in any of the identified phases of the divestiture (e.g., preannouncement, announce to Day 1, post-Day 1). HR and business leadership will define the timeline based on the specifics for the transaction in question.

13.1   Step 1: Define and Segment the Target Population

The divesting company should complete a talent segmentation specifically related to the divestiture, which is different from a talent assessment that may be conducted under business-as-usual circumstances.

The primary purpose of the talent segmentation is to identify the employees who drive value to the business and whose turnover would create risks to business continuity or critical customer/partner/vendor/alliance relationships. These identified employees could include:

- Key employees critical to the ongoing success of the remaining entity
- Seasoned employees with the experience required to successfully lead through the divestiture planning and execution phases
- Employees required to accomplish short-term transaction-related activities (e.g., transitional employees)

By identifying these employees, a company can take the first step toward developing the right retention strategy that will support its divestiture activities.

13.2   Step 2: Determine Retention Award Eligibility

For the above categories of talent/employees—all of which can be identified as key to the success of the divestiture—HR leaders should consider the following factors when determining the right type of retention award:

- *Leadership roles:* Operations-related positions that affect business continuity, such as recruiting and onboarding employees and maintaining engagement teams
- *Unique skill sets:* Positions that require skills in high demand, especially in certain geographies
- *Availability of skill set in external labor market:* Ability to replace a skill set with talent from the external labor market should turnover of a key employee occur
- *Performance levels:* Consistently high performers with high potential in future business operations
- *Institutional knowledge:* Employees with critical knowledge about business processes not readily available through other avenues
- *Relationship owners:* Employees with in-depth relationships with critical external parties (e.g., key customers, government officials, industry leadership, industry alliances)
- *Location:* Employees at locations and/or countries critical to business operations and strategy

Retention decisions should consider whether the employee brings a critical skill set not easily found in the market.

To aggregate the input gathered through the talent segmentation process and better prioritize employees for special retention consideration, it is helpful to plot employees based on their perceived business and retention risk, as follows:

Employees who are critical to ongoing business continuity are considered high-performing talent and, as such, are often a high priority for retention.

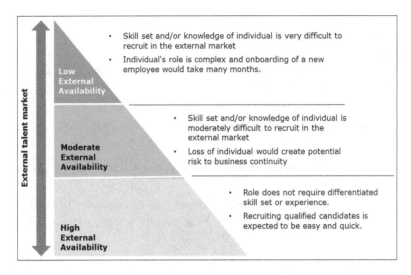

Fig. 13.2 Dynamics in a Talent Market

13.3 Step 3: Determine the Appropriate Retention Awards for Key Employees

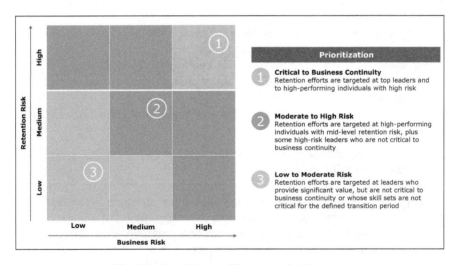

Fig. 13.3 Prioritization of Employees for Retention

Next, the divesting entity must determine the appropriate retention award for each key employee and should consider both financial and nonfinancial incentives.

13.3.1 *Financial Retention Awards*

Since each divestiture is different and, by nature, has different strategic priorities, no two financial retention plans are the same. In order to optimize talent retention, each financial retention award should be carefully calibrated against the specific needs and timeline of the transaction.

When HR leaders first sit down to build a financial retention award program, they should consider the following key questions:

- What is the most appropriate retention period?
- What budget does the company need to set aside for financial retention awards?
- Are other financial retention vehicles already in place (e.g., existing long-term incentive awards, severance for transitional employees)?
- What amount of financial award is required to retain top talent beyond the financially reinforced retention period?
- Does the financial retention award program need to be a one-size-fits-all solution? Or should individual factors (e.g., high-demand skills) influence the size of awards for certain employees?

Effective financial retention award programs share the following characteristics:

- They are specifically tailored to meet the company's needs
- They provide meaningful financial rewards that incent the employees to remain
- They are offered to employees after deliberate and proactive consideration by HR leadership

13.3.1.1 Specifically Tailored

Financial retention award programs must be tailored to the specific talent retention needs of the company. The types of financial awards can and should vary based on the environment and employees in question.

Examples of tailored financial retention awards include:

- Traditional retention bonus:
  - The goal is the long-term retention of key employees who are critical to the successful completion of the divestiture and/or future success of the remaining organization.
  - Awards are often contingent upon:
    - Continuous employment throughout the retention period
    - Satisfactory performance
    - Accomplishment of individual or workstream transaction goals
  - Awards are typically paid out through cash and/or equity.
- Stay bonus:
  - The goal is the retention of critical employees for a defined period of time.

- Awards are offered to employees who are critical for a limited period of time until a process, program, project, or transition service is transitioned or completed; for these awards there is a defined employment end date.
- Awards are typically paid to employees as either a lump sum or salary continuation, along with any severance (and signing of a general release), upon their separation from the organization.
- It is often expected that at the end of the stay term, employees are released from the organization.
- Completion bonus:
  - The goal is to retain key contributors through the completion of the transaction.
  - The awards are generally only paid to a few executives and other key contributors (e.g., executives in corporate strategy, business development, HR) integral to the completion of the transaction.
  - Awards are typically paid upon successful completion of the divestiture.

Employees may react in different ways to specific awards; therefore, understanding your target employee population and what drives their overall retention is extremely important. Senior leadership should consider the suite of award types and make decisions based on what would have the most value to their targeted employees.

13.3.1.2   Meaningful

Financial retention awards must be significantly more than what targeted employees could realize by pursuing employment with competitors. To maximize the likelihood of employees remaining with the organization, the size of the payout and the duration of the retention period must be taken into consideration. The longer the desired retention period, the larger the award required. For retention periods longer than 12 months, interim payouts should be considered.

13.3.1.3   Deliberate

Employees should not automatically be offered financial retention awards. Not every research and development (R&D) employee is critical to the next product release, not every sales representative has critical client relationships, and executives are generally not irreplaceable solely based on their level within the organization. The most effective organizations make proactive decisions on who should receive a retention award based on a detailed review of the workforce.

13.3.2   *Nonfinancial Retention Efforts: Engaging Leadership and Motivating Talent*

Financial retention programs, while critical to keeping top talent during the divestiture process, may still not be enough to retain key employees. HR leaders should also strive to create the right employment experience; otherwise, the key talent the company needs for its future success may leave once retention awards are paid.

As such, it is important for a company to also consider certain nonfinancial awards when defining its overall employee retention strategy.

Active leadership engagement plays a critical role when key talent is deciding whether to stay with an organization. In that sense, managers play a key role in assessing employee potential and turnover risk, clearly articulating organizational and transactional goals, and helping engage the necessary resources that can deliver success.

The means by which managers can take on active roles in retaining key talent include:

- *One-on-one meetings with employees.* A simple yet powerful way managers can demonstrate organizational and managerial support is to hold regular one-on-one meetings with employees to provide updates on the direction of the new organization and discuss how employees are coping with announced changes. At times, these conversations will also discuss the increased workloads for impacted employees. Some employees may be asked to not only continue to deliver against their day jobs but also help the organization separate as part of transaction planning. Through these one-on-one meetings, managers can assess the current state and identify issues that require escalation and resolution at a higher level.
- *Special assignments.* Managers can enhance employee engagement by providing high-potential talent with certain special assignments, including:
  - Internal development opportunities
  - Introductions to new leaders in the organization
  - Opportunities to engage in cross-functional strategic initiatives
  - New career opportunities within the company
  - External development via conferences or certificate programs
- *Targeted development opportunities.* A divestiture is a unique opportunity for top performers to step up and help the business deliver against the transaction goals. Roles will be created within the transaction structure that are filled by employees tapped to help drive divestiture activities. These experiences can be career accelerators that allow high-potential employees to contribute in new ways to the success of the business.
- *Special exposure and visibility to senior leadership across the corporate functions who are helping to lead the divestiture.* Corporate leadership will continuously monitor the progress of the overall divestiture as the remaining organization tracks toward Day 1. As such, employees engaged with supporting the

transaction may gain exposure to the senior leadership team and be able to build relationships that last.

13.4   Step 4: Execute Retention Via Effective Change Communications

Successfully executing a retention strategy involves rolling out the overall retention program with targeted and effective change communications. Mitigating the sensitivities around retention requires developing a detailed communications plan.

At a global level, senior leadership should openly acknowledge and message the material changes ahead of the divested or to-be-divested business while also emphasizing the opportunities the remaining entity will have going forward and how critical the current talent is for the realization of these goals. This creates the foundation for talent retention efforts that are anchored with effective communications going forward. Customized communications should be developed and released to the unique audiences within the organization.

Key considerations for messaging include:

- Leadership:
  - Leaders should consistently address concerns that employees may have about staying with the company through the transaction.
  - Messages can be shared at an overall company level through regular employee newsletters, as well as in-person meetings, executive road shows, town halls, and round tables.
- Managers:
  - Managers should reinforce and personalize messages coming from the leadership team by meeting one-on-one with employees and describing the means by which the retention plan will be rolled out.
  - Messages can be shared in one-on-one meetings, individual goal-setting, and career planning conversations
- Human Resources:
  - HR should focus on coordinating all communications to ensure consistency across various functions.
  - HR should provide guidelines and feedback to both leadership and managers on how best to communicate, including establishing best practices to ensure messages cascade down in a thoughtful and consistent manner.
  - HR should encourage questions from leaders and employees throughout the process, as well as respond to and document frequently asked questions (FAQ).

While each stakeholder has a defined role in the retention communication strategy, it is important that messaging from all groups is consistent and aligned with business objectives.

13.5   Step 5: Establish an Ongoing Governance Structure

As a business enters into the early stages of divestiture planning and begins designing the overall employee retention strategy, it is a leading practice to establish an ongoing governance structure to monitor execution throughout the transaction. This structure could be set up as a cross-functional committee that includes key stakeholders from across the business who are directly involved in divestiture planning, as well as those not directly involved with the transaction.

Key activities this cross-functional committee could oversee include, but are not limited to, the following:

- Reviewing and approving recipients of financial retention awards at the onset of divestiture planning and on an ongoing basis thereafter
- Monitoring the overall retention budget
- Ongoing monitoring of the effectiveness of current retention strategies
- Monitoring attrition and turnover to identify employee groups that may require additional retention efforts as the transaction progresses
- Overseeing the retention strategy communications campaign
- Coordinating the release of financial retention award payouts
- Coordinating the timely release of transitional employees

A single cross-functional committee that manages the execution of the employee retention program will help ensure accountability at the leadership level through a clearly defined body that owns the program—should issues and/or questions arise. In addition, centralizing the decision-making process and execution will help ensure there is only one holistic strategy, versus the various functions developing their own independent retention strategies and operating in silos.

13.6   Conclusion

Delivering a successful divestiture includes maintaining business continuity throughout the planning and execution phases to ensure the remaining entity is set up for success on Day 1 and beyond. Retention of critical talent is a perennial business focus, but the importance of retention is even more heightened during a transformative event such as a divestiture. The complexities of a divestiture make it difficult to successfully execute the employee retention strategy, but by taking into consideration the steps highlighted throughout this chapter, a company can take the first step toward developing a strong retention strategy and plan—and best position a business for success across all phases of the divestiture.

Case Study: 13

Background

A US-headquartered medical device company providing biologics and minimally invasive solutions to orthopedic surgeons decided to divest a small business unit. The divestiture represented approximately 10% of revenues and 15% of the company's employees.

Challenges

The company operated as a fully integrated business across all functions as well as supply chain and commercial. Business development and human resources were tasked with:

- Determining the talent needs of each function for the remaining organization (i.e., post-divestiture) in terms of both headcount and capabilities
- Identifying the talent that is critical to the success of the remaining organization (and also identifying the portion of the workforce that would be divested with the transaction)
- Reviewing the need for financial retention awards and designing a talent retention plan
- Identifying and in some cases develop nonfinancial retention tactics to support the retention planning and enhance employee engagement during the transaction planning phase

A critical objective for senior management was also to optimize the operating model and workforce of the remaining organization beyond the carve-out of the divestiture.

Approach

The team of business development and human resources leaders began their work early in the transaction planning process by outlining to senior management the objectives and suggest approach for the process.

After having achieved alignment with senior management, the team engaged each of the functional leaders in conversation about:

- Go-forward capabilities the function will provide to the organization post-divestiture
- Corresponding talent needs
- Key talent in their function
- Resources required for any transition services

Human resources came prepared to each of the meetings and presented current and projected future costs for the function as well as relevant benchmark data for industry peers.

Suggested talent needs for each function as well as identified key talent were subsequently reviewed, debated, and agreed upon in a series of senior management calibration session.

- Finance used the calibration session outputs to build up the go-forward financials for the remaining organization.
- HR reviewed the identified critical talent and identified retention risks.

In the next phase, HR developed a retention program that consisted of both financial retention awards and several nonfinancial engagement approaches:

- Financial.
  - Key talent
    - Review of existing retention levers such as unvested long-term incentives and in a few cases tuition reimbursement.
    - If existing retention levers were considered not sufficient to assure retention, supplemental retention awards were extended for a 6-month period.
  - Resources required for transition services
    - Review of existing retention levers such severance payable upon release.
    - If projected severance payment at the end of the transition services was not sufficient, a supplemental stay bonus was extended.
- Nonfinancial.
  - Robust change management and communications plan: The company committed to a comprehensive plan for manager and employee readiness for the divestiture with a foundation of open, transparent, frequent, and direct two-way communication
  - Engagement of some of the most critical talent (across all levels) in cross-functional projects on the CEO's agenda
- In the implementation phase, HR executed retention award and stay bonus agreements and monitored ongoing employee engagement during the divestitures planning as well as post-transaction close.

Impact/Results

The company was able to successfully close the divestiture with a leaner operating model and the critical talent to support the organization future. With the retention plans in place and highly visible leadership, employee and manager engagement remained solid throughout the transaction, and voluntary turnover did not materially increase over prior periods.

Chapter 14
Shaking Things Up: Reorganizing

Global deals present global challenges. A divestiture with many countries in scope requires significant effort by human resources (HR) and many other corporate functions to successfully manage these specific global challenges. This often includes the managing of diverse compensation policies, foreign and domestic regulations, and union and other collective labor contracts, as well as organizing (and at times reorganizing) the transaction across different cultures. Significant time and effort is required to coordinate the divestiture across multiple countries, employee populations, and jurisdictions.

At the start of divestiture planning for a global transaction, it is typically HR's responsibility to define the activities required to deliver a successful Day 1, such as:

- Enable a smooth employee experience with minimal disruption to the employee population and the business.
- Manage data specific to employee movements and job transitions, including decisions related to the organization as defined by corporate leadership.
- Determine the country and local requirements for all types of employee transfers.
- Establish global guidelines, where possible, and execute at the local/country level, if required.
- Ensure data integrity.
- Coordinate activities and dependencies between various workstreams.
- Understand the specifics of the divestiture transaction (e.g., asset versus share deal) on a country-by-country basis and its implications on core HR activities.

By focusing on these activities, HR, in coordination with the other partner workstreams (e.g., IT, finance, legal, tax, etc.), will be able to develop an executable plan to manage through the complexities of the divestiture.

© Deloitte Development LLC 2018
J. Joy, *Divestitures and Spin-Offs*, Management for Professionals,
https://doi.org/10.1007/978-1-4939-7662-1_14

In a global divestiture, HR is typically responsible (in coordination with the acquiring company) for driving completion of a number of core activities, including:

1. Prepare for and drive the *employee information and consultation (I&C) process* across all countries, including consultation with established works councils and/or unions. Of note, the acquiring company will also have specific responsibilities with regard to their works councils and/or unions. These responsibilities will need to be owned by the acquiring company and can be executed in partnership with the divesting company.
2. Determine *offer letter/transfer letter requirements* for every employee who is identified to be "in scope" for transfer to the buyer, and execute the development and delivery of offer/transfer letters. As with the I&C process, the acquiring company may have certain requirements that will need to be met, and again, the acquiring company and the divesting company can work in partnership to ensure all requirements are met.
3. *Manage dependencies* across all workstreams according to the established transaction timeline and path to Day 1, including total compensation, organizational design, and legal requirements.
4. Serve as the *single source of truth for all employee data*, including the tracking of employee acceptances and rejections as they move through the defined offer/notification process, where applicable.

Building a strong plan to deliver against these core activities will help position the company to successfully execute the closing of the divestiture (Day 1) and beyond.

14.1 Prepare for and Drive the I&C Process Across All Countries, Including Consultation with Established Works Councils and/or Unions

When assessing the complexity of a potential divestiture, it is important to understand the in-scope global footprint (e.g., the specific requirements for every country that is in scope as part of the transaction). For example, works councils are organizations that represent employees at the local level in many countries outside the United States—a majority of these are located in the EMEA region (Europe, Middle East, and Africa). While works councils cannot block a company's plans, they can significantly obstruct and delay the divestiture timeline and process. Works council consultation in Europe, otherwise known as the information and consultation (I&C) process and employee offer/notification requirements, will most often vary by country. In some jurisdictions, this is a mandatory step, while in other jurisdictions the obligation only arises when changes to the terms and conditions of employment are contemplated. In all jurisdictions, affected or potentially affected employees must be identified before the process can begin.

As indicated earlier, the responsibilities and expectations for a company going through a divestiture are different from the responsibilities and expectations for a company acquiring another business. The topics that a company undergoing a divestiture ("seller") must address with works councils and/or unions will depend on the nature of the transaction.

At a high level, I&C typically should include the following information:

- The identified date when an employee will officially "transfer" to the acquiring company, the new employer's name, and the reasons for the transfer.
- Legal, financial, and social consequences for affected employees.
- Changes that will impact employees after their transfer to the acquiring company.
- Business plans for the remaining company, if available.
- Legal entity structure and timeline (e.g., if legal entities are transferring in whole to the buyer, if employees will be integrated into existing legal entities at the buyer, etc.), if available.
- Organizational design for the remaining company, if available.
- Note: During the early stages of a divestiture transaction, it may not be feasible to communicate all of these components at one time to the works council representatives. It is the responsibility of the HR, labor relations, and legal teams to construct a timeline for when such information can be legally shared and communicate that to the appropriate works council representatives.

Clearly, the above is just a high-level summary. It is important that the legal and labor relations teams on the ground clearly understand the type of deal and the defined parameters of the transaction. Different types of deals (i.e., asset versus share) carry different implications for HR and tie directly into the I&C process. The requirements for HR will vary, depending on the nature of the defined deal structure.

Understanding the type of deal the divestiture entails is critical to developing a detailed strategy for approaching the employee I&C process.

At the start of the I&C process, the HR, labor relations, and legal teams will need to clearly outline the I&C strategy and present this to the appropriate works councils—where required. Delivering a clear I&C strategy is one key to a successful transition. Failure to comply with I&C requirements can cause delays and lead to increased costs. While each company's approach to I&C must be customized to the specifics of the transaction, there are a few key considerations:

14.1.1   Understanding the Scope of the I&C

- Identify the entities (e.g., unions in the Americas and Asia Pacific, works councils in Europe) that require consultation at the start of divestiture planning.
- Understand the expectations of every entity that requires consultation.

- Determine the I&C responsibilities of the company as the seller, and set the I&C strategy.
- Determine the I&C responsibilities of the buyer, if the divested business will be acquired by another company.
- Develop a detailed I&C plan, including timing implications, and have all key stakeholders, including the legal department, review and approve the plan.
- Ensure the priorities for consultation with unions and works councils are understood across the company.

14.1.2   Driving the I&C Process

- Identify and consult with employee representatives and trade unions.
- Define the company's legal obligations for the works councils/unions within each country.
- Understand the type of deal (i.e., asset versus share) the divestiture entails.
- Focus on key messages linked to divestiture milestones and key decisions:
    - Build the bottom-up messages in coordination with employee representatives.
- Continuously align and liaise with the buyer.

As a company enters into the early phases of divestiture planning, HR leadership must understand the roles and responsibilities of the key players, including stakeholders participating in the works council I&C process. The following graphic provides a high-level view of the stakeholders often involved, as well as their typical responsibilities:

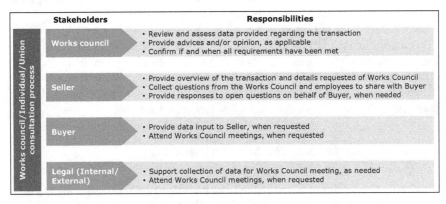

Fig. 14.1 Stakeholders and Responsibilities

The above are not meant to be an exhaustive list of all key stakeholders. There will also be critical local and country leaders helping to drive the process.

Prior to the first works council meeting, HR and the legal teams must gather specific details about key areas. Typically, HR takes the lead in this process, with support from the internal and external legal team, as needed. Some of these areas are highlighted below. It is important for the legal team to weigh in on areas that will be consulted on prior to any discussion with works councils.

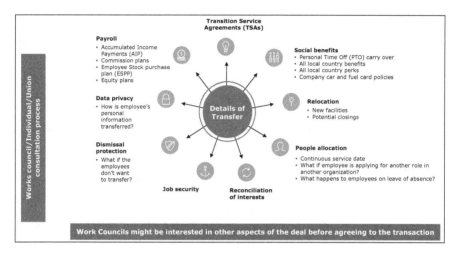

Fig. 14.2 Details of Transfer

Divestiture planning cannot begin until all required works councils have signed off and approval has been granted. Should planning begin without their approval, the divesting company may be setting itself up to be delayed by the works council's/union's final decision until the required court hearings take place, which could push the approval significantly past the established timeline for the divestiture planning process.

In the end, works councils must have information about what is changing on Day 1, as well as changes to any specific employment terms and conditions (T&C). Ensuring the company, the legal team, and the labor relations team are prepared to approach the I&C process with a defined and coordinated strategy is essential.

14.2   Define the Employee Transfer Strategy, Define the Offer/Transfer Letter Requirements for Every In-Scope Employee, and Execute the Development and Delivery of Offer/Transfer Letters

In order to execute the transaction and formally transfer or off-board in-scope employees, the divesting company must define the employee transfer strategy and the plan to develop and distribute the required offer letters/transfer letters to the affected employee, per local requirements. As with works council requirements, the defined employee transfer strategy, and associated offer/transfer letter requirements, will vary by country.

At a high level, the key steps required to define the employee transfer strategy by country include:

- Confirm the legal transaction plan, transfer method, process, and documentation needs of each applicable country—note this is likely to change throughout the divestiture process; thus, continuous coordination with the legal team is key.
- Understand the transaction deal type (i.e., asset versus share).
  - The transfer process will vary based on the identified deal type (e.g., whether employees can be transferred versus terminated and rehired).
- Identify data points required to prepare employee notification packets based on the legal requirements of each applicable country.
- Create the offer letter/notification packets.
  - Employee offer letter/notification requirements will vary based on the type of transfer.
  - Based on the transaction type (e.g., stock purchase), an employee may be required to "accept or reject" through a true offer letter process.
  - In other nonstock purchase transactions, an employee may only need to be "notified" of the transfer of employment to the buyer.
  - At times, this activity may be driven by the acquiring company, in partnership with the divesting company.
- Confirm the delivery confirmation method (i.e., e-signature vs. manual signature) for the notification documents in each applicable country.
  - Local legal requirements also dictate what to give employees and the required format (e.g., email, hard copy) to successfully transfer employment.
  - For certain countries, it is required that documents are signed with a "wet signature" by employees
- Determine the scenarios in which employees refuse to transfer and confirm with legal what employees are legally able to do if they do not consent to transfer.
  - In certain instances in which an employee refuses to accept a transfer, the company will be liable to pay severance if the employee is terminated.
- Identify the severance requirements of each applicable country.
  - In certain countries, employees may be entitled to statutory notice and severance depending on the type of transfer.
- Confirm whether employees can be transferred while on leave of absence.
  - In some countries, the company must wait until employees return to work prior to formally transferring the employee.
- Release the offer/notifications, manage the offer/notification process, and track the offer letter/notification delivery and acceptance and rejection status.

After the employee transfer strategy is defined, a critical next step will be to develop the content that will be included in the required offer/transfer letters.

The divesting company will not be in a position to develop the employee transfer documentation until the following components are defined, as many of these components are required to be included in the documentation itself.

- *Organizational design/HR business partners (HRBPs)*
  - ○ Timing of business unit organizational design decisions
  - ○ Organizational modeling tool data, if applicable
  - ○ Collaboration approach on consultation and notification process
- *Total compensation*
  - ○ Data related to new offers and any other compensation, benefits, equity, and T&C changes
  - ○ Timing of annual merit increases
  - ○ Severance planning
- *Talent acquisition*
  - ○ General hiring practices, including maintenance of the organizational structure for new hires, resignations, and internal transfers
- *Legal*
  - ○ Legal entity restructuring approach and timeline
  - ○ Internal legal counsel guidance
- *Global mobility*
  - ○ Immigration impacts for transferring employees
  - ○ Clarification on where and how expatriates transfer as part of the transaction, including home/host country legal requirements
- *Workplace*
  - ○ Facility and work location changes that impact employee data
- *HR systems*
  - ○ Data management support
  - ○ Requirements for operational cutover and system implications
  - ○ Organizational modeling tool support, as applicable
- *Local HR*
  - ○ Works council consultations and/or union negotiations
  - ○ I&C negotiation processes
  - ○ Reduction in force (RIF) planning and workforce planning
- *Country/local legal requirements*
  - ○ Certain countries have specific notification timing requirements that must be met in order to transfer employees, such as:
    - ▪ 30 days in advance of transfer
    - ▪ 60 days in advance of transfer
    - ▪ In good time

○ These requirements should be considered when building the overall offer and transfer notification timeline.

Again, all of the above may not be formally included in the content of an offer/transfer letter, but it is a best practice to address the above and understand the deal implications of the above, prior to initiating the content development phase of this process.

Throughout the employee notification process, it is important to engage with both the internal legal team and an outside legal advisor. One of the keys to success for a divestiture is to work with a legal advisor who has a truly global reach and can provide advice on both the legal implications of the deal transaction and the specific requirements, on a by-country basis, that should accompany any documents developed and distributed to in-scope employees.

14.3 Manage Dependencies Across All Areas According to the Established Timeline, Including Total Compensation, Organizational Design, and Legal Requirements

When developing the timeline for distributing transfer documentation, HR leadership must effectively manage all dependencies and identify any potential timing risks.

Key dependencies that will likely have an impact on the employee transfer strategy include:

1. Waves of organizational design decisions
    (a) Organizational design decisions are typically made by level, starting at the top of the organization.
    (b) The company should plan for at least 30 days between finalizing organizational decisions and the point employee consultations and/or notifications can begin.

2. Timing of local works council consultations/union negotiations, as applicable
    (a) In most cases, the employee transfer process cannot begin in a country until any and all consultation requirements are closed; I&C must close prior to the release of any formal transfer documentation.

3. Performance review cycle and/or merit cycle
    (a) Performance reviews may be utilized as a vehicle for verbal/informal notifications—this helps to streamline the EE communications process.
    (b) Business leadership will need to determine the impact of the merit cycle on the notification process.

4. Staggered announcement versus big bang announcement for both verbal/formal notifications
   (a) A country by country rollout plan along a set timeline is a leading practice for distributing employee transfer documentation.
   (b) By phasing the process by country, the overall workload is kept at a more controlled and feasible level—this may require managing employee expectations or confusion/anxiety through upfront communications.
5. Timing by when data needs to be finalized for HR systems cutover
   (a) There may be different effective dates for organizational structure and managerial changes, depending on the business unit. Typically changes to shared functions are not made until operational Day 1.
   (b) Employees will need to be mapped to legal entities, locations, cost centers, and pay groups as part of the data conversion.
6. Specific jurisdiction requirements/regulations
   (a) The teams that are involved in the defining the employee transfer plan will need to review the employee transfer country step list (provided by legal) to understand country-specific activities and timing requirements.
7. Entity formation timing for asset deal countries
   (a) Certain countries may be delayed closing due to legal entity set up lead times and, therefore, will need to identify and track delayed transfer employees.

Understanding the core dependencies and building a cohesive timeline that takes all of these factors into consideration is the first step in defining a successful employee transfer strategy that can be rolled out across all in-scope countries and deliver to the established Day 1 transfer date.

14.4 Serve as the "Single Source of Truth" for All Employee Data, Including the Tracking of Accepts and Rejections, as Applicable

Once the offer/transfer notification process has been initiated, a critical component for the team driving this work will be to maintain the employee data file that will be the "single source of truth."

Key responsibilities as part of this effort include:

- Create and update an employee headcount report on an ongoing basis.
  - Intent of this file will be to provide a day-by-day reflection of:
    - Offer/transfer accepts and rejections
    - New hires
    - Terminations
    - Delayed transfers (e.g., garden leave, leave of absence)

- Provide required employee data to other workstreams as needed, including benefits, HR systems, payroll, global real estate, and tax/treasury (for opening balance sheet validation purposes).
- Provide updated transfer headcount to necessary partners to define required severance implications.
  - For certain countries, severance is a required component should an employee choose to reject transfer.
  - A cross-functional team from HR and finance is typically engaged in monitoring rejections globally and determining severance implications in the countries where this is required.
- Identify countries at "risk" for business continuity due to high employee rejections.

As this data file will feed many downstream partners, it is important that there is one file, owned by one team to ensure that duplicate files are not being shared.

14.5   Conclusion

In a divestiture with a diverse country footprint, successfully transferring the identified in-scope employees is a measurement of success. A well-defined and structured transfer strategy and plan—from managing the I&C process through finalization of the final employee transfer file—is required in order to execute this transfer across all in-scope countries effectively. The larger the global footprint of the company, the more complex the employee transfer plan and the more critical the separation planning phases will need to be.

Case Study: 14

Background

A Fortune 50 client, global multinational information technology company providing hardware, software, and services to consumers, small- and medium-sized businesses (SMBs), and large enterprises, including customers in the government, health, and education sectors. In an effort to be ahead of the anticipated industry consolidation, the organization publicly announced plans to divest its largest business unit which represented approximately 50% of the workforce and 30% of revenues.

Challenges

The human resources (HR) team was tasked with supporting the on-time carve-out for the 112,000 employees and supporting HR divestiture-related activities across all HR workstreams, including benefits, compensation, HR systems, payroll, labor relations, go-live HR experience, and org design. The global presence and size of the divestiture led to many key challenges that had to be mitigated, including:

- Information and consultation in 24 countries in 26 weeks, including negotiations in some of the most complex countries (i.e., France, Germany, Austria, the Netherlands)
- Obtaining agreement and consent from the buyer regarding the terms and conditions to be presented to works councils (WCs)
- Carve-out of 112,000 employees, with a particular focus on the enabling function employees, within the defined cost envelope for each function and business
- Distribution of 48,000 offer letters across 63 countries and tracking of offer rejections and associated severance costs
- Ongoing tracking of employee company alignment and deviations from intended company designation due to exception scenarios prohibiting the movement of employees to their intended company, such as offer rejection, leave of absence, garden leave, pending visa acquisition, etc.

Approach

The program and teams were structured to mitigate the above challenges primarily through the establishment of dedicated support teams with clear roles and responsibilities, defined processes and escalation paths, weekly alignment, and status meetings with consistently updated dashboards.

At the outset of the divestiture, a focused 3-day workshop brought the leaders from each of the above teams together to discuss their proposed timeline of key milestones so that all interdependencies could be uncovered and any disconnects could be identified. For example, when all milestones were mapped on a large timeline, it quickly become obvious that the timing of offer/notifications for Country X had to be pushed back because the works council discussions would not be far enough along to commence offer/notification.

More specifically, some of the key approaches by workstream were:

Organization Carve-Out: a strict and fair process that carved-out employees based on percentage of time devoted to a business, with particular attention paid to enabling function employees supporting multiple business units. Carve-out decisions were made by business/function leaders with support for HR business partners.

Labor Relations and Works Council: significant authority was given to the in-country experts to interact with country works council within the guardrails set out by the global labor and employee relations workstream. Weekly meetings with the buyer and an agreed upon timeline for answering questions and providing consent allowed for tight timelines to be met and appropriate information to be provided to WCs. A weekly dashboard from countries to global project management enabled identification of issues and an escalation path for speedy resolution.

Offer/Notification and Offer Rejection Tracking: the dedicated team outlined the country requirements and timing constraints by country in a matrix that was made available to all workstreams. Once initiated, the team tracked all offer acceptances and rejections through an easily accessible dashboard.

Impact/Results

The team was able to successfully close all works council negotiations within the tight timeline, distribute all offer/notifications on time and without error, and manage the constant flow of designation change requests in order to position the company for successful and on-time divestiture.

Chapter 15
Legal Entity Operating Structure

15.1 What Steps Are Necessary to Prepare for Legal Entity Readiness?

Legal entity formation is critical to transaction execution because it is a prerequisite for all other milestones, including the establishment of tax registrations, bank accounts, and reconfigured IT systems. Some of the other key activities necessary to set up and operationalize a new legal entity include HR information consultations, indirect procurement contract separation, and the testing of IT, payroll, finance, and HR systems.

One of the more complex and interdependent steps in the transaction execution process is the confirmation of product and trade compliance. This includes registrations with local and national government agencies to:

- Ensure importer/exporter infrastructure and capabilities are established.
- Ensure no social and environmental-related barriers to market access exist.
- Ensure compliance with global trade, import/export, safety, telecommunications, social, and environmental regulatory requirements.

Once this step is completed, the final step requires:

- Completion of the opening balance sheet by parent company's controllership team
- HR's sign-off on benefit go-live readiness, including migration and testing
- Legal team to sign the separation agreement and transfer employees to the divested entity

Legal entity readiness is critical and complex due to two main factors:

- Long lead-time activities required.
- Coordination among several interdependent workstreams and stakeholders is necessary.

© Deloitte Development LLC 2018

J. Joy, *Divestitures and Spin-Offs*, Management for Professionals,
https://doi.org/10.1007/978-1-4939-7662-1_15

Typically, the longest lead-time activities occur at the beginning of the divestiture process, including legal entity formation and registration, which involves setting up direct and indirect tax IDs and establishing bank accounts for the new legal entity. In some jurisdictions, these activities can take as long as 6–10 weeks. Similarly, downstream activities also take time and preparation, including testing IT, HR, and payroll systems. These activities must be closely coordinated with end-state requirements; the timing of these activities is critical to effective transaction execution. There are other activities that require long lead times, such as managing the separation of indirect procurement contracts, as well as controllership activities related to carve-out financial statements and opening balance sheets. Hence the necessary cross-functional coordination, communication, and decision-making must be seamless and precise to enable the timely completion of these activities.

Legal entity readiness activities with long lead times are performed by multiple workstreams—legal, tax, treasury, finance, controllership, indirect procurement, HR, payroll, IT, and product/trade compliance—each operating under a separate work plan to achieve the same goal to ensure that the new legal entity is ready to transact business on Day 1.

Figure 15.1 showcases some of the interdependencies that typically exist in the formation of a new legal entity. Large divestitures often require establishing new legal entities across several jurisdictions, each of which may have slightly different regulations, thereby adding to the complexity. In a large divestiture, sometimes as many as 200 new legal entities may need to be formed.

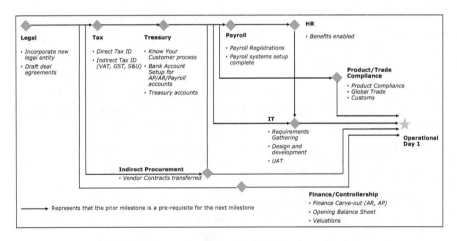

Fig. 15.1 Transaction Execution (TE) Interdependencies

Addressing these workstream interdependencies throughout the transaction execution process can enable a tax-efficient transaction and a seamless legal separation. The following five key focus areas are critical to the planning process:

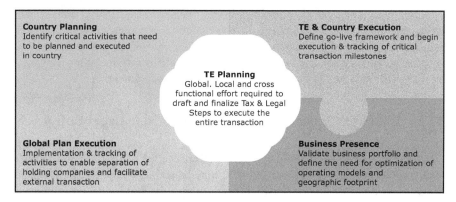

Fig. 15.2 Transaction Execution (TE) Focus Areas

As mentioned earlier, each jurisdiction in which a new legal entity must be set up will likely have its own regulations and nuances. For example, in China, in addition to the normal duration to file the product and trade compliance registrations necessary for legal entity setup, additional time is required to translate all the applicable forms into Chinese. Bureaucratic delays across countries can also have a ripple effect on interdependent activities and push the setup of the new legal entity behind schedule, thereby slowing down the entire transaction execution process. Anticipating and planning for these delays can prevent them from becoming major setbacks.

Common Regulatory Requirements Across Countries

Regulatory requirements in China can lead to long lead times. Tax ID registrations are sometimes delayed by the government, making it difficult to set up bank accounts for the new legal entity. Work-arounds such as leveraging the seller company's bank account until bank accounts are set up for the new legal entity simply do not work in China. These government delays can be costly, affecting the stock price of all entities involved in the M&A deal and increasing the volatility of the deal itself.

In Europe, works council delays can push the entire transaction into a holding pattern until the council deems the separation acceptable.

Russian regulations require explicit customer approval to migrate contracts, and failing to migrate a significant portion (typically 90%) of contracts implies the deal cannot close.

Additionally, opportunistic joint venture partners who leverage the timing to negotiate optimal outcomes for themselves can stymie the transaction.

Rapid and efficient divestiture execution begins with tightly orchestrated workstream milestone execution. In the largest and most complex divestitures, it is essential to have a global cross-functional transaction execution workstream that acts as a central coordinator for the various other workstreams, including legal, tax, treasury, HR, payroll, IT, supply chain, and indirect procurement.

15.2   Issues to Consider When Creating a New Legal Entity

Companies often misjudge the time and effort needed to establish and register legal entities during a divestiture. While it may be a simple process in the United States, typically taking a day or two, the same cannot be said for countries in other parts of the world. Due to regulatory and administrative requirements, setting up a legal entity or a registered branch can take anywhere from weeks to months in certain regions.

Early preparation that includes a detailed assessment of the lead times and requirements for each jurisdiction in which a new legal entity must be established is key to meeting Day 1 goals, since it will help the companies involved in the deal to identify potential risks early and develop contingency plans well in advance. But despite all these efforts, companies may still find themselves at risk of not meeting Day 1 goals due to new legal entity setup delays. In such instances, explore alternatives, such as utilizing a dormant entity within the company's legal structure to represent the divested entity until the new legal entity can be set up.

Costs Resulting from Shared Telecommunications Network Infrastructure

In various jurisdictions, local regulations regarding the sharing of telecommunications network infrastructure can add unforeseen challenges to the setup of a new legal entity. In India, Brazil, and the United States, sharing IT infrastructure in call centers (even in cases of split real estate sites) may result in additional regulatory concerns and higher taxes (sometimes as much as 28–30%) applied to a business that was not in fact in the telecommunications industry. Due to these complexities, additional legal restructuring, IT infrastructure costs, and real estate strategies are required to address these specific regulations, adding to the already complex separation process within these countries.

Obtaining direct and indirect tax identification numbers for the new legal entity can also be cumbersome in some jurisdictions. In India, for example, value-added tax (VAT)—a form of indirect tax—is collected and governed by the state government, and each state has specific rules based on the type of goods manufactured or sold. A company has to obtain VAT registration in each state in which it intends to conduct business, and processing times can range from 3 to 6 weeks after all required documentation has been submitted, including incorporation documents and lease agreements. A delay in completing the VAT registration process can prevent a company from selling in that state. Given the dependency on the legal incorporation documents and delays that can be encountered in the incorporation process, there is a risk of not being able to operate and sell products on Day 1. One mitigation tactic to use while VAT registration remains in process is to sell and ship goods from states in which VAT IDs have already been obtained into areas in which VAT registrations are not yet complete.

Timelines are largely dependent on government and tax authorities, but investigating and utilizing all opportunities to expedite the tax registration application, including preparing the tax registration forms and having all required documents ready for submission as soon as the legal entity is formed, can potentially speed up the process. It is critical, especially in developing and emerging markets, to start the tax registration process as early as possible and set up flexible deadlines that leave room in the schedule for delays caused by unforeseen issues.

When it comes to treasury activities, operationalizing a legal entity requires securing bank accounts for the departments needed to run the business, including payroll, treasury, accounts payable, and accounts receivable, among others. But opening a bank account requires both the successful registration of the new legal entity with the government, as well as the tax registration of the new legal entity. Any delays in document availability will delay the opening of bank accounts, since banks must complete extensive know your customer (KYC) procedures for each entity, which can take from 4 to 16 weeks, depending on the country. All banks need both legal and tax activities to be completed for the new legal entity before the bank accounts can be set up. The legal entity and tax registrations are prerequisites in the KYC process; thus, a slipup anywhere in the legal entity setup timeline can have a domino effect across the entire transaction.

India Transaction Execution Case

Regulatory hurdles in India presented particular challenges for a company involved in an M&A transaction. After a lengthy legal entity incorporation process, obtaining the required direct and indirect tax registrations took more than 3 months due to regulatory constraints, which then led to delays in establishing bank accounts. Separating the telecommunications network infrastructure prior to Day 1 was also challenging as local regulations stipulated physical networks must be separated by deal close. Local authorities also required the company to undergo product retesting and recertification—a process that took more than 6 months—due to the rollout of a new brand logo. All of these hurdles led the company to implement a contingency plan that allowed it to continue conducting business at deal close.

Once bank accounts are opened, they still need to be tested to ensure they are ready to support cash flow from transactions, which adds pressure to the divestiture timeline. Companies experiencing delays when opening bank accounts for new legal entities in certain jurisdictions should consider exploring a contingency strategy in which the divested entity/new legal entity uses the seller company's bank accounts to execute transactions until bank accounts for the divested entity/new legal entity are opened and operationalized. This contingency is subject to local legal and tax considerations and requires some manual work-arounds to separate payments, collections, and accounting entries between the two entities.

Product and trade compliance (i.e., global trade compliance, importer/exporter customs compliance, safety regulatory compliance, and social and environmental compliance) is also dependent on the availability of legal, tax, and treasury documentation, and any delays can cause ripple effects to an already lengthy compliance process. In Brazil, for example, the approval time needed for product recertification is about 6 months, and if the process is not complete by deal close, a company may be unable to conduct business. To help minimize risk, prioritize high-revenue and high-margin products for recertification before all other products. The rollout of new branding and logos often associated with divestitures can have product and trade compliance implications as well. In India, a new brand or logo will require product retesting, recertification, and new registration requirements. This is a very lengthy process and can put a company at risk for missing Day 1 goals. Negotiating with authorities for a waiver or grace period can ease the burden of these compliance requirements.

Another compliance issue that requires a well-developed plan is the establishment of separate physical telecommunications infrastructures. Due to the technical complexity involved, there is usually not enough time to establish physically separated networks by deal close. In these instances, an arrangement should be put in place for the seller company to provide telecommunications services to the divested entity under a transition service agreement (TSA), with the length of the TSA varying by jurisdiction and subject to government authorizations and regulatory approvals. Highly restrictive governments, such as Saudi Arabia, typically offer a transitional period of 6 months or less post-deal close to achieve full separation. Permissive regulatory governments, such as the United Kingdom, may offer transitional periods exceeding 6 months.

Employment compliance issues should also be considered, and local requirements should be addressed early in the transaction execution process. In Europe, for example, works councils are prevalent, and their approval must be obtained before separation activities can begin. Complex and long consultation processes with works council can potentially delay deal close, Day 1 goals, and employee transfers. Companies should complete all pre-work within legal and labor constraints to ensure divestiture activities kick off as soon as approval is received from the relevant works council.

Other potential legal entity readiness challenges include legal and functional name changes required due to trademark laws, IT system separation, user acceptance testing, and contract transfers, which in certain countries, such as Russia, require customer consent and signatures. It's important to develop a detailed cross-functional legal entity readiness plan that identifies and aligns interdependencies across various functions, with mitigation plans for potential problem areas. Tight coordination among all teams and dedicated tracking of critical separation milestones will help ensure successful and timely transaction execution.

15.3 Leading Practices: Vision, Planning, and Execution

As discussed, legal entity readiness and creation are complex due to lead times, interdependencies, and the broad range of cross-functional stakeholders involved. This complexity is compounded by the number of jurisdictions involved. Based on extensive experience with large and complex divestitures, it is essential to have a vision and a set of guiding principles to aid in separation readiness, proper planning, and a dedicated transaction execution team to drive effective execution. The following sections provide additional leading practices on each of these key topics.

15.3.1 Develop a Focused Vision to Aid Legal Entity Separation

A clear vision is the start to effective transaction execution. The vision for the divestiture should begin with the end goal in mind and include the activities most important to the divested entity. To help ensure legal entity readiness for large-scale divestitures and transformations, develop tangible and quantifiable guiding principles, including:

- Nonnegotiable separation date
- Ensuring the transaction is tax-efficient

Clear guiding principles will give stakeholders an anchor on which decisions and trade-offs can be made, as well as help reduce the time and deliberation required for decision-making, which is critical when it comes to legal entity readiness and transaction execution.

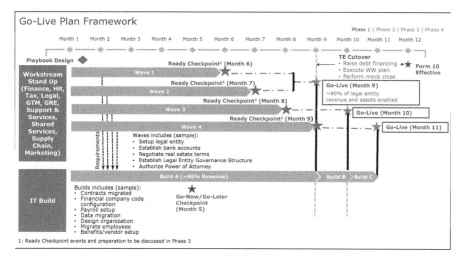

Fig. 15.3 Sample Go-Live Framework

15.3.2 Create a Comprehensive Country Divestiture Plan

Go-live schedules for each country in which a new legal entity must be established should be established within the first 3 weeks of the transaction execution process to help ensure the new legal entity is ready by Day 1. The go-live schedules will serve as reference points for cross-functional teams and help speed up the decision-making process. Stakeholder approval of each go-live schedule is essential to ensure all relevant business units are in agreement on the milestone dates noted in the schedule and can execute upon their separation plans accordingly. Approval is especially needed from critical functions such as legal, tax, finance, HR, and IT. Figure 15.3 highlights a wave-based approach to setting up a go-live schedule for each country in which a new legal entity must be established.

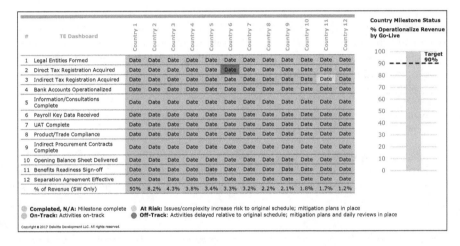

Fig. 15.4 Sample Country Readiness Dashboard

The wave plan begins with a comprehensive country-by-country Tax Legal Step Plan (TLSP) anchored on the most tax-efficient transaction. Subsequently, legal and controllership teams take the lead in reviewing the tax step plans to determine any obvious barriers to feasibility. In-country business and other functions are involved across each country to ensure that a cross-functional feasibility assessment is completed for TLSP implementation. These in-country reviews should focus on addressing one key question—"What do you need to accomplish to adhere to the wave plan?" Local teams are expected to clearly define interdependencies, incremental costs, key roadblocks, and country-level milestones during this assessment period.

It is typical to face resistance from program's cross-functional stakeholders during this effort as they may feel that they do not have enough information to build the country-level plans. A guiding principle in such cases is to prioritize speed over elegance. Teams should focus on establishing a baseline country plan with the level of information available and then set specific operational and financial impact thresholds to avoid unnecessary change. To help with this, a stringent change control process should be established so that only those items impacting the business beyond the agreed upon thresholds are processed for changes.

Although a divestiture itself is highly complex, it can benefit companies to also make some critical business operating changes during the separation process. This can decrease costs and resource utilization for the company in the long run because operational efficiencies are achieved earlier in the life-span of the divested entity, as well as at the reconfigured seller company. A classic example centers on optimizing business presence in certain geographies. M&A events including divestiture can be used to rethink a company's global footprint as the entire organization is more receptive to change. For example, a company undergoing a global divestiture decided to streamline its geographic footprint and rationalized its legal entity presence from operating in 118 countries down to operating in 62 countries. For countries where legal entity presence was not maintained, the business was transferred to third-party partners, and the legal entities were liquidated. The key is to determine which decisions have greatest financial implications and try to come to an agreement on them as soon as possible.

Certain complex geographies require innovative solutions to fast-track the planning timeline. For example, in France where negotiations with works councils can sometimes delay the legal entity readiness process, work-arounds should be built into the go-live schedule for that country. One alternative to fast-track the process in long lead-time countries such as France is to consider acquiring a preexisting legal entity within the country that already operates with works council approval and aligns with the future divested business, then rolling the divested entity into that preexisting legal entity, rather than going through the tumultuous process of creating an entirely new legal entity for the divested entity.

Federal Businesses Transaction Execution Case

In spin-merge transactions, complexities arise when the business being spun off is acquired by an entity with foreign ownership or headed by a CEO from a foreign country. A recent multibillion dollar spin-merge transaction required major restructuring of deal covenants in order to separate the commercial and US government business. This separation is mandated by the Committee on Foreign Investment in the United States (CFIUS), an interagency committee authorized to review transactions that could result in control of a US business by a foreign person, in order to determine the effect the transaction may have on the national security of the United States. The regulatory hurdles and government approvals needed during the transaction execution process may delay the already lengthy separation timeline.

15.3.3   Execute Diligently

The larger a company, the more complex the separation will be, and the more stakeholders will be involved. In order to manage decision-making with a large set of stakeholders, a dedicated transaction execution team needs to be put in place. The team will be responsible for driving the overall set of activities as well as keeping the various functional and cross-functional workstreams on track for the timely execution of the activities. To adhere to the strict execution timelines, a formal change control process should be put in place that enables requestors to evaluate the necessity of a change and provides record keeping so that inquiries about how and why decisions were made can be tracked. The challenge in implementing a change control process is ensuring that all teams (on a global and local level and from all functions) are aware of the process and abide by it. Thorough communication of the change control process as well as a list of key contacts is necessary to help ensure effective change control implementation.

Cross-functional calls, meetings, and workshops should be conducted throughout the transaction execution process to enable discussion and help ensure timely completion of separation milestones. A key leading practice is to conduct periodic in-person workshops throughout various phases of the execution timeline. These workshops should discuss go-live issues and should be attended by cross-functional and cross-regional leadership. Furthermore, timely and efficient communication of separation status updates is necessary. The country readiness dashboard presented in Fig. 15.4 should be shared with teams and executive leadership to show the progress of various functions in completing separation milestones.

15.4   Conclusion

Divestitures are complex due to the challenge of managing many interdependent cross-functional activities. In particular, legal entity readiness is among the most critical activities in the separation timeline as there is no single owner of the work, subsequent separation activities cannot begin until the new legal entity is established, and navigating complex regulatory and procedural hurdles across jurisdictions is necessary.

There will always be jurisdictions that are tougher than others. Knowing which issues to expect during a divestiture and establishing an effective transaction execution team are necessary to resolve the separation challenges that will inevitably arise. Having a clear vision for the divestiture, anticipating issues in complex jurisdictions, quick planning, and thorough and diligent execution of workstream tasks to accomplish separation milestones are key practices that can help ensure divestiture success.

Case Study: 15

Background

As one of the global leaders in aluminum mining and production, the client was an industry leader specializing across the complete metal value chain from mining and refining of natural resources like aluminum and bauxite to producing finished rolled and engineered aluminum products and solutions for some of the largest OEMs in the world. Following increasing market pressures along with agitation of activist investors, management concluded in late 2015 to separate into two distinct organizations—an Upstream Co. focusing on mining and refining natural resources at competitive costs and a Value-Add Co. focusing on growth in the industrials and lightweight aluminum manufacturing.

Challenges

The transaction execution team was assembled to facilitate and drive functional execution of the tax step plan, regulatory filings, and country readiness activities, including, but not limited to, legal entity formations, asset movements, tax registrations, bank account set ups, opening balance sheets, carve-out financial statements, payroll setup, product/trade compliance registrations, cross-functional issue resolutions, and IT system changes. Many of these activities were subject to lengthy and unpredictable lead times, adding to the importance of rapid decision-making and effective execution of activities and putting at risk the timely completion of the separation milestones. Additionally, seemingly simple decisions (e.g., branding) would have profound downstream impacts on key business processes such as shipping and trade compliance, requiring close cross-functional coordinating and planning across all milestones. Yet, even with close cross-functional coordination, country- and region-specific nuances, such as local country regulatory license and permit requirements and local works council negotiations and approvals, continued to add complexity to the deal.

Approach

The transaction execution and country execution readiness team needed to quickly mobilize to establish structure (including cross-functional contacts), charters, cadence, and milestone planning to ensure LD1 readiness in a relatively short timeframe. In order to help coordinate overall delivery of ~50 key milestones across each of the over 150+ legal entity changes worldwide while continuing to account for interdependencies and country-specific nuances, tax considerations, and risks, the team developed a cross-functional matrix to track progress at both the region, country, and entity level. Serving as the primary mechanism for reporting and tracking for both new legal entity formations and name changes, the matrix captured the completion dates and status for each key milestone per legal entity. The resulting matrix became a sophisticated and powerful tool that allowed the team to easily access, update, and analyze the nearly 4500+ individual milestones, not only allowing for quick assessment of overall progress but also downstream implications on any delayed and/or at-risk activities (critical for reacting to and planning for obstacles in countries with long lead times and/or challenging political landscapes). Delivery of milestones leveraged a phased approach based on regional/country regulatory requirements, complexity, and lead times to avoid the risks associated with a "big bang" event.

Meeting cadence included weekly cross-functional and separation team meetings with both functional and country workstream leads; weekly region-specific calls to address detailed plans and corporate reorganization activities, progress, and country nuances; and ad hoc special topic working sessions as required. Key outputs included an executive dashboard, decision log, legal entity name mappings, country and separation trackers, and go-live readiness checklists.

Impact/Results

In completing a successful separation, the transaction execution team was vital to achieving a tax-efficient separation in one of the most complex divestitures, requiring the formation of 12 new legal entities (NLEs) and 100+ legal entity name changes across 28 countries. Cross-functional coordination enabled not only the formation and name changes of all entities but also completion of other key activities such as tax registrations, bank account setups, IT form and system updates, works council consultations, and trade compliance filings prior to Legal Day 1, ensuring customer and supplier continuity and minimal disruption to the business.

Chapter 16
Managing Banking and Treasury Implications During Divestiture

16.1 Banking and Treasury Implications of a Separation

Traditionally, the main responsibilities of a company's treasury function have revolved around protecting the company's liquid assets and helping finance perform its core operations. In recent years, however, these responsibilities have evolved and expanded. Many C-suite executives expect today's treasury functions to serve as strategic advisors to finance, the chief financial officer (CFO), and the overall business. Now more than ever, treasury executives and professionals must stay in front of rapidly shifting business requirements to support growth, liquidity, financial risk management, and marketplace performance expectations.

Treasurers are critical partners to C-suite executives and strategic advisors on mergers and acquisitions (M&A) transactions, especially helping to ensure separations are successful. The separation of a business from an organization is complex and time sensitive and involves many regulatory authorities. During a separation, key activities for the treasury function include financing the spin entities with enough funds for operations and helping to ensure the soon-to-be-divested entity is ready and fully functional on Day 1. Typically, the treasury is either a centralized function or centrally managed with multiple global centers. A centralized treasury function provides cash visibility, forecasting, and positioning, as well as a cost advantage for funding activities, investments, and risk management activities.

In many public divestitures, a business unit is sold as a stand-alone business. This involves creating a new business from the ground up, including a new treasury organization. This is a complex task, particularly since the time to sale and separation is committed to the board of directors and investors and there can be costs from missing the deadlines. The treasury should consider all aspects of setting up a new fully functional treasury for the soon-to-be-divested entity to serve the new business. This is especially important in case the new business plans to run the treasury as is without integrating with its own treasury for a foreseeable future.

© Deloitte Development LLC 2018
J. Joy, *Divestitures and Spin-Offs*, Management for Professionals,
https://doi.org/10.1007/978-1-4939-7662-1_16

During separation, executive management of the selling company should evaluate whether to create an entirely new treasury organization for the divested entity or mirror (create exact copy) the existing treasury function. While creating a new treasury function may align with the purchasing company's setup, it can take much longer and cost more than mirroring the existing setup. A lot of coordination with the purchasing company and the divestiture team is required to set up a net new treasury organization. If the intent and terms of the sale are to create a new organization with a new set of systems and processes, it may provide a valid business case to build a new treasury function. In many cases, the divested entity's treasury is created as a mirror of the seller company's treasury and runs in parallel for a few months before the official sale date. This mirror setup includes employee structure, processes, policies, strategies, operations, systems, vendors, and banking relationships to support the new organization. The contracts with vendors and banks are created in the name of the selling business and are transferred to the new company on the sale date.

The divested entity may take on its own debt to continue operations or engage in other financing deals if needed, update its working capital requirements, or enhance its risk management profile and strategies. The new organization and treasury should update the regional and global footprint of the divested entity's operations, which will likely require adjustments to banking relationships, funding models, cash concentration pools, and an increased focus on cash visibility to support the newly created business.

During a divestiture, the seller company's treasury function must perform multiple activities concerning banking and systems to achieve a successful separation. These separation activities are particularly complex, time consuming, and dependent on multiple third-party partners and service providers.

The treasury function's primary objective is to establish banking relationships for new legal entities set up for the divested entity. This includes bank accounts, lines of credits, and other services. Similarly, the treasury systems, including cash management and ERP systems and the IT infrastructure required to support them, need to be stood up to support the operations of the new treasury organization.

These two activities run in parallel and involve interdependencies that make them extremely complex and resource intensive.

16.2   Banking Separation and Its Implications

Choosing banking partners to build out the account structure of the divested entity is a critical decision for the treasury team. Banking partners directly affect the cost and timing of the separation, so it is important to consider the following:

- *Existing versus new relationships:* There are many benefits when utilizing existing relationships to build out the new banking structure. In some cases, the evaluation of new banking partners may be necessary based on the location of the divested entity and its existing relationships or balance of trade considerations.

- *Footprint of the banks:* Whether banking partners meet the requirements of global business operations is a factor that can influence their ultimate selection.
- *Services offered:* Banking partners will need to be vetted to confirm they provide all the services that will be required by the divested entity such as lockbox operations, accounts payable processing, automated funding structures such as zero balance accounts (ZBAs), and integration with the divested entity's technology system infrastructure including treasury management systems.
- *Banking partnerships of the buyer company:* If the divested entity is being sold to a company with relationships with same banks, the buyer company's banking partnerships can aid in a timely and successful integration with its current operations.
- *Future bank account structure:* In addition to considering these factors, a separation provides the seller company with the opportunity to assess its current bank account structure to ensure it is still efficient.

Figure 16.1 provides an example of the existing account structure of a company.

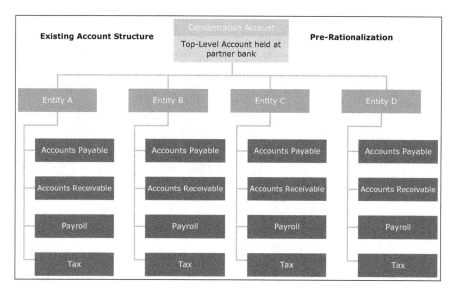

Fig. 16.1 Existing Account Structure of a Company

The divested entity needs an efficient account structure. Figure 16.2 provides an example of a future account structure.

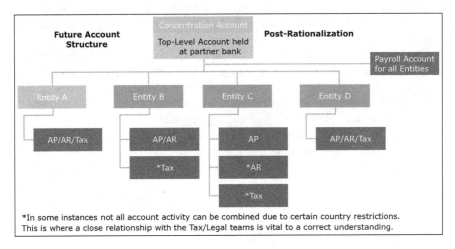

Fig. 16.2 Future Account Structure

- *Teaming with tax and legal:* When developing a banking plan for a separation, a close connection is required between the treasury, tax, and legal teams. Input from the tax and legal teams is critical for decisions around business units that need to be incorporated for the entity to be divested during the separation. Insights into the legal and regulatory requirements in various jurisdictions are crucial to a successful separation. These insights will directly affect the treasury team's decisions when choosing banking partners and setting up account structures. The tax and legal teams also aid in the preparation and execution of key documents such as articles of incorporation and certificates for incumbency.
- *Teaming with information technology (IT):* Treasury must also maintain a close relationship with the IT team that supports configuration of treasury management systems (TMSs). Configuration demands can be very significant during separation, and the treasury takes a lead role in driving these configurations to completion. Treasury should foster two-way communication with the internal IT team to help address any issues that may arise.
- *Teaming with accounts payable (AP) and Accounts Receivable (AR) Teams:* AP/AR teams can also influence the treasury team's decisions on banking partners. The specific needs of these teams can lead to a preference for one banking partner over another. Occasionally, the needs of the AP/AR teams are not completely aligned, and their preferences for banking partners may diverge. In such cases, the treasury team should weigh the options on both sides when selecting banking partners.
- *Banking design efficiency opportunities:* To gain efficiencies, the seller company's current bank account structures can be mirrored for the divested entity. This allows for a seamless transition as the same business processes used by the seller company can be utilized to manage the divested entity's accounts. The mirroring process should not be entered into blindly, however, as the seller company's

banking structures may have become inefficient and its bank accounts may need to be consolidated to create a more cost-effective bank account structure.

- *Communication with banking partners:* After analyzing the bank account structure required by the divested entity, it is imperative to open lines of communication with banking partners in a timely manner. While banks line up their resources, the treasury team can gather the documentation the banks will need to begin the account opening process. The treasury team needs to manage the account opening and novation process to help ensure continuous progress. The treasury team should hold regular meetings with banking partners to allow for the timely exchange of information and provide a forum to address any issues.

> *While undergoing a separation, a Fortune 100 company was significantly challenged by the sheer volume of documentation required to open several hundred bank accounts that would be required for the separating entity. The treasury team implemented a detailed process and timeline to manage the effort. Additionally, the treasury team met regularly with banking partners to address any roadblocks in the account setup process. In the end, the treasury team's efforts to implement a strong plan to manage the account setup process and maintain open lines of communication with banking partners resulted in a successful separation.*

- *Testing:* Once the target banking structure has been decided upon, accounts have been opened, and systems have been configured, the transaction project team should work in lockstep with banking partners, IT, and operations team, including cash management, AP/AR, payroll, and accounting to test the whole setup. Prior to the separating entity going live and transitioning to a stand-alone operation, the treasury team should ensure all operations are running as expected.

> *While standing up the separating entity, the treasury team for a Fortune 100 company had to ensure banking partners supported payment processing, confirmations, and bank statements via their treasury management system (TMS). This process required the coordination of banking partners, the IT team, and the operations team across time zones. By regularly communicating with banking partners and addressing failed tests and other issues with the operations and IT teams in real time, the required adjustments could be made on the same day. Accounts and systems were retested until the tests were successful. This was an iterative process involving banking partners, the IT team, the operations team, and the treasury team, but the treasury team's coordination of the effort helped make the separation a success.*

The critical path items in a typical bank account setup process include:

1. Business defines the need for an account.
2. Potential banking partners are reviewed based on their alignment with the separating entity on the following factors:

   (a) Location
   (b) Services offered

   (c) Local regulations
   (d) Balance of trade considerations

3. A banking partner (or partners, if necessary) is chosen for the separating entity.
4. Legal and tax teams prepare know your customer (KYC) documentation.
5. The chosen banking partner is asked to set up bank accounts and other services for the separating entity.
6. The chosen banking partner opens accounts and configures services.
7. The new bank accounts are configured in the internal systems (i.e., TMS and enterprise resource planning (ERP)) of the separating entity.
8. New bank accounts are tested to ensure funds flow and statements are received as necessary.

Note: Opening bank accounts requires an incorporated legal entity. The creation of legal entities may require significant lead time in certain foreign jurisdictions and should be considered when creating the timeline for account opening.

Depending on the separating entity's complexity and banking partners, the process can take anywhere from 2 months to 7 months. Care must be taken to control the process and obtain all regulatory documentations well in advance to avoid delays.

16.3   System Separation and Implications

Treasury systems consist of a complex web of third-party systems and in-house developed systems that must be configured to work with systems maintained by vendors and banking partners. The new treasury function must be able to fully engage and operate these systems on Day 1. Ten key considerations for treasury system separation include:

1. System separation strategy
2. Banking connectivity and bank portals
3. Third-party and vendor connectivity
4. Licensing agreements for the divested entity
5. Setup of the divested entity's new treasury system
6. Data migration
7. Testing and certification
8. Data and user cleanup
9. System and data archives
10. Temporary service agreements (TSAs)

Each of these considerations, which are discussed in detail below, is pivotal to the successful standup of the new treasury organization.

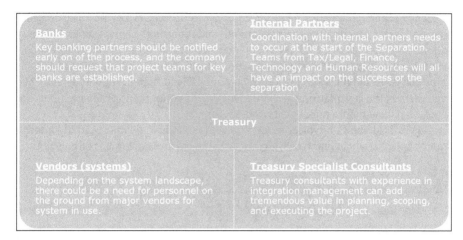

Fig. 16.3 Treasury Divestiture Team

16.3.1 System Separation Strategy

Developing a treasury system separation strategy is key to a successful divestiture. The treasury system influences the entire organization, including business decisions related to operations, business processes, support requirements, and data sharing. There are five options for creating a new treasury system:

1. Transform the seller company's treasury system
2. Implement an entirely new treasury system for the divested entity
3. Use the buyer company's treasury system
4. Physically clone the seller company's treasury system
5. Logically separate from the seller company's treasury system

Transforming the seller company's treasury system for the separating entity is similar to implementing an entirely new treasury system for the separating entity. It can be a valid option if a new treasury system landscape is required for the sale of the separating entity.

Using the buyer's treasury system requires coordination with the buyer company. It can be a valid option if the buyer company is willing to work together with the seller company and modify the design of its treasury system to incorporate the needs of the separating entity. Sometimes using the buyer's system is not permissible or feasible during the sales process.

The two remaining strategies, physically cloning the seller company's treasury system ("physical separation") and logically separating from the seller company's treasury system ("logical separation"), are the most commonly used options. Physical separation involves cloning the seller's existing system from the ground up, adding new or additional hardware for the separating entity, implementing all necessary software, and configuring everything for the new treasury system setup. Logical separation utilizes the seller's existing hardware and software but creates a logically separated area for the divested entity to operate. A key factor to consider during logical separation is user separation and reporting. Logical separation only allows an entity access to its own data by its own users. System and vendor architecture must allow logical separation in order for it to work. Both options have their pros and cons and must be considered carefully. The duration, support agreements, and users of the new platform, as well as the legacy configuration of master data, are areas to review before making a final decision.

Figure 16.4 shows a typical treasury system landscape. In an organization, many more applications can interface with the TMS, but only a sample set is displayed here.

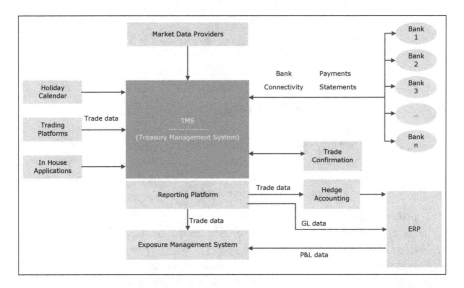

Fig. 16.4 Typical Treasury System Landscape

In a typical logical separation of a treasury system, a new area or group must be created in TMS and all the supporting in-house and vendor systems to logically create the divested entity's treasury system landscape. A key requirement is keeping the users and data of the two entities separate from each other. Although the interface infrastructure can be shared between applications, care must be taken to clearly distinguish the data between the two entities. It is also important to make sure that the TMS and other vendors are aligned with the strategy and the vendor licenses allow the company to implement this setup.

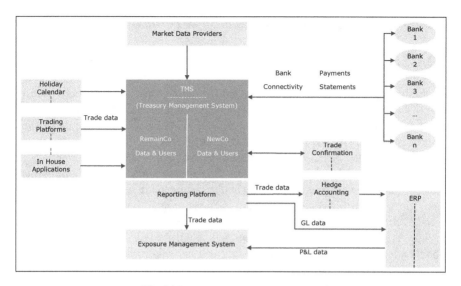

Fig. 16.5 Treasury Systems Landscape

During a typical physical separation of a treasury system, an exact clone of the seller company's entire treasury system landscape is created for the divested entity using new or existing hardware, as displayed in Fig. 16.6.

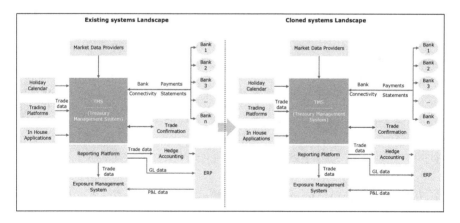

Fig. 16.6 Typical Physical Separation of a Treasury System

16.3.2   Banking Connectivity and Bank Portals

Banking connectivity is critical for treasury operations. Most TMS and ERP systems are connected to multiple banks either directly or through SWIFT. Depending on the new bank relationships established for the divested entity, it may need to establish similar bank connectivity. The IT and business teams should discuss the timelines involved because the setup required to enable payments and the flow of account statements, as well as establish the physical connectivity between the divested entity and banks, can require 2–6 months depending on the maturity of bank and the connectivity method used. Some new banks or jurisdictions may require complex system setup that may not be completed in time for Day 1. In such cases, contingency plans must be agreed upon between all stakeholder entities.

Bank portals are used by many companies for operational activities as well as a backup for processing treasury payments and viewing account activities. New bank portals are required for the divested entity and can take significant time approximately 3–6 months to set up; therefore, the setup should be planned with partner banks well in advance of Day 1. Typically, the setup involves adding new accounts and new users to the newly created bank portals. After the setup, the new users are provided with login credentials and security tokens entitling them to proper rights to the accounts. Many banks may require additional user documentation to fulfill anti-money laundering (AML) and other regulatory requirements; thus, a dedicated team of bank portal administrators is required to coordinate and complete all steps in time for Day 1.

16.3.3   Third-Party and Vendor Connectivity

Most treasury systems interface with vendors and third-party systems. Some of the typical vendors include market data providers, trade confirmation and settlement services, exposure and risk management specialists, and hedge accounting specialists. Depending on the separation strategy, replicating the interface or creating a new interface may be necessary. The strategy, requirements, and timelines for implementation of the interfaces and vendor systems must be discussed with vendors early in the separation process to achieve the project timelines.

16.3.4   Licensing Agreements for the Divested Entity

The seller company maintains several licensing agreements with third-party treasury vendors. During the separation process, if any of these third-party licensing agreements are required by the divested entity, then changes to the agreements may be required. The IT team should discuss any changes to vendor licensing agreements with the procurement and legal teams.

Some licensing agreements may prohibit the implementation of a logical separation strategy. In most cases, a new license may be required between vendors and the divested entity. Typically, the licensing agreement secured for the divested entity is a replica of the existing licensing agreement the vendor has with the seller company, but the terms and conditions should be reviewed carefully. If the current license is for multiple years with many discounts, the vendor may not offer the same discounts to the divested entity or may ask for a longer commitment.

If the ultimate strategy is to merge the divested entity's new treasury system with the buyer's treasury system in the near term, then it is prudent to renegotiate the terms and conditions of licensing agreements accordingly. Renegotiation can take a long time to finalize; thus, it is important to engage vendors in this effort as soon as possible. Additionally, renegotiation must be handled very carefully as some vendors may attempt to maximize the agreements in their favor by leveraging the separation timeline and the divested entity's dependency on their services. One global company had to pay millions for a new license that just provided the divested entity with a few months of usage of a vendor system.

16.3.5 Setup of the Divested Entity's New Treasury System

Once the strategy for the new treasury system has been decided upon by the seller company, the buyer company, and the divested entity, and all vendors and third parties have been engaged in the setup process, it is time to finalize the setup strategy for the divested entity's new treasury system. The pros and cons of various strategic options should be discussed with all stakeholders. One option is to set up the divested entity data in the seller company's existing treasury environment and then clone or replicate that data in the new treasury system. This will help create a working setup for the divested entity and support transactions that take place before Day 1. The other option is to set up the divested entity's data only in the new treasury environment. This is a cleaner approach as it allows the new treasury system to be designed to fit the requirements of the divested entity. But this approach also has pitfalls as it can take time to agree on a new design, which creates the risk of not having the system ready in time for Day 1 or pre-Day 1 activities.

16.3.6 Data Migration

In a typical separation, the divested entity starts with legacy data such as account balances; thus, it is important to plan for data migration activities, beginning with collecting the static and transactional data that needs to be migrated. A key decision must be made on how to migrate the data, which can be done manually or using tools to perform bulk uploads. Since static and transactional data changes up to the go-live date, data migration must be done in lock step with business activities.

The data migration should be tested, and mock cutover and data migration sessions should be conducted to ensure a smooth go-live.

Typically, data migration starts a few days or weeks prior to the go-live date and includes the bulk upload or manual entry of data, followed by continued incremental adjustments until go-live. Sometimes final adjustments may be required after go-live. Given that the data must be accurate and complete, many validation and reconciliation routines and tools must be developed to ensure the divested entity's new treasury system has all the required data to be fully operational on Day 1. This activity requires great alignment and coordination between the IT, treasury operations, AP/AR, payroll, and accounting teams. Dedicated resources should be identified and assigned to migrate and validate the data before and after go-live. A formal sign-off should be obtained to ensure no data is missing for the divested entity in conjunction with the go-live date.

16.3.7   Testing and Certification

As with any new system, it is critical to thoroughly test the new treasury system to certify its readiness prior to the go-live date. End-to-end testing procedures should be completed to certify the full life cycle of treasury activities working in the new system. It is very important to coordinate with internal teams such as AP and AR, as well as align the scope and timeline of testing activities with vendors. Many times vendors will need to mobilize a high-performing team to support the short timelines of such activities. Vendors are typically amenable to mobilizing these teams to meet the timelines as it presents an opportunity for them to expand their customer base with the divested entity. These activities also provide vendors inroads into working with the buying company as well. Proper testing documentation should be maintained with sign-off and approvals from key executive management team members responsible for the operations before certifying the system is ready. The executive team can be from the divested entity if they have been identified or from the selling company if not.

16.3.8   Data and User Cleanup

Once the new treasury system is ready for the divested entity, the seller company should ensure that there are no residual data or users from the seller company attached to the new system prior to handing over the systems to the buying company. Typically, a user audit is conducted on the new system and bank portals to ensure that only users of the divested entity or buyer company, if necessary, have access to new treasury system.

16.3.9   System and Data Archives

Often, the divested entity may need access to the seller company's historical data for future audit requirements. This requirement can create a long-term liability for the seller company; thus, the treasury, tax, and legal teams must decide on how to manage it. The seller company may agree to provide the divested entity with relevant historical data to support an audit for a certain period of time after the transaction close date. Alternatively, the seller company may provide the divested entity with a copy of relevant historical data as either a data dump or a system archive.

16.3.10   Temporary Service Agreements (TSAs)

In most separations, for regulatory and tax reasons, the divested entity should be able to operate as a stand-alone company for at least 3 months prior to the sale date. This necessitates the seller company operating two sets of treasury and operations systems for at least 3 months.

16.4   Summary of How to Design and Stand Up a New Treasury System

When developing a plan to stand up a new treasury organization for the divested entity, many factors should be considered. Some features of the seller's treasury system may be mirrored in the divested entity's new system, while others may not be required. For example, if the divested entity's business is largely domestic, minimal Forex currency exchange requirements will be necessary; thus, the Forex features of the seller's system may not be mirrored in the divested entity's system. All features of the seller's system should be analyzed to determine which of them will be required by the divested entity. This will bring efficiency to the forefront of the design for the new system. This can be achieved by paying close attention to the tenets described here.

- Banking partners should be selected carefully by rationalizing account opening decisions and focusing on efficiencies that can be gained by adding ZBA structures or creating multipurpose accounts (i.e., AP/AR) in the new system.
- System separation strategies should be created with efficiencies in mind. Utilization of the seller's existing infrastructure (i.e., logical separation) can save time and money. However, a new treasury environment set up for the divested entity may allow the implementation of modern elements, such as utilizing the cloud and other new technologies.

- Third-party vendor systems should be analyzed to ensure they function efficiently with the new system. The pared-down structure of the divested entity's new treasury system can lead to the removal of vendors not needed by the divested entity.
- The setup of both transitioning and remaining employees may be done on the each entity's banking portals and internal systems. This will help during the testing phase, but the users belonging to the selling company should be removed during the cleanup process when the separation occurs, and the systems are handed over to the buying company.
- Personnel TSAs can also be utilized when standing up the new treasury organization as institutional knowledge of the seller company's employees can be imparted to new operators at the divested entity once it is operating on its own.

16.5   Conclusion

The treasury team should act as both an adviser and key driver of separation activities since the treasury team operates at the intersection of back end systems that drive financial decisions and the banking partners and vendors that can make those decisions a reality.

The treasury team's coordination of separation activities with the IT, tax, legal, procurement, and finance teams is critical. The treasury also engages and works closely with banking partners and vendors to help ensure the build-out of the new treasury function for the divested entity is successful.

Case Study: 16

Background

A multinational large and complex technology company with business in consumer and enterprise hardware, software, and services with annual revenue of more than $120B, divesting business resulting in two $60B companies focused on consumer and enterprise services.

Challenges

The company's treasury had older treasury technology platforms coupled with many homegrown applications, relationships with hundreds of banking partners with thousands of bank accounts, and highly customized processes making it very challenging to meet the committed divesture deadlines.

Approach

In order to achieve successful divesture in the limited time, multiple options were considered to separate the systems and processes for the remaining and new company. The key objective at this stage was to deliver on time, with minimal change for the organization and systems while implementing efficient processes.

The company worked with advisors to help solve the issues on two fronts—systems and banking relationships. The treasury team worked with AP, AR, tax, and legal teams to optimize the account structure. The team found opportunities for the remaining company and the new company to reduce the number of accounts and associated cost, while it also cleaned up stale data and resolved audit issues. For systems, the two main options considered were cloning the systems and processes or setting up a new treasury with new system and processes. Given the tight timeline and resource constraints and other benefits, the clone option was preferred. The company created two clones of the legacy platform, with improvements to bring efficiencies in the system but with minimal change for the team.

Impact/Results

The clone strategy allowed the remaining and the new company achieve reduction in number of accounts and bank fees, setup of automated cash pools, cleanup of the systems, simplified, straight through and automate processes and trained teams to use the systems efficiently. In the end, both of the companies' treasuries achieved simplified banking and system landscape and clean data with enhanced reporting, making the treasury team's job efficient to support the businesses' objectives.

Chapter 17
Legal and Tax Aspects of Divestitures

Selling (part of) your business has many legal implications to be observed that you should have on your radar screen from the very beginning of the divestiture process.

17.1 Strategic Goals of the Divestiture

Before sellers start a divestiture process, they should keep in mind that the strategic goals behind the divestiture usually would impact the transaction structure to be chosen. Therefore, it is important that potential sellers consult with advisors about their motivation to sell. You may want to concentrate on your core business, plan your corporate succession, or simply want to improve your equity basis and liquidity; if your advisors know your goals, they can help advise you on the most effective legal transaction structure suitable to achieve your goals.

17.2 Asset Deal Versus Share Deal

In an asset deal the seller retains possession of the legal entity and sells the individual assets of the business, whereby in a share deal the seller sells the shares in the entity itself.

Whether the business shall be sold by way of an asset deal or by way of a share deal might sound like an easy question in the first place. Especially if the whole business to be divested is already merged or united in one entity with no other business units involved, a share deal may be the best choice.

However, in situations, where an asset deal seems to be the best option, one should always look at the situation from various angles before making a final decision.

J. Joy, *Divestitures and Spin-Offs*, Management for Professionals,
https://doi.org/10.1007/978-1-4939-7662-1_17

Tax law aspects definitely need to be considered but also public law aspects (environmental, social security etc.), labor law aspects, mandatory employee participation aspects (depending on the jurisdictions involved), transaction cost aspects, internal consent requirements, required third-party consents, and governmental pre-emptive rights (depending on the jurisdiction involved), just to name a few. Please refer to Sect. 2 (below) for further considerations regarding asset and shares deals.

17.2.1   Choosing the Right Sales Process: "One on One" Versus "Limited Auction"

One of the first decisions to be taken in a divestiture process is whether you want to sell the unwanted business by negotiating exclusively with one particular party ("one on one") or whether you want to sell the business in the course of a limited auction and invite various interested parties to negotiate.

While the latter may allow you to optimize the purchase price and other relevant conditions through maximum competition, it can also have downsides like higher transaction costs, higher effort required for information to be gathered and then scrutinized, and a rather long and complex transaction process.

The exclusive, tailor-made sales process with just one party may in many cases run faster and more flexibly, and it may be easier to keep the contemplated sale as confidential in a one-on-one sale than in a limited auction process. Not being able to compare multiple offers from various bidders can be a downside of a one-on-one sale.

Common steps of both sales processes can briefly be summarized as follows:

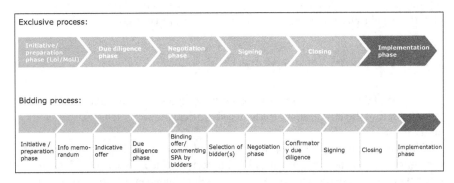

Fig. 17.1   Course of M&A Transaction

17.3   Transaction Preparation Steps

Before the transaction begins there are many aspects that should be organized during the preparation phase. It is time to assess potential carve-out measures for the business to be divested.

Such measures could include the liquidation/merger of dormant subsidiaries, the consolidation of the group structure, and the demerger of side activities into a new entity as well as the settlement or carve-out of ongoing or lingering disputes.

In case of a contemplated bidding process, the preparatory steps may also include the carrying out of a financial vendor due diligence that aims at the identification of potential carve-out topics and at the compilation of tax and legal fact books, which may also be handed to each bidder at the beginning of the due diligence phase. Such vendor due diligence reports and fact books can reduce the transaction costs of potential bidders in the first phase of due diligence and may therefore attract more bidders to join the process. Carrying out a vendor due diligence is not a must and is more often seen with the sale of larger complex targets than for smaller divestitures. It is, however, an effective approach to help prevent the common phenomenon that after the due diligence phase and during the negotiations the bidder usually knows the target better than the negotiating parties of the seller.

In parallel, the seller's M&A advisors will often prepare a (often anonymized) teaser and information memorandum about the Target to be handed over to potential bidders at an early stage of the transaction.

The first document exchanged between the seller and each bidder is generally the nondisclosure agreement ("NDA"), where the parties agree not to disclose information on confidential and proprietary information. Despite having signed a binding NDA, sellers should be very cautious about forwarding information to potential bidders in order to protect the target's business secrets and know-how and to ensure compliance with antitrust and cartel laws. As a rule of thumb, the more advanced the bidding process and negotiations become, the more information may be disclosed. Sellers have to be aware that some bidders might be more interested in gathering information about the target than actually buying it.

In case of an exclusive divestiture process with only one bidder involved, parties would after the first exchange of financial key figures and company data enter into some form of Letter of Intent ("LoI"), Memorandum of Understanding ("MoU"), or term sheet—all terms refer to more or less the same type of document and agreement.

The LoI/MoU or term sheet sets out the common understanding of the parties as to the key terms of the deal or at least the steps and methods that shall lead to these terms. Unlike the NDA, the LoI/MoU is usually non-binding with respect to its key provisions and should confirm that seller and buyer have a common understanding about the main deal parameters before both parties invest more time and money in the due diligence process. Additionally, the psychological effect of such non-binding MoU should never be underestimated, as parties can feel committed to the agreed terms, although they know that such terms are legally not binding. The seller, if he/she already knows what is important, should try to address key conditions already in the MoU phase to clearly define its most important cornerstones for the deal right at the beginning of the sales process.

The MoU usually covers topics like a summary of the transaction parameters, a first purchase price indication, a general description of the purchase price calculation mechanism (locked-box vs. closing accounts mechanism), likely closing conditions, exclusivity (if any), and a time table for the next steps (due diligence, first draft of the share purchase agreement (SPA)/asset purchase agreement (APA), signing, etc.).

17.4   Due Diligence

During the due diligence phase, potential buyer(s) will usually explore the legal, tax, financial, commercial, technical, and environmental risks with respect to the target and its business.

Usually the due diligence phase precedes the negotiation phase; however, these phases may also overlap to some extent. In any event, it is important from a seller's perspective to provide for sufficient time to set up the data room. This process ties up a lot of resources and at the same time only a few people are privy to the divestiture plans, which makes this process even more challenging and requires good planning.

The buyers will categorize their due diligence findings. While some of their findings may have to be dealt with prior to closing of the transaction, others may have an impact on the purchase price or the liability regime under the share or asset purchase agreement. Hence, if issues are identified in the early stages of the sales process (e.g., during the setup of the data room or prior), it is advisable for the seller to consider solutions and/or develop a narrative which can be communicated to buyers during their tax due diligence.

In a one-on-one scenario the buyer generally sets out the information which should be reviewed in a due diligence request list. While the seller may be reluctant to disclose certain information at an early stage, it is in the interest of the buyer to receive complete information as soon as possible. On the other hand it may also be beneficial for the seller to grant broad insight in order to limit its liability on the basis of the purchaser's knowledge of the disclosed facts. In this respect, the content of the data room should be frozen and documented at the end of the due diligence. In some jurisdictions it is common to even attach the content of the data room to the deal documentation in form of a data room DVD evidencing all disclosed information.

For most deals a virtual online data room will be set up and hosted by one of the few recognized professional data room providers. Physical data rooms in which document folders are made available for review on site are no longer standard but are generally used for smaller deals or in specific situations, such as providing highly sensitive data. Commonly the data room also provides for a Q&A tool in which the buyer can request further information or demand further explanation of certain information. The seller should allocate resources for this Q&A process (either internally or externally) early enough. In larger transactions more than 100 questions might be dropped each day that need to be reviewed and answered correctly and thoroughly. Often in an auction scenario, the seller may restrict the number of questions each bidder can submit to secure an orderly process.

When setting up the data room, several organizational topics need to be considered, such as access and user rights for both the seller and the buyer team, staffing of the Q&A team, provision of data room rules and procedures setting out the points of contact, access and user rights, access time, printing and storage regulations, etc.

Setting up a data room and processing the enquiries under the Q&A tool should be conducted with great care, not only because of the legal restrictions explained further below but also to avoid misleading or incorrect information, which can—in extreme cases—even lead to the buyer's right to challenge and reverse the later purchase agreement for willful deception. Furthermore, there may be related liability risks which are to be avoided. An efficient data room process may also project organizational control and efficiency which reflects favorably on seller.

Three legal aspects are of particular relevance for the due diligence process: confidentiality and data protection, consequences for the seller's liability, and competition law aspects.

As the seller will provide confidential information and may provide sensitive information, the seller should insist on signing NDAs prior to exchanging information obliging the buyer to keep the provided information confidential (not only during the term of the agreement), not to exploit such information for its own benefit, and to return or destroy disclosed information after review. A breach of the confidentiality agreement should be penalized. This may particularly be important in situations where the parties are active in the same field of business and/or the transaction does not close. If the parties are active in the same field of business, in particular if they are competitors, competition law restrictions have to be taken into account to avoid prohibited sharing of information or the impression of prohibited anticompetitive arrangements.

When providing information the seller should consider applicable data protection rules and ensure that disclosed information does not contain protected data such as seller's employees' personal data. Such data may only be disclosed in anonymized form, e.g., by redacting relevant documents, during the due diligence phase.

Particularly, in situations where the potential buyer is a competitor of the seller or the target or is otherwise active in the same field of business and the risk of an exploitation of sensitive information to the seller's detriment is particularly increased, a clean room may need to be structured to control the disclosure of competitively sensitive information to a limited number of participants (a so-called clean team), with any output/analysis from the clean room subject to antitrust legal review as agreed to by the parties. Such clean team should consist of neutral experts collectively engaged by the seller and the buyer, and they are instructed not to disclose any of the reviewed information except in a summary due diligence report restricted to the disclosure of the evaluation of the due diligence findings. Please refer to Chapter 10 "Working Under the Tent: Confidentiality and Restricted Information Disclosure" for more details on clean room and the functioning of the clean team.

17.5   Negotiating the Deal: Key Aspects

Following the due diligence or in the last phase of the due diligence, the parties start negotiating the share/asset purchase agreement and all its ancillary documents. The latter often also includes a transition(al) service agreement ("TSA") to help ensure that the acquired business can effectively be operated by the buyer after closing. In many cases HR services, IT services, and certain bookkeeping services cannot simply be switched over to the buyer on day 1 after closing. The buyer may need time to implement its own (centralized, group-wide) administrative and IT services. Therefore the TSA is quite essential for the buyer in order to maintain a smooth transition period.

In a bidding process, the first draft of the transaction documentation would be prepared by the attorneys of the seller, and with its (final) bid each bidder must hand in a first markup of such documentation. In the following phases of the auction process, the attorneys of both sides usually negotiate one or two further rounds via markups before the parties sit together to discuss and negotiate open topics.

The most important topic of the negotiations is the purchase price and the purchase price calculation mechanism, although at least in an exclusive sales process the latter has most likely already been agreed upon in the LoI/MoU. Sellers (especially in Europe) sometimes insist on a locked-box mechanism to effectively fix the purchase price at signing, and as such, it will not be adjusted after closing, irrespective of any negative or positive developments of the business between the time period between signing and closing. Buyers usually aim for a closing account or completion account mechanism with net debt and working capital adjustments; according to which the parties only agree on a preliminary purchase price to be paid at closing that will be adjusted at a later stage, depending on the cash, debt, and working capital of the business to be divested at the closing date. Should the buyer accept a locked-box purchase price, which is rather rarely seen in the USA (roughly in 15% of all deals), the parties generally agree on strict governance and no leakage provisions to make sure that the seller does not negatively influence the value of the business between signing and closing given the buyer has already been committed to pay a fixed purchase price at closing.

The second most important negotiation topic is the representations, warranties, and indemnities to the benefit of the buyer. While there is usually no doubt that the seller must guarantee the full, unrestricted, and unencumbered ownership in the shares to be divested, the rest of the range of warranties and representations is dependent on the negotiations between seller and buyer and more or less dependent on the economic power and individual situation of each party involved. The seller would be well advised not to accept a purchase price offer before knowing the representations, warranties, and indemnities (the latter usually agreed upon for tax, pension, and environmental matters and for those subject matters that are already known by both parties) the buyer would want to get in exchange, because the higher the purchase price, the more guarantees a seller usually has to grant.

In order to further control the liability of the seller, sellers should always try to insert liability limitations into the liability sections, in particular, an overall financial cap on their liability. In order to help prevent small claims of the buyer during the warranty period, seller should try to get a so-called de minimis provision; this is an agreement according to which only claims exceeding a certain amount per each single claim will be considered. Another means is the so-called "basket" provision, which sets out a requirement that the total of all claims the buyer makes must exceed a certain amount in order to be suitable for a claim against the seller. With both means, de minimis and basket, sellers will only be liable when it comes to justified and significant claims but do not have to waste their time with numerous tiny and unimportant claims. In most jurisdictions, it is common that such restrictions are not applicable to tax, environmental and title representations, warranties, and indemnities.

In terms of liability limitations, the seller should try to insert a provision into the share purchase agreement according to which the buyer shall not be entitled to a claim in case the respective circumstances forming the basis of the claim have been disclosed to the buyer in the course of the sales process (e.g., in the due diligence phase).

Usually the closing of the deal is subject to the fulfillment of certain closing conditions. The most common—and in most countries mandatory—one is antitrust clearance. While this statutory obligation can usually not be waived by the parties, other closing conditions can be structured so that, depending on whose interests are protected by the respective closing condition, the protected party can waive the respective condition or the parties can jointly waive a condition. Common closing conditions are, in particular, releasing of securities and guarantees, cutting of cash pooling arrangements, cutting of intercompany services, and intellectual property (IP) separation.

17.6 Particularities of Divestitures of Listed Companies

The acquisition of shares in listed companies (public M&A) is subject to comprehensive regulatory requirements which do not apply to the acquisition of shares in private companies. Such regulatory requirements are primarily addressed to the buyer and the target company but have a large indirect impact on the structuring of the divestiture process by the seller.

Many jurisdictions provide for an obligation of the purchaser in case of public M&A transactions to submit a public tender offer to all shareholders of the target company. In case of a public tender offer, the purchaser is obliged to issue an offer document in accordance with comprehensive requirements in terms of content and form which outlines the background, conditions, terms, and consequences of the public tender offer and which is subject to a detailed review by the public authorities. Furthermore, the purchaser and the target company are subject to various publication obligations.

Particularly extensive requirements apply to takeover offers (where the purchaser aims for acquiring control, in the listed target company) and mandatory offers (where the purchaser has acquired control). In those cases and depending on the jurisdiction involved, the purchaser must offer a consideration in accordance with minimum purchase price requirements which are mainly based on the recent average stock exchange price for the shares in the target company.

Divestitures of listed companies are rarely seen, and a seller will therefore very likely not have to deal with the additional pitfalls of the sale of a listed company.

17.7   Particular International/Cross-Border M&A Aspects

While the general M&A process for the divestiture of a non-listed business is designed generally the same all over the globe, the devil lies in the details and local formalities. While shares in a US entity can be transferred by private deed, the transfer of shares in a German limited liability company, for example, need to be notarized to be valid, and the notary needs to read aloud the whole deed to all parties, sometimes for several hours. In other jurisdictions physical share certificates need to be exchanged, and in Russia certain companies must have more than one shareholder, or at least its sole shareholder must in turn have at least two shareholders. Restrictions for foreign investors may exist for certain industries, and the mandatory involvement of union representatives might delay a deal for several months as different jurisdictions bring along different hurdles and obstacles that the seller needs to overcome to successfully divest its business.

Especially in cross-border M&A transactions, it is important to consider engaging appropriate legal and tax advisors with a global footprint before undertaking any active step in the divestiture process, as you might not be aware of the legal problems that arise in the different countries in question or the tax burdens or even potential tax savings that might apply.

17.8   Tax and Transaction Implications

When divesting of a division or a line of business ("Target"), there are a myriad of income and non-income tax considerations which span the lifecycle of the transaction from the planning period to execution phase to the post-transaction period. In addition, and depending on the footprint of Target, there may be US ("United States") and non-US/local country tax considerations. The following are samples of relevant tax considerations in the context of a Target with a global footprint.

17.8.1 Pre-transaction Restructuring

As referenced in other chapters of this book, where Target includes legal entities which are not wholly dedicated to Target's business (i.e., mixed entities), pre-transaction legal restructuring may be required to neatly package the entirety of the Target business to effectuate a more efficient sales process. The pre-transaction restructuring could take the form of distributions or contributions of assets (including the shares of legal entities), and very likely these transactions will either result in immediate or deferred tax consequences.

In addition, these transfers may be cross-border, thereby implicating the tax laws of multiple countries. Furthermore, depending on the agreed-upon acquisition structure, any pre-transaction restructuring will likely be of interest to a buyer who will want to assess the tax basis of the acquired assets and/or the potential risks to which it may succeed when acquiring Target. Therefore, tax advisors should be part of the discussions of any pre-transaction restructuring to avoid or ameliorate the potential for adverse tax consequences.

17.8.2 Transaction Execution

To divest of Target, the parent entity ("Seller") in general has three transaction options: (1) an asset sale, (2) a stock sale, and (3) a spin-off. Each transaction alternative has different consequences to seller and a buyer. Additionally, Seller may consider a combination of these transactions to effectuate the divestiture, or, as noted further below, a structure where a legal sale of shares is treated as an asset sale for tax purposes.

17.8.2.1 Asset Sale

In General

In the context of an asset sale, Seller will recognize a tax gain or loss based on the difference between the consideration received (purchase price plus assumption of liabilities) and the tax basis in the divested assets. Depending on the nature of assets sold, taxable gain or loss will either be treated as ordinary or capital. For example, gain associated with the sale of inventory or resulting from depreciation recapture will be treated as ordinary, while gain associated with the sale of goodwill may be capital in nature.

Buyer will take a purchase price (plus assumed liabilities) tax basis in the acquired assets. To the extent the acquisition results in a step-up in tax basis of Target's assets, Buyer will have a tax benefit of additional depreciation/amortization tax deductions on a go-forward basis. Furthermore, in general, the historical income tax liabilities associated with the operations of Target will remain with Seller in an asset sale and not transfer with the Target assets to Buyer.

Synthetic Asset Sale

As mentioned in other chapters of this book, opportunities exist whereby Buyer legally acquires the equity of Target but receives the benefits of the asset purchase (i.e., stepped-up tax basis in assets). From a US perspective and subject to satisfying certain requirements, these synthetic transactions include:

- A Section[1] 338(h)(10) transaction which can occur when a seller sells the shares of an S corporation or the shares of a subsidiary in seller's US consolidated tax group to a US corporate buyer. Note that a Section 338(h)(10) election is not available where either Seller, Target, or Buyer is domiciled outside the USA.

- A Section 338(g) transaction which can occur when a seller sells the shares of a corporation. Note that a Section 338(g) transaction usually involves a US corporation acquiring the shares of a foreign corporation which results in a step-up in the tax basis of the assets of the foreign corporation. If Target is treated as a controlled foreign corporation ("CFC") (i.e., a foreign corporation in which one or more US shareholders (i.e., US persons who own 10 percent or more of the voting stock of the foreign corporation) own more than 50 percent of the stock of the foreign corporation, by vote or value, on any day during the taxable year) for US income tax purposes, gain recognized on the deemed asset sale generates additional earnings and profits ("E&P") (i.e., the measure of a corporation's economic ability to pay dividends to its shareholders) and may give rise to subpart F income (i.e., passive income and several other categories of income derived from transactions that can be used to shift profits from the US parent or a related foreign subsidiary to a CFC) and a taxable deemed dividend from the CFC Target to Seller. However, for foreign tax credit (i.e., a tax credit for income taxes paid to a foreign government) purposes, it is noted that a Section 338(g) transaction does not apply for purposes of determining source or character of the gain recognized by Seller on the disposition of the CFC Target.

- A Section 336(e) transaction is similar to a Section 338(h)(10) transaction; however, this transaction does not require Buyer to be a US corporation.

- The sale of equity of an entity which is disregarded for US income tax purposes (a "DRE"). From Seller's perspective, this will be treated as sale of the assets of Target. Similarly, Buyer will be treated as acquiring the assets of Target.

The sale of the equity of a DRE may also occur in the context of a foreign corporation. For example, if a second-tier CFC makes an election to change its US tax classification to a DRE, then a disposition of the lower-tier DRE by the first-tier CFC is treated as an asset sale as opposed to a stock sale on the basis that the first-tier CFC is deemed to be the owner of the second-tier CFC's assets immediately after the check-the-box election. Further, any gain realized on the asset sale

---

[1] All references to "Section" in this report refer to the Internal Revenue Code of 1986, as amended, and the Treasury Regulations thereunder, unless otherwise noted.

constitutes gain from the sale of property used in the parent CFC's trade or business. On this basis, the gain generally is not considered subpart F income of the first-tier CFC and, therefore, is not taxable as a deemed dividend to Seller.

Note that state and local jurisdictions may not follow the synthetic asset sale treatment, and therefore, the tax result may be different on a state/local level. Consultations with a state tax specialist are recommended.

Seller should consider the potential of the above transactions as they can deliver incremental value to a Buyer via the stepped-up tax basis in Target's assets and therefore may present an opportunity to extract additional purchase price from Buyer. In practice, we recommend that Seller understand at the outset of the divestiture process the potential benefit of delivering stepped-up tax basis to a buyer. This will help Seller and its financial, legal, and tax advisors to assess the best approach to marketing the benefit and strategize about extracting the additional value from a buyer.

17.8.2.2 Stock Sale

In General

In the context of a stock sale, Seller will recognize a tax gain or loss based on the difference between the consideration received and the tax basis in the Target shares. Seller's gain or loss on the sale of assets is treated as a capital gain or loss.

A Buyer will take purchase price tax basis in the acquired shares, however a carryover tax basis in Target's assets. Furthermore, Target may remain liable for pre-close tax matters, among other liabilities, and therefore Buyer (as the new owner of the shares of Target) may ultimately be liable for Target's pre-close tax liabilities. A buyer will often seek protection for these pre-close tax liabilities through indemnification provisions in the purchase agreement. Despite what may be stated in the purchase agreement, the legal liability of pre-close taxes may reside with Target/Buyer in the context of a share transaction.

Sale of Stock of a Foreign Corporation

Gain from the disposition of stock of a foreign corporation by US Seller is treated as a taxable dividend to Seller if at any time within the last 5 years the corporation was a CFC and Seller was a US shareholder of the foreign corporation.

Dividend treatment is limited to the extent of the untaxed E&P of the CFC but also generally includes the E&P of any lower-tier CFCs owned by the CFC. This allows US Seller to convert stock gain into a dividend which may have increase US Seller's foreign tax credit position for foreign income taxes paid by the CFC.

Stock Disposition of a Lower-Tier CFC

Gain realized by a first-tier CFC on the disposition of stock of a second-tier CFC is immediately taxable to the US parent. The gain is treated as passive basket subpart F income at the first-tier CFC level unless it is recharacterized as a deemed dividend to the extent of the second-tier CFC's previously untaxed E&P. Under these circumstances, the gain/deemed dividend may be treated as general basket subpart F income at the first-tier CFC but only to the extent that the dividend is treated as being distributed out of the previously untaxed E&P derived from the second-tier CFC's active trade or business.

17.8.2.3   Spin-Off Transactions

In General

Another type of divestiture transaction is a spin-off. A spin-off is a distribution by a parent corporation of the shares of a controlled (i.e., ownership of at least 80 percent of the shares entitled to vote and 80 percent of the number of each class of shares) subsidiary to Seller's shareholders. The distribution may take the following forms: (i) a pro rata distribution of a controlled subsidiary's stock by the parent corporation to its shareholders, i.e., a spin-off; (ii) a non-pro rata distribution of a controlled subsidiary's stock by the parent corporation to certain shareholders in exchange for the parent corporation's stock, i.e., a split-off; and (iii) a distribution of a controlled subsidiary's stock to shareholders in liquidation of the parent corporation, i.e., a split-up. In addition, a spin-off transaction may be preceded by a separate but related transaction in which the parent corporation making the distribution first transfers assets to the controlled subsidiary which may be pre-existing or newly formed (please see above for further detail regarding pre-transaction restructuring).

US Spin-Off Transactions

If the relevant facts exist and if properly structured, a US spin-off distribution should not result in any immediate adverse US income tax consequences. *However, these divestitures are complex undertakings, and many requirements must be satisfied to qualify for tax-free treatment. Although not an exhaustive list, certain of the requirements are as follows:*

- The distributing corporation (i.e., for purposes of the spin-off discussions, this entity is referred to as "Parent" and referred to as "Seller" elsewhere in this chapter) must have control of the distributed corporation (i.e., Target) immediately prior to the spin-off.
- Immediately after the distribution, Parent and Target must each be engaged in an active trade or business for at least 5 years.
- The distribution must not be used principally as a device for distributing historical earnings.
- Parent must not have acquired control of Target within the preceding 5 years in a taxable transaction.
- Parent must distribute all the shares and securities of Target.
- There must be a corporate business (i.e., nontax) purpose for the spin-off distribution.
- The pre-distribution Parent shareholders must maintain adequate continuity of interest in both Parent and Target following the distribution.
- There must be continuity of business enterprise.

The potential benefits of a tax-free spin-off are powerful to Parent, Target, and Parent/Target shareholders. However, if the transaction does not meet the numerous requirements (those mentioned above and others that may be dependent on specific facts relevant at the time of the transaction), the transaction could be recast as a taxable distribution to both Parent and Target. As such, if Parent is considering a spin-off transaction, it is advisable to seek the counsel of a tax advisor. In some situations, the US Internal Revenue Service ("IRS") may provide an advanced ruling on certain aspects of the spin-off transaction and thereby reduce the tax risk associated with a spin-off.

Cross-Border Spin-Offs

In the cross-border context the transactions indicated below are of relevance.

US Distributing Corporation Spins Off Foreign or US-Controlled Subsidiary to Foreign Shareholders

A US distributing corporation recognizes gain on a spin-off of a foreign-controlled corporation's stock but not on a spin-off of a US-controlled corporation's stock. Gain recognized by the US distributing corporation on a spin-off of a foreign-controlled corporation's stock is recharacterized as a taxable deemed dividend to the extent of the US distributing corporation's share of the foreign-controlled corporation's previously untaxed E&P.

US Distributing Corporation Spins Off Foreign-Controlled Subsidiary to US Shareholders

A US distributing corporation must recognize built-in gain inherent in the stock of a foreign-controlled subsidiary (i.e., the excess of the value of the stock over the tax basis in the stock) under circumstances in which the domestic distributing corporation spins off the stock to an individual US shareholder but not necessarily to a corporate US shareholder. Gain recognized by the US distributing corporation in regard to a spin-off of a foreign-controlled corporation's stock to an individual US shareholder may be recharacterized as a deemed dividend to the extent of the foreign-controlled corporation's previously untaxed E&P.

Where the US shareholder is a domestic corporation, the US distributing corporation does not recognize gain inherent in the stock of the foreign-controlled corporation to the extent that the US shareholder inherits the US distributing corporation's tax basis and holding period in the stock of the foreign-controlled corporation that is distributed in the spin-off. This helps ensure that a deemed dividend is preserved on any future sale of the stock of the foreign-controlled corporation by the US shareholder immediately after the distribution. To the extent that there is a basis or holding period differential in the stock of the foreign-controlled corporation pre- and post-spin-off, a taxable deemed dividend may be triggered from the foreign-controlled corporation to the US distributing corporation.

Foreign Distributing Corporation Spins Off Foreign- or US-Controlled Subsidiary to US Shareholders

There are two separate rules in regard to a foreign distributing corporation's spin-off of its subsidiary's stock to US shareholders. The application of each rule depends on whether the spin-off is a pro rata (i.e., a spin-off) or non-pro rata distribution (i.e., a split-off). These rules, which are very complex, are briefly discussed below. The general policy behind each rule is to preserve the deemed dividend attributable to each of the US shareholders with respect to the stock of the foreign distributing corporation and the stock of the controlled subsidiary (that existed prior to the spin-off) post-spin-off. A reduction in the deemed dividend attributable to a US shareholder may result in a taxable deemed dividend to that shareholder immediately following the spin-off.

In regard to a pro rata distribution, the US shareholders must apportion tax basis between the stock of the foreign distributing corporation and the stock of the controlled subsidiary to the extent necessary to preserve the deemed dividend attributable to each US shareholder with respect to the stock of each corporation that existed prior to the spin-off. As indicated above, to the extent that there is not enough basis to apportion between the stock of the two corporations, the US shareholders are treated as receiving a taxable deemed dividend. It is noted that a deemed dividend from one corporation to the US shareholders results in a basis increase in the stock of the other corporation.

Since a non-pro rata distribution generally leaves a US shareholder with ownership over only one subsidiary after the split-off distribution, tax basis cannot be apportioned from the stock of one corporation to the other. Therefore, the US Treasury Regulations require that a US shareholder includes in its gross income a taxable deemed dividend equal to the deemed dividend attributable to the US shareholder pre-spin-off but lost in the corporation that was split-off. It is noted that a deemed dividend from the split-off corporation to the US shareholder results in a basis increase in the stock of the retained corporation.

17.8.3 Tax Attributes

For US purposes, tax attributes (e.g., E&P, tax credits, and net operating losses) do not transfer with Target in connection with an asset transaction. However, in the context of a share transaction, tax attributes do transfer with Target.

When Parent is selling the shares of Target and Target and Parent file a consolidated income tax return (e.g., Target, Parent, and potentially other entities file one income tax return and report the income, loss, and deductions of all entities who join in the consolidated tax filing), Parent and Target will need to identify and quantify the tax attributes that will transfer to a buyer such that (1) Buyer can report/utilize those tax attributes post-transaction and (2) Parent can remove the tax attributes from its financial and tax books and records.

Therefore, for example, net operating losses or credit carryovers of Parent must be allocated and apportioned to Target based on its relative contribution to those items. The calculation of the amount of the tax credits and losses that go with Target can become complicated, especially where the requisite information/historical bookkeeping has not adequately been maintained.

Furthermore, the tax basis in Target's assets will carryover with Target to the post-transaction period (i.e., when owned by Buyer). However, note that the deferred tax assets and liabilities of Target will not carryover with Target as these balances will be recalculated in connection with purchase accounting (i.e., revised book balances as compared to carryover tax basis balances). Although it may seem to be a straightforward exercise, the determination of the tax basis in Target's assets is often challenging especially when Target's operations are contained in mixed entities.

17.8.4 Other Tax Considerations

In addition to the above, there are other tax considerations Seller should keep top of mind as it considers a divestiture transaction even though some are germane to the post-transaction period. These considerations include:

- Pre-transaction settling of intercompany balances between Seller and Target

  ○ Oftentimes, Target and Seller have intercompany relationships and balances which, for various reasons, Seller or a buyer may want to unwind prior to the divestiture transaction. There may be associated complexities that make this process more difficult than anticipated. For example, Seller's accounting for intercompany transactions may not be closely monitored and therefore the settlement process may evolve into also having to verify the related balances.

- Transfer taxes

  ○ From a US perspective, transfer taxes may apply in the context of an asset sale. This is generally the case when vehicles and real estate are involved; however, a broader sales tax may also apply to the transfer. To the extent there are non-US aspects of Target, local country transfer taxes should also be considered. Further note that certain non-US jurisdictions (e.g., China) may impose a transfer tax on the indirect transfer of a subsidiary.

- Tax reporting aspects of the transaction or transactions

  ○ Very likely there will be tax reporting aspects of the divestiture transaction and any related pre-transaction restructuring. The tax reporting can include statements or forms which will have to be included with the income tax return of the year for which the transactions were completed. Monetary penalties may apply to the extent the statements and/or forms are not completed/filed.

  ○ From a US perspective, these forms and statements include (but are not limited to) the following:

    ▪ Form 8594 (Asset Acquisition Statement)—this form is used to report a sale (or purchase) of a group of assets that comprise a trade or business if goodwill or going concern value attaches (or could attach) to the assets.

- Form 8023 (Elections under Section 338 for Corporations Making Qualified Stock Purchases)—this form is used to make an election under Section 338 (as described above) if a corporation makes a qualified stock purchase (i.e., acquires at least 80% of the value and vote of the shares of another corporation).
- Form 8883 (Asset Allocation Statement under Section 338)—this form is used to report information about transactions involving the deemed asset sale of corporate assets under Section 338. Note that, as of the timing of this writing, the Internal Revenue Service has not created a separate form for Section 336(e) transactions (as discussed above), and the Form 8883 should be used for this purpose.
- Spin-Off Statements—in the context of a spin-off transaction, Parent is required to include a statement with its federal income tax return for the year of the spin-off which includes (among other things) the following:

  - The identification of Target
  - The date of the spin-off
  - The aggregate fair market value and tax basis of Target shares (immediately before the spin-off)

- Calculating the gain/loss on the divestiture transaction

  - For income tax reporting as well as financial reporting purposes, Seller will have to calculate its tax gain or loss on the divestiture transaction. The gain or loss is calculated as the difference between the consideration received (e.g., purchase process plus assumed liabilities) and the tax basis in the divested assets/shares. As mentioned above, for an asset sale, the determination of the tax basis in Target's assets is often challenging especially when Target's operations are contained in mixed entities.

  - However, in the context of a share sale, tax basis is not as straightforward and oftentimes requires a separate analysis (especially if Target is not newly or recently formed). Among other things, all of Target's historical income tax returns will be required to calculate tax basis in shares for US purposes.

17.9   Conclusion

Although divestiture transactions are generally driven by commercial reasons, legal and tax aspects of such transactions should remain top of mind as opportunities may exist to generate additional value based on legal and/or tax considerations. To better position a divestiture transaction to benefit from these potential benefits, legal and tax disciplines should be included in related transaction discussions starting with the initial planning phases.

Case Study: 17

Background

A US-based, $30 billion, publicly traded multinational company in the hospitality industry operates in more than 100 countries through its company-owned equity operations, as well as through franchising and licensing to third parties. Its Country X operations are one of the company's largest.

Over the course of several years, the company entered into transactions to increase its franchise and licensing footprint while disposing its company-owned operations, including:

- Increase its franchise and license percentage and reduce the amount of company-owned operations.
- Monetize one of its operating units in Country X ("Company X Unit").
- Focus capital investment on its remaining core businesses and other emerging markets.

The company entered into a plan to spin-off its Company X Unit to its shareholders. After the spin-off transaction, Company Z Unit became a third-party franchisee.

Challenges

The tax and legal challenges faced by the company in its spin-off of Country X Unit included:

- Minimize US and non-US income and indirect tax, including Country X tax, associated with the pre-spin transaction to position the Country X entities and assets for the spin-off.
- Structure the spin-off itself such that it qualifies for tax-free treatment under US federal income tax rules
- Maintain consistency in the franchise and license agreement with Country X Unit (e.g., royalty rates and other terms and conditions), other third-party vendors, and company-operated franchise and license agreements.

Approach

The plan and approach to the spin began with a review and understanding of the Company's purpose for engaging in the transaction, prioritizing goals, identifying potential challenges, and identifying potential solutions to those challenges. It was critical to obtain thorough data in order to make sound decisions in due diligence as well as planning for post-spin integration. This information includes but is not limited to:

- Financial data (including tax attributes)
- Shareholder data
- Business history
- Business model (product flows, contractual arrangements, cash flows)
- Impact on incentives (federal, state, local, non-US)
- Incorporation documents
- Previous tax returns

- Trial balances
- Documents to calculate potential tax liabilities

Once key information was gathered and analyzed; it was important to develop a feasibility, design, and implementation plan to execute the transaction such that the company's prioritized goals are balanced with the realities of meeting the presented challenges. As part of this, the company focused on confirming impacts in the USA, Country X, and other non-US jurisdictions, obtaining tax rulings where necessary and available, putting in place favorable third-party and intercompany financing, and consulting with various business groups across functions (e.g., legal, controllership, treasury, supply chain) to help ensure cross-functional dependencies are considered throughout the transaction.

Impact/Results

Most of the pre-spin transactions were either tax-free for US federal income tax purposes or, if taxable, the tax was able to be directly offset with credits for foreign taxes paid on the transaction and other foreign operations. In some of the affected countries outside of the USA and Country X, advanced tax rulings are available in order to obtain certainty of tax-free treatment in connection with the transaction.

- Although minimization of US and other country taxes were a priority in the transaction, most critical was the need to minimize Company Z's taxes based on the positioning of Country X entities and assets. Country X's tax rules are ambiguous with respect to transfers of legal entities and include significant built-in gains in the Country X entities and assets. A tax on the transaction would have materially changed the economics of the spin-off. Company management, with assistance from US and Country X tax and legal advisors, was able to get informal clearance from Country X tax officials that the proposed transaction would be tax deferred.
- As the spin-off satisfied the requirements to be tax-free for US federal income tax purposes (e.g., control, device, active trade or business, distribution, business purpose, continuity of interest, continuity of business enterprise), company management and its tax and legal advisors were able to get comfortable with the idea that the transaction should be tax-free. It should be noted that in many cases in which significant tax is in question, it is advisable to also request an advanced ruling from the IRS in order to get certainty of the US federal income tax treatment of a transaction.
- Although Country X Unit sought to minimize the royalty rate to be applied to its Country X operating revenue post-transaction, the company and its tax and legal team were able to demonstrate (a) that the ownership of the intellectual property being franchised and licensed to Country X Unit was owned and controlled by the company and not Country X Unit and (b) the royalty rate being charged under the franchise and licensing agreement was appropriate, given the value of the intellectual property rights being conveyed and the importance of its use in the operations of the Country X Unit business. As a result, the company was able to include a royalty rate in its franchise and license agreements with Country X Unit, consistent with the rate charged to its other franchisees.

Chapter 18
Accelerating Divestitures Through Minimal Rebranding

A company's brand represents its identity. For customers and partners, the brand is synonymous with the company itself. The brand is also an extension of the company's products or services. It often takes years for a company to build a brand, and once it is built, it is very important for the company to maintain its brand equity.

18.1 Need for Rebranding During Divestiture

When a business line is not profitable or misaligned with the company's overall growth objectives, a divestiture enables the company to spin it off in order to focus on higher growth areas. Rebranding reinforces this effort and helps the company realign its business objectives to match brand perceptions. Rebranding becomes vital when the seller company is trying to:

- Appeal to a particular customer segment.
- Create a business strategy with brand resonance.
- Recover from a negative event (e.g., corporate scandal) that harmed the company's reputation, since rebranding can help create a positive image for the company.
- Distinguish itself from its competitors.

There are four common rebranding scenarios for the seller company, based on the nature of the mergers and acquisitions (M&A) transaction:

1. A divestiture in which the seller company retains its original brand
2. A separation in which the seller company alters or modifies its original brand
3. A transformational divestiture in which the seller company creates a new brand
4. A portfolio transaction in which no brand changes occur

© Deloitte Development LLC 2018

J. Joy, *Divestitures and Spin-Offs*, Management for Professionals,
https://doi.org/10.1007/978-1-4939-7662-1_18

The divested entity must also rebrand itself. Although it starts off associated with the seller company's brand, the divested entity must quickly define its own brand identity to signal to customers and investors that it is no longer part of the seller company. The divested entity gets to position and adapt its rebranded identity to match its business strategy, products, and services. The new brand communicates the future vision for the divested entity to all customers and stakeholders.

This chapter will focus on the most common rebranding scenario in which the seller company retains its original brand, but certain trademarks are transferred to the divested entity as part of the M&A deal and can no longer be used by the seller company after a certain date or time period.

18.2   Rebranding Requirement

Upon the first announcement of the M&A deal, the seller company must establish ground rules and a timeline under which the divested entity can leverage the seller's brand. These rules should apply to existing branding and new use of the brand post-deal announcement.

Detailed guidelines and a timeline for the use of the seller company's trademarks and brand logo by the divested entity must be determined before the deal closes. These guidelines and timeline will allow the seller company to drive and monitor the rebranding effort by the divested entity and help ensure a complete disassociation with the seller company per the agreed timeline (by Day 1 or by a specified duration post-Day 1).

The rebranding effort is a monumental task that involves numerous critical steps, including but not limited to, conducting a rebranding impact assessment, identifying the rebranding scope and requirements, and executing rebranding to completion. Additionally, since the timeline to Day 1 is usually short (i.e., 3–6 months), it is important to prioritize and identify the minimal rebranding requirements for Day 1.

The level of effort associated with rebranding varies based on the customer-facing nature of the seller company. Companies with a vast presence in business to consumer (B2C) business such as retail businesses and banks must be very careful when rebranding themselves to avoid dilution and confusion among customers. For such companies, the rebranding timeline for the divested entity is typically short, ranging from 3 to 6 months. To highlight the extent of effort involved in rebranding customer-facing businesses, consider the rebranding effort required for a typical bank. To prepare for rebranding, the bank must send customers notices about the changes, new checks with the rebranded bank logo, new ATM cards, and new Internet-banking platforms. For business to business (B2B) companies, rebranding may take more than 12 months.

The following tables summarize the rebranding requirements for each type of brand use:

Table 18.1   Rebranding Efforts That Requires Cessation of Use of the Seller Company's Logo Within a Stipulated Time Period

Type of brand use	Examples
All use of trademarks, including: • External uses • Internal uses	• Products, inventory, packaging, software interfaces
	• Product documentation such as manuals, legal guides, warranties, data sheets, and user agreements
	• Signage used on buildings and at trade shows
	• Websites, domains, customer portals, service applications, online help, and other online applications
	• Marketing assets and collateral such as advertisements, promotional materials, brochures, images displayed to users, white papers, and social media accounts
	• Email signatures, letterhead, office forms, invoices, business cards, labels, training materials, PowerPoint templates
	• Copyright notices
Use of the seller company's business name	• Use in any legal entity names
	• Use in any business or doing business with seller company's name
	• Portals and materials prepared and used by the divested entity or hosted on the divested entity's behalf
Other obvious or externally visible uses	• Uses in programming code that are highly visible to the public; for example, when the seller company's logo is not buried or embedded in lines of programming code along with text or numbers
	• Internal systems and portals used or viewable by third-party vendors or the public
	• Internal systems and portals that create output (that references the seller company in areas such as field, record, or location identifiers) that is visible to third-party vendors or the public
New uses	• Inclusion of the seller company's trademarks as new identifiers in programming code, systems, or databases

Table 18.2 Rebranding Requirements That Necessitate Implementation of TSAs

Type of brand use	Examples	Rebranding requirement
Internal or functional uses that are accessible or viewable by the public and customers	• The seller company's name embedded only in programming code or a URL (not use in traditional domain names) as part of a longer string or as a data field, if required to support the architecture of existing data systems, provided there is no attendant name or branding visible on user interfaces that are visible and accessible by the public and customers	• No action required for any such uses if already covered under a transition service agreement (TSA) between the seller company and the divested entity
		• For any uses not covered under a TSA, no change is required to existing uses if steps are taken to restrict the ability of the public and customers to view or access the references to the seller company's name or branding; however, the divested entity cannot introduce new uses after close
Internal or functional uses that are NOT accessible or viewable by the public and customers	• Embedded trademarks in programming code that are not visible or viewable by the public or customers	• Divested entity should make changes as soon as it is practically possible
	• Pre-close and historical documents strictly used internally such as manuals, internal memoranda, and trainings	• For all of these materials, the references to seller company needs to be removed from any updates or new versions produced

Table 18.3 Uses of the Seller Company's Products or Textual Non-trademarks That Do Not Need to Be Rebranded

Type of brand use	Examples
Use of seller company's products	• Continued use of the seller company's products by the divested entity that bears the seller company's trademarks on the products as purchased, e.g., use of seller company's servers with seller company's trademark for the divested entity's computation needs
Textual non-trademark use	• Use in documents such as securities, regulatory filings, emails, and speeches to accurately describe the historic or current relationship between the divested entity and the seller company

18.3   Rebranding Process and Activities

The following are the major steps associated with rebranding:

18.3.1   Step 1. Create a Rebranding Strategy

- Assess the seller company's current marketing strategy to ensure the rebranding effort is in alignment with the marketing strategy.
- Perform a rebranding impact assessment (i.e., implications to customers, revenue, cost and effort estimations, and legal and tax implications).
- Select a rebranding strategy that aligns with the seller company's marketing strategy and the rebranding impact assessment.

18.3.2   Step 2. Perform Rebranding Prework

- Define the scope of both the internal and external rebranding effort.
- Collect asset inventory that will require rebranding.
- Define rebranding requirements based on the type of branding used, as well as the associated timeline; rebranding efforts should be categorized under one of the following scope requirements:
  - Stop using the seller company's logo within a stipulated time period.
  - Require a TSA to allow usage of the seller company's logo for an extended timeframe post-Day 1, or obtain a commitment from the divested entity to make changes as soon as practically possible.
  - No rebranding requirements associated with the seller company's products or textual non-trademark usage.

18.3.3   Step 3. Prepare the Rebranding Plan for Execution

- Select a rebranding partner (an outside firm with extensive experience in rebranding with a stellar track record of successful rebranding) to assist with the rebranding effort
- Create a rebranding execution plan that includes the timeline, governance structure, inventory of rebranding elements, and rebranding requirements

18.3.4   Step 4. Execute the Rebranding Plan

- Perform quality control of all rebranding exercises.
- Collect key metrics to measure rebranding effort and execution.
- Execute change management through awareness sessions and internal/external communications to address concerns of employees, customers, and shareholders (if applicable) and assure them that rebranding will have minimal impact on their business or day to day lives.
- Monitor and track rebranding effort and completion.

18.4   System (Application) Rebranding

Planning for application rebranding should begin early in the deal process, since it usually takes longer than other rebranding activities. A step-by-step process to perform application rebranding effectively by Day 1 follows:

Step 1. Finalize the application separation strategy, including rebranding across planning, design, development, testing, and cutover of IT application, to avoid duplication of effort.

Step 2. Take inventory of the seller company's and the divested entity's IT applications, along with the correct disposition for each application.

Step 3. Conduct application blueprinting exercise to finalize the future IT landscape. The application blueprinting exercise will help identify applications that will be in scope for rebranding by Day 1.

Step 4. Filter the applications identified in Step 3 using the following framework to determine the rebranding scope and effort:

(a) No rebranding required for an IT application, if legal dispensation can be obtained
(b) Minimal rebranding required for an application, if text disclaimer can be added communicating that the divested entity is no longer part of the seller company
(c) Some rebranding required for an application, if the company name changed, but there were no logo changes
(d) Full rebranding required for an application if the company name and logo both need to be changed

Step 5. Based on the rebranding scope and effort determined in Step 4, identify detailed rebranding requirements for each IT application.

Step 6. Execute the rebranding effort required for each IT application based on the detailed rebranding requirements identified in Step 5.

Step 7. Perform testing to ensure the IT applications have been successfully rebranded. The testing effort and test cases will vary based on the rebranding effort and scope determined in Step 4; for instance, testing may include reviewing the application screen or printed material to ensure the seller company's name and logo have been successfully changed.

Step 8. Once testing is complete and application goes through the cutover process which is the final set of activities and processes involved in bringing logical or physical separation of application to fruition (for more details, refer to "Chapter 24, Cutover: Getting Ready for the Launch"), perform final check to ensure applications were rebranded correctly with no issues.

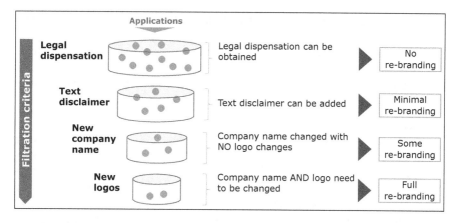

Fig. 18.1 Filtration Criteria to Identify Rebranding Scope and Effort

18.5   Conclusion

Rebranding during a divestiture is vital as it helps define the divested entity's brand identity that gets communicated to its employees, customer, and investors. Rebranding requires considerable effort and time. Divested company should work with the seller company to establish detailed guidelines, requirements, and timelines for the use of seller company's trademark and brand logo. It is important for the two parties to clearly articulate and agree upon minimal rebranding requirements that can be implemented by Day 1. Divested entity should follow the four-step process laid out in this chapter to help with the rebranding strategy, planning, and execution for effective rebranding with minimal impact to the divested entity's business. Special emphasis should be given to application rebranding as it is usually the most complex and requires more effort/time compared to rebranding of other assets types.

Case Study: 18

Background

An international bank with more than 5 million customers; 20,000 employees; and 10 million credit cards in operation embarked on a US$5 billion divestiture of its operations in Brazil, which required rebranding.

Challenges

Since the timeframe to Day 1 was short, it increased the complexity of rebranding multifold:

- Need for business agility and to avoid significant business impact necessitated a different approach with a huge focus on identifying and prioritizing minimal rebranding requirements
- Need for alignment with all the third parts involved on the program (e.g., payment getaway and ATM provider) regarding disclaimers and rebranding implementation, cost, and timeline, having in mind the client's disruption and legal requirements
- Need to ensure cross-functional dependencies are captured and the discontinuity of a product or service will be reflected on the rebranding communications

Approach

Key business stakeholders, legal team, and IT implementation team were engaged to identify rebranding requirements. In order to complete accelerated rebranding by Day 1 and protect the seller company's brand, these requirements needed to be prioritized into a list of minimal rebranding requirements that must be achieved by Day 1 for each asset type. Refer to Table 18.4 for details on minimal rebranding requirements for each asset type (e.g., credit cards, printed material etc.).

Business stakeholders and the IT implementation team jointly discussed and prioritized the IT applications that required rebranding to drive the application rebranding schedule. Once the IT implementation team executed the application rebranding, the IT implementation team worked with business stakeholders to perform testing to ensure that rebranding was successfully executed.

Clear communication between business stakeholders and the IT implementation team helped ensure risks and issues were identified and resolved quickly.

Impact/Results

As a result of the rebranding approach, the bank accomplished the following:

- Ready for Day 1 within 3 months of announcement
- Effectively met the rebranding requirements for Day 1
- Protected the seller company's brand on Day 1
- No significant impact on the divested entity's business
- Complete remaining rebranding as part of the TSA exit and post-Day 1 implementation within 3 months of closing

The following tables provide an overview of the minimal rebranding requirements identified by the bank's stakeholders, legal team, and IT implementation team:

Table 18.4 Minimal Rebranding Requirements Identified by Asset Type

Assets	Minimal rebranding requirements
Credit cards/checks	• Do not rebrand existing credit cards until credit card migration is achieved in accordance with the terms of the sales and purchase agreement (SPA)
	• New credit cards or checks may continue to be issued with the seller company's logo. A letter with a legal statement should be attached along with the new credit card notifying customers that the credit card is not a credit card of the seller company
Printed material	• All new printed material (e.g., customer documentation, correspondence, statements, and marketing material) should clearly tell customers they are contacting the divested entity and not the seller company
Real estate assets (branches/ATMs)	• Seller company's logo may remain on buildings and inside branches for the duration of the TSA, but must be removed upon TSA exit
	• Merchandising material will remain unchanged until the TSA exit
	• A trademark licensing agreement (TMLA) is required for 60 days post-separation to remove photos on walls inside buildings and branch locations as well as advertising
Technology platforms	• Internet banking will be partially rebranded
	• For mobile banking, TMLA required until TSA exit as it is not possible to rebrand mobile banking prior to TSA exit
Other assets	• Public website—Seller company's domain needs to be available during the entire migration phase to support regular operation of internet and business banking (i.e., 90 days post-separation)
	• Intranet—Post-day 1, all global links between the seller company and the divested entity must cease when the TSA commences
	• Call center—A recorded message communicating that the divested entity is no longer part of the seller company should be implemented for customers at the first access point for the divested entity's products or services

Chapter 19
Managing Customer and Partner Transitions During a Separation

19.1 Overview

In this chapter, we will investigate the complexities of managing customer and partner transitions during a separation. In response to a 2013 survey, more than 76% of business executives stated that customer and supplier relationships were a major challenge when executing or considering a divestiture.[1]

Here's why: The transition of existing customers and partners is logistically intensive, requires thorough planning, and can have a material top-line impact. If not managed well, the business may face disruptions, negative stakeholder experience, and revenue leakage due to competitor poaching. Additionally, customers and partners will attempt to renegotiate more favorable terms as the balance of power shifts, and this could have material financial impacts. Last but not least, separations pose a unique opportunity to generate value through the creation of symbiotic multiyear partnerships. These partnerships are generally significantly accretive to the topline over a 3–5-year period and can drive immediate growth momentum for the newly separated companies. However, differences in priorities can make for difficult negotiations.

The complexity and effort required to ensure customer and partner readiness are often underestimated and overlooked. In broad terms, there are three components to seamless customer and partner readiness:

1. Sharing the vision and generating excitement about the new portfolio to drive top-line growth. Marketing and communication efforts through the course of the separation are critical to achieve this.
2. Customer and partner operational readiness which involves the tactics of setting up the newly separated entity into customer and partner systems so that transactions can occur seamlessly post close (also referred to as vendor setup).

---

[1] "Divestiture Survey Report 2013: Sharpening Your Strategy," Deloitte Consulting LLP, January 1, 2013. Accessed February 8, 2017

© Deloitte Development LLC 2018
J. Joy, *Divestitures and Spin-Offs*, Management for Professionals,
https://doi.org/10.1007/978-1-4939-7662-1_19

3. Unlocking value through the creation of preferred vendor agreements between the two companies.

Significant and material value is locked within customer and partner transitions, and only through planning and disciplined execution can it be unlocked. In this chapter, we will explore the strategies, tactics, and best practices needed to unlock this value.

19.2   Getting the Basics Right

The critical basic dimensions to successful customer and partner transitions include:

- Understanding the long poles in the tent that are must-haves for enabling the vendor setup transitions
- Having a differentiated strategy by stakeholder type
- Engaging actively with the business in order to bring a P&L lens to customer and partner transitions and

Enabling a disciplined feedback loop with those in the field that arm the management team with a retrospective reporting capability as well as a forward-looking predictive mechanism.

Understand the long poles Customer and partner readiness can take long time (months to years) to plan and execute; it is imperative to understand the long poles in the tent to manage this process effectively against a robust timeline. To do this, start from the end date or go-live date, and work backwards to identify the long poles and build the execution plan.

For example, collecting vendor setup data is one of these long poles—although tactical in nature, it is time-consuming because of the multiplicity of information needed. Customers and partners need to have access to new legal entities, bank accounts, and tax IDs in order to be able to set up the newly formed company as a vendor. This information in turn requires several months of coordinated functional planning and execution to get prepared, which leaves a narrow window of time for customer and partner transition management.

It is important to accelerate and decouple those aspects that can be managed independently (e.g., sharing the overarching strategy and approach with customers and partners, training the sales teams) from the aspects that have dependencies (e.g., where vendor setup data is needed).

Additionally, many companies do not have reliable customer master data, which is also critical to affecting the transaction. The timeline must include the functional precursors and the functional interdependencies early in the process to ensure timeline completion.

Lastly, the timing and execution plan must allow for as much time as possible for customers and partners to actually execute vendor setup (setting up the new entities in their systems) as this is extremely time-consuming when done at scale.

Have a segmented strategy Large global customers and partners that have complex operations and represent a large proportion of revenue typically require white glove service. Sales leaders need to engage them early and drive coordinated discussions through the countries they are present in. This requires a significant amount of lead time and preparation. Many of these large customers and partners will attempt to renegotiate contracts or ask for additional guarantees or investments to cover the cost of operational changes. Each of these discussions will take time and possibly even leadership escalations.

On the other hand, the long tail of smaller customers and partners requires a more pipeline-focused approach. Vendor setup will be simpler for these accounts, but managing the sheer volume of the long tail translates into significant time and effort. Aligning near-term efforts to those cases where a deal is in the pipeline helps to direct resources to where it counts most.

The most amount of focus must be paid to the top customers and partners that drive 80% of revenue as these will typically be the toughest to transition but will have the largest bearing on the revenue outlook of the new entity. Start early with these customers, enable an efficient feedback loop, engage globally for large global customers and partners, and drive progress to ensure no disruption to the pipeline.

Last, but not least, federal, state, and local governments require special attention as these contracts require multistep and lengthy novation processes. And the timeline must account for these specific complexities as well.

Enabling a disciplined reporting mechanism and feedback loop Transitioning thousands of customers across geographies and time zones can be extremely difficult to keep pace. To effectively manage the transition, it is really important to understand where customers and partners are in the transition cycle and when they are expected to complete in order to predict impact to revenue and resources needed for exception handling and to hold the sales teams accountable for vendor changes.

For a recent large $9B divestiture, this was managed as follows:

- Day-by-day burn down charts to indicate when customers and partners would migrate over
- Web-based tool that was accessible by the central project management team, region leaders, and the sales teams—included current state, projected closure dates, and any impediments to transition on an account by account basis
- Regular updates to the regional sales leadership and EVP of sales in order to drive momentum when lacking

Business engagement and ownership Comprehensive business engagement is critical to drive to successful outcomes. The account and sales leaders are the first line of defense with customers and partners and are primarily accountable to explain the transition journey to customers and partners, provide them with the necessary information needed to enable the transition, and ensure that the transition is completed within the required time. But business engagement goes well beyond this tactical execution:

- Building a prioritized plan: Ensuring that resources are focused on where they count most, e.g., large customers or near-term pipeline, difficult customers, customers and partners that are strategically important, etc.
- Driving the call to action: Sales teams are more liable to respond to the call to action when it comes from within their management chain.
- Focusing on the quarter: Ensuring that customer and partner readiness activities align with the quarter timing and focus.
- Making difficult trade-offs: Balancing investment asks from customers and partners with the strategic importance of those customers and partners. For example, in a recent technology sector separation, a top 20 customer voiced significant concerns and made a number of asks, ranging from investments to complete vendor setup, parent company guarantees as they were uncertain of the ability of the newly separated company to seamlessly conduct business, and a request to review detailed and confidential financial information to assess the financial viability of the new business. In this particular case, the solution involved significant interaction and engagement between executive sponsors of both companies and sharing of critical/confidential information to get to a positive outcome.

Risk mitigation The goal of 100% customer and partner separation by Day 1 is usually difficult to achieve because of the complexity and the volume of contracts. In light of this, it is prudent to establish a risk mitigation strategy—which includes the ability to receive and process misdirected payments or misdirected orders for contracts that are delayed or permanently stranded. Typically, it is just a question of time to get delayed vendor setup. However, occasionally, a few contracts will become permanently stranded, meaning that they are not going to set up the new company for future business. In such cases sub-contracting is an option that can be leveraged in order to not lose the business related to those contracts, if both parties agree.

19.3   Creating Incremental Value Through Preferred Partnerships

One of the largest sources of value generation from separations comes from structuring preferred vendor agreements between both companies. These are essentially commercial agreements between both companies and, although materially accretive for each company, are difficult to negotiate because of different priorities and conflicts of interest. The value of these arrangements can vary greatly depending on the size of the business and the synergistic go-to-market opportunities. For example, for two similarly sized deals, the value of commercial agreement struck ranged from >$1B to ~$200M due to the size and nature of the business.

Partnership and reciprocity This is perhaps the most material principle in establishing mutually beneficial commercial agreements. When both parties agree to create a symbiotic agreement in the spirit of reciprocity, agreement can be reached effectively and quickly. However, if the spirit of partnership and reciprocity is breached, mutually beneficial agreements can be extremely difficult to reach.

To MFN or not to MFN is the question Agreements can be structured as MFN (most favored), similarly situated or arms-length agreements. Most favored clauses can drive significant synergistic goals but would have commercial impact (e.g., margin impact) to both sides as the agreement helps achieve joint goals in a mutually beneficial and friendly way. There are limitations to what MFN clauses can solve for because the benefits of those arrangements could legally extend to other contracts with MFN clauses. Hence, MFN clauses must be crafted with a lens to overall financial exposure while solving for shared goals.

At the other end of the spectrum, arms-length agreements may solve for the commercial impacts of MFN terms but also represent the loss of a unique, once-in-a-lifetime separation opportunity to create unique and mutually beneficial goals.

Establish a clear legal framework Establish and agree on the framework of legal documents quickly as this will determine how and where energy is spent, for example, how much negotiation should occur at each individual statement of work versus the overall master commercial agreement.

Establish an effective governance and operating model Determine which decisions and choice points should be made centrally as part of the master agreement versus what decisions should be made in a disaggregated manner by each product owner.

Understand the balance of trade Usually at the starting point of the negotiation, it is critical to understand what intercompany relationships exist pre-separation and are material to business in the future and where future sources of value can stem from. The process of creating an inventory of existing intercompany relationships can be extremely time-consuming and error-prone as some of these relationships may be embedded deep within the operations of the organization. Therefore, plan for adequate time to conduct an effective sweep, and anticipate needing change control as more relationships are unraveled. Having visibility into both revenue and margin impacts of the balance of trade can provide significant leverage. For example, are you selling products that are strategically important to the other company but do not generate material revenue or margin for you?

Plan for today with a view of the future Forecasts are often more optimistic than reality. Create the balance of trade and negotiating basis with the current state in mind, but create incentives to drive future strategic goals and targets. For example, will increasing margin drive increased revenue for certain strategic products? Are there revenue commitments that may be possible with a different margin arrangement?

Understand the tradeoffs Establish scenarios with different optionality, and use these as a mechanism to horse-trade against different positions. Have a view of a preferred and balanced option that would be mutually beneficial to both parties, and drive toward that.

Establish a timeline As in the case of any other M&A planning and execution activity, have a clear sequence of steps with dates and owners for each. Leverage the timeline as a road map to get to closure, but do not make concessions to adhere to the timeline. The timeline should serve as a guidepost to determine the degree of progress made.

19.4   Re-aligning Partnerships

As companies divest and downsize, they will need to make strategic decisions to recalibrate and balance their go-forward portfolio with their partners. In most cases, several legacy relationships will no longer make sense following an analysis of revenue, margin uplift, company adoption, etc. To effectively determine the go-forward approach to partnership realignment requires intimate knowledge of pre-deal relationships, including the variables involved with shifting intercompany trade agreements to commercial agreements.

- *Revenue.* The proportion of top-line revenue enabled by a partner is the single most important piece of information used in deciding which partners to prioritize. Sales enabled by such partners are generally incorporated into the revenue synergy plan and lend some degree of predictability to sales forecasts post-Day 1. Preserving these partnership relationships should be a top priority.
- *Strategic direction.* Implicit in the decision to divest a business unit is the idea that some opportunity or organizational shift is worth pursuing. Partner relationships need to be evaluated with respect to this new direction (i.e., new customer profiles, different product *portfolios*, geographic rebalancing).
- *Complexity.* Complex partnerships, for example, depend on how partners tend to buy products (i.e., centralized versus decentralized) or their reach (i.e., regional versus global), which may impact the demand for attention and resourcing. Such partnerships should be considered in the context of the company's long-term objectives and be prioritized accordingly.

Using these factors to evaluate partnerships will help optimize the customer and partner portfolio of the respective companies.

19.5   Conclusion

Managing partnerships with customers and suppliers, though a challenge, is essential to a successful divestiture. It is valuable to maintain business continuity and critical to create a foundation for long-term growth.

Case Study: 19

Background

A Fortune 100 technology company with $33 billion in revenue was pursuing two simultaneous divestitures and needed support managing customer and partner relationships and contracts.

Challenges

The company had thousands of customer and partner accounts between the two divested business units, and the account setup process was heavily dependent upon information not entirely in the company's control (e.g., tax registrations). Timely setup of these accounts was critical in order to ensure that there was no disruption to business. Due to the dependency on external information and a short carve-out timeframe, the actual window to ensure customer and partner readiness was extremely narrow.

Approach

The company developed a strategy that prioritized key customers and partners and minimized disruption to the business. The core to this strategy was quickly assembling a customer and partner readiness (CPR) team. Initially, this team focused on the company's top 100 global partner and customer accounts, prioritizing these accounts for setup to minimize disruption to the business. Not all information required to set up partners and customers for success was within the company's control (e.g., updates to legal entity names); instead, the team focused heavily on factors within the company's control (e.g., vendor negotiations, legal support) to properly manage risks and timelines.

To further minimize risk throughout this process, the company developed two key tools for education and management: a webinar series and a customer/partner portal. The webinar series was targeted at account executives and focused on aligning all participants on how to communicate key divestiture information and the upcoming milestones for customers and partners, as well as how to address common concerns from partners. The webinars helped ensure that communication with partners was consistent and clear, thus boosting their confidence during the transition. The customer/partner portal was an externally facing website listing FAQs, country-specific vendor setup sheets listing the new legal entity information to enter into procurement portals, and timelines of changes during the divestiture.

The rubber hit the road in the months leading up to close and as readiness inched toward the 80% completion stage. Several large accounts requested for incremental asks to complete the process—parent company guarantees and investments, detailed walk-through of the process, requests for different terms, and in one case a request for detailed and confidential financial data. Through daily follow-ups, active engagement from the regions and business and sales team, and discussions between the C-suite of the newly formed entity and customers and partners, the team was able to drive closure to most accounts by close, leaving a handful of accounts as delayed at the end of close.

Finally, the team set up a process for misdirected cash and invoices to ensure business continuity for the few cases where vendor setup was behind schedule or where incorrect orders were placed after the close and despite vendor setup.

Impact/Results

The customer and partner readiness team was critical to successfully managing expectations and effectively communicating key information to relevant partners. By prioritizing the company's top 100 global accounts, the team ensured that the majority of revenue was closely monitored and top accounts were reassured about their relationship with the seller company and/or divested business. The customer/ partner portal facilitated the setup process by maximizing customer and vendor self-service while providing access to FAQs. This strategy allowed for successful customer/partner setup and minimized the impact of misdirected revenue.

Chapter 20
Managing the Application Separation Life Cycle

20.1 Overview

When a company announces a business divestiture or separation, the information technology (IT) applications that support its processes must be separated as well. The process of separating IT applications during a divestiture or separation is referred to as application separation. This chapter details the action necessary to successfully plan for and execute application separation.

A divestiture or separation relies heavily on application separation strategy and planning before initiating execution and hence requires a clearly defined application separation life cycle (ASLC). There are four overarching phases to the application separation life cycle:

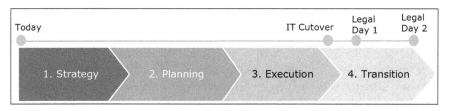

Fig. 20.1 The Four Phases of Application Separation Life Cycle (ASLC)

1. *Strategy*: The vision and guiding principles for application separation are estab-lished during this phase. Prioritization of additional requirements beyond the separation, such as regulatory requirements, is considered as well.
2. *Planning*: This phase consists of baselining the current application landscape, categorizing the comprehensive list of applications, evaluating the impact of application separation on current business processes within each function, and preparing the tools and processes necessary to initiate execution.

© Deloitte Development LLC 2018

J. Joy, *Divestitures and Spin-Offs*, Management for Professionals,
https://doi.org/10.1007/978-1-4939-7662-1_20

3. *Execution*: With a foundational strategy and planning in place, application separation execution can begin. Execution involves many activities within the following sub-phases of application separation:

- Requirements analysis
- Design
- Development
- Testing
- Cutover

4. *Transition*: During execution, some applications undergo "logical separation" as opposed to "physical separation." For example, some applications are separated as is using changes in access control (logical separation) as opposed to replicating entirely new instances of existing applications (physical separation). During this phase, logically separated applications are managed further. Additionally, all applications within the scope of the divestiture or separation are further evaluated for transformation or replacement by modern and lower cost alternatives.

The activities highlighted in the above phases will be described in further detail throughout this chapter. Several examples and leading practices from industry will also be shared. A strong understanding of all phases of the application separation process is vital to the smooth execution of a divestiture or separation of any size, scale, or complexity.

20.2   The Traditional Software Development Life Cycle (SDLC) Is Well Structured, But Is It Enough for Application Separation?

The traditional SDLC consists of six phases: requirements analysis, design, development, testing, deployment, and maintenance. Each phase serves as input for the next. Requirements analysis involves documentation and analysis of business and system requirements. These requirements are utilized to design and then develop a system in individual units. The system is then tested as a whole prior to deployment after which maintenance or support is provided in the future.

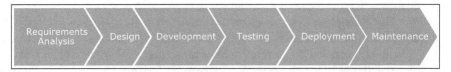

Fig. 20.2 The Traditional Software Development Life Cycle (SDLC)

The traditional SDLC was originally created for a stand-alone software implementation effort. Divestitures or separations require additional application strategy and planning activities for successful execution.

The application separation strategy must be clearly defined to address the nuances of the technology landscape in which the companies involved in the transaction—the seller company, the divested entity, and possibly the buyer company—will operate on or after Day 1. Sufficient planning is required to:

- Understand the current application landscape of the entities involved.
- Define how each application will be separated.
- Determine how each application separation will affect business processes.
- Prepare for successful execution.

Thus, in the context of a divestiture or separation, the traditional SDLC needs to be replaced by the ASLC.

The Application Separation Life Cycle (ASLC)

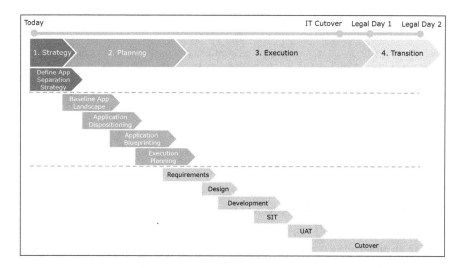

Fig. 20.3   The Application Separation Life Cycle (ASLC)

The application separation life cycle consists of four overarching phases—strategy, planning, execution, and transition. Each of these phases is further described in the sections below.

20.3   Phase I: Application Separation Strategy

An effective application separation strategy includes an approach that will not only minimize disruption to existing business processes but also reduce the risk, time, and effort required to separate applications prior to Day 1.

While the goal is to separate applications shared within the existing landscape, some applications may not be well positioned to support the entities involved in the transaction on Day 1. In such cases, separation serves as an opportunity to replace applications with lower cost and less complex alternatives that include better support (e.g., cloud-based applications). However, the majority of existing applications will be separated as is to accommodate an accelerated timeline. Enhancing the future state of the application landscape is considered a post-Day 1 activity.

The key question the application separation strategy must address is *will the majority of applications shared between the entities involved in the transaction be separated physically or logically?*

The summary below defines physical versus logical separation, as well as explains how each applies to a divestiture or separation:

Table 20.1 Sample Application Blueprinting Template

Shared application separation strategy	Applicable deal size and structure
Physical separation: complete separation of application functionality, data, and supporting infrastructure	• Separation of two large equally sized businesses • Example: goal is to create two stand-alone businesses that operate independently on Legal Day 1
Logical separation: partial separation of application functionality and data	• Divestiture of a smaller-sized business when compared to the original company • Example: company being divested may be merged with a buyer, requiring application separation during an interim or transitionary period

The application separation strategy forms the lens by which planning activities will be conducted during the next phase of application separation.

20.4   Phase II: Application Separation Planning

With an application separation strategy in place, it is time to plan for execution. Planning brings structure, order, and visibility to the application separation process. This phase results in a clear view of applications in scope for separation, business processes supported by each application, and dispositions (application separation options) assigned to each application to further categorize separation activities during execution.

Application separation planning activities are divided into the following phases:

Fig. 20.4 Application Separation Planning Activities

- *Baseline application landscape*: In this phase, a comprehensive list of applications is collected and categorized, resulting in an application inventory that serves as a central repository for application information throughout execution of separation activities.
- *Application dispositioning*: In this phase, application dispositions, which describe the ways in which applications will be separated, are defined. Additionally, applications are assigned to their appropriate dispositions.
- *Application blueprinting*: In this phase, IT and business units engage in blueprint interlock sessions to plan for separation activities in a way that minimizes their impact on business processes. This results in application blueprints that highlight the interaction between business processes and the applications that support them.
- *Execution planning*: In this phase, which occurs prior to executing application separation, project planning templates and tracking tools are set up to track the progress of separation activities.

Each of these phases is described in further detail in the sections that follow.

20.4.1 Baselining Application Landscape

A major obstacle faced while executing application separation is the lack of end-to-end visibility into the application landscape. Understanding the application footprint is often challenging for the following reasons:

- Absence of a centralized well-managed application repository
- Limited, incomplete, or inaccurate documentation describing application ownership, business criticality, application technology, usage, and functionality
- Incomplete understanding of application infrastructure mapping

A baseline understanding of the current application landscape will help execution teams make informed decisions while planning for execution. The phases below aid in mapping a strong application baseline landscape to avoid initiating application separation with little or no information about the current state of the company's application landscape.

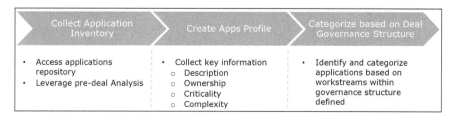

Fig. 20.5 Baselining Application Landscape

20.4.1.1   Application Inventory Collection

Teams should not reinvent the wheel when developing an application inventory. Most IT organizations maintain an internal repository of applications. If an application inventory already exists, it can be repurposed. If an application inventory does not exist, it must be built, and building an application inventory is an iterative process. Any and all pre-existing application information is collected from available sources, cleansed, and organized into a central repository.

During application inventory collection, all applications owned or managed by the company are identified. Some applications may be owned by the company but have limited IT involvement or support; these are referred to as shadow IT applications. Such applications were procured by the business without prior approval from IT, and a clear system of record and ownership may not exist. In large companies, the number of shadow IT applications is often comparable to the number of applications owned by IT. For example, a large technology company with 1900 IT applications also identified 1550 shadow IT applications in its technology landscape.

To help the business separate applications and identify IT dependencies, the IT team educates the company's business units on collecting a business-owned application inventory. It is important to note that the business is ultimately responsible for creating and managing execution plans for these applications in preparation for Day 1.

20.4.1.2   Application Profile Creation

The quality of information in the application inventory, not the quantity, drives effective decision making for application separation. While collecting too little information is not ideal, gathering too much information may lead to confusion. It is essential to create profiles for applications that provide just enough information to ultimately summarize their purpose. Listed below are some key attributes to include when creating application profiles:

Table 20.2 Application Profile Creation

Attribute	Description or example	Attribute	Description or example
Application inventory ID	Identifier issued to an application slated for separation	Function	Example: human resources, finance, supply chain
Application name	Name of the application	Supporting business process	Example: hiring, purchasing, pricing, order management
Application description	Description of what the application does	Risk category	Low, medium, high
Vendor name	Vendor name for the application, if applicable	Business criticality	Normal, mission critical, entity essential
Data center location	Data center where the application is hosted	Workstream	Workstream that owns the application
Estimated number of users	Number of users that currently use the application	Sub-workstream	Sub-workstream that owns the application
Complexity	High, medium, low	Business owner	Name of business owner
Approximate number of interfaces	Number of interfaces for the application	IT contact	Name of the key IT contact for the application
Country location	Country where the application is used	Business owner	IT team or business team that owns and manages the application
Authentication	Mechanism used by the application to authenticate users, e.g., Lightweight Directory Access Protocol (LDAP)	Authorization	Authorization policy used by the application to grant access to users, e.g., Active Directory(AD)

20.4.1.3   Categorization Based on Deal Governance Structure

Categorizing applications by "workstreams" defined within the deal governance structure helps to establish application ownership. Applications are further categorized by the business units they support in addition to the functions they enable to establish application usage. This helps in developing a comprehensive understanding of all applications before they are dispositioned.

20.4.2   Application Dispositioning

The application disposition provides the method by which the application will be separated on Day 1. There are typically between five and seven options for application disposition. Application disposition will ultimately determine whether, after separation, an application belongs with one of the companies involved in the transaction or should be shared by two or more entities involved in the transaction. Using a freshly categorized and profiled application inventory, business unit and IT owners should work together to determine the disposition for each application.

When considering the factors that contribute to application disposition, it helps to broadly categorize applications based on how the entities involved in the transaction will use them:

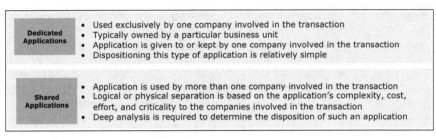

Fig. 20.6   High-Level Application Categorization

20.4.2.1   Defining Application Dispositions

While divestitures and separations vary in deal structure, complexity, and timeline, the range of options for application dispositions is generally constant. The table below provides a general range of application disposition options used for application separation:

Table 20.3 Application Disposition Definitions

Category	Disposition	Definition	Criteria
Dedicated	Retain	Application is retained by remaining company. No transfer of ownership is required	• Application used exclusively by one company • No shared data between the two companies • Minimal separation effort
	Give and go	Application is moved as is from current location to a target location	• Dedicated application is used exclusively by the other company • Ownership is transferred from one company to the other
Shared	Extract and retain	Application data is extracted and provided to one business, while the application is owned by the other	• Application functionality is not required by the business being divested or separated • Historical data may still be required
	Configure in place	Application shared between the separating companies is separated logically by configuration	• Application shared between the two companies • High complexity and hardware cost associated with creating two physically separate application instances • Single application instance shared by both companies on Legal Day 1
	Clone	Further divided into two categories: 1. Clone and go: Clone shared application completely with underlying data 2. Clone, cleanse, and go: Clone shared application and cleanse sensitive data	• Application is shared between the two companies • All data can be transferred from one company to the other • Losing data integrity is a key risk
	New build	An entirely new application is built for one of the separating companies to replace the existing application	• Application shared between the two companies • Complexity and cost to build are generally lower than the cost to separate • If needed, data is extracted, transformed, and loaded from legacy application

20.4.2.2 Assigning Dispositions to Applications

There is no one-size-fits-all approach to assigning dispositions to applications. Every approach to dispositioning may differ based on deal structure, regulatory requirements, historical data requirements, and data sensitivity, to name a few of the many factors. Additionally, initially chosen dispositions may change as new information is received over time. However, having too many factors may lead to unwanted complexity in determining dispositions. The following decision tree provides a framework for initial dispositioning.

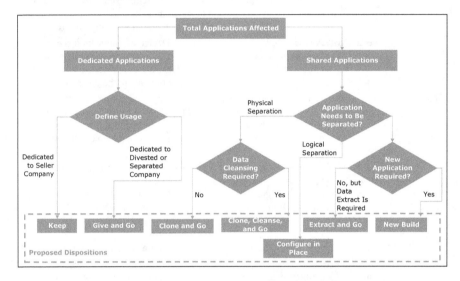

Fig. 20.7 Application Dispositioning Decision Tree

Although this framework will help determine the disposition of an individual application, it is essential to factor in additional dependencies when considering the spread of dispositions across the entire application landscape.

20.4.2.3 Key Considerations While Assigning Dispositions to Applications

1. *Align Dispositions with a Focus on Legal Day 1*
   The goal of application separation is to minimize disruptions to business processes on Day 1. Since application separation activities allow application functionality to be modified, many IT teams think of application separation as a means to achieve their future-state or end-state architecture goals. This approach can set application separation up for failure because future-state application architecture goals are rarely achieved within an accelerated separation or divestiture timeline. In practice, teams should only exercise the "new

build" disposition option as a last resort when there is absolutely no other option for application separation.

2. *Interlock with Upstream and Downstream Applications*

Applications do not operate in silos. They interact with other applications, thereby creating dependencies on each other for the flow of information before (upstream) or after (downstream) receiving data. The disposition of an application not only affects its path to Day 1 but also affects the path other applications take to get to Day 1.

For example, during the divestiture of a business unit at a Fortune 50 technology company, an order processing application was cloned and required more than ten interfaces to be rewired with surrounding systems. This not only increased the effort required for surrounding systems but also added complexity to testing and go-live.

3. *Dependency on Infrastructure*

Application separation can create additional costs for new IT infrastructure, depending on the number of physically cloned applications. A clone disposition is ideal if the application is portable and easily deployable to other locations. However, if the cloned solution requires impractical IT infrastructure or is cost prohibitive, configuring in place may be preferred as the application disposition.

4. *Going the Manual Route*

Sometimes it is best to disposition a shared application as "retain" or "give and go" even when the application will not solely be used by one company. For example, during the divestiture of a business unit at a large technology company, an invoicing application used in 27 countries across both the seller company and the divested entity was dispositioned as "retain," meaning the invoicing application would no longer support the invoicing processes of the divested entity post-Day 1. Why was this decision made?

The divested entity used the application to issue invoices to a handful of customers in Korea but recognized the cost of cloning the application far outweighed the benefit of supporting invoices for its customers. As an alternative, the divested entity decided to manually issue invoices to customers using a manual tool.

5. *Obtaining Sign-off from Both IT and Business*

Once the IT team initially dispositions applications, it is essential for the team to obtain sign-off from the applicable business units to help ensure alignment. It is not unusual for business units and IT to have multiple discussions to achieve consensus on application dispositions, which may slow down the momentum to initiate project execution. To expedite this, deep-dive sessions between the parties involved are encouraged. As a rule of thumb, execution-related effort for application separation must commence only after both IT and applicable business units sign off on the disposition for each application.

20.4.3   *Application Blueprinting*

After application dispositions have been confirmed by both IT and the applicable business units, the next step is to conduct application blueprinting. So far, the planning phase has focused on assigning dispositions to applications. Application blueprinting will help plan for the impact of application disposition on business processes supported by the application.

Blueprinting provides all teams (i.e., business units and IT) with a common understanding of the changes needed to achieve successful separation from a business process and application perspective. There are three sub-phases to application blueprinting as follows:

Fig. 20.8 Application Blueprinting Phases

20.4.3.1   **Document Business Processes by Function in Blueprinting Templates**

There are several functions within a business unit, including IT, human resources (HR), legal, treasury, finance, and procurement, among others. As a first step, IT and business unit teams should list detailed business processes associated with each function. These are usually captured in blueprinting templates at a level of detail consistent with the existing documentation within the company. While some companies use custom business processes to define the internal workings of their functions, others use standardized business processes. As a general rule, business process templates should capture three levels of detail to sufficiently plan for separation execution. Having identified the business processes within each function, the next step is to identify the applications that support them.

Table 20.4 Sample Application Blueprinting Template

Functional overview		Current process overview					Process detail		
Workstream	Sub-workstream	Process	Activity	Application name and ID	Day 1 disposition	Business requirements	Sensitive data elements	Geographies affected	Criticality
<Insert workstream name>	<List sub-workstream>	Provide a complete list of processes/ elements or major activities for functional area	Briefly describe how this process is currently performed	List key applications/ infrastructure to enable this process and a unique identifier for the application	<Day 1 disposition of the application>	Specific business requirement on how disposition should be carried out	Data elements that are sensitive per legal, regulatory, or business requirements	List the geographies/ countries affected	<High/ medium/ low>
Example									
HR	Organizational design	Experienced hire recruiting	Day 1 new hire training program	Application A (114389) Application B (114390)	Clone, cleanse, and go	Only extract employees that will belong to the buyer on Day 1	Personally identifiable information (PII), such as employee home address	Special consideration needed for Germany and France	High

20.4.3.2   Map Business Processes to Applications

Once all of the business processes are added to the blueprint templates for each function, business and IT teams meet to discuss how IT applications support business processes within each function. These meetings are called blueprint interlock sessions. For example, an application with a disposition of "clone," which supports the "hire-to-retire" business processes, is represented in a blueprint, along with its disposition as shown in Table 20.4 above. The impact of application separation on the business processes (hire to retire in this case) can be discussed in a blueprint interlock session, which is a joint session between IT and business teams.

20.4.3.3   Conducting Blueprint Interlock Sessions

Blueprint interlock sessions consist of one or more joint discussions between business units and IT. There are various objectives for an interlock session, but the guiding principle is to review and understand how application dispositions may affect business processes. The end goal of an interlock session is to de-risk the application separation and validate any assumptions. Blueprints are reviewed by function and compared against the application disposition to shed light on any gaps. These sessions also identify external dependencies when physical infrastructure, hardware, dependent systems, vendors, and contracts are discussed.

Although blueprinting interlock sessions are typically 1 or 2 days long, follow-up work is often required to finalize and align the blueprints. The ten tips provided here can help establish this alignment at a fast pace, so IT and business units can shift their focus to execution.

Ten Tips to Consider for Running a Successful Blueprinting Session:

1. *Conduct session dry runs in preparation for working blueprinting session.*
2. *Business unit and IT teams should be identified in advance to lead the discussion.*
3. *Prioritize applications that support critical processes.*
4. *Accelerate past lengthy conversations on issues by placing them in a parking lot.*
5. *When issues arise, assign owner(s) and due dates.*
6. *Separate what is required from what is convenient.*
7. *Identify what is NOT going to be done, such as not focusing on resource requirements, project costs, or financials.*
8. *Decisions made by the business unit and IT teams should be thought of as binding.*
9. *Have a notetaker to capture decisions, action items, and salient meeting minutes for publishing after the session.*
10. *Follow-up discussions will be required to keep track of open items until closure.*

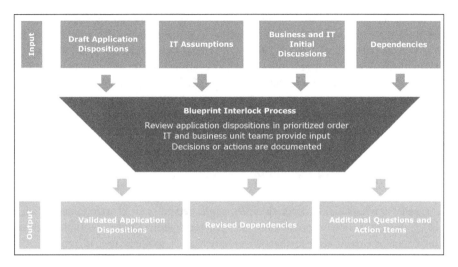

Fig. 20.9 Input and Output of Blueprinting Sessions

20.4.4   Develop Execution Plans

The next step after finalizing application dispositions and blueprints involves developing execution plans.

This phase includes the setup of the project execution templates and tracking tools necessary to measure execution progress and alert the IT and business unit teams of upcoming risks and issues. While the objectives are simple, the steps to effectively manage project planning and reporting are complex and further expanded upon in Chapter 22, "Managing IT in Divestiture: Orchestration, Instrumentation and Measurement."

20.5   Phase III: Application Separation Execution

Execution is the core of the redefined SDLC. The goal is to develop and deploy planned separation activities in a fixed timeframe to achieve application separation. Execution is divided into the following sub-phases:

20.5.1   Requirements Analysis

Requirements analysis for application separation relies heavily on application dispositions and application blueprints. Often, the timeline for requirements analysis overlaps with the planning phase of the separation process.

During the course of a divestiture, shifts in strategic priorities or regulatory policies may result in additional application separation requirements. For example, during the divestiture of a business unit at a Fortune 50 technology company, applications supporting federal agencies were logically separated from the commercial business units they supported to comply with federal policies. Such requirements are captured and executed in the forthcoming phases of the redefined SDLC in an accelerated timeline based on when the requirements are identified. Typically, such requirements affect a subset of the applications and not the entire application landscape.

20.5.2 Design and Development

Design for application separation is a slight departure from traditional software design. In a divestiture or separation, design for application separation is built based on application separation requirements which rely heavily on application disposition.

The development phase consists of making a set of application code changes required to execute application separation requirements and design which were previously aligned with the disposition of an application.

During the design and development phase, IT teams consider nuances of the business processes supported by each application to ensure that critical business functions are not disrupted by application separation. For example, a system supporting the order management process for the supply chain function may have a disposition of "configure in place." This system will need to process orders for two separating companies which will share a single application instance on Day 1. Orders which consist of a combination of products belonging to both separating companies, known as mixed orders, must be accounted for and separated as well. In such cases, IT teams often build an additional layer of logic within the application to address or block mixed orders during the time of the separation. Such complex changes are designed, developed, and tested comprehensively during application separation execution.

20.5.3 Testing

Testing for separation consists of the following steps:

- Identifying testing scope and approach
- Baselining testing applications timelines and cycles
- Clarifying key responsibilities
- Establishing entry and exit criteria
- Creating and executing test cases

The key difference between the traditional SDLC and the ASLC lies in what is being tested. Application dispositions determine the testing scope and the type of testing required for each application. For example, some applications with a disposition of "give and go" may only require verification of rebranded screens, whereas applications with a disposition of "clone, cleanse, and go" may require comprehensive testing of end-to-end functionality as well as regression testing. Table 20.5 below describes how testing scope varies by application disposition. It is essential to note that testing for application separation is a broad concept, and activities specific to this phase are discussed in more detail in Chapter 23 "Testing: Making the IT Separation Foolproof."

Table 20.5 Application Disposition Testing Scope

Category	Disposition	Definition	Testing scope
Dedicated	Retain	Application is retained by remaining company. No transfer of ownership is required	• Rebranding changes where necessary • Access to the application • Connections with interfacing applications
	Give and go	Application is moved as is from current location to a target location	• Rebranding changes where necessary • Access and navigation within the application • Connections with interfacing applications • Automated processes executed in a batch
Shared	Configure in place	Application shared between the separating companies is separated logically by configuration	• Rebranding changes where necessary • Access and navigation within the application • Connections with interfacing applications • Automated processes executed in a batch • Data integrity and separation
	Extract and retain	Application data is extracted and provided to one business, while the application is owned by the other	• Rebranding changes where necessary • Access and navigation within the application • Data separation, cleansing, and integrity • Connections with interfacing applications • Automated processes executed in a batch • End-to-end process testing
	Clone	Further divided into two categories: 1. Clone and go: Clone shared application completely with underlying data 2. Clone, cleanse, and go: Clone shared application and cleanse sensitive data	
	New build	An entirely new application is built for one of the separating companies to replace the existing application	• Same as extract and retain and clone • Regression test to validate customizations to the new application • Stress and performance testing of the new application and associated hardware

20.5.4   *Cutover*

In the context of application separation, cutover refers to the final set of activities and processes involved in bringing logical or physical separation to fruition. This is the final phase prior to which application separation goes "live" and requires a life cycle of its own. Chapter 24, "Cutover: Getting Ready for the Launch" dives deeper into this topic," dives deeper into this topic, but at a high level, the cutover life cycle is divided into three sub-phases:

- Pre-cutover execution
- Cutover execution
- Post go-live

Pre-cutover execution focuses on planning efforts to support cutover window activities. Cutover execution is the most important phase and encompasses the activities required to separate applications belonging to the seller company from those of the divested entity. Post go-live ensures systems are stable and business processes are running as per plan.

20.6   Phase IV: Application Separation Transition

An application with a disposition of "configure in place" often requires a sizeable amount of transitionary effort post-Day 1. Since these applications are not physically separated from the ground up, the same application instance is used by both the seller company and the divested entity, and this is documented contractually during the course of the divestiture. The application is utilized as a service from seller to buyer, or vice versa, and to manage these services, both the buyer and seller must create transition service agreements (TSAs).

Applications that need TSAs are generally highly complex and cannot be separated within the timeline of Day 1. However, TSAs usually end after a fixed-period post-Day 1, and managing transitions involves a unique set of complex activities. Chapter 30, "Transition Service Agreements (TSA): Approach to De-risk Divestitures," sheds more light on TSAs and their nuances.

Additionally, all applications within the scope of the divestiture or separation are further evaluated for transformation or replacement by modern and lower cost alternatives. Chapter 27, "Transform as You Separate," dives deeper into this topic.

20.7   Conclusion

After describing the unique set of activities required for successful application separation, there is no doubt that application separation requires a redefined SDLC. It is also evident that the application separation process consists of several complex activities spread out across four phases—strategy, planning, execution, and transition. The application separation process provides a structured approach to help ensure that all entities involved in the transaction are set up for success on Day 1.

In a few phases of the application separation process, the underlying sections are addressed in more detail in the forthcoming chapters. It is also important to note that successful application separation is heavily dependent on IT security and infrastructure, concepts that are addressed later in this book.

Case Study: 20

Background

When a large technology corporation announced that its business units will be separated into two stand-alone entities, the information technology (IT) applications that supported its processes are needed to be separated as well. The company had $20B+ in revenue and consisted of several functions and business processes supported by 2000+ IT applications. Application separation at this scale needed to overcome a series of challenges prior to Day 1.

Challenges

1. A system of record for application separation did not exist. The current system of record for applications was inadequate, contained outdated information and wasn't set up for application separation as a tool. Teams executing the transaction had little or no visibility into the application landscape as a whole.
2. Application ownership was unclear, as teams were unaware of which organizations or business functions were supported by each application. Furthermore, ownership defined within the current system of record was not aligned with transaction governance structure.
3. Ownership of business-owned applications was not clear as well. In addition to existing IT applications, 1000+ business applications were identified and needed to be separated.
4. There was ambiguity in application separation strategy, specifically in the following areas:
   (a) A standard list of options clearly describing the methods by which applications can be separated did not exist.
   (b) For the vast majority of applications that were shared between the separating companies, there was uncertainty in whether they will be separated physically (e.g., creating a clone) or separated logically (e.g., user access changes).
   (c) The impact of application separation on existing business processes was unknown.

Approach

1. An application inventory was set up as a separate tool to baseline the application landscape. A dedicated team was created to manage and refine the new application inventory.
2. Applications were categorized based on workstreams and sub-workstreams defined as part of the separation governance structure, and a single owner was identified for each application.
3. Business-owned applications were identified and tracked separately. These applications were separated by the functional teams that owned them.
4. Ambiguity in application separation strategy in each area was addressed:

   (a) Application dispositions were defined, which consisted of a range of options for separating each application with detailed descriptions and application criteria.
   (b) Guidelines were provided to prescribe when shared applications should be separated physically or logically. For example, applications were cloned when complete separation of application functionality, data, and supporting infrastructure was required. This is more common during the separation of two equally large-sized companies into two stand-alone entities that operate independently as opposed to the divestiture of a smaller-sized business unit.
   (c) Dispositioning exercises were conducted, and application dispositions were tracked within the newly set up application inventory.
   (d) Blueprinting sessions were conducted with IT and business teams to understand the impact of application separation on the business processes that were supported by each application.

Impacts/Results

1. Application dispositioning exercises led to structured execution planning, since project plans were created at an application level based on their dispositions.
2. Application inventory setup and dispositioning led to structured execution tracking and reporting, since execution progress was tracked based on application ownership and disposition.
3. Blueprinting sessions helped identify application separation business process impact, and the functional teams were aligned with IT prior to initiating requirements and design for execution.
4. Going into requirements and design, teams understood the methods by which applications were going to be separated, allowing for a smooth transition from planning to execution.
5. All IT applications were separated successfully and support the business processes of both stand-alone entities today.

Chapter 21
Simplifying IT Infrastructure Separation

21.1 Introduction to IT Infrastructure Separation

IT infrastructure separation is often considered a complex, time-consuming, and expensive component of a divestiture program.

An organization's IT infrastructure supports various day-to-day activities that are pivotal for business operations. All IT functions, including processes, applications, information security, and end-user operations, are heavily dependent on infrastructure components. Hence, preemptive planning to separate the IT infrastructure is paramount to the success of the divestiture, as well as the future IT infrastructure design of the divested entity (the "NewCo").

21.2 IT Infrastructure Separation Objectives

The key objectives for both the seller and buyer companies are to achieve Day 2 separation on schedule, at low cost, and with minimal impact on end users and the business. Meticulous planning and diligent execution of IT infrastructure separation activities contribute to the achievement of these objectives. IT infrastructure separation is often a central determinant of the cost and duration of transition service agreements (TSAs). Moreover, for the NewCo, IT infrastructure planning and strategy directly affect the stand-up of the new organization.

© Deloitte Development LLC 2018   241
J. Joy, *Divestitures and Spin-Offs*, Management for Professionals,
https://doi.org/10.1007/978-1-4939-7662-1_21

Table 21.1 Objectives of Infra Separation

Primary objectives of IT infrastructure separation
• Minimal impact to the parent company's IT infrastructure environment, business, and end users
• Seamless transition of IT infrastructure from the parent company to the NewCo
• Legal and contractual requirements for the implementation of Day 1 and Day 2 IT infrastructure separation
• Establishment of a stand-alone IT infrastructure by the NewCo on Day 2 that is completely separated from the parent company's IT infrastructure

IT infrastructure components are intricately intertwined; thus, effectively separating these components during a divestiture is essential to the success of the transaction. Every business-critical application and end-user service is dependent on the normal functioning of the IT infrastructure. Additionally, a divested

> • IT infrastructure separation costs are significant components of the total separation costs.
> • IT infrastructure separation costs depend on the scope, scale, and complexity of the transaction.

business unit often shares IT infrastructure services with the parent company even post-Day 1. Considering these challenges, achieving the objectives for IT infrastructure separation within a short timeline is highly challenging.

21.3   IT Infrastructure Separation Phases

A well-defined vision and strategy for IT infrastructure separation must be developed at the start of any complex divestiture or spin-off transaction. It is critical for the leadership of the IT infrastructure separation team to focus on all aspects of IT infrastructure separation, starting with IT blueprinting.

IT infrastructure separation should follow the following three-phased approach:

1. Strategy—Develop an IT infrastructure separation strategy and blueprint
2. Separation Planning—Identify and formulate IT infrastructure separation projects
3. Separation Execution—Execute Day 1 and Day 2 IT infrastructure separation plans

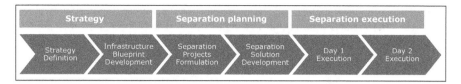

Fig. 21.1 IT Infrastructure Separation Phases

This chapter will take a deep dive into each of these three phases as well as discuss common IT infrastructure separation challenges and leading practices derived from a history of divestiture experiences.

21.4   Phase 1: Strategy

Defining the IT infrastructure separation strategy and vision up front is critical to the success of any divestiture or spin-off transaction.

21.4.1   IT Infrastructure Separation Strategy

Defining the IT infrastructure separation strategy helps establish the scope, schedule, resources, and transition costs essential for Day 1 readiness and transaction close. During this phase, the buyer and seller must envision their primary goals for the infrastructure separation on Day 1 and Day 2. The buyer and seller should determine the areas of the infrastructure that must be separated by Day 1, as well as whether the infrastructure should be fully separated or whether TSAs should be put in place to allow for partial separation of the infrastructure.

- A typical IT infrastructure separation strategy calls for the creation of separate and distinct IT environments for the parent company and NewCo, while maintaining shared domains for shared services and TSA obligations.
- Select non-shared services and applications that present minimal risk to the parent company should be separated and migrated into NewCo's hosting facility prior to Day 1.

21.4.2   Key Activities for the Strategy Phase

- *Define the End State*
  - Strategize the end-state layout of the IT infrastructure for the NewCo—the point at which the divested business unit is completely separated from the parent company.

- The type of divestiture, which is determined during the due diligence phase (i.e., before deal signing), plays a significant role in defining how the IT infrastructure will be separated.

• *Common Types of Divestitures*

Table 21.2   Types of Divestiture

Type of divestiture	IT infrastructure separation strategy
Carve-Out: A company divests a business unit to a strategic or financial buyer **Carve-Out**	• Key IT infrastructure is separated from the parent company and maintained by the divested business unit • A strategy is developed to merge the divested business unit's IT infrastructure with the buyer's IT infrastructure • A one-way Active Directory (AD) trust may be put in place between the parent company and the carve-out entity to allow infrastructure functions to work on Day 1
Spin-Off: A company divests a business unit that becomes an independent stand-alone entity **Spin-Off**	• It is critical to visualize the end state of the spin-off entity during the strategy phase as it must be able to operate independently by Day 2 • A two-way AD trust may be put in place between the parent company and the spin-off entity to fully stand up the spin-off entity's stand-alone IT infrastructure

• *Define IT Infrastructure Separation Goals for Day 1 versus Day 2*

Multiple factors affect the IT infrastructure components that must be separated on Day 1 (by legal close) versus Day 2 (full separation):

- Duration and time restriction between deal signing and Day 1.

- Legal, regulatory, and information security requirements for separation—certain IT infrastructure components—must be separated from the parent company by Day 1 to prevent NewCo from accessing confidential areas of the parent company's network.
- NewCo's business requirements may compel certain key IT infrastructure components to be provided by the parent company until NewCo's IT infrastructure is self-sufficient.
- Impact to end users—separation of IT infrastructure on Day 1 may disrupt the day-to-day business operations of both entities; thus, leadership may develop a phased approach to IT infrastructure separation to absorb the impact.

- *Fine Tune End-State Vision and Strategy*

  It is common to focus on Day 1 separation objectives; however, in order to develop a reliable IT infrastructure separation strategy, it is important to visualize the end state and plan accordingly during the strategy phase. During a divestiture, the parent company's infrastructure landscape does not go through significant transformation. However, the parent company must strategize to ensure that separation activities do not affect the rest of the business.

  The NewCo must develop a clear view of the key end-state IT infrastructure components it needs in order to function. The end-state vision should map the point of departure and the point of arrival for each infrastructure component.

- *Refine and Finalize the Critical Path to Divestiture*

  The key outcome of the strategy phase is to identify the critical activities required for IT blueprinting, Day 1 planning, and the development of separation plans. Both the parent company and the NewCo should collaborate to determine these critical activities.

- *Estimate High-Level Costs and the Divestiture Timeframe*

  Overall separation costs and timeline requirements are critical in determining the IT infrastructure separation strategy for Day 1. Due to the complexities related to the business, regulations, and time constraints, IT infrastructure separation on Day 1 should meet basic contractual requirements, while post-Day 1 IT services must be defined in a TSA.

21.4.3   IT Infrastructure Blueprint Development

Key Deliverable The IT blueprint is one of the most critical outputs of the pre-Day 1 planning phase. The IT blueprint is utilized throughout the course of the IT infrastructure separation and captures the current-state infrastructure details of the parent company and maps them to the Day 1 strategy and end-state vision.

> The IT blueprint outlines the full scope of IT infrastructure services required by the NewCo. Each service must be analyzed to determine whether it can be separated by Day 1 or whether a TSA will be required for continued use.

Facilitates Day 1 and Day 2 Scope and Decisions IT blueprints provide a holistic view of all the IT components that need to be separated, as well as the extent of separation required for Day 1 and the end state.

Provides Guidance for Identifying Shared Versus Dedicated IT Infrastructure Services The IT blueprint development process helps develop an action plan to help ensure an issue-free Day 1 and minimal user impact related to separation activities. Details gathered during the IT blueprint phase also help the IT separation team understand the infrastructure services that are shared across business units versus infrastructure services dedicated just to the NewCo. This information is critical to finalizing plans for Day 1 and Day 2 and to develop TSAs.

A typical IT blueprint captures the following:

Current-State Landscape	**As-Is Information**
• IT components such as data center, network, and end-user computing • Sub-processes • Shared or dedicated IT services • Vendors used	• As-is scope of services • Critical cross-dependencies between applications and business functions • Dependencies affecting in-flight projects
IT Infrastructure Separation Options and Dependencies for Day 1 and Day 2	**Cost and Separation Projects**
• List of Day 1 and Day 2 separation options • Preferred Day 1 and Day 2 options • Critical Day 1 and Day 2 dependencies • TSA requirements	• Base costs and run costs • Project charter and corresponding options analysis • Proposed point-of-arrival solution

Key Considerations for Developing an IT Blueprint

• Developing the IT blueprint, although it is a joint deliverable, requires significant commitment from the parent company's IT team since most of the data gathered relates to the current-state IT infrastructure.
• It is critical that key stakeholders and current-state IT infrastructure leaders provide approval before proceeding to the planning phase.
• The Day 2 (end-state) strategy must be determined for each IT component during the IT blueprinting process in order to identify which IT infrastructure services will require TSAs post-Day 1 and how long after Day 1 the separation will be finalized.
• When estimating run costs, consider the dis-synergies resulting from the separation, including additional circuit costs, separate data centers, and separate directories.

21.5   Phase 2: Separation Planning

21.5.1   Separation Project Formulation

The goal of separation planning is to identify the separation projects required to successfully separate the IT infrastructure in accordance with the scope plans for Day 1 and Day 2. Key activities include:

1. Identifying and prioritizing projects based on identified scope and the IT blueprint
2. Assigning project managers and resources from the parent company and NewCo to each project
3. Determining key dependencies with non-IT infrastructure projects
4. Determining interdependencies among infrastructure projects
5. Determining the sequence of projects to develop a high-level road map and program milestones

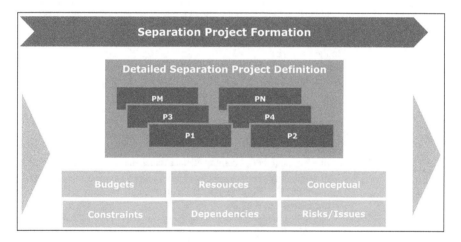

Fig. 21.2   Separation Project Formation

The desired outcome of the separation project formulation phase is presented in Fig. 21.2.

Creating project plans is essential for IT infrastructure separation. In particular, upstream and downstream dependencies must be considered, especially since some of the dependencies may involve external vendors or teams outside of the IT infrastructure space.

Further details around project planning and reporting for divestitures can be found in Chapter 22, "Managing IT in Divestiture: Orchestration, Instrumentation, and Measurement."

21.5.2   Developing Separation Solutions

• *Comparing Solutions Based on Various Dependencies*

IT infrastructure separation often involves dependencies with other separation workstreams (i.e., human resources), which increases the need to get it right. When planning for IT infrastructure separation, the entities involved should consider the type of divestiture involved—carve-out or spin-off—to determine the impact on the parent company's current-state IT infrastructure and the NewCo's future-state IT infrastructure.

• *Constraints that Influence Finalization of Solutions*

Some core infrastructure components to consider in a divestiture include:

Table 21.3   IT Infrastructure Considerations for a Carve-Out

Core infrastructure component	Divestiture considerations
Networks	• Will NewCo need to change IP addresses? For carve-outs, are there overlaps with the buyer? • Are facility changes needed for comingled sites and what is the impact to the network? • Are external and internal domain name system activities required for separation?
Data center	• What is the data center strategy for NewCo (i.e., cloud, on-premise, colocation)? For carve-outs, how does the chosen strategy integrate with the buyer's strategy? • How comingled are the data centers and what will be required to separate them? • Will a large number of comingled data centers have an impact on TSAs?
End-user computing	• Will each entity keep its existing directory services and establish a trust connection? For carve-outs, what timeframe will directory services integration occur (i.e., Day 1 or Day 2)? • What is the email/collaboration strategy for NewCo (i.e., O365, on-premise)? • Will users keep their existing workstation assets and receive new images? • Will users need new mobile devices or need to install software on their existing devices?

• *Using Options Analysis to Determine the Preferred Execution Option*

Options analysis allows the IT separation team to develop up to three solutions for each separation project. For example, an options analysis for wide area network (WAN) acceleration may include duplicating the current-state environment or selecting a more cost-effective WAN acceleration solution. The criteria commonly evaluated for each option include:

– Estimated time to deploy the solution
– Costs (one time and recurring)

- Items in and out of scope
- Benefits and risks
- Alignment with guiding principles for the program

- *Key Infrastructure Separation Projects*

    A few infrastructure separation projects have significant downstream dependencies and impact overall TSA exit timelines and, thus, require significant effort and long lead times to plan and strategize. These are classified as "key infrastructure separation" projects; some of the common examples are:

    (a) Authentication and authorization of IT infrastructure
    (b) Data center and IT infrastructure readiness
    (c) Local area network (LAN)/wide area network (WAN) separation
    (d) Unstructured data separation

    This section provides insight into key infrastructure separation projects, as well as presents common pitfalls and considerations.

(a) *Authentication and Authorization for IT Infrastructure and Applications*

    During IT separation (Day 1 and Day 2), the first priority for leadership is to ensure that NewCo's access to key applications and infrastructure services is not impacted. This is enabled through proactive planning and implementation of Day 1 solution for directory services such as Active Directory (AD).

    Directory services (AD) is the core of an organization's IT infrastructure landscape, providing two crucial services—a secure authentication platform and enforcement of policies. Authentication and authorization are required to verify user credentials and grant access to an entity's resources.

    Hence, implementation of NewCo's directory services (AD) infrastructure and AD Domain is typically the first critical path milestone toward separation of overall infrastructure services or applications. It is preferred for NewCo to build a greenfield AD infrastructure and a new Domain and migrate RemainCo user accounts and workstations, servers, etc. to the NewCo's Domain. Migration of directory objects is time-consuming and requires meticulous planning. Until full separation of infrastructure and applications (between Day 1 and Day 2, synchronization with RemainCo's Directory Service is maintained through a trust. Trust between domains is maintained to allow authentication and synchronization of accounts and attributes between domains.

    Implementing a solution for directory services (AD) by Day 1 is a critical predecessor to the advancement of other infrastructure separation events like end-user computing, collaboration tools, and even separation of applications. Additionally, directory services (AD) are a key dependency to ensure successful testing of Day 1 NewCo applications, in order to facilitate test user and machine accounts in the new domain.

    Considering criticality of establishing directory services, it is important that NewCo's data center and network connectivity between two companies are in place to host or support NewCo's directory service.

Due to the impact this key infrastructure project has on other workstreams, a Day 1 strategy must be defined in early stages of IT separation planning. Successful separation of directory services and seamless access to applications primarily depends on development of cross-company forest and domain trust blueprint, finalization of end state of the directory services (AD) environment for Day 1 and Day 2, and identification of cross-company application access blueprint.

The common pitfalls and considerations associated with this key project are:

- *Underestimating Cost to Stand Up of New Directory Services (Active Directory, AD) and Migration to New Domain*
  Directory services (AD) implementation, establishing of trust, and domain controllers in various geographic regions should be considered in hardware, software, and resource cost estimates for Day 1 and Day 2. Estimates should include the costs to migrate applications, end users, workstations, and hardware to the new environment.

- *Lack of Detailed Logistics Planning for User and Workstation Migrations*
  User and workstation migrations are typically the most complicated and time-consuming activities for separation due to their high impact on business and end users. Detailed logistics planning and early alignment with business stakeholders is key to helping ensure the timely completion.

- *Implementing Security Controls During Directory Services (AD) Trust*
  Security measures and compensatory controls must be implemented prior to activating trust between two organizations. Third- party tools can be used to accomplish this. The CISO may require constant monitoring and logging of data to ensure only authorized accounts have access to the parent company's IT environment.

(b) *Data Center and IT Infrastructure Readiness*

If the parent company owns or leases its own data center, it is important to determine how to split the data center between the parent company and the NewCo. This will depend on the terms of the transaction and how the applications are split across the data center. Once the data center separation strategy is determined, downstream considerations for servers, storage, and network must be mapped out. The common pitfalls and considerations associated with data center project are listed below:

- *Short Timeframe to Develop Facility and Hosting Strategy*
  Develop a facility and hosting strategy early due to long lead times to - procure hardware from various vendors, finalize contracts for hosting services, engage managed services and obtained required licenses. Data center facility stand-up becomes a quick dependency for other separation projects, but it is important to note that unless a clear data center strategy is defined the network design cannot be defined and finalized.
  Additionally, for most deals, due to legal constraints, servers and storage supporting the separation cannot be hosted on the buyer's facilities prior to Day 1.

- *Ability to Quickly Scale Server and Storage Availability*

The separation of shared applications may lead to an increased demand for servers and storage over a short period of time, hence rapid assessment of infrastructure support for shared applications is essential. An approach to quickly scale to meet server and storage demand must be defined.

If new hardware is required to meet server and storage demand, orders must be placed early to accommodate lead times. Off-premise solutions (i.e., cloud solutions) to build servers may be considered to scale quickly.

- *Underestimating the Effort Required to Move to the Cloud*
  Effort required to migrate from On Premise to Cloud solutions is often underestimated. Additional time must be factored into the plans to configure and test the new environment. Be aware of public cloud limitations such as the operating systems supported by the cloud solution, regulatory limitations, and bandwidth requirements to move data.

(c) *Local Area Network (LAN)/Wide Area Network (WAN) Separation*

Data network separation, primarily LAN/WAN separation, is another key infrastructure separation project, especially due to the long lead times required to procure and turn on new circuits, complexity in design and execution, and large-scale impact to progress of other separation efforts. Detailed network designs, Day 1 transition plans, and Day 2 exit strategies for global networks must be developed at an early stage. Key stakeholders from both the parent company and the NewCo, including information security, legal, and IT infra-structure leaders, should approve network separation solutions prior to the detailed plan development.

Issues with network separations could cause breach of security, regulatory non-compliance, impact to business/users, disruption to business-critical appli-cations and services, and third-party connectivity issues. Due to the long time-frame to exit, data network separation often requires a TSA that will need to remain in place until all other dependent IT infrastructure and application are separated. The common pitfalls associated with this key project and how you can address them include:

- *Long Lead Times to Order Circuits and Network Equipment*
  New circuit and equipment requirements must be quickly identified and ordered to meet Day 1 and Day 2 timelines. Project plans must account for long vendor lead times. Alternative options should be considered to mitigate the need for new circuits by Day 1, for example logical separation of net-works instead of full network severance by Day 1, or using existing RemainCo network devices instead of new orders (through asset transfers).
- *Redundancies Related to Private IP Addresses*
  Assess the parent company's IP space and the acquiring entity prior to Day 1 to determine if there are private IP address conflicts. Network engi-neers must design to ensure there are no IP collisions or conflicts in the Day 1 or Day 2 solutions.

When developing a plan, consider the number of assets affected, level of effort required to update, as well as the impact on end users and the business. Any changes to IP addressing of assets.

- *Late Engagement with Legal and Information Security to Determine Network Separation Requirements*

  For LAN/WAN separation, engage Legal teams early to identify countries and regions in which physical network separation is required prior to Day 1. Certain countries have strict telecommunication laws that require separation solutions to adhere to specific guidelines, which must be considered during Day 1 and Day 2 solution development. For example, there are specific requirements for the distribution of VoIP traffic, proxy server location, and IP address registration.

- *Inadequate planning to implement firewall and manage firewall rules between the Parent Company and NewCo*

  Network traffic between ParentCo and NewCo should traverse firewalls to control and monitor user access during the TSA period (between Day 1 and Day 2). Access to ParentCo must be governed through proper firewall rule management. Firewall management process is complex and involves multiple stakeholder inputs such as Application owners, Business, Info Sec and Legal teams.

  The IT infrastructure separation team can add firewall rules as it goes through the software development life cycle and testing phase to allow controlled access to the parent company's environment.

(d) *Unstructured Data Separation*

Unstructured data is commonly generated when using end-user computing services such as email, collaboration tools, home drives, or other file-sharing mechanisms. Separating unstructured data is one of the key infrastructure separation projects due to the complexity as well as importance in dispositioning data between the parent company and the NewCo as well as classifying data as sensitive or nonsensitive. The common pitfalls and considerations associated with this key project include:

- *Underestimating the Effort Required to Separate Unstructured Data*

  Separation of unstructured data is complicated due to the complex entanglement of permissions, ownership and usage. Tools available in the market cannot be utilized to identify and classify unstructured data ownership.

  Pre-Day 1 Legal agreements must be created about data ownership, classification and data transfers. These agreements should be guide the solutions for separation of unstructured data. Logically separate data, if physical separation is not possible by Day 1.

- *Delayed Alignment with Business, Legal, and Information Security*

  Solutions for unstructured data related to migration of collaboration tools (e.g. SharePoint), file shares, and email, should be aligned with Business, legal, information security and respective technology owners. Alignment of these solutions are a rigorous time consuming process and require detailed analysis, hence efforts should be initiated during early strategy/planning stages.

21.6   Phase 3: Separation Execution

21.6.1   Day 1 Execution

Once the Day 1 approach is determined, the execution phase begins, which is outlined in this section.

- *Requirements*

  The requirements for execution of each separation project will be defined by the transaction. During this phase more detailed infrastructure separation requirements are gathered from IT, the business, the NewCo, and the acquiring entity, as applicable. Some of the key questions to answer include:

  - What is the scope of affected items (i.e., number of users, assets, applications, sites)?
  - What are the upstream and downstream dependencies?
  - Are there any business-mandated requirements or constraints?
  - What is the high-level integration strategy?
  - What are the implications for Day 1?

- *Design and Build*

  During the design phase, a detailed design is created for the Day 1 separation approach, which includes design artifacts that vary based on the infrastructure separation solution. The project plan, resourcing, and budgeting should be determined based on the design. During the build phase, changes planned during the design phase are implemented. Similar to design, build activities vary based on the scope of separation projects.

- *Test*

  Compared to application separation, testing is more limited for IT infrastructure separation projects. Unit and integration testing are common, with a few projects requiring user acceptance testing (UAT). End-user facing projects typically require UAT to verify the impact on end users before cutover.

  The scope of testing performed prior to Day 1 is limited by legal requirements. Tests requiring connectivity to the acquiring entity must be vetted by the legal team. As a result, comprehensive connectivity testing may not be possible until Day 1. Activities specific to this phase are discussed in greater detail in Chapter 23, "Testing: Making the IT Separation Foolproof".

- *Cutover*

  In the context of IT infrastructure separation, cutover refers to the final set of activities required for separation. In IT infrastructure separations, end-user communication prior, during, and after cutover is important due to user impact.

  From a change management and operations perspective, it is important to prepare for an increased volume of IT changes to support the transaction. Also, additional coordination with end users and vendors may be required, particularly for end-user facing projects. Chapter 24, "Cutover: Getting Ready for the Launch," dives much deeper into this topic.

21.6.2   Day 2 Execution

The key objective for Day 2 is to successfully exit all IT infrastructure TSA obligations and operate on independent infrastructure services and platform. During the period between Day 1 and Day 2, multiple infrastructure projects are executed to gradually phase out the use of shared IT infrastructure as services and systems are migrated. As infrastructure services are separated from the parent company during Day 2 execution, a new IT infrastructure platform is progressively established for the NewCo, or, based on the type of separation, the buyer starts supporting the IT infrastructure requirements of the separated business unit. Hence, Day 2 requires meticulous solution development which eventually shapes the infrastructure of the separated company.

21.7   Conclusion

IT infrastructure separation planning and execution are important to help ensure a successful separation. The separation project timelines vary significantly. Some projects require quick execution early in the transaction timeline, such as implementing server environments to enable applications, while other projects require a longer timeframe for execution, such as network (LAN/WAN) separation. IT infrastructure separation projects have direct impact on business and end users, which not only adds to the complexity in execution but also demands intricate planning and coordination with key stakeholders through all phases.

Case Study: 21

Background

A Fortune 100 global banking and financial services company had a need to divest its credit card business and required restructuring of its data center infrastructure to support for the carve out of all core data center, network/security infrastructure, and application components to enable the successful transition of TSAs. Scope included the following:

- Support the transition of the credit card portfolio.
- Ensure that IT operations is managed according to performance-level agreements.

- Support RemainCo corporate card services for commercial/wholesale banking clients and retail and small business cards.
- Support the transition of 6,000 organizational resources.
- Build a state-of-the-art disaster recover (DR) data center.

Challenges

There were numerous challenges with a divestiture this size including coordinating the migration dates into a new data center without disrupting the day-to-day business operations. Initial discovery showed inconsistencies with the data coming from multiple sources, resource constraints, the aggressive timelines of the TSA exits, and the transfer of assets (physical and people). Even with these challenges, focus could not be lost to achieve the following:

- Maximize the number of systems and applications that can be separated by Legal Day 1 (LD1).
- Minimize the timeframe to complete remaining separation activity.
- Remove as much liability as possible from both companies.
- Identify cross-functional dependencies to ensure full separation.
- No impact to any businesses during separation activity.

Approach

Divestitures typically involve many parts of an organization where costs and timelines can be significant; therefore, a rigorous approach is necessary to architect, plan, and execute the effort. Our application and data center migration approach was to ensure business-aligned IT. The proven migration dimensions provided the framework for validating the proposed strategy to ensure industry leading guiding principles for successful migrations.

Impact/Results

The results were incredible and there was not a single disruption to the business. Overall, there were ~10 data centers that were divested (partially or fully). A new data center was built to support the divesting companies IT operations; 12,000 physical assets and 300 IT employees transferred; processed 6,000+ change orders; migrated 1,700+ applications, 10,000 active directory groups, 8,500 mail and domino access groups, and 3,000 assets within the divested company; data separation of 1,200 (500 gb) physical tapes, 1,800,000 tape volumes (evaluated), 750,000 tape volumes (identified/copied), and 1,000,000 DASD files (identified/copied); developed 3 cross-company secure networks; segmented primary and backup data centers; evaluated 300,000 lines of traffic traversing through the firewalls; analyzed 600 firewall rules and successfully decommissioned the rules upon exit; and built 585 database instances, 100 FTP database instances, and consolidated 200 SQL licenses.

Chapter 22
Managing IT in Divestiture: Orchestration, Instrumentation, and Measurement

22.1 Standardized Tracking

During a divestiture there are several key components that need to be managed at both the executive and project levels. Teams should take a structured and standardized approach to carving out the business unit to ensure full separation and business continuity following the divestiture.

One major challenge is tracking the separation of IT applications. Management teams should identify high-level metrics relevant to the executive committee. These metrics should include project planning status categorized into logical groupings such as by business units or workstreams. The purpose of these metrics is to provide a clear indication of the health of the program on a frequent basis. Additionally, metrics should be tracked at the most detailed level, which would be at the level of each individual project plan; however, the presentation of these metrics must be rolled up to a few key areas in order to provide data to executives and draw meaningful conclusions about program health.

The IT portion of the divestiture must be broken down into small, digestible pieces of work. One approach is to leverage project management tools and create a project plan for each impacted IT application. The project plan is developed to define the scope of work and list of activities required to logically separate a given application from the remaining business, based on the disposition type. This approach will help ensure the necessary applications that are frequently tracked and separated from the existing entity on Day 1. However, simply having a project plan for an application will not provide a detailed view into the risks it poses to the divestiture or business continuity. It is imperative to consistently track the same elements across all project plans. Each project plan should have the same level 1 activities in order to implement executive-level program tracking. However, at the second or third level of detail of the project plan, each plan will have a different set of activities unique to a particular application. The project management tool is the most

© Deloitte Development LLC 2018
J. Joy, *Divestitures and Spin-Offs*, Management for Professionals,
https://doi.org/10.1007/978-1-4939-7662-1_22

effective way to focus on execution activities. The use of real-time reporting from project plans helps in tracking progress efficiently as data never lies.

Additionally, the project planning methodology must align with the timeline of the divestiture, the complexity of IT application separation, and the project managers' familiarity with various project planning approaches. For example, under the waterfall method, the management team identifies the key milestones that each plan will track as well as formulate a program-level timeline to track progress.

22.2   Project Planning Milestones

To maintain a granular-level view, a project plan should be developed for each application, rather than a group of applications. Under the waterfall method, standardized and relevant key milestones should be identified for each application. At the beginning of a divestiture program, a program timeline needs to be developed in order to help ensure that all IT activities are complete by Legal Day 1. In order to track to the program timeline, each high-level milestone is given a start and end date that each project plan will need to track to. For specific applications that have key dependencies on other business functions, an exception process will be required that rationalizes the need for modification of the timeline. The high-level milestones should include the following:

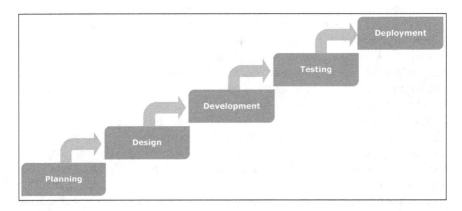

Fig. 22.1 Project Planning Milestones

1. *Planning*—This phase includes outlining the activities required to prepare the application for separation, such as developing a project charter that sets the tone for the work, finalizing the budgeting and resourcing needs required to separate the application, scoping the IT and business requirements, and receiving sign-off from all parties to move forward with the next phase of work. The planning phase also includes identifying the hardware and infrastructure required to run the application.

2. *Design*—This phase includes activities associated with finalizing design decisions, such as branding changes, the data retention and cleansing strategy, user access changes, and network considerations for specific applications. Design activities should be completed and signed off by both IT and business stakeholders to ensure alignment across the organization prior to the start of the development phase.

3. *Development*—The time required for the development phase is dependent upon the time needed to separate a given asset. For example, cloning an asset for the divested entity will require not only data cleansing but additional tasks such as building an entirely new instance of the application and associated interfaces.

4. *Testing*—The testing phase should follow a two-step approach. In a divestiture, it is important to have system integration testing (SIT) completed separately from user acceptance testing (UAT). Although both are part of functional testing, SIT focuses on testing the application as well as downstream and upstream integrated applications linked to the application, whereas UAT focuses on whether users will be able to work with the application. Reporting for this phase should include the tracking of defects and test case pass rates in order to assess and prevent potential problems that may arise during deployment.

5. *Deployment*—Deployment includes the key planning activities related to cutover as well as the activities required for the application to cutover on Day 1. Cutover is the process of executing a list of specific activities required for the ultimate logical separation of applications. A business continuity plan is required for each application, and IT should collaborate with the business to ensure that IT application separation will not negatively affect key business activities. Activities during the cutover execution phase are critical and should be completed in a sequential manner to ensure the application can go live within the allotted timeframe and the two entities can effectively separate on Day 1. Reporting for deployment activities requires very specific dashboards including reports to track critical path assets, issues and delays, timing of cutover activities, and high-level execution statistics by sub-workstream.

22.3 Deployment Tracking

The process of logically separating applications and completing activities for a successful go-live requires substantial coordination and tracking. The separation activities during a divestiture or spin-off can be executed in waves to ensure an approach where learnings and best practices can be leveraged from one wave to another. The deployment process includes a set of activities that are required to execute cutover for each application. Depending on the type of application and the disposition type, the activities can either be quite detailed or high-level if significant changes are not required.

During the period of deployment, which can last approximately one month for each wave depending on the dependency of critical path applications and the peak activity levels, accurate tracking of task progress as well as issues is imperative. There is a limited window of time for each application to start and complete their cutover activities and typically there are several applications that are dependent on data from other systems. A delay in one application can have a domino effect on other application cutovers if not managed effectively.

For this reason, real-time tracking at a task level and application level is required. The command center requires the use of several dashboards such as those that track task level completion, issue level tracking, and executive level reporting. The task level dashboards track detailed cutover tasks including the start time, percentage completion, and end time of the task in addition to the priority level of the application to which the task is tagged. This allows the command center to assess the importance and impact of a task that is running behind, based on the categorization and priority level of the application.

Effective issue tracking is also crucial to help ensure visibility and resolution. When an issue is logged, the application teams, command center, and infrastructure teams should have immediate visibility to conduct an impact assessment on upstream and downstream applications. Documentation of issues and the resolution plan leads into executive reporting during the deployment phase.

Based on the level of activity and number of critical assets going live on a given day, executive reporting is scheduled to brief all stakeholders, both IT and Business, on the progress of deployment. The daily reporting cadence, which at times can be twice per day, depending on the level of activity, is an important forum where issues can be discussed and the resolution can be aligned among the key IT and Business leads. In addition to the issues, the executives should be briefed on the health of the deployment activities and the progress that has been made across the group of assets within a given wave. A reporting template should be leveraged which includes high level statistics of cutover activities, a summary of the urgent or high issues aligned to each sub-workstream as well as any class issues identified. This should also include a deep dive into each of the critical path assets and the progress being made on the deployment of these applications. Stakeholders are particularly interested in the daily reporting of deployment because of the potential impact it can have on business operations and continuity. The goal is to have alignment between Business and IT on the cutover tasks as well as the timing of these activities.

22.4 Tracking Tools

A key leading practice for a divestiture is to ensure all teams involved are aware of the information available to them with regard to project progress as well as understand the source of truth for IT activities. Key tracking tools used in several divestitures include:

1. *Project Management Tool*—This is the foundational planning tool, such as Microsoft Project Server, for all IT aspects of a divestiture. This tool can house all application-specific project plans used by project managers on a daily basis

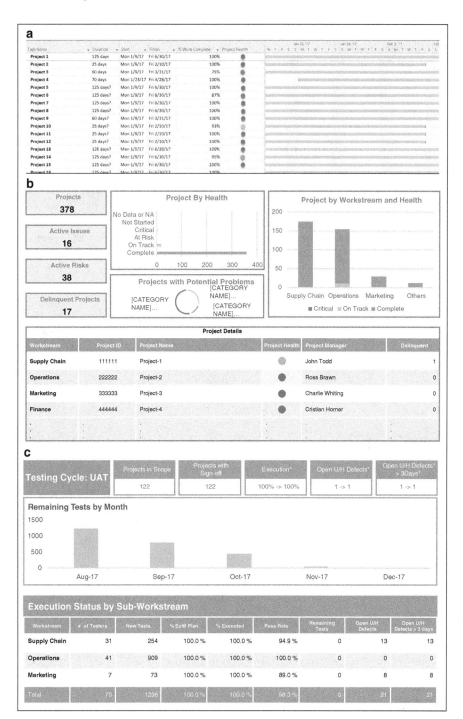

Fig. 22.2 Project Tracking Tools

and serve as the single source of truth for the underlying data, key milestones, and executive reports.

2. *Budgeting Tool*—Budgeting and resourcing tools, such as Project Portfolio Management, should be leveraged from the beginning of the IT separation process to track project-specific resources, such as employee time, and keep the program financially aligned with the budget allocated to each specific workstream. This tool tracks budget allocations against expenditures on a weekly basis, which can allow variances to be resolved quickly.

3. *Reporting Dashboards*—Project plan reporting can range from wide-ranging executive-level reporting to very detailed activity-specific reporting. Therefore, developing standardized metrics using real-time tools is essential. Such metrics provide a visualization into the key components of information that are relevant to various groups. A real-time dashboard can be helpful in several ways, including helping ensure the project plans remain on schedule and bringing transparency across all levels of the organization.

22.5   Conclusion

In order to effectively manage a divestiture, an understanding of underlying data and metrics is imperative. Management of the key data and access to relevant data sources are required for effective execution of activities for applications in scope. Data discipline will enable effective executive reporting and rigorous tracking to help ensure the program meets key targets and milestones.

Case Study: 22

Background

A large multinational IT company generating more than $50 billion in revenue decided to spin off one of its subsidiaries to another technology services company. The IT applications, which had to be separated, were highly integrated between parent company and the subsidiary.

Challenges

The complexity of monitoring al the IT projects, which were kicked off to execute separation of applications, within the divestiture timelines posed challenges as outlined below:

Scope:

- 400+ IT projects covering ~700 applications, involving ~800 IT FTEs, and being executed from multiple geographies

Timeline:

- Day 1 was 10 months post the deal announcement; hence all the intermediate milestones had to be monitored over a span of 10 months.

Other Complexities:

- Metrics and reports had to be detailed enough to identify even granular issues like delayed task for a specific project while also had to be rolled up at a business unit level to present an overview to the executives.
- Three months after the transaction announcement, the parent decided to divest another business unit to a different buyer with base of operations on a different continent. Hence, parallel IT projects were kicked off to execute separation of applications specific to other business unit being divested. It was critical to track both sets of IT projects accurately.

Approach

A dedicated reporting team was formed to develop, publish, and modify (as needed) the reports used by the stakeholders—Divestiture Management Office, business unit heads, and respective project managers. The reporting team was also responsible for actively identifying underlying patterns as observed in the reports and notifying stakeholders about root causes. In some of the instances, reporting team even worked with the stakeholders for resolving the systemic issues.

A program timeline was developed, at the start of the divestiture program, to ensure that all IT activities are complete by Legal Day 1. This timeline was further subdivided into high-level milestones—start and end dates for phases in waterfall model of Software Development Lifecycle (SDLC). All individual project plans were tracked against these milestones in various reports. Any planned deviation from these milestones required an exception process. A project missing these milestones without planned exception was flagged.

All the reports had "Microsoft Project Plans" for individual projects as the source of truth. Some of the key reports used to monitor overall program health were:

- Quality and Completeness—Evaluating projects for parameters critical from a readiness perspective for successful execution
- Project Execution—Tracking the health and percentage completion of all the projects against program timelines and identifying projects that are at risk of getting delayed
- Application Inventory—Tracking multiple parameters for every application and tracking the changes made to the parameters on a daily basis

Impact/Results

Timely and accurate reporting enabled stakeholders to:

- Identify issues specific to projects and/or systemic issues and develop mitigation strategies
- Predict, by comparing projected and actual completion percentages for project execution tasks, potential delays in projects and take correct steps to ensure adherence to program timelines

Mitigation actions were taken for all the risk prone projects as a result of efficient monitoring with relevant reports. As a result, all the IT projects were completed within program timelines.

Chapter 23
Testing: Making the IT Separation Foolproof

23.1 Introduction

Divestiture transactions demand a complex and wide-ranging set of changes to business-critical information technology (IT) systems. These IT changes go through a software development life cycle (SDLC) that includes designing, building, testing, and deploying the changes. These changes must move through the SDLC quickly to avoid disrupting business for the divested entity and the seller company on Legal Day 1. Most IT teams are not accustomed to this size, scale, and complexity of changes required while being in a race against the clock. Testing teams engaged in divestitures are responsible for ensuring that the existing IT applications and infrastructure components are able to separately recognize and support legal entities, customers, suppliers, employees, product lists, and processes that are split between the seller and the divested entity. Additionally, testing teams must also operate under extreme time constraints to minimize defects and risk to transaction close. This complexity increases exponentially with the size of the IT landscape and puts an enormous burden on testing teams to go above and beyond in planning and executing the required activities.

Some of the IT modifications typically involved in the transaction include changes to network configurations, procurement and setup of new IT infrastructure, migration or cloning of existing applications, development of new application interfaces, and the separation and cleansing of data. To manage these wide-ranging changes in a highly compressed timeframe, testing teams must use well-defined test management practices to develop and execute detailed and exhaustive testing plans. These practices include implementing large-scale organization-wide releases of changes, leveraging a shared pan-organizational approach, and orchestrating multiple teams across different time zones to align on a single objective. This chapter dives deep into the key practices that successful testing teams use to help ensure a risk and issue-free separation for the buyer, seller, and divested entity.

© Deloitte Development LLC 2018

J. Joy, *Divestitures and Spin-Offs*, Management for Professionals,
https://doi.org/10.1007/978-1-4939-7662-1_23

23.2   Testing During Separations

Although most organizations have gone through multiple IT implementations and deployed changes to their IT applications in the past, the size and scope of changes required during a separation event are unprecedented. Thoroughly testing the changes before Day 1 is critical to business continuity of multiple business entities. All of the changes must be individually validated during development and then combined together and tested as a whole to ensure the divested entity and the seller company can process business transactions successfully on Day 1.

Planning for testing all the application and infrastructure changes required for Day 1 readiness should begin as soon as the disposition of various components of the post-close IT environment is determined. On the application landscape front, testing usually focuses on validating changes to business rules, business-driven changes, logical data segregation and access changes for shared applications, and data migration, cleansing, and branding changes for cloned applications. While these changes may not seem complex to test, the testing team must have a well-defined plan to manage the scale of effort required in the short period of time available to complete this work. The following sections present key success factors for planning and execution of the testing effort for a separation event.

23.2.1   Test Planning Phase

1. *Single program testing timeline*: The timeline for the testing phase should be driven by the overall separation timeline. To manage against the compressed timeline, testing teams should strive to set hard deadlines for key testing milestones. It is imperative that the Divestiture Management Office that oversees all activities for a successful separation defines a program-level timeline for the testing phase and socializes that timeline to all testing teams across the organization. All testing teams must understand and follow the same testing timeline in order to avoid missed milestones, suboptimal coordination, or miscommunication. In rare scenarios, exceptions can be made to allow teams to follow different timelines dictated by the testing methodology (e.g., agile versus waterfall) or to manage dependencies with other enterprise programs.

2. *Standardized testing and planning strategies*: Although creating test strategies and plans may be an everyday job of test managers, most organizations have testing methodologies that differ across business groups or application teams. For the purposes of meeting Day 1 separation goals, the testing approach and strategy should be centrally planned by a Core Testing program management team. Having a program-level approach for testing helps ensure that a standard approach and timeline can be followed across all testing effort in scope. A well-established testing approach for a separation should include:

   • Guidelines to manage testing scope
   • Definition for range of severity for defects

- Short service level agreements (SLAs) for fixes
- A fast escalation process for defect fixes and retesting

3. *Focus on data security*: One of the most important focus areas of the testing phase is to ensure that access to the seller company's data and the divested entity's data is appropriately segregated among the two entities. Guaranteeing data integrity and confidentiality is critical to the success of a separation event. For this, designing user access controls at an application level in a timely manner is essential. However, it is even more essential to have the testing team participate in the user access and data security design phase in order to allow the team to drive the testing strategy based on user separation design. Key areas to consider when defining user access and data security include:

   - Which applications will only be accessed by the seller company, the buyer company, or the divested entity? Which applications will continue to be accessed by more than one entity post-separation?
   - How will access be segregated (i.e., through application-level access, Active Directory changes)?
   - What data can users access at different access levels?
   - Which users cannot access data because they are part of the divested entity?
   - What new user profiles (different roles for different sets of users) and levels of access are required for both the seller and the divested entities?

   To help ensure robust test execution, it is important to validate both positive test scenarios (e.g., users expected to have access should be able to access the applications/systems) and negative test scenarios (e.g., users that should not have access post-separation should not be able to access the applications/systems) to ensure that appropriate levels of access and authorization are implemented and enforced to support the separation.

4. *Timely planning for test environment readiness*: Setting up environments for testing is a task that requires careful planning, budgeting, and resource allocation. The testing plan should account for the appropriate amount of time and resources required to have the environments configured, the application code migrated, and data created and loaded to start test execution as planned. For a large portfolio of applications, there might also be a need to plan for new environments to be provisioned and configured to support parallel testing for performance and system integration. Beyond the testing environment setup, foundational elements like setting up appropriate access of environments through Active Directory need to be included in the planning.

5. *Focus on end-to-end (E2E) business flow testing*: The purpose of testing is to simulate the future state in a controlled environment and rectify any issues or defects before moving changes into production. A separation event typically enforces some change in the way a business process is executed by the entities involved. For example, applications that supported a particular step in a particular process may no longer be used by one entity, or a new business step may need to be supported by existing applications. In order to move changes into production with the highest level of confidence, testing teams should represent post-close

scenarios as accurately as possible for both the seller and the divested entities. Documenting and thoroughly testing E2E business flows that simulate how transactions and data will flow through the core business operations of the two entities are critical to avoid issues of post-separation. A few examples of E2E business flows include lead-to-order, order-to-cash, record-to-report, and hire-to-retire processes.

6. *Support for data migration*: For separation scenarios in which data from the seller's systems must be migrated to the divested entity's target systems, it is critical to have an effective model for data extract, transform, and load (ETL) activities in place prior to testing. Representatives from data architecture, data and integration design, and the testing teams must analyze and plan for data transformation and transfer to target systems to reduce defects encountered during testing of data migration.

7. *Mobilization of business users for user acceptance testing (UAT)*: Business users are an integral part of the testing life cycle as they have a deep understanding of IT and business process changes implemented for the separation event. A key challenge for business validation and sign-off for Day 1 readiness is that business users are busy planning and executing separation of business operations, which constraints their bandwidth to participate in UAT. It is therefore critical to set expectations with business users early in separation execution planning on their key responsibilities and time requirement for the testing effort. Business users should be responsible for test case and data validation, approval, and execution, as well as the final certification of UAT results. Nominating a senior business executive as an overall UAT lead upfront helps in identifying the key business participants for the testing effort and helps establish leadership support for the required time commitment.

8. *Cutover simulation planning*: The post-testing cutover phase helps ensure that the IT systems are ready to support the end-state operations of the separated entities. By simulating the steps needed to deploy IT changes into production, risks associated with the cutover phase can be mitigated. Simulations are not a traditional component of a testing cycle, but they are a critical success factor for complex separation transactions. During simulations, the sequenced activities planned for Day 1 "move to production" are executed in a controlled environment. The execution of each individual task is timed, and issues are logged for root cause analysis and correction. Performance of at least two or three simulations is recommended to incorporate lessons learned from each exercise, as well as to allow participants to rehearse their activities so they know what to do during the actual go-live of the IT application and infrastructure landscape.

23.2.2 Test Execution Phase

1. *Defect fix prioritization*: Testing teams usually test all the defined test scripts, but not all scripts end up finding a defect in the application being tested. To prioritize the development team's efforts to fix defects, it is important for the testing team

to define a standard way of measuring defects, including providing a clear catalog of defect types and defect criticality thresholds, as well as driving an organization-wide understanding of these boundaries. A timeframe within which a defect type should be fixed should also be adhered to by all teams.

2. *Daily tracking of test execution*: Assuming the appropriate testing strategy has been defined, developing a centralized process with toolsets to monitor and track testing progress is critical to speed up test execution activities. A structure with dedicated resources to monitor the daily execution of testing activities and testing teams trained in the status monitoring process is key to managing test execution.

3. *Executive reporting of testing progress and issues*: In order to establish the appropriate level of urgency and drive quick decision making through executive channels, it is imperative to frequently report on the test execution progress to Divestiture Management Office (DMO) leadership. These reports should communicate test execution against plan, defects identified, defect resolution status, test cases executed per person, and timeline for resolution. Detailed metrics reports enable the leadership team to remove roadblocks, as well as enhance visibility into the testing team's progress.

23.3 Testing Phase Deliverables

Test planning and execution for a separation can be somewhat simplified by focusing on a few key testing phase deliverables discussed below.

23.3.1 Testing Strategy

Typically, application testing teams affected by a separation have not have worked together before; thus, there is a strong possibility that each application testing team has its own testing strategy and list of applications that are required to be tested. It is essential to align the testing strategies used across all teams into one common testing strategy. For example, all teams should have the same entry and exit criteria and similar test execution targets.

To ensure that all teams have the same general guidelines, a well-defined testing strategy document should be shared with all teams that not only provides general testing guidelines but the flexibility to address exceptions using novel approaches. The testing strategy document should cover the following key areas:

- Program scope and timeline
- Different dispositions and disposition-specific testing guidelines
- Testing approach
- Program and testing governance structures
- Testing phases and detailed timelines

- Communication cadence
- Reporting metrics
- Testing execution process

As part of the testing strategy, testing guidelines must be defined for applications based on the application dispositions. In addition to any functional changes that need to be tested, other aspects typically not covered in regular testing cycles must be addressed, including:

- Rebranding changes
- Interface verifications (with new and cloned systems)
- Access, authorization, and navigation
- Security testing
- Data integrity testing

23.3.2   Testing Approach

Test Coverage

In most separations, testing teams are new to the IT separation experience. Due to the time constraints under which testing must be completed, first-time teams tend to rely on their existing test scenarios for testing separation-related IT changes. This approach usually leads to more testing than required. To plan and execute the testing effectively, it is critical that teams downsize their test beds for separation-specific scenarios.

Rightsizing the test cases will provide teams with more time to test relevant scenarios and help engage the appropriate level of resources to support test planning and execution.

Performance Testing

Performance testing is a key area that must be covered in the testing approach. In a typical separation, many applications are cloned to support the divested entity. Standing up a cloned application requires new infrastructure that needs to be assessed from a performance perspective based on multiple factors, including:

- Volume of data and transactions to be supported by the application
- Capacity and location of the infrastructure

23.3.3   Testing Governance

The test governance structure usually used during regular product or process changes will not work in a separation testing environment due to the differences in scope, the compressed timeline, and the scale of testing efforts required for a separation. Testing a full portfolio of applications requires increased oversight and coordination to help ensure all teams responsible for test execution are moving in lock step. Additionally, successful testing requires strong engagement and ownership from both the business and IT teams, as well as the clear assignment of responsibilities among the different teams.

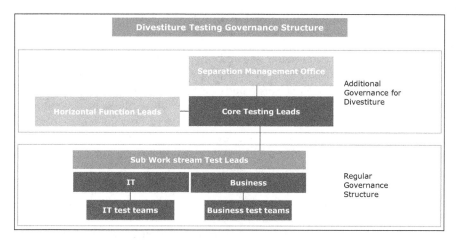

Fig. 23.1 Testing Governance Structure for Divestitures

Figure 23.1 depicts a typical governance structure to support the testing phase of a separation.

Once the governance structure is defined, the next step is to define the responsibilities for each of the roles in the governance structure. The roles and responsibilities for both IT and business teams in the testing governance structure are as follows:

Table 23.1 Testing Roles and Responsibilities

Roles	IT responsibilities	Business responsibilities
Global testing leaders	• Develop the testing strategy, processes, and tools • Ensure all testing activities are carried out in alignment with program requirements and the overall schedule • Work closely with the Divestiture Management Office (DMO) to periodically report testing status to key stakeholders	• Assess the testing strategy from a business perspective • Work with key stakeholders to get their sign-off on the testing strategy
Core Testing leaders	• Own end-to-end testing across all workstreams and regions • Ensure successful end-to-end test execution and manage defect escalations for end-to-end testing	• Oversee UAT testing case development and execution at the business unit level • Work with sub-workstream leaders to monitor progress and raise risks, if any
Sub-workstream test leaders	• Manage all testing activities (e.g., test planning) within sub-workstream • Drive definition of golden transactions for end-to-end processes across business units and product lines • Work with regional and country resources to ensure their needs are addressed • Manage escalations of defects and test execution at the sub-workstream level	• Identify the business processes and functionalities that need to be covered during UAT testing • Work with business users to create test cases, load test cases to the execution tool, and identify and create data • Manage day-to-day UAT testing activities

23.3.4   *Reports Used to Monitor and Track Testing Activities*

Reporting on separation testing should be planned and executed at the program level as all testing teams must track their progress against a common set of milestones. Execution and defect status reports must be standardized using automated tools and recorded in a centralized location to enable all stakeholders to monitor the status. Testing teams should all follow the same defect severity guidelines to ensure program-level reports are generated and reviewed using a common lens. This level of instrumentation enables effective visibility, management, and timely guidance to steer the testing effort and keep it on course.

Key performance indicators (KPIs) are at the heart of successful instrumentation and help ensure both the execution and governance teams are aligned on the most relevant metrics to determine testing progress and success. Weekly and monthly targets must be defined for each KPI, and each testing team must adopt KPIs before execution starts. Specific KPIs must be defined based on the nature and scope of testing. For example, if applications are cloned for the divested entity, relevant KPIs include data cleansing and access segregation.

Below is a non-exhaustive list of common testing KPIs and suggested targets:

Table 23.2   Common Testing KPIs

Type	Metric	Description
Test execution	Test execution rate	Compares the current number of tests executed against the daily target
	Test execution burnup	Graphical view of the number of tests executed against target, including a view of those passed against the pass rate target
	First run pass rate	Pass rate percentage of the tests upon first run; it provides an initial quality indicator
	Current pass rate	Current percentage of tests in a passing state out of the total executed
Defects	Open and close rate	Rolling weekly average of opened and closed defects
	Open defects by severity	Number of open defects by severity pending repair
	Fixed defects by severity	Number of fixed (not closed) defects and requirement changes by severity pending closure by testing
	Defects submitted vs. closed weekly	Number of defects closed within the same week submitted provides a weekly trend of defects submitted
	Open defects and affected tests	Sum of the affected tests associated with the sum of open change requests (CR) by assigned team
	Defect state churn rate	Number of times the defect state changes from fixed to open

23.4   Conclusion

Testing can play a significant role in de-risking and helping to ensure business continuity during a separation event. Regardless of the maturity of testing teams in executing testing cycles for changes to an IT environment, they may be surprised when confronted with the organizational scale, compressed timeline, and diversity of testing efforts required to ensure IT readiness for separation on Day 1.

Preparing for a successful testing effort requires diligent focus, deep planning, and effective execution to overcome the scale, timing, and complexity challenges inherent to a Day 1 readiness scenario. Standing up the appropriate testing strategy, deliverables, governance, and reporting mechanisms can support the seller company, the buyer company, and the divested entity in achieving a smooth transition to post-close operations.

Case Study: 23

Background

The separation of a major business unit of a Fortune 100 company affected a large portfolio of 450+ applications shared between the seller company and the divesting business unit. The IT team had 9 months to get the IT portfolio ready for Day 1. Separation of IT systems took 3 months to plan, leaving only 9 months to complete the design, build, and test the required changes.

Challenge

Application changes were scheduled for release across three phases, with a large portfolio of 300+ applications going live within the initial 6 months itself. Application teams had only 3 months to execute the entire scope of testing activities for this portfolio. At the start of the test planning effort, each team brought its own unique testing process that they had been following for years. This created the complexity of quickly establishing and aligning the various teams on a shared testing approach, progress and quality reporting dashboards, and common program timeline.

Approach

At the outset, a detailed testing roadmap at the program level was established, to finalize key testing phases and the timelines for each. This program-level testing roadmap was then shared across testing teams, thereby enabling them to plan for detailed planning and execution and raising issues in advance for any risk or roadblocks they might face in meeting these timelines. Roles and responsibilities for testing governance and execution were defined for the overall governance model, and key stakeholders at multiple organization levels and across both the seller and divested entities were identified for each role.

Kickoff meetings were conducted for IT leaders, business leaders, and application project managers to generate awareness and alignment on the program-level testing strategy, governance model, execution approach, reporting tools, and status meeting cadence. Common test execution guidelines were defined for various testing teams to plan their testing scenarios and minimize issues. Teams were given clear guidelines on:

- Where to load test cases
- The naming structure of folders and test cases
- Weekly execution targets
- Periodic project plan updates
- Testing readiness and execution guidelines

Detailed dashboards depicting testing progress in real time were made available to all teams on a daily basis. Applications falling behind schedule were identified in daily status meetings, with a focus on problem solving and removing barriers to execution. Weekly reports were compiled and shared with the program-level leadership and testing governance team to drive accountability at the most senior levels in the organization.

Impact/Results

The massive testing exercise covering a portfolio of more than 300 applications was successfully completed within the 3-month timeline. More than 40,000 system integration testing (SIT) cases and more than 38,000 UAT testing cases were planned and executed with a pass rate of more than 99 percent. Testing success was a major factor in ensuring operational readiness of the application portfolio on Day 1.

Chapter 24
Cutover: Getting Ready for the Launch

24.1 What Is Cutover?

WILL I BE ABLE TO SHIP MY PRODUCTS?
CEO, Multinational Enterprise IT Company

CAN I CLOSE MY BOOKS?
CFO, Multinational Enterprise IT Company

In any divestiture or separation, deal execution is critical to achieving Day 1 success. Deal execution often draws the most attention from leadership due to its associated risks and impact on shareholder value. Cutover forms the crux of deal execution.

Cutover, an essential element of the divestiture or separation life cycle, focuses on executing the plans required for Day 1 readiness, including, but not limited to:

- Separation of people, processes, and systems
- Provision of transition services agreements (TSAs)
- Ensuring the separation does not negatively affect customers, suppliers, or employees

Comprehensive project management, data-based decision-making, and risk-weighted judgment are required to ensure a successful transition to Day 1, while simultaneously safeguarding business continuity during the cutover process.

> *The separation of a $100 billion company into two Fortune 50 companies required the cutover of a complex IT landscape involving more than 2000 applications shared between the two entities.*
>
> *The two entities relied heavily on IT for day-to-day operations:*
>
> 1. *More than 80% of revenue flowed through the supply chain ecosystems for both companies.*
> 2. *About one million transactions with a combined value of more than $500 million were executed daily.*

© Deloitte Development LLC 2018
J. Joy, *Divestitures and Spin-Offs*, Management for Professionals,
https://doi.org/10.1007/978-1-4939-7662-1_24

24.2   Types of Cutover

Cutover is a sequential process tangled with several dependencies that takes thorough planning, skilled implementation, and ongoing training and support. There are three major approaches that are widely adopted for cutover execution.

24.2.1   Big Bang

Under the big bang cutover approach, all Day 1 cutover activities are executed in one stretch, including implementation of all cutover-related code changes and the simultaneous migration of employees and customers from RemainCo to their respective information technology (IT) landscapes. Big bang is the fastest of all cutover approaches. It requires the shortest implementation time and minimal rework since all code changes are done with the final state in mind. Users can be migrated to their respective IT systems immediately; thus, multiple clones of applications and data are not required, which leads to minimal redundancies—a huge incentive for companies to choose the big bang approach.

However, despite all the potential benefits, companies tend to stay away from this approach due to the high risks involved. In a large and complex separation, IT processes and systems tend to be heavily interconnected, and failure in one part of the system can quickly cascade across the overall IT landscape. If the application scope and complexity of the separation are relatively simple or if cutover speed is of the utmost importance due to legal constraints or the nature of the deal, then companies should consider adopting the big bang approach.

24.2.2   Phased Approach

Under the phased cutover approach, divestiture of business and IT landscapes occurs in "waves" to minimize the risk of failure. Multiple factors such as geographical spread of separating entities, application complexity, and transaction timeline are used to determine the activities required during each phase. A phased approach ensures all critical details are factored into the planning process, which makes it a better risk management option than the big bang approach, especially for complex business and IT environments.

Despite its risk management benefits, the phased approach is time consuming and costly. Business and IT teams need to implement ad hoc or throwaway processes and code changes to separate the seller company and divested entity. For example, if the lead-to-cash process is separated in two phases, then business teams must manually maintain customer orders during the transition period. Lead-to-cash IT applications must be changed to accommodate these temporary business process changes, which are then reverted back once the separation is complete.

24.2.3   Combination Approach

Ideally, a company will adopt a combination of the phased approach and the big bang approach to ensure effective risk management and speed of execution. There are usually certain business simple sub-processes and applications that can be separated in one single release, which makes a controlled big bang approach effective for these areas, while a phased approach can be used to separate more complex IT processes.

24.2.4   Choosing an Appropriate Approach

Thus to summarize, the appropriate cutover approach depends on the risk appetite of the company and the complexity of the IT and business landscape.

Each of the three approaches requires a well-defined strategy for a successful cutover. Rushing through the planning process can transform what should be a beneficial business initiative into a fire drill exercise and crisis. The cutover process is driven by both business and IT teams; thus, a streamlined strategy is needed to ensure consistent and efficient execution.

24.3   Defining a Cutover Strategy

The overall cutover strategy combines both the business and IT cutover strategies, each of which deal with different aspects of cutover. However, they need to complement each other to ensure effective cutover execution.

24.3.1   Business Strategy for Cutover

The business strategy for cutover is driven by transaction execution requirements, financial agreements, and the divestiture timeline, among other factors. The business cutover strategy focuses on three primary areas:

- Impact of application downtime on business processes
- Internal and external communication management
- Legal entity readiness

The company must assess and manage business functionality during cutover execution, especially during downtimes, as well as communications to external stakeholders, including customers, partners, and vendors. A special team should be set up to manage communications, including crafting messages about the divestiture for external stakeholders. This team should include staff from the CIO's office to ensure transparency and a clear understanding of IT-related issues and requirements.

Legal entity readiness—the process of establishing a legal name and status for the divested entity in all necessary jurisdictions—is a prerequisite for cutover. Key business activities required for legal entity readiness of the divested entity include tax registrations, the establishment of bank accounts, human resources (HR) consultations, contract separation, and user acceptance testing (UAT) on IT, payroll, finance, and HR systems. An entity cannot go-live without having all requirements in place. Additionally, it is critical to develop a robust finance operating model that aligns financial resources across the portfolio of financial services and sub-functions (e.g., revenue accounting within controllership, payroll within finance).

In addition, the business functions play a key role in defining the IT strategy, including participating in user acceptance testing of the software development life cycle (SDLC). During cutover planning phase, the business functions develop an inventory fulfillment and payables management plan to ensure supply chain processes are not affected during cutover execution. Moreover, the executive team manages the hiring of new personnel during cutover. The executive team also sets up a business command center to provide complete support during cutover execution.

24.3.2   IT Carve-Out Strategy for Cutover

The IT carve-out strategy includes a plan for the disposition of applications that play important roles in cutover execution, as covered in detailed in Chapter 20—"Managing the Application Separation Lifecycle." A summary of IT cutover activities based upon application disposition follows:

Table 24.1 IT Cutover Activities by Application Disposition

Category	Disposition	Definition	Cutover Activities
Dedicated Applications	Retain	Application is retained by the seller company. No transfer of ownership is required	• Data cleansing • Security information changes
	Give and go	An application is moved as is from its current location to a target location	• User migration • Data cleansing • Information security changes • Data migration • People readiness • Network changes
Shared Applications	Extract and retain	Application data is extracted and provided to one entity, while the application is owned by the other entity	• User migration • Data migration • Data cleansing • People readiness
	Configure in place	An application shared by the buyer company and the divested entity is separated logically by configuration	• User migration • Data cleansing • Information security changes • Data migration • People readiness • Network changes
	Clone	Further divided into two categories: 1. Clone and go: Clone shared application, as well as the underlying data 2. Clone, cleanse, and go: Clone shared application and cleanse sensitive data	• User migration • Data migration • Information security changes • Data cleansing • People readiness • Infrastructure installation
	New build	An entirely new application is built for one of the separating entities to replace an existing application	Clone • User migration • Data cleansing • Information security changes • Data migration • People readiness • Infrastructure migration Transform • User migration • Information security changes • Data migration • People readiness • Infrastructure installation

Below are brief definitions of key cutover activities:

1. *User Migration*: User migration involves moving users to new emails and IDs to segregate their access to the IT systems and applications of the two separating entities. For a new build, authorized users will be granted access to the newly built system. However, for shared applications, users moving from the seller company to the divested entity will be given new IDs that grant them access to the divested entity's system and applications.

2. *Data Extraction and Migration*: Data migration involves the transfer of transactional and historical data from the seller company to the buyer company in accordance with the service agreement signed by the two entities. Data extraction involves identifying and pulling data in a format agreed upon to enable separation. This data is then migrated from the source or staging area and loaded into the destination system. Data migration is one of the most critical and time-consuming activities during cutover and requires developing a data migration strategy that is consistent with infrastructure capacity of the destination system and the amount of data being transferred.

3. *Data Cleansing*: Data cleansing is the process of detecting and removing inaccurate or unnecessary records from a record set, table, or database. Incomplete, incorrect, or inaccurate parts of the data are identified and replaced, modified, or deleted. Data cleansing can be performed interactively with data wrangling tools or, alternatively, through processing. Data cleansing is required when cloning an entire application.

4. *People Readiness*: People readiness involves creating awareness among employees about future changes in the organizational structure and reporting hierarchy of the company, as well as training employees on any new procedures planned as part of the reorganization. Effectively managing people readiness is a key driver of divestiture success. Some companies establish a cross-functional divestiture management office (DMO) to guide people readiness activities.

5. *Information Security*: Information security is key to a successful IT cutover strategy. Information security involves effectively managing the processes, tools, and policies necessary to prevent, detect, document, and counter threats to digital and non-digital information. The information security strategy should incorporate the relevant people, processes, and technology needed to address security challenges. Key information security activities include granting user access, implementing user authentication processes, performing vulnerability scans, and implementing or updating cybersecurity features.

6. *Infrastructure Migration*: Infrastructure migration is the process of transferring the seller company's data center environment to the buyer's data center operating system. It is a daunting task that involves complex hardware, software, and network technology. Infrastructure migration and installation activities are discussed in details in Chapter 21—"IT Infrastructure – Data centers, Network and Infrastructure Planning."

Both business and IT cutover strategies are often interlinked at critical points and must be aligned with each other in order for the overall cutover to be successful. Due to the tight coupling of business and IT activities, it is imperative to combine the business and IT cutover plans at critical intersecting points. These plans should then be tested through mock implementations or paper-based simulations to validate their effectiveness. Leaders from both IT and business should oversee this combined effort.

24.4 Cutover Approach: All You Need to Know

Imagine a stunt plane performing an extremely difficult backflip at an air show packed with onlookers. The crowd holds its breath as the pilot purposely stalls the plane's engine and expertly tumbles the aircraft backward over itself and then erupts in thunderous applause at the successful maneuver. Such a feat requires the utmost timing and precision. A fraction of an error could be the difference between life and death. In the world of divestitures, similar precision is required when performing a cutover. The entire cutover life cycle can be divided into the following three phases:

- *Pre-cutover Phase*: Focuses on planning, development, and testing
- *Cutover Execution*: Executes the activities needed to separate the entities
- *Post-Cutover Phase*: Ensures systems are stabilized and business processes run as planned

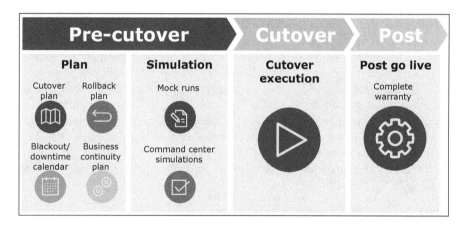

Fig. 24.1 Three Phases in the Cutover Life Cycle

24.5 Pre-Cutover Phase

Pre-cutover consists of planning and simulating the IT and business activities required for cutover, including building a production environment and designing business processes to support the cutover window. Pre-cutover testing validates cutover execution-related activities against the technical requirements of the two separating entities. The activities performed in the pre-cutover phase lead up to cutover execution, and potential issues with cutover execution-related activities are identified and resolved during pre-cutover.

Key deliverables produced during this phase include a project schedule or work breakdown structure (WBS), a communication plan, a security plan, and a contract guidelines.

24.5.1 Cutover Planning

A cutover plan starts with developing the application blueprint. The level of interdependencies between the applications, shared infrastructure, and comingled data of the separating entities, as well as the complexity of business processes (i.e., manual vs. automated), targeted for separation will determine whether cutover can be achieved in one big bang implementation or should be performed using a phased approach.

> *A key consideration for cutover plan is creating the cutover plan for orchestrating the entire cutover. Should Sales applications be separated first or should it start with HR applications? The cutover plan also needs to consider the business activity calendar to ensure minimal disruption. Business activities (i.e., month-end close, quarter-end close, holidays, and quote-to-cash close) play a key role when planning for the cutover.*

Application and Business Readiness Activities

An application readiness assessment must be completed to ensure key deliverables and crucial milestones are achievable. From an IT perspective, the application readiness assessment includes UAT, provisioning and testing of new hardware (e.g., servers, storage), coordination with interdependent applications, submission of security-related changes required for both divested and RemainCo entity to the security and infrastructure team, analysis of network capacity to determine the data migration schedule, and developing recommendations to avoid network slowdown or breakage during cutover execution. The overall objective application and business readiness activities are to minimize the impact of cutover to customers and partners.

Blackout/Downtime Impact Assessment

Blackout estimation starts with identifying the seller company's business processes and mapping them to the IT application inventory. The first step is to identify the business processes that are not stand alone. Various industry-specific process frameworks are available to use for blackout and downtime impact assessment. Once the business processes are identified, they need to be reviewed by the business functions so that company-specific (RemainCo and NewCo) changes can be made. A sample output of the business process identification exercise is shown in Fig. 24.2.

Process (L1)		Sub-process (L2)
A. Customer experience (lead to cash)	---→	A.1 Customer Setup and Leads Capture Partner Enablement A.2 Quotes Submitted A.3 Orders Submitted A.4 Orders Built, Shipped & Invoiced A.5 Financial posting to General Ledger
B. Employee experience (hire to retire)	---→	B.1 Payroll and Benefits B.2 Expense Management B.3 Requisition to Hire B.4 Transfer through Retirement B.5 Training
C. Financial close (record to report)	---→	C.1 Transaction Aggregation C.2 Adjustments and Reconciliation C.3 Internal Reporting and Consolidation C.4 External Reporting
D. Supplier/vendor experience (procure to pay)	---→	D.1 Requisition and Purchase Order Creation D.2 Receive Goods and Invoices D.3 Vendor Payments D.4 Claims and Disputes
E. New product introduction (design to deploy)	---→	E.1 Engineering and Design E.2 Product Registration E.3 Change Order and Bill of Materials E.4 Procurement E.5 Deployment E.6 Pricing and Finance
F. Customer services and support (services delivery)	---→	F.1 Assisted Support/Support Delivery F.2 Service Definition and Entitlement

Fig. 24.2 Sample Output of Business Process Identification

Once business process identification is complete, applications must be mapped to business sub-processes and ratified by the application owners and business function leads. Next, business and IT teams need to jointly decide on the changes required for the cutover and estimate the blackout period, which is an iterative process as the estimates should be revised and compressed with each iteration. Several techniques can significantly reduce the initial blackout estimates, including plan walk-through and review, mock move to production (MTP) simulations, and brainstorming creative solutions with functional and technical teams. A sample blackout estimate for the lead-to-cash process is shown in Fig. 24.3.

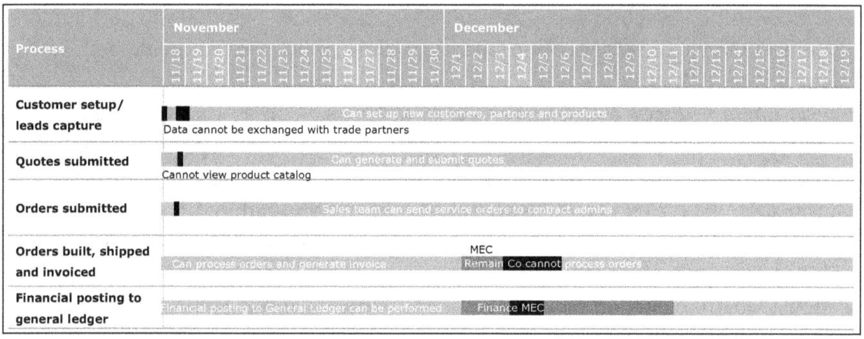

Fig. 24.3 Sample Blackout Estimate for the Lead-to-Cash Process

Finally, proper planning is required to put a business continuity plan (BCP) in place that mitigates potential business risks. A BCP is a predefined plan on how to run critical business processes during planned or unplanned blackouts or downtime. One of the key objectives of a BCP is to limit business disruption and impact. The company must be prepared to mitigate the possible failure scenarios that may occur during cutover.

In parallel to the blackout exercise, the company must start building a critical path for the cutover by reviewing major dependent activities within and between applications to understand which applications are critical to overall business operations.

Develop the Integrated Cutover Plan (ICP)

The ICP is a sequenced plan for the completion of all critical path business and IT cutover tasks, and it includes detailed timing and duration estimates to migrate functionality into production. The ICP helps the company manage the complexity of the overall cutover plan by focusing only on a few critical applications that form the critical path for business continuity. The cutover plan for all other assets will need to align with the ICP. In a separation that involved approximately 1500 applications, it will typically take the cutover team about 60 to 90 days to develop and finalize the ICP. Multiple workshops with business and IT applications teams must be conducted to develop and finalize the ICP. Application teams must then perform multiple reviews of the finalized ICP and conduct a pressure test to ensure it can hold up in the cutover environment.

Plan by Asset Category and Disposition

Each of the three phases—pre-cutover, cutover execution, and post-cutover—must have its own cutover plans, but not all applications in the IT landscape have the same level of criticality or complexity. When developing a cutover plan for each application, consider:

1. *Baseline Tasks*: Each application disposition and category of asset should have a framework of baseline tasks that must be completed. For example, all applications that have the clone, cleanse, and go disposition will require data cleansing tasks.
2. *Additional Critical Tasks*: Certain critical assets, such as a multi-instance SAP enterprise resource planning (ERP) system, may require the performance of certain critical tasks specific to each instance. This is because these tasks may be critical to the business and, hence, must be closely monitored.
3. *Dependencies (for Linkages)*: Applications referenced in the ICP must be analyzed for their upstream and downstream dependencies with other applications. Upstream dependencies refer to activities that must be completed before cutover tasks can begin on an application. Downstream dependencies refer to cutover tasks that an application must complete before subsequent tasks can begin.

The components of a cutover plan for an application include:

- Task identification
- Task milestones
- Task start time
- Task end time
- Completion percentage
- Predecessor

A sample cutover plan template is shown in Fig. 24.4. This template is used primarily for tracking and reporting the status of cutover tasks to executives. Multiple tools are available to create and maintain these cutover plans (e.g., Microsoft Project Servers).

Task Mode ▼	Unique ID ▼	Status Formula ▼	Task Name ▼	Duration ▼	% Complete ▼	Resour Names ▼	Start ▼	Finish ▼
1	133	▶	◢ Pre-Cutover Activities	2488.65 hrs? 99%			Tue 6/26/12	Mon 10/8/12
2	134	◉	▷ Data Cleansing in 11i	441.73 hrs 100%			Mon 9/10/12	Fri 9/28/12
94	161	◉	▷ Resolution of Critical Issues	720.87 hrs? 100%			Fri 8/10/12	Sun 9/9/12
109	163	◉	▷ Internal/External Communications	2488.65 hrs? 100%			Tue 6/26/12	Mon 10/8/12
205	466	▶	◢ Techical Infrastructure	627.62 hrs? 99%		DBA	Thu 9/6/12	Tue 10/2/12
206	467	◉	Back-up GOLD [Database Applications]	31.52 hrs 100%		DBA	Thu 9/6/12	Sat 9/8/12
207	468	◉	Clone GOLD to R12 Prod [Including DBA Chei	5 hrs 100%		DBA	Sat 9/8/12	Sat 9/8/12
208	469	◉	Update XML poolsize to 6 and Run Autoconf	6674 mins 100%		DBA	Thu 9/13/12	Tue 9/18/12
209	470	▶	▷ Connectivity between 11i production and R1	105.02 hrs 99%		DBA	Mon 9/10/12	Fri 9/14/12
214	475	◉	Send SysAdmin password, app passwords, ti	5 mins 100%		DBA	Fri 9/7/12	Fri 9/7/12
215	485	◉	Create Read ONLY database access	5 mins 100%		DBA	Fri 9/7/12	Fri 9/7/12
216	486	◉	Install EBS Printers-PROD	126.08 hrs 100%		DBA	Sat 9/8/12	Thu 9/13/12
217	487	◉	▷ Turning R12 Prod	171.7 hrs? 100%			Fri 9/7/12	Fri 9/14/12
220	490	◉	▷ RSA Pre Set-up-Prod	320 hrs? 100%			Sat 9/8/12	Fri 9/21/12
227	497	◉	▷ Markview Pre Set-up-Prod	67.22 hrs? 100%			Mon 9/10/12	Thu 9/13/12
244	514	◉	▷ AdventX Pre Set-up-Prod	20 hrs? 100%			Thu 9/13/12	Fri 9/14/12
249	515	◉	Export Sterling PROD Configs & Services	37 hrs 100%		XYZ	Tue 9/11/12	Wed 9/12/12
250	526	◉	Install Sterling Schema	28.47 hrs 100%		XYZ	Mon 9/17/12	Wed 9/19/12
251	516	◉	Configure Sterling adapter and import sterlir	29.62 hrs 100%		XYZ	Mon 10/1/12	Tue 10/2/12
252	517	◉	*Delete* Configure Sterling adapter	34.47 hrs 100%			Mon 9/17/12	Wed 9/19/12
253	518	◉	FIN: External ACLs (JP Morgan, etc.)	0.08 hrs 100%			Mon 9/17/12	Mon 9/17/12

Fig. 24.4 Sample Cutover Plan

A cutover governance structure is required to ensure project teams update and complete their project plans in a timely manner.

Cutover Governance Structure

The cutover governance structure will drive end-to-end cutover planning and execution. The key reason to establish a governance structure is to efficiently manage all components of the cutover program, including application readiness and command center execution. Some components, such as the command center, have their own governance structure. A sample governance structure is outlined in Fig. 24.5.

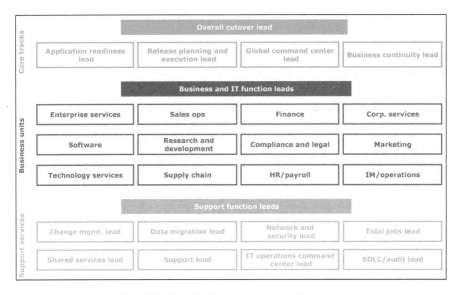

Fig. 24.5 Sample Cutover Governance Structure

The governance structure is divided into three parts:

- Core Leadership—The core leadership team focuses on cutover planning, command center strategy, and the coordination of support functions to provide a framework for data collection and cutover deliverables, as well as to monitor and track cutover-related risks and risk mitigation plans.
- Business Units—IT and business function leaders serve as the points of contact responsible for cutover plans. They work with individual project managers to ensure cutover planning is completed at the project level.
- Support Services—Support function leaders assist with process simplification. For example, the IT operations leader is in charge of the IT operations command center, which works with the global command center to triage issues.

Governance leaders must ensure a rollback plan is in place as part of the cutover plan for each asset.

Rollback Plans

In standard IT project management parlance, a cutover plan is laid out to ensure that specific changes are deployed in the appropriate order without interrupting other processes. Additionally, a rollback plan must be created to return services back to their last working state in case the rollout does not execute successfully.

The development of rollback plans depends on the risk appetite of the company, the scope and complexity of the divestiture deal, and the IT application landscape. Rollback plans are not mandatory for all companies. Even in the most complex deals involving more than 600 applications, a company may decide against developing rollback plans if the IT application landscape is too distributed and complex. In such cases, the cutover execution team must be extra cautious and ensure nothing goes wrong or, alternatively, follow a two-key approach to cutover execution.

The two-key approach, also known as the nuclear validation process, should be designed to achieve a high level of accuracy in executing tasks for critical path applications. All actions must be completed in the presence of two authorized people at all times.

24.5.2   Cutover Simulation

Cutover simulation is a formal trial run of the cutover plan that includes triggering, executing, and validating durations, interdependencies, and the sequence cutover actions.

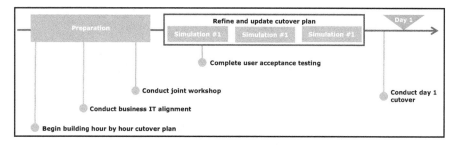

Fig. 24.6 Sample Cutover Simulation

There are three key types of cutover simulation:

- Mock MTP simulation
- ICP simulation
- Command center simulation

Mock MTP Simulation

MTP involves making changes to IT applications and data in the production environment. However, before executing MTP activities, it is essential to simulate the detailed steps required to execute changes in individual systems in order to identify issues and make final adjustments to the cutover plan. Such a simulation is called a mock MTP simulation.

Systems that may add to cutover downtime should undergo multiple mock runs to reduce their blackout estimates. Mock runs must be tracked at the application level. The final blackout estimates for critical systems should be used to refine the cutover plans of dependent systems. Mock runs are also used to identify network capacity constraints. Below are some best practices for conducting mock MTP simulations:

- Multiple mock MTP runs should be executed in preparation for production cutover.
- The most complex and risky functions should participate in all mock MTP runs.

- Rollback plans must be pressure tested during mock MTP runs.
- Release managers to encourage the IT and business functions and infrastructure teams to foster an environment of collaboration; for example, to address network capacity constraints, IT team work with infrastructure team to stagger applications that need high network availability.

Command Center Simulation

The command center simulation is a structured trial that emulates events and processes likely to be encountered during cutover that involve IT, business unit, and functional personnel. The objectives of the command center simulation include:

- Testing the sequencing and dependencies in the ICP against the command center
- Validating the command center operating model, including communications cadence
- Refining the command center playbook to ensure cutover readiness

ICP Simulation

Based on the scale and complexity of the company's change management process, resource availability, and risk appetite, the ICP simulation should be conducted using a paper-based or system-based approach or a combination of the two. A paper-based simulation is basically a role playing exercise that follows the end-to-end ICP in a sequential manner for key systems and their interdependencies. A system-based simulation is the execution of a subset of the ICP on a production-like environment. Figure 24.7 outlines these two approaches in more detail:

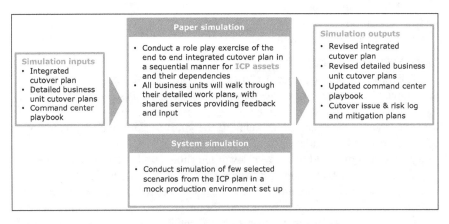

Fig. 24.7 Paper-Based vs. System-Based Simulations

Command Center Structure

To facilitate tracking of cutover progress and triaging of cutover issues, a multi-tiered command center is setup. The entire planning and testing phase of pre-cutover culminates with the command center setup, which occurs immediately prior to cutover execution. The command center should lead all cutover-related communications and provide timely updates to executive leadership. The top layer of the command center is called the global command center (GCC). The IT operations and business unit teams work under the GCC as part of a business unit command center (BU CC). During the pre-planning phase, the command center location and governance structure are finalized, and a meeting cadence is set up for the remaining cutover phases. Figure 24.8 depicts a sample two-tier command center.

Fig. 24.8 Sample Two-Tier Command Center

24.6   Cutover Execution

Strong planning, leadership, and simulation exercises are the basis of successful cutover execution. Three aspects of effective cutover execution include:

- Cutover plan execution and command center operationalization
- Asset categorization and issue management
- Issues monitoring and resolution

Cutover Plan Execution and Command Center Operationalization

An hour-by-hour cutover plan is developed during the planning phase. During execution, release managers manage the progress toward critical plan milestones by updating the percentage completion of each task in the plan. The command center starts operating during the cutover execution phase and monitors these updates.

The command center's primary mission is to protect the company's assets by serving as a central point of contact in actively managing cutover execution, coordinating cross-functional communication through meeting cadence, and escalating cutover issues. A lot of decision-making within the command center is based on application categorization.

Application Categorization and Issue Management

Not all applications in the IT landscape have the same level of criticality or complexity. To aid in the planning process, assets must be categorized into multiple buckets. Asset categorization for each application includes vendor categorization (i.e., proprietary, third party, or developed in-house), obsolescence ("sunset date") and legacy considerations, estimated users at the parent or seller company and the divested entity, business criticality, data criticality (i.e., how sensitive is the data used by the application), rebranding requirements, disposition, customer considerations (i.e., if application is used by customers), and regulatory impact. Based on these factors, assets are grouped into multiple categories to simplify prioritization and management.

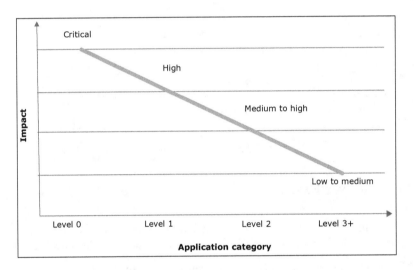

Fig. 24.9 Application Categorization

Issue management involves a sequence of processes that vary based upon the category of the asset, as follows:

Table 24.2 Issue Management Processes by Asset Category

Asset category	Category description	Escalation to command center	Escalation to GCC	Escalation to senior leadership
Level 0	• Applications with a high impact on revenue, third parties, internal operations, and/or brand	• All issues should be escalated to the command center within 15 min	• Critical path timeline is impacted	• Top 10 customers/ partners are impacted
Level 1	• Applications with a high impact on company operations	• Issues that affect the cutover timeline by more than 1 h should be escalated to the command center within 15 min	• Critical path timeline is impacted	• Escalation based on GCC discretion
Level 2	• Applications with a medium to high impact on business unit level operations	• Issues that affect the cutover timeline by more than 1 h should be escalated to the command center within 15 min	• Critical path timeline is impacted	N/A
Level 3	• Applications with a low to medium impact at the workgroup or department level	• Issues that affect the cutover timeline by more than 1 h should be escalated to the command center within 15 min	N/A	N/A

Cutover Execution Reports and Meeting Cadence

Reporting covers trends and estimates for cutover completion based on cutover project plan status. Multiple reports are generated during cutover to keep a close eye on cutover activities. Hence, the frequency to generate these reports is high. Generally, cutover team generates these reports. Reports can be manually pulled or auto-generated, based upon maturity of the reporting tool being used. The reports are needed as inputs to various managing and controlling processes, and, as such, these reports are shared with senior executives, GCC staff, and technical staff during checkpoint meetings, per the meeting cadence. Checkpoints meetings monitor the overall health of cutover execution and the project. If execution is not progressing as planned, corrective action (i.e., time extensions and rollbacks) is taken.

The command center meeting cadence established during the pre-cutover phase comes into action during cutover execution. It is a best practice to utilize defense readiness condition (DEFCON) levels, an alert system used by the US armed forces, during cutover execution to measure the cutover period criticality on a particular day, which can range from high criticality (DEFCON ONE) to low criticality (DEFCON FOUR). Each particular day of cutover execution is mapped to a DEFCON level based on the number of tasks ending on that day, the number of applications in cutover execution on that day, and the number of critical applications needed during a blackout period. On days rated DEFCON THREE or DEFCON FOUR, the frequency in which reports are generated is low, but may scale up to 4-h interval checkpoint calls between the GCC and the business unit command center during days involving highly critical tasks (i.e., DEFCON ONE and DEFCON TWO). Figure 24.10 defines the DEFCON levels in detail.

DEFCON Levels	Descriptions
DEFCON One Highest level of criticality	• Highest volume of cutover tasks • Execute four hour status updates and reporting • Two executive updates per day
DEFCON Two High level of criticality	• Medium volume cutover tasks • Execute four hour status updates and reporting • One executive update per day
DEFCON Three Medium level of criticality	• Low volume cutover tasks • Execute eight hour status updates and reporting • One executive update per week
DEFCON Four Low level of criticality	• Very few cutover tasks • Normal staffing operations • Normal status and reporting

Fig. 24.10 DEFCON Levels

Each day of cutover is mapped to a DEFCON level. Figure 24.11 demonstrates how DEFCON levels are typically distributed over the cutover execution phase.

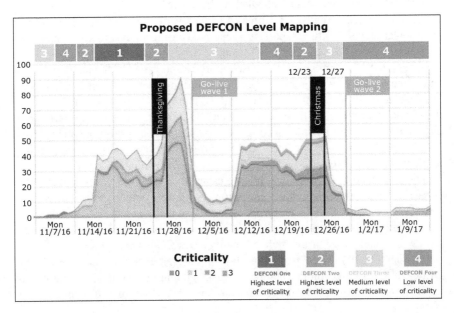

Fig. 24.11 Proposed DEFCON Level Mapping

Issue Monitoring and Resolution

To track and manage cutover tasks and issues, cutover dashboards are maintained as part of command center cadence which is established in pre-planning phase. For a small separation deal (typically, 50–100 applications), dashboards are built in Excel, and the cutover progress data is updated by application teams in SharePoint. However, for complex cutovers with more than 500 applications in scope, online dashboards are setup which give a near real-time picture of the cutover status of applications.

When an issue is discovered, typically it is logged in an issue management tool. The issue is assigned to a particular application owner. The application owner reviews, resolves, and finally closes the issue. In case the application team needs additional help, the command center teams step in to provide the required support.

The command center should use the following guidelines to prioritize open issues:

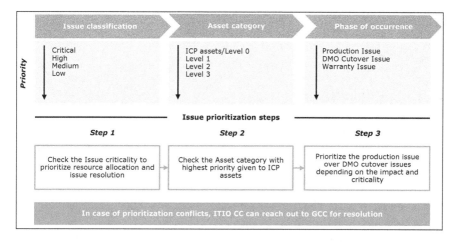

Fig. 24.12 Deciding Issue Priority

Cutover Go Versus No-Go: A Final Checkpoint

Before executing cutover, the final cutover go vs. no-go decision must be made by Program Leads based on a checklist that includes UAT sign-offs; communications with partners about the impact of changes, mitigation steps, and failure points; and the effect of legal factors such as branding, logo changes, and trademarks. Once the final go vs. no-go decision is made, then cutover execution can begin.

24.7   Post-Cutover Phase

After business processes and IT systems are separated, the applications may be unstable and require close monitoring. Adequate training tools, resources, and planning are required to educate users on how to use the new environment.

The post-cutover phase focuses on managing and supporting post-Day 1 functionality and transaction activities to ensure business continuity and adherence to all contractual, legal, and compliance obligations. This phase should establish a structure with appropriately skilled people, tools, and procedures to manage and support the production environment.

Key activities include:

1. *Hyper Care*: This occurs immediately after cutover execution and involves the maintenance and operational support of the new system, including staffing up for user support and issue management and building system health maintenance and operational monitoring plans.
2. *Training and Communication*: Training plays a key role in a successful cutover and can be achieved effectively through a train-the-trainer approach. Train-the-trainer model enables experienced personnel to educate and impart knowledge to a less-experienced resource to deliver courses, workshops, and seminars as required.
3. *Command Center Close*: This occurs at the conclusion of post-Day 1 support after all exit criteria have been achieved, and it should take place as quickly as possible after Day 1.

24.8   Residual Risks

Even after putting all checks and balances in place, some risks will remain that are systemic in nature. These are called residual risks. In objective terms, residual risks can be measured by the cost the company will incur as a result of such vulnerabilities. There are two types of residual risks:

1. *Counterparty Risk*: The risk to each party in a contract that a counterparty will fail to oblige the terms of the contract.
2. *Execution Risk*: The risk of not completing cutover execution within the agreed-upon cost limits and timeline.

A risk management framework should be implemented to ensure:

- Transaction risks are consistently and continually assessed on both an individual and portfolio basis.
- All relevant risk types are considered and integrated (e.g., insider risk, reputational risk, strategic risk).
- Risks relevant to all transactions must be captured in a risk and control library that is embedded into the project.

Under the waterfall risk management framework, standard reporting of risks and issues and clear risk thresholds, escalations, and acceptance processes provide appropriate management awareness, engagement, and approval of the risks on both an individual and portfolio basis.

Under the big bang approach, standard minimum controls for generic risks and key risk indicators (KRIs) are implemented to consistently manage and monitor the control environment throughout the life cycle of the transaction.

24.9   Conclusion

Developing a sequenced ICP (with both business and IT tasks) for critical path applications and performing simulations and pressure tests on the ICP are critical to the success of the cutover. By paying close attention to small details across functions, estimating blackouts appropriately, and performing cutover activities precisely will help the business functions and IT teams achieve complete sign-off from Executive leadership on Day 1 with no rollbacks in cutover execution.

Case Study: 24

Background

A global CPG company decided to undergo a major spin-off—a near-50/50 split—due to their increasingly diverging businesses and market conditions. The typical divestiture focuses on making sure that both businesses operate effectively on Day 1. But, this company's view was much wider: Business models, organizational designs, and go-to-market models all were changed in addition to the separation and stand-up.

Undergoing multiple simultaneous transformations made for a highly complex IT separation and required an airtight cutover plan. To achieve that, the company embarked on a rigorous IT cutover planning phase.

Challenges

IT cutover planning was highly complex due to the following challenges:

- *Vast Application Landscape*: Company had 9 ERP instances and 500+ applications with significant interdependencies.
- *Day 1 Infrastructure Scope*: Beyond ensuring flawless Day 1 network access for both companies and enabling TSAs through intercompany network access, remote access infrastructure had to be greatly expanded for a concurrent outsourcing effort.
- *Global Reach, Regional Complexity*: A highly regionalized cutover strategy was needed due to the nine region-specific ERPs. However, the regional plan had to be harmonized globally due to a high degree of cross-application interdependency.
- *Minimal Room for Error*: Cutover timing and task durations needed to be precise to ensure all IT work was completed within the strict operational blackout window.

Approach

Given the complexity of this deal, IT started cutover planning early to ensure a successful Day 1 go-live:

- *Cutover Planning Process Confirmed (4 Months Prior to Day 1)*: The IT DMO aligned all IT global and regional leads on the cutover planning approach and timeline.
- *Project-Level Draft Cutover Plans Complete (3 Months)*: Project teams jointly defined the IT cutover strategy with their functional counterparts and prepared draft master cutover plans.
- *IT Cutover Planning Session (10 Weeks)*: IT leads and SMEs from around the globe gathered to align on (1) task sequencing, (2) key IT and business dependencies, and (3) risks, mitigation, and contingencies.
- *IT Mock Cutovers (8 Weeks)*: Two dry runs pressure tested the feasibility of completing each task on time with the right resources.
- *Program-Level Critical Path Complete (6 Weeks)*: The IT DMO and IT separation project teams refined and finalized the IT cutover critical path.
- *Cross-Functional Cutover Road map Walk-Through (4 Weeks)*: IT participated in a cross-functional cutover road map walk-through to align across all business functions.
- *Mock IT Cutover (3 Weeks)*: All IT stakeholders participated in a cutover simulation, to refine timing estimates and ensure that cutover execution could complete within the system blackout window.
- *Final Cutover Preparation (2 Weeks)*: The IT DMO stood up global and regional command centers to execute on the minute-by-minute plan.

Impact/Results

The Day 1 go-live was essentially a great success: IT executed a flawless cutover—no technical issues encountered! After the 4-day blackout leading to Day 1, the separated businesses continued their full operations seamlessly.

Key lessons learned:

- *Start Early.* Creating a minute-by-minute, fully-sequenced plan always takes longer than expected; starting early will help avoid oversights.
- *Know Your Business Dependencies.* Seamless orchestration of business and IT activities is necessary for a successful cutover; identify business dependencies early on and ensure complete alignment: What is needed, from whom, and by when?
- *Practice, Practice, Practice.* Leverage planning workshops, road map walk-throughs, and mock cutovers to iteratively "practice" the cutover—only then will you have full confidence in your plan.
- *Hope for the Best, but Plan for the Worst.* Consider all risk factors and mitigation steps, define rollback procedures in case of a failed cutover (including "go/no-go" time cutoffs), and ensure that leadership is represented in the command center to make critical decisions immediately.

Chapter 25
Command Center: Setting Up Round-the-Clock Monitoring During Cutover

25.1 Command Center: Overview

Cutover is one of the most critical and complex phases of a divestiture. To help manage the complexity, it is important to set up dedicated teams and processes to govern cutover execution. This setup is known as a "command center."

A command center is a central coordination unit that oversees cutover activities, facilitates coordination across teams (i.e., multiple information technology (IT) and business teams), and resolves issues through effective decision making. If a cutover involves multiple regions (e.g., Asia-Pacific (APJ), Americas (AMS), and Europe and the Middle East (EMEA)), more than one command center may be required, each acting as a central hub that oversees a specific region.

Command center activities include:

- Managing cutover execution of IT and business milestones (e.g., application code release, business validation, go-live)
- Coordinating cross-functional communications between vendors and partners
- Monitoring downtime of business processes and IT applications
- Serving as a single point of escalation for change management and critical issues

Generally, the objective of a command center is to help ensure a successful cutover for a separation or divestiture by providing direction and clarity on cutover-related issues, assessing risks, and executing actions to resolve issues quickly. Hence, not establishing a command center can pose a great risk to the success of a divestiture.

However, a command center does not provide support for non-cutover-related issues (e.g., production issues), does not serve as help desk support, and is not responsible for the frontline execution of cutover activities, which are performed by business and IT applications teams.

© Deloitte Development LLC 2018
J. Joy, *Divestitures and Spin-Offs*, Management for Professionals,
https://doi.org/10.1007/978-1-4939-7662-1_25

25.2   Command Center: A Framework

In order to set up a command center, a robust framework is needed to manage all aspects of the cutover—people and organization, operating procedures, and reporting and metrics.

25.2.1   People and Organization

People and organization are cornerstones of the command center framework and include the following:

- *Structure*: The first order of business is to establish a command center structure that defines the team and the communication flow. Generally, a command center is organized into a multi-layer hierarchy. The number of levels in the hierarchy is primarily driven by the scale of the cutover and the organizational structure of the company. At a minimum, the command center should have two hierarchy levels, in which the lower-level coordinates with the IT teams for activities related to the cutover plan and the upper level acts as final escalation point for critical issues.
- *Roles and Responsibilities*: Each command center team should have clearly defined roles and responsibilities established using either the RACI model (responsible, accountable, consulted, and informed) or the CAIRO (consulted, accountable, informed, responsible, and omitted) model. We recommend the CAIRO model for quickness of decision making.
- *Staffing*: Staffing in command center involves mapping resources (i.e., people from IT and business teams) to all the defined roles. Depending on the criticality and volume of cutover activities, a company can decide to have dedicated resources staffed for command center or have resources focused part time on command center and part time on other businesses as usual activities.
- *Training*: All command center resources should be trained prior to the command center launch. The command center planning team should develop training materials and playbooks as well as conduct simulations to familiarize the resources with command center operating procedures and methodology.

25.2.2   Operating Procedures

Operating procedures are essential to an effective command center framework and include the following:

- *Criticality Levels*: The criticality level for a cutover activity indicates the level of active monitoring and leadership involvement required during cutover. Criticality levels are typically based on the cutover task volume and criticality of the applications undergoing cutover. For example, when critical applications (e.g., enterprise resource planning (ERP) or finance IT systems) undergo cutover, they are labeled with the highest criticality level.

- For example, a Fortune 500 company decided to set up command centers for its separation cutovers using defense readiness condition (DEFCON[1]) levels, an alert system used by the US armed forces, which can range from high criticality (DEFCON ONE) to low criticality (DEFCON FOUR).
- *Location*: The command center location is typically based on:
  - Number of countries affected by the cutover
  - Where the majority of teams are located
  - Logistical challenges such as travel time, office space, and network connectivity

  Key responsibilities of the command center include:

- *Reporting*: A reporting cadence is defined based on the criticality level of the cutover tasks involved. Activities with a high criticality level may require round-the-clock reporting between leadership and execution teams.
- *Change Management*: Change management refers to the management of changes to the cutover plan, which can have a major impact on the overall cutover schedule due to multiple downstream interdependencies. One missed task can cause hours of delay to all downstream go-live activities.
- *Issue Escalation*: The command center serves as a centralized point of issue escalation for cutover execution teams. The command center communicates escalation points for critical and non-critical applications and establishes guidelines for top-down and bottom-up issue escalation.

A standard method of tracking cutover progress and communicating the status of cutover activities and issues to stakeholders is essential to an effective command center setup. Clear reporting metrics and tools to track command center operations are necessary for this.

25.2.3   Reporting and Metrics

- *Key Performance Indicators (KPIs)*: KPIs measure the overall progress of the cutover and alert leadership to any cutover issues. Some common KPIs include metrics for the number of total applications that have completed cutover, the

---

[1] The US armed forces use an alert system called defense readiness condition (DEFCON). The system uses a five-level scale to indicate the criticality of different scenarios, with level 1 indicating situations of global severity such as nuclear war and level 5 indicating normal peace time situations.

number of open issues, the number of late/backlogged tasks, and the number of applications in blackout.

- *Reporting Dashboards*: Automated dashboards can help save time during complex and large cutovers by highlighting cutover progress, off-track tasks, and issues. For small divestitures, command centers can track cutover progress manually through conference calls and emails.
- *Reporting Cadence*: The reporting cadence helps maintain consistent communication between the command centers and leadership teams through status calls, handoff calls (between regions), and progress reports. A well-defined cadence identifies stakeholders and defines the frequency of calls and status reports.

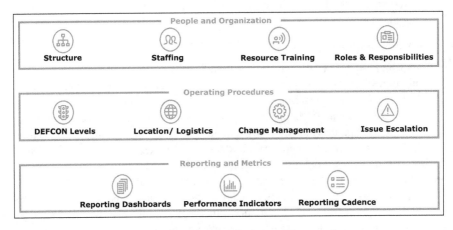

Fig. 25.1 Command Center Strategy Framework

The above framework serves as a guideline. Each transaction is unique and poses different challenges. Hence, it is impossible to adopt one singular approach. Instead, the above framework should be revised based on the complexity of the in-scope cutover. Five factors that drive the complexity and magnitude of the entire command center strategy include:

1. *Organization Size*: An organization's size helps determine the operating procedures and staffing levels required for the command center. Large organizations with complex applications need a strong governance structure and skilled IT and business resources for the command center.
2. *Organizational Structure (Levels of Operation)*: In many organizations, the business either has its own IT teams (e.g., finance IT team, supply chain IT team) or a centralized IT team, which need to be factored into the organizational structure.
3. *Volume and Criticality of Applications Undergoing Cutover*: The volume and criticality of applications undergoing cutover defines the level of and staffing needed for the command center.

4. *Location and Logistics*: The location of the command center should balance the geographical distribution of application teams and leadership. The ideal location should have leadership presence to help ensure fast decision making.

A deep dive into the components of the command center will help clarify its responsibilities.

25.3   People and Organization

During a divestiture, it is not just IT applications that are separated but also employees and assets (i.e., offices, equipment). The cutover of IT applications and employees can pose a huge risk to the transaction. For example, employees who are being let go by the parent or seller company may lose the incentive to proactively work on cutover activities and may choose not to cooperate. The command center strategy must manage such challenges.

25.3.1   Command Center Structure

Command centers are usually geographically distributed and multitiered. If the leadership team and cutover execution teams operate out of a single geographical location, a two-tiered command center can be set up. However, if the leadership and cutover execution teams are located in different geographical locations, a global command center should be established with a "follow-the-sun" (i.e., a round-the-clock model in which issues can be handled by and passed between command centers situated in different time zones across the world to increase responsiveness and reduce delays) model in which each command center is responsible for a specific region.

Establishing at least a two-tier command center structure is recommended, with the highest chain of command dominated by the global command center (GCC), which is responsible for acting as the topmost escalation point and providing updates to executive leadership. The second tier is at the business unit (BU) level, which is closer to execution and helps the execution teams with resources, infrastructure, and information support. A single-layer command center structure should generally be avoided as there are different stakeholders across organization levels and geographies that need to be managed.

Key functions of Tier 1 command centers (e.g., global command center in Fig. 25.2):

- Leads communications and provides timely updates to executive leadership and external stakeholders (e.g., customers and partners)
- Manages and maintains the master schedule of the cutover program

Key functions of Tier 2 command centers (e.g., IT infrastructure, IT applications, and business teams):

- Supports frontline execution of activities across application and business teams
- Manages the daily schedule of cutover activities
- Directs resources to the appropriate teams as and when requested
- Logs and supports triaging of cutover issues

In many organizations, the IT operations team is separate from the IT project team. The IT operations team focuses on IT service operations related to application support, infrastructure, and help desk support. In such cases, a three-tier command center structure can also be established in which the GCC is responsible for acting as the highest escalation point, while the IT operations command center is responsible for working with business teams and providing updates to the GCC. Business and IT teams can still reach out to the GCC directly but will be expected to work more closely with the IT operations command center team as the immediate point of escalation and support.

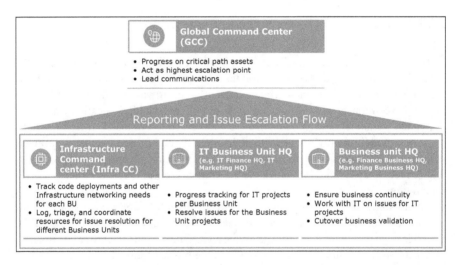

Fig. 25.2 Command Center Structure

A high-tech Fortune 50 company wanted to separate into two companies under 12 months in order to focus on its core competencies and better compete in the market. The company had an extremely complex IT landscape with four data centers, more than 65,000 servers, and more than 2,500 applications shared between the separating entities. The business relied heavily on IT for day-to-day operations.

80 percent	>1.5 million	$2 billion
Revenue flows through the supply chain ecosystems of both entities	*Transactions executed daily with a net worth of $500 million*	*Worth of sales orders held in queue for processing during a 6-day downtime*

A multitiered and multiregional 24X7 command center approach was followed for the critical separation cutover.

A *global command center (GCC)* was set up under the CIO's office to manage the global nature of the cutover. The GCC acted as the highest escalation point for all cutover-related issues.

An *IT command center (ITCC)*, which reported to the GCC, coordinated resources for issue resolution directly with the various business units or business sub-workstreams (SWS). Each business unit (BU) consisted of two dedicated SWS headquarters—IT headquarters and business headquarters. The 2 BU headquarters worked on the ground with the application teams and coordinated directly with the ITCC.

The structure can be explained better with the help of the following figure.

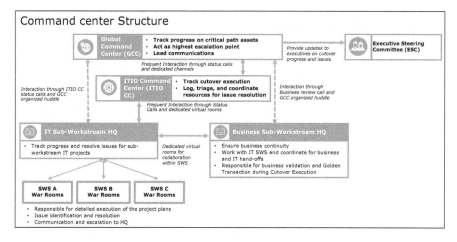

Fig. 25.3 Command Center Roles

25.3.2 Staffing

When finalizing the command center staffing levels, consider the following two things:

- Roles and responsibilities needed in the command center
- Criticality levels based on complexity and volume of applications undergoing cutover

Based on these factors, critical roles should be staffed during criticality level 1 and criticality level 2 when the most critical applications for the business unit are undergoing cutover.

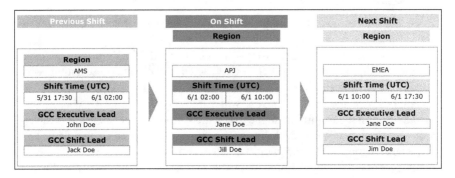

Fig. 25.4 Sample Command Center Staffing Roster

25.3.3 Resource Training

Simply staffing the command center with employees will not make the command center successful; instead, those employees must be trained on the different command center operating protocols in order to quickly assess the impact and act on cutover-related issues. This training is done through mock cutovers, simulation exercises, and workshops.

25.3.4 Command Center Roles and Responsibilities

Role definition models such as RACI or CAIRO should be leveraged to define command center roles and responsibilities. The CAIRO model is a responsibility assignment matrix that enables fast decision making by removing people not required in decision making.

There are multiple threads in a command center, including issue, milestone, and task tracking, as well as business engagement, communications, reporting, and logistics. The RACI and CAIRO models can be used to distribute the roles and responsibilities for these different threads. Figure 25.5 uses the CAIRO model to assign roles and responsibilities for issue management.

Category	Activity	Global Command Center Roles						
		GCC Executive Leader	Master Scheduler	GCC Regional Leader	Shift Lead	Analyst	Enterprise Architect	Cutover Team Member
Issue Management	Document issues encountered during cutover	I	O	A	A	R	C	O
	Triage and prioritize issues during cutover	A	O	R	R	R	C	O
	Diagnose and resolve issues during cutover	A	O	R	R	R	C	O
	Communicate of issue resolution status	C	O	R	A	R	C	O
	Engage workstream leaders for escalated issue resolution during cutover	A	O	R	R	C	C	O
	Escalate cutover issues requiring executive committee approval	A	O	A	R	C	R	O
	Monitor issue aging and escalate to command center leadership	I	O	A	A	R	I	O

| Legend | C | Consulted | A | Accountable | I | Informed | R | Responsible | O | Omitted |

Fig. 25.5 CAIRO Model for Global Command Center Roles

Command center roles can be broadly divided into three categories: leadership roles, subject matter experts (SMEs), and facilitators and execution teams.

- *Leadership Roles*: There are two primary types of leadership roles: cutover leader and master scheduler.
- The cutover leader is responsible for the following:

  - Global point of contact for overall cutover execution, decision making, reporting, and escalation management
  - Provides regular updates to executives and drives investigation of class issues as needed
  - Responsible for business continuity and risk reduction

  The master scheduler is responsible for any changes to the master cutover plan. In case of any changes to the plan for an application, the master scheduler assesses the impact of the change on other interdependent systems and processes and approves the change or requests a hold based on this assessment.
- *Subject Matter Experts (SMEs)*: SMEs come from various business units (i.e., supply chain, finance) and have expertise and knowledge of the business processes, applications, and data needed by the business unit. SMEs should be staffed both at the business command center level and the GCC level. The GCC typically staffs more experienced people in the organization, preferably from upper management (e.g., regional delivery leader) since they directly interact with executives and must have the authority and influence to remove organizational roadblocks. In case of any cutover-related issue, the SMEs play a crucial

role in understanding the impact, getting resources together, and providing a solution.

- *Facilitators and Execution Teams*: The facilitators in the command center bridge the gap between the leadership team and the execution teams on the ground. They have expertise in command center operations and processes, proactively monitor execution progress, and expedite issue escalation to help ensure timely action from leadership. Since not all organizations have a flat structure, bridging the communication gap becomes very important for the high-risk operation of a command center in which every moment matters. Key responsibilities of facilitators include:

  - Providing analysis support and regular updates to the cutover leader
  - Monitoring and reporting on cutover activities and issues
  - Escalating any issues to shift leaders

The execution teams include representatives from IT and the business who actually move the needle by performing and closing tasks like business validation, data migration, making code changes, and handing off interdependent applications. Project managers from the business unit's IT team also form part of this team as they are responsible for tracking progress and updating the status of all finished tasks for their projects.

25.4 Operating Procedures

Before a command center is operationalized, a command center training manual or playbook should be created highlighting the rules of the road. This playbook will help each command center member understand key procedures and reporting cadences to leadership.

25.4.1 Command Center Criticality Level

Cutover is the most important part of any separation execution, and criticality levels provide a way to measure the criticality of the cutover period. Based on cutover activities (i.e., number of tasks ending on a day, number of applications in cutover execution on a particular day, number of critical applications in blackout), each day of cutover execution is mapped to one of the criticality levels in the DEFCON model.

Key potential benefits of using the criticality level approach are outlined below:

- Provides a clear communication to all stakeholders in the command center on the level of alertness required.
- Useful in managing expectations and has helped to ensure the right level of preparedness in the command center for orchestrating cutover.

Based on the criticality level, a command center can operate in physical or virtual mode; for example, for a high criticality level scenario, it is almost always necessary to have a physical command center. However, if the criticality level is low (i.e., few applications undergoing cutover), the command center may operate virtually.

DEFCON Levels	Descriptions
DEFCON One Highest level of criticality	• Highest volume of cutover tasks • Execute four hour status updates and reporting • Two executive updates per day
DEFCON Two High level of criticality	• Medium volume cutover tasks • Execute four hour statues updates and reporting • One executive update per day
DEFCON Three Medium level of criticality	• Low volume cutover tasks • Execute eight hour statues updates and reporting • One executive update per week
DEFCON Four Low level of criticality	• Very few cutover tasks • Normal staffing operations • Normal status and reporting

Fig. 25.6 DEFCON Levels Defined in a Fortune 500 Separation Cutover

25.4.2 Command Center Location and Logistics Strategy

The command center is usually staffed 24X7, and depending on the spread of resources, it could be global or regional. To provide an example, in a recent divestiture deal for a Fortune 50 high-tech company based in the United States, three physical command centers were set up in the APJ, EMEA, and AMS regions to facilitate cutover activities in these respective regions. The command centers were set up in three regions because the applications that were part of the deal had end users and application teams from multiple countries across the globe. A round-the-clock, follow-the-sun model helped the company oversee and monitor the progress of the cutover. If the scope of the transaction is less complex and only involves countries from nearby geographies (e.g., the United States, Mexico, and Canada), it may be more efficient to set up only one physical command center.

25.4.3 Change Management Control Process

During cutover, changes made to one project plan or schedule may affect the cutover of interdependent applications and have an adverse effect on the entire cutover timeline. Project plans must undergo a change management process for any changes in task schedule once the cutover execution has started. Typically, a workflow-based process or tool should be developed to request and manage changes.

25.4.4   Issue Escalation

Issues can be escalated using either a top-down (i.e., the GCC finds an issue and escalates it to the concerned business unit) or bottom-up (i.e., business units reach out to the GCC for help on cutover-specific issues) method. Since cutover issues can have significant business impacts, it is necessary that all teams involved in cutover realize the importance of proactively monitoring and escalating issues. The worst possible scenario occurs when teams are sitting on an issue trying to resolve it, when escalating it through the proper command center channels would help resolve it. Hence, specific guidelines should be established so that all teams understand the escalation process and escalation point.

25.5   Reporting and Metrics

Command centers need real-time reports to assess issues and take quick actions. Organizations can use online reporting tools or create custom dashboards to track project milestone updates during command center operation. These project plans should be maintained by their respective project managers using project planning tools. Project managers can update each milestone of the project plan as and when the related cutover activities are completed. Time is a critical factor, and minutes lost due to delayed reporting could result in disruption to the business.

25.5.1   Reporting KPIs

Before the command center is operationalized, it is critical to define KPIs to track progress. KPIs for the GCC should be different than those used in lower-level command centers. The GCC is more interested in understanding the impact of issues on the overall cutover schedule and key milestones such as go-live. The GCC may not care about a delay in a cutover task that does not have a material impact on the cutover schedule. Similarly, command centers at lower level should use more granular KPIs to anticipate any issues.

25.5.2   Real-Time Reporting Dashboards

If the scope of a cutover is large and complex, developing real-time dashboards can save a lot of time and hassle during cutover. For small divestitures, command centers can track cutover progress by manually updating data from multiple sources. While this process can be slow, tedious, and prone to errors due to the manual steps involved, it is a workable solution when not a lot of applications are involved. However, if the scope of the cutover includes more than 100 applications, web-based dashboards should be set up to track progress using visualization tools.

Criticality	Count of Applications	Not Started	In Process	Complete	Red	Amber	Green
Cutover Progress Dashboard							
Mission Critical	2	0	2	0	0	0	2
Business Critical	34	10	12	12	2	0	10
Moderate	22	10	2	10	0	0	2
Low	68	20	9	39	0	0	9
Total	126	40	25	61	2	0	23

Fig. 25.7 Sample Reporting Dashboard for Tracking Cutover Progress

25.5.3 Reporting Cadence

The command center should follow a strict reporting cadence both for upward (i.e., reporting to leadership) and downward (i.e., reporting to business and application teams) communications. In a recent divestiture deal, a Fortune 500 company set up three global command centers in three different regions and had shift handoff calls (e.g., AMS hosts handoff call at the end of its shift and gives an update to APJ, the next region on duty). Apart from these calls, executive calls took place on a weekly or biweekly, depending on the criticality level of the task. Figure 25.8 depicts the call cadence for level 1 tasks (i.e., DEFCON ONE) that are at the highest level of criticality. The meeting cadence should be simplified with fewer checkpoint calls once the activity level drops to criticality level 2 or below.

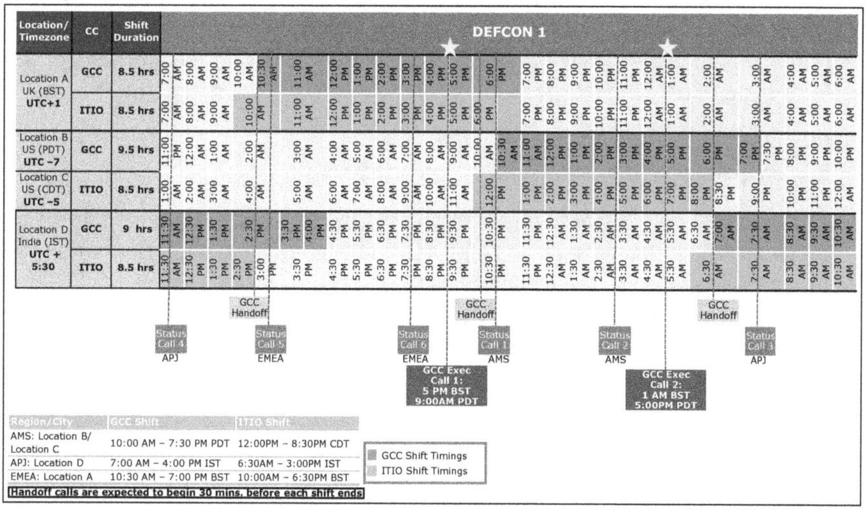

Fig. 25.8 Sample Command Center Criticality Level and Staffing Model

25.6 Conclusion

The command center plays a critical role in minimizing operational risks and increasing business continuity during the final stages of executing a separation or divestiture. For the command center to be successful, it should be able to integrate people, processes, and tools to drive a proactive response to risks and issues. What separates a mediocre command center from a successful command center is the ability to proactively assess risks, understand issues, and leverage appropriate responses to resolve the issues. Organizations that implement successful command centers can avoid pitfalls like an emergency shutdown and help minimize disruption to the business on Day 1.

Case Study: 25

Background

A US-based global technology company agrees to enter a joint venture and sell a majority stake in its China server, storage, and services business to a China-owned company to create a new entity valued at ~$4.0B. Key drivers include the ability to more effectively penetrate the local market and align with buyer's core business strength. Objectives include successful separation of three in-scope business units from seller's portfolio, no disruption to other local Chinese's business managed by seller and no disruption to seller's own in-flight separation activities.

In order to facilitate a smooth Day 1 cutover, an integrated central Separation Management Office (SMO) was established to drive cutover planning and Day 1 orchestration. Overall scope of IT planning included transition of ~8000 employees, 143 applications and related infrastructure, facilities moves, and transfer of end-user compute (EUC) capabilities.

Challenges

Key challenges were centered on two primary areas:

1. IT separation and business planning on an aggressive timeline with significant regulatory compliance requirements including alignment with Committee on Foreign Investment in the United States (CFIUS).
2. Setting up a global IT command center straddling multiple time zones to coordinate activities with both the seller organization (US based) and buyer organization (China based) with stakeholders from business and IT.

Approach

A global "follow-the-sun" command center was stood up to drive a multi-cutover Day 1 plan across 13 workstreams including go-to-market, sales, finance, HR, supply chain, IT, legal, compliance, and other essential business functions.

- *Multiple Cutovers*: Due to aggressive timelines and complexity in the expected future-state business processes, a two pronged cutover was established with an

China time	US time PST	\<Month\> / \<Day\>
7 – 8 a.m.	4 – 5 p.m.	
8 - 9	5 – 6	IT Only Sunrise call
9 - 10	6 – 7	Sunrise call
10 - 11	7 - 8	
11 – 12 p.m.	8 – 9	
12 - 1	9 - 10	
1 - 2	10 - 11	
2 - 3	11 – 12 a.m.	
3 - 4	12 – 1	
4 - 5	1 - 2	
5 - 6	2 - 3	
6 - 7	3 - 4	
7 - 8	4 - 5	Workstreams status reports due in at 7 PM to Command Centre
8 - 9	5 - 6	
9 - 10	6 - 7	IT Only Sunset call
10 - 11	7 – 8	Sunset call
11 – 12 a.m.	8 – 9	Command Center dashboard and broadcast email sent out

Fig. 25.9 Representative Daily Schedule: Exhibit 1

early "operational cutover" phase to pressure test the joint seller/buyer business processes and ensure business continuity and an official "legal close" cutover for full separation. A robust set of accelerators were leveraged to assist with planning the operational cutover where both IT systems and data between business teams would mimic post-Day 1 operating model.

Investment in detailed task level cutover planning, capture of contingency plans, and application checklist reviews with a robust cross-functional governance model helped address proper cutover readiness.

- *Global Command Center*: Due to the global nature of the divestiture, a 24/7 cross-functional command center was set up with sunrise and sunset calls (held in Beijing, CN, local time) to manage cutover activity, incident management, and daily leadership reporting. Multiple war rooms (including a war room for IT) were used to manage function-specific activities with a strong governance model to manage cross collaboration and appropriate escalation to the command center.

Function-specific cutover tasks were managed locally by functional teams, and incidents were addressed by the respective functional war rooms. Necessary high or critical severity incidents and issues would be discussed on AM (sunrise)/PM (sunset) calls and subsequently escalated to the command center by email. Primary communication models included hosted command center calls and 24/7 dial-in conference bridges to report and escalate identified incidents. Minimal blackout periods were used with the exception of finance and HR to support data conversion and validation exercises.

Detailed staffing models, incident logs, status reports, and escalation/process flows were leveraged to maintain consistency across the large distributed ~150 person cutover team.

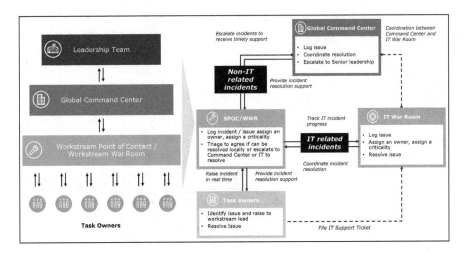

Fig. 25.10 Command Center and War Room Structure and Incident Management: Exhibit 2

Impact/Results

Based on the approach used, legal cutover resulted in minimal to zero impact to business operations with all major issues and incidents identified and rectified during the operational cutover phase. Regulatory requirements were fully satisfied, and effective communications kept buyer and seller informed.

Command center rigor and follow-the-sun model enabled achievement of aggressive timeline and flawless Day 1.

Chapter 26
Protecting the Organization During Vulnerable Times

26.1 Importance of Cybersecurity in a Divestiture Transaction

26.1.1 Cybersecurity Risks with Divestiture Transactions

Most organizations need to secure their networks from both outside and within the business, as well as in the cloud, but during a divestiture, merger, or acquisition, this need for cybersecurity gets elevated. The organization is in a state of flux throughout the transaction period, with significant changes to the enterprise network and security configurations, user profiles, and business-critical applications that may be opening the door to cyber threats.

M&A transactions including divestitures offer cybercriminals an increased attack surface, and this has caused many companies to experience cybersecurity breaches that ultimately damage their reputations, company valuations, and customer loyalty, not to mention the lawsuits. For example, in the midst of an acquisition, a Fortune 500 company suffered a large breach of user information. The organization was criticized for its late disclosure of the breach and its insufficient response. As a result, the company is facing several lawsuits, as well as an investigation by the Congress in the United States. This is over and above the tremendous blow to the company's reputation and its brand value.

Unfortunately, this organization is not alone.

As another example, regulators with the US Securities and Exchange Commission (SEC) are currently investigating a group of hackers suspected of breaking into corporate email accounts; stealing confidential information, such as details about transaction details and valuations; and then proceeding to use that information to engage in insider trading. In coordination with this effort, US regulators have asked at least eight publicly listed companies to provide details about their data breaches.

© Deloitte Development LLC 2018
J. Joy, *Divestitures and Spin-Offs*, Management for Professionals,
https://doi.org/10.1007/978-1-4939-7662-1_26

The unusual move by the SEC reflects increasing concerns about cyberattacks on US companies and government agencies.[1]

In a divestiture transaction, as two or more companies separate their IT assets, a compromised seller's system could potentially leave the buyer's systems and network exposed to the same vulnerabilities and threats. For instance, a large telecommunications company recently announced that computer systems at its newly acquired cable company were compromised, potentially exposing sensitive customer information to theft and abuse.[2]

26.1.2 Business as Usual or New Net Risk?

Since the key focus in a divestiture or separation is the actual execution of the divestiture in a fast-paced manner, clients often wonder why their standard business practices, cybersecurity posture, processes, and infrastructure are not sufficient during the transaction.

A huge component of transaction activity is transferring and separating people, processes, and technology between two or more organizations that are a part of the transaction. Such a huge undertaking brings an increased level of risk that one company will inadvertently integrate a large portion of IT infrastructure from the other company that may have already been breached by cybercriminals. Although the risks may remain somewhat the same, the risk profile, landscape, and associated magnitude will likely increase significantly as the result of the transaction and the visibility in the press.

Although there is a business-as-usual (BAU) component to cybersecurity, entities involved in the deal should not think cyber activity and associated threat levels will remain the same during and after the transaction. Special considerations must be given to cybersecurity as a result of the changes introduced during the process of integrating or unwinding the two companies. This chapter will consider:

1. Cybersecurity matters that affect organizations undergoing M&A transactions
2. The cybersecurity approach of the new company resulting from the transaction, including current versus residual risk and security posture
3. Case studies and leading practices to help plan the next steps

---

[1] "Exclusive: SEC hunts hackers who stole corporate emails to trade stocks," Sarah N. Lynch and Joseph Menn, Reuters–Technology News, June 23, 2015, http://www.reuters.com/article/us-hackers-insidertrading-idUSKBN0P31M720150623

[2] "Telstra says newly acquired Pacnet hacked, customer data exposed," Colin Packham and Kenneth Maxwell, Reuters–Technology News, May 20, 2015, http://www.reuters.com/article/us-telstra-pacnet-cybercrime-idUSKBN0O50WM20150520

26.2   Establishing the Cyber Risk Profile

In addition to measuring steady-state operational risks, a separation or divestiture transaction necessitates an enhanced level of risk assessment by management. Samples of risks often included in the new company's risk profile are as follows.

Table 26.1   Risk Area and Description (Example)

Risk area	Description of risks
Identity and access management (IAM) active directory (AD)	Shared IAM AD risks 　Risk of elevated privileges 　Risk of data breaches, both internally and by third parties 　Risk that data and/or applications will be misused
Network segmentation (site)	Comingled site risks 　Increased risk of attacks by malicious insiders 　Increased risk of data breaches due to bridging of networks and IT infrastructure 　Misuse of data and/or applications
Network segmentation (data center)	Shared network risks 　Increased risk of attacks by malicious insiders or third parties 　Increased risk of data breach 　Misuse of data and/or applications
Vulnerability management	Shared vulnerability risks 　Risk of exploiting a vulnerable application 　Risk of data breach

These risks represent some of the main areas of concern that organizations must deal with during and after a divestiture. Clearly, the new company that emerges from the transaction will not have the same risk profile as the original companies.

26.2.1   Existing Cyber Risks Versus Net New Cyber Risks

The executive management of the company involved in a divestiture must determine the corporate profile of the new company following the transaction. From a cyber risk perspective, before making any changes or performing any mitigating actions, it is essential for the executive management of the company involved in a divestiture to understand the existing cyber risks (pre-transaction) the original companies face versus the combined net new cyber risks that the new company face as a result of the transaction.

The cyber risk profile of the new company that emerges from the transaction is established by understanding the pre-transaction cyber risks that carry over to the new company, as well as any new cyber risks introduced as a result of the transaction. Once these risks have been cataloged, and prioritized, appropriate and adequate steps can be taken to mitigate them.

26.2.2   Demonstrating Changes in Risk Level Due to Divestiture

Risks can be categorized based on severity of impact and likelihood of occurrence for the different risk profiles within the organization's IT systems.

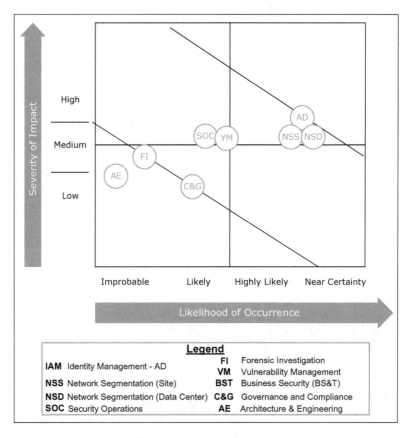

Fig. 26.1 Sample Risk Profile

In addition to measuring steady-state operational risks, a separation transaction necessitates an enhanced level of risk assessment and management. Additionally, it is imperative that the cyber team outlines common risks resulting from transactional activity and the then project the impact of risk mitigation efforts used to manage those risks.

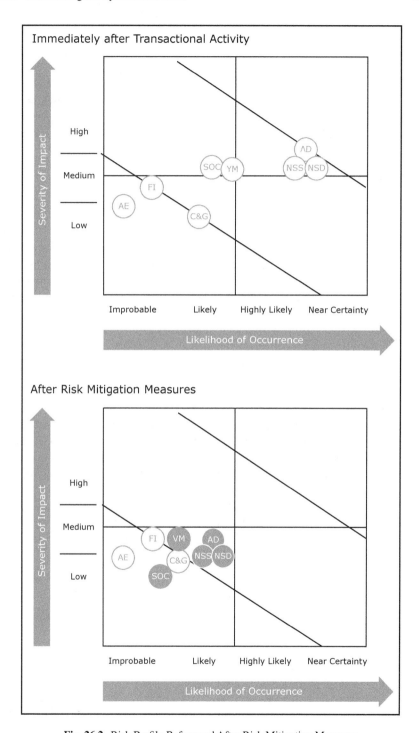

Fig. 26.2 Risk Profile Before and After Risk Mitigation Measures

In order to minimize risk, having an accurate assessment of the following is important:

1. Cyber risks existing before transactional activity is announced
2. Cyber risks introduced as a result of transactional activity
3. Risk mitigation measures required to bring the cyber risks in line with acceptable limits so they do not pose a threat to the transaction or the future of the new company, including associated countermeasures and associated one-time costs

26.3   Enumerating Cyber Risks in a Transaction

26.3.1   Cyber Risk Framework and Applicability to Divestiture

Divestiture transactions are bound by extreme time constraints, and organizations must quickly and continuously adapt to the changes brought about by these disruptive events. In many cases, companies are expanding or contracting their organizational to newer engagement models. All of these actions inherently create cyber risk. However, it is imperative to proceed with these transaction-related changes as rapidly as possible while mitigating the cyber risks.

Organizations should deliberately decide which applications require tighter cybersecurity and which applications can be secured through business-as-usual cybersecurity principles. Using a risk-based analysis, organizations can determine what to focus on in terms of alleviating cybersecurity risks. Cyber incidents manifest themselves not only via technology systems but also impact critical business operations. Cyber monitoring for systems, applications, and people should be enhanced during the transaction so that the attacks can be detected in an expedited manner and the organization is able to mitigate any transaction or operational risk.

Aggressively addressing cybersecurity risks will help in building confidence with a broad range of stakeholders (i.e., customers, business partners, regulators, and employees) involved in the transaction. The executive management of the companies undergoing a transaction should understand that cyber risk is a strategic issue in the context of a divestiture. Organizations should address the increased threat by:

1. Taking a strategic and structured approach to cyber resilience and communicating with all key stakeholders on how to manage cyber risks
2. Focusing resources on what matters most and driving the value of cyber investments
3. Separating the target state for cybersecurity vs. what is important to get the transaction done with adequate cyber risk controls in place (Day 1 goals)

In order to characterize and prioritize the cyber risks introduced as a result of the transaction, it is important to use a comprehensive framework to ensure all the various aspects of cybersecurity are addressed. The framework should touch upon key areas of cybersecurity within the following three areas of cybersecurity governance.

Fig. 26.3 Cyber Risk Framework Key Areas

Each of these key areas can be further broken down into the subareas to create a cyber risk framework which can serve as a tool by the means of which organizations can identify and address the key cybersecurity issues faced in divestiture transactions.

This framework represents the length and breadth of cybersecurity areas commonly in play during divestiture transactions and has been used by organizations successfully to identify, mitigate, and manage risks resulting from these disruptive events.

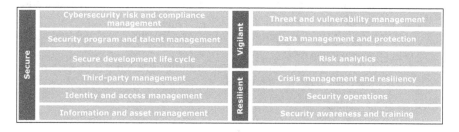

Fig. 26.4 Cyber Risk Framework

26.3.2 The Important Areas in Cybersecurity (Based on Cybersecurity Framework)

First, enumerate cyber risks related to the important areas affected by the transaction, the most common of which include the areas identified in green in Fig. 26.4.

26.3.2.1 Risks Related to Identity and Access Management

Identity and access management (IAM) helps with the enablement of the right individuals to access to the right resources as per the need to access.

The IAM workstream includes a number of components often affected by divestiture, such as:

- *Directory services*: The following are the risks and considerations associated with the directory services:

    – Decision around creation of a new active directory (AD) or creation of new identities to share the existing active directory
    – Trust-related decisions between the AD of the new company and the original entity
    – Data access decision between

- *Single sign-on*: The following are the risks and considerations associated with the single sign on

    – Management of seamless authentication managed in applications undergoing changes as a result of the transaction
    – Risk of lack of application access or lack of availability

- *User provisioning and management*: Authentication, authorization, and privilege access management:

    – User provisioning methodologies for Day 1
    – Risk of cross provisioning, such as the remaining company provisioning access to the new company
    – Managing manage application authentication and authorization in preparation for the transaction
    – Managing the risk of an increased chance of cyberattack if privileged access is not handled adequately
    – Managing toxic combinations within identities created as a result of the transaction

- *Segregation of duties*:

    – Risks related to segregation of duties
    – Managing toxic combinations within identities created as a result of the transaction?

26.3.2.2 Risks Related to Threat and Vulnerability Management

Threat and vulnerability management is a practice and a process of identifying, prioritizing, reporting, and remediating vulnerabilities in an IT environment, especially in operating systems, applications, software, firmware, etc.

During the transaction, the cybersecurity and network security of the system become vulnerable to cyber threats as the result of several transaction-related activities. These activities will inevitably create changes to the operating system, applications, and networks of the companies involved in the transaction, whether it is RemainCo, SpinCo, or NewCo. These changes will most likely introduce high-risk vulnerabilities into these IT components that must be addressed in order to mitigate the cybersecurity risk.

The vulnerability management workstream includes a number of components often affected by an M&A transaction, such as:

1. *Cloning Existing Applications for the New Company*

   • Risk of high-risk vulnerabilities in cloned applications
   • Measures that have to be taken to patch the vulnerabilities prior to Day 1

2. *Splitting Applications for the Remaining Company from the New Company*

   • Managing vulnerabilities introduced as result of splitting the applications?

3. *Providing Applications as Is to the New Company*

   • Managing high-risk vulnerabilities that exist within the applications that must be remediated prior to handing them over to the new company

4. *Preparing Applications for TSA Activities*

   • Managing any vulnerabilities that result from changes that have occurred within the applications as a result of TSA activities

26.3.2.3   Risks Related to the Security Operations

A security operations center (SOC) is a centralized unit that deals with security issues on an organizational and technical level. An SOC within a building or facility is a central location from which staff use data processing technology to supervise the site. During a divestiture, several activities take place in the SOC that require increased monitoring and detection standards that should consider the following factors:

• Monitoring of security operations for Day 1 threats
• Understanding the change in cyber threat landscape as a result of the deal
• Risk related to disgruntled employees and other internal threat actors to carry out cyberattacks
• Strategy to will the company split the security operations infrastructure such as SIEM (security information and event management) and antivirus protection

26.3.2.4   Risks Related to Data Management and Protection

Data loss prevention defends against potential data breaches and data exfiltration transmissions by monitoring and blocking unauthorized parties from accessing sensitive data while in use (endpoint actions), in motion (network traffic), and at rest (data storage). In data leakage incidents, sensitive data is disclosed to unauthorized parties either through malicious intent or an inadvertent mistake. Sensitive data includes personally identifiable information (PII), company information, intellectual property (IP), financial information, protected health information (PHI), credit card data, and other information.

Deliberate or inadvertent disclosure of sensitive data during a divestiture can not only jeopardize the transaction, but also business continuity, brand reputation, and future success. Mitigating controls must be put in place to help ensure that such nefarious activity does not happen. The key aspect to consider for data leakage prevention is addressing the increased risk of sensitive data leakage caused by the divestiture?

26.3.2.5   Risks Related to Network and Site Segmentation

Network segmentation, as it relates to the creation or carving out of a network space in M&A and divestiture transactions, refers to either:

1. Carving out a small subset of network segmenting for the purposes of creating a new network for the new company
2. Carving networks out of an existing network for the purposes of merging them together to create a new network for the new company
3. Merging network segments into a larger network for the purpose of creating a new network for the new company
4. Handling firewall changes to ensure optimal cybersecurity policies are followed

Site segmentation refers to segregating the physical sites between the new company and the remaining company.

There are several factors that should be considered when carving out or creating a new network or splitting the sites:

- Strategy of the network being carved out for the new company and/or the spun-off company
- Definition of controls for proper network and site segmentation, keeping cybersecurity in mind
- Management of the firewall changes handled to ensure optimal cybersecurity policies are followed
- User segmentation changes that need to be considered
- Definition of controls are in place for network and/or site segmentation

Network Segmentation (Site/Data Center)

Comingled or shared site risks:

- Increased risk of insider threat attacks
- Increased risk of data breach
- Misuse of data and/or applications

26.3.2.6 Risks Related to Cybersecurity Risk and Compliance Management

Preparing for changes in cyber compliance and the regulatory landscape is a key to the success of the divestiture.

There may be several compliance and regulatory changes the new company will face, including the following:

1. Business market and geographic changes
2. Industries the new company will operate in
3. Changes in the new company's client base
4. Changes to the types of products and services the new company offers
5. Changes to the types of data the new company may be required to store

26.4 Why Are Regulatory Changes and Compliance So Important in an M&A Transaction?

Net New Compliance Factors

Understanding the compliance strategy in place as a result of the divestiture and the factors to consider as a result of the changes, for example:

- A NewCo can be subject to new compliance factors due to change in the business requirements and the kind of data it processes. An example is the introduction of cybersecurity compliance that did not exist before the transaction, such as PCI DSS (Payment Card Industry Data Security Standard).
- A compliance such as this can be introduced if the NewCo has to process credit card information post the acquisition of a new company.

Compliance Data Segregation

- Understanding if there is any compliance-related or PII/PHI data that needs to be segregated as a result of the divestiture

Data Residency

Data residency refers to the physical or geographical location of an organization's data or information. Data residency also refers to the legal or regulatory requirements imposed on data based on the country or region in which it reside. A divestiture may create data residency-related issues in case there are any data residency issues that need to be handled based on the changes in geography in which the NewCo will operate.

The next sections will provide a step-by-step approach on how to manage cybersecurity risks, as well as create a plan of action in light of the M&A or divestiture transaction, followed by a real-world case study.

26.5   Mitigation Approach

Cybersecurity can be approached in various ways; however, the approach must be structured, defined, and measurable and must lead to risk reduction. When combined with the cyber risk framework, these steps can help organizations set the direction to prioritize, execute, and measure an effective cybersecurity model.

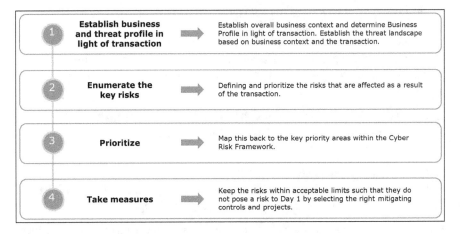

Fig. 26.5 Proposed Approach

26.5.1   Step 1: Define the Organization's Current Cyber Threats Based on the Cyber Threat Landscape

It will greatly help if the organizations undergoing a transaction identify and prioritize cyber risks. The first step in effective cyber risk determination is to define the organization's cyber threat landscape, which is a mapping of all possible factors that could pose threats to the organization.

Using a threat model is based on the MITRE Corporation's Common Attack Pattern Enumeration and Classification (CAPEC) model. CAPEC is a comprehensive dictionary and classification taxonomy of known cyberattacks that can be used by analysts, developers, testers, and educators to advance community understanding and enhance defenses. This threat model considers who may want to attack the organization (threat actor), how the attack may happen (technique), what assets may be targeted (crown jewels), and how vulnerable these assets are to exposure (surface). The result is a measure of an organization's exposure to particular threats.

The following diagram represents a sample threat landscape exercise that should be used by an organization to understand the threat actors; how they may target the company; their tools, techniques, and procedures; how they may exploit the organization's IT challenges; and the potential impact they may have on the transaction and the organization's business continuity.

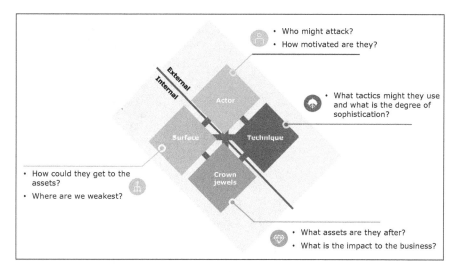

Fig. 26.6   Sample Threat Landscape Exercise

The result of this threat landscape exercise will be the enumeration of the top threats to the organization resulting from the transaction. For example, a sample threat landscape could include the following:

R1 – Sensitive data disclosure	R5 – Internal/Ext. fraud
R2 – Data integrity compromise	R6 – Reputation Risk
R3 – Internal function disruption	R7 – Regulatory Compliance Risk
R4 – External facing service disruption (DDoS)	R8 – Third party risks

Fig. 26.7   Threat Landscape Sample Output

Once the threat landscape is defined, the organization proceeds to the next step, which is defining and prioritizing the risks that are affected as a result of the transaction.

26.5.2   Step 2: Define and Prioritize the Risks that Are Affected as a Result of the Transaction

Completing the threat landscape exercise is key to understanding the top risks facing an organization. A major component of this exercise is prioritizing the identified threats as T1 through T10 on the risk heat map (see Fig. 26.8) and enumerating the risks introduced as a result of the transaction.

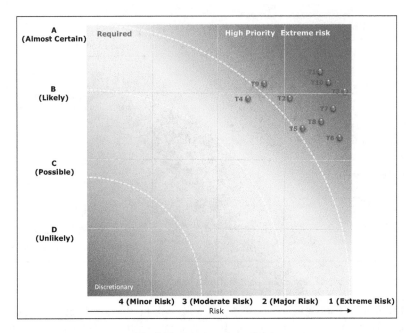

Fig. 26.8 Prioritization of Risks

This risk heat map helps organizations visualize the threats and understand the prioritized risks.

26.5.3   Step 3: Map This Back to the Key Priority Areas Within the Cyber Risk Framework

An organization should consider the areas within the cyber risk framework that are key to the transaction and aligned to the key threats. Some areas that should be considered high-priority targets during M&A and divestiture transactions are highlighted in red in the cyber risk framework as per Fig. 26.10.

26.5.4   Step 4: Keep the Risks Within Acceptable Limits Such That They Do Not Pose a Risk to Day 1 by Selecting the Right Mitigating Controls and Projects

Last but not least, the risks must be kept to an acceptable level, so they do not pose a risk to Day 1.

After defining the acceptable risk level for the organization, review the status of each risk defined in Step 3. If a risk is within an acceptable risk level, then no additional measures are necessary. However, risks that are above the acceptable level need to be addressed in a prioritized fashion, using a slew of measures.

26.6   Wrapping It Up

M&A and divestiture transactions can be disruptive events for organizations and can exponentially increase cybersecurity, technology, compliance, and operational risks.

Due to the overwhelming impact of such transactions on a company's assets, including business processes, information, and people, early incorporation of cyber risk management activities into the M&A life cycle may reduce the strains of cyber risk and compliance.

The same approach toward cybersecurity-related risks does not apply to all organizations engaged in M&A transactions. Therefore, it is important to understand the components of the transaction. Identifying synergies early on between M&A objectives and cybersecurity, technology risk, and compliance drivers can enhance and accelerate the overall separation and/or acquisition process, as well as interim planning and execution efforts.

We recommend integrating cyber risk management components into the M&A life cycle to help ensure success.

Case Study: 26

Background

In a dynamic business environment with challenging growth and margin pressures, a leading US-based software and data center service provider sought to achieve near term and sustainable cost benefits by selling two parts of its business (i.e., the software business and the data center business) across two transactions. These divestitures would free up resources to invest back into the business, evolve strategic sourcing competencies, and drive sustainable process efficiencies and cost improvements.

The end-to-end spin and merge efforts (divestiture), involved creating two parallel spin companies—one for the services business and one for the software business. The scope of work included setting up a Divestiture Management Office and leading the transaction to its full completion from an IT perspective.

The cybersecurity function was identified as a key area of both transactions that increased the cyber risk profile of the company. In addition, there was a possibility that the acquiring entity might audit the company's business units.

Challenges

The key problem areas that needed to be addressed were as follows:

1. Two transactions were being executed in parallel, and cybersecurity function was a central function that provided services to both business units that were being divested.
2. The team managing the cybersecurity function had to identify the most efficient strategy around active directory separation.

3. The applications transferring over to the new company had to be fully functional and include single sign-on capabilities with no degradation in user experience.
4. The team managing the cybersecurity function had to identify the most efficient strategy around SIEM/SIOC separation, as well as maintain continuity of operations.
5. The cyber risk profile had to be reduced to a minimum between the entangled sites and the three companies involved in the deal.
6. Net new vulnerabilities were identified as a result of the following separation activities:

   (a) Cloning the applications
   (b) Providing existing applications to the new company
   (c) Preparing the applications for TSA

7. Network space had to be carved out for the two new company organizations, keeping in mind the heightened cybersecurity risks.
8. Aggressive timelines led to certain pressures on which cybersecurity risks to prioritize in the given time period.

Approach
The following were the high-level steps followed:

To deliver your assessment, we will follow a process consisting of five phases, encompassing your business, threats and capabilities. The result will be a transformation roadmap which will guide your organization towards the target state.

① Establish Business Profile in light of transaction	② Conduct Threat landscape Assessment	③ Enumerate the key risks	④ Prioritize	⑤ Take measures
Establish overall business context and determine Business Profile in light of transaction	Establish the threat landscape based on business context and risks	Defining and prioritizing the risks that are affected as a result of the transaction	Map this back to the key priority areas within Deloitte Cyber Risk Framework	Keeping the risks within acceptable limits such that they do not pose a risk to Day 1 by selecting the right mitigating controls and projects

Key activities

• Understand the key services provided by Cyber Security to each of the businesses being divested • Leverage a top-down as well as a bottom-up approach to determine the current state of cyber capabilities • Interview business stakeholders to identify what matters to the organization from a cyber perspective i.e., its crown jewels • Determine the enterprise level or LOB level cyber risk appetite • Determine the day 1 disposition for each of the Cyber Security services	• Identify threat actors and techniques relevant to the organization and the industry • Using the identified threat actors, define specific threats that may be relevant to the enterprise or specific crown jewels within the enterprise • Determine exposure to threats based on business, technology and related characteristics of the organization	• Map threats to top risks that are faced by the organization in light of divestiture • Understand the solutions that are required to address these solutions • Determine the solution, as it relates to day 1 for the following: – Active directories – SIEM – Certificate Authority – Single Sign On (SSO) – Data loss prevention – Vulnerability Management	• Determine target state maturity and acceptable risk levels scores based on the overall understanding of: – Business/IT context – Threat landscape and exposure – Industry/peer maturity – Risk appetite • Identify the TSA/MSA for the cyber services that will be required by Newco post day 1 • Roll out projects for: – Lowering risk profile for vulnerabilities – AD day 1 strategy – SIEM day 1 strategy – SSO day 1 strategy – Certificate Authority day 1 strategy – Projects related to authentication, authorization	• Analyze and organize the recommendations into discrete projects, taking into account priority level • Define project attributes such as budget & resource estimates, timelines and dependencies. • Execute and measure the projects for day 1. • Carve out a fully functional Cyber security function for the carved out unit

Fig. 26.9 Threat Landscape Sample Output

We leveraged the above methodology to develop an understanding of the client's threat and risk profile, as well as the business units being carved out and the risks faced by the organization and mapped them to actionable outcomes. Between the two transactions, there were 28 projects identified for cybersecurity remediation in order to get to Day 1 successfully with an acceptable level of cyber risk exposure. In addition, 10 TSA agreements were identified between the two transactions.

The risk mitigation measures were mapped either to a Day 1 strategy or a future-state strategy. The following figure represents an example of the outcomes around the risk mitigation measures. In this example we worked with the client to determine that instead of accepting a massive risk for 12–18 months, there will be an initial risk for Legal Day 1 + 5 weeks; gradually and systematically risk levels shall be reduced within 6–7 months after Legal Day 1.

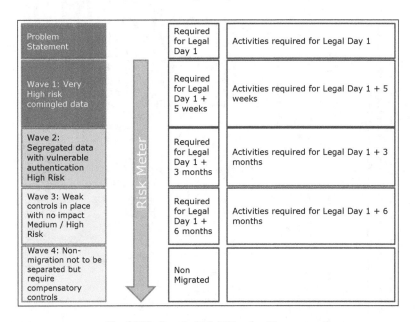

Fig. 26.10 Sample Risk Mitigation Measures

Impact/Results

The client was able to overcome a particular set of challenges related to the two transaction agreements, including dealing with aggressive timelines related to the transaction and successfully delivering on the cybersecurity expectations of three parties (organizations); in addition, the client was able to develop Day 1 strategies and execute projects by completing the transaction in time, completing the necessary activities to address the cybersecurity risks:

- Firm up TSA requirements and agreements for cybersecurity—where required.
- Help the organization maintain a cyber risk posture throughout both transactions.
- Help the organization with regulatory and compliance concerns from a cybersecurity perspective.

Chapter 27
Transform as You Separate

Divestiture transactions provide organizations with unique opportunities to transform and optimize their business processes and operating environments; however, without a well-planned integration strategy, many companies cannot capitalize on these fortuitous events.

In most acquisitions, the buyer company follows a bolt-on integration approach in which the acquired entity continues to use its legacy processes and systems. This approach can leave the buyer with a bloated infrastructure full of redundant resources and information technology (IT) systems that negate possible synergies and efficiencies from the acquisition and may result in suboptimal business processes and IT spend.

Similarly, after a typical divestiture, the seller company is stranded with an oversized infrastructure originally built with the divested entity in mind, including IT applications that are no longer suitable for the remaining business. Also, the seller company usually shares IT applications with the divested entity for some timeframe after the divestiture.

Additionally, many companies—buyer companies, seller companies, and divested entities—often use their own in-house, customized IT systems to cater to business requests. These IT systems may not follow the best architecture principles regarding scale, security, and design, resulting in deviations from industry leading practices.

All of these conditions force companies involved in divestiture transactions to use varied systems and processes to conduct business across different geographies and lines of business, which can lead to an abundance of inefficiencies, including an inconsistent customer experience, increased operational overhead, and eventual erosion of shareholder value.

© Deloitte Development LLC 2018

J. Joy, *Divestitures and Spin-Offs*, Management for Professionals,
https://doi.org/10.1007/978-1-4939-7662-1_27

Some examples of issues faced by companies include:

- Inability to bundle products between the seller or parent company and the divested entity
- Manual order management and long processing time due to disparate IT systems
- Inaccuracies in sales pipeline forecasts
- Long and complex financial reconciliation process
- Lack of comprehensive executive reporting
- High cost of IT infrastructure and maintenance for both seller and buyer company

Software as a service (SaaS) solutions offered by cloud service providers can help alleviate many of these issues and accelerate the completion of the transaction itself, which, in effect, will allow the company to focus on its core objectives—growth, profitability, and customer satisfaction.

SaaS solutions can deliver out-of-the-box functionality that requires minimal customization, thereby significantly reducing the go-live timeline and easing the pressure to recover the one-time costs of the divestiture. The flexibility offered by SaaS solutions can serve as a divestiture or separation readiness engine, allowing a company to easily carve out a business unit.

During the last decade, cloud service providers have matured and expanded their product offerings, providing more stable and secure SaaS solutions. As a result, many businesses are increasingly embracing SaaS solutions to run critical business processes with higher efficiency and reduced operational expenditure than in-house solutions. SaaS solutions are based on industry leading practices; thus, they follow optimized business processes for specific industries and subsectors. Additionally, SaaS solutions generally require little on-premise infrastructure for support, allowing companies to roll them out quickly.

Key potential benefits of SaaS solutions include:

- Homogenous business process across geographies leading to lower operational costs
- 360 degree view of the customer, which gives every information about a customer and is a core value proposition of the SaaS sales solution
- Single system to track sales opportunities and leads
- Increase in upsell and cross-sell opportunities across geographies leading to better customer conversion rates and higher customer satisfaction
- Centralized revenue recognition across the company that allows sales transactions to be recognized the moment they are completed
- Reporting functionality that provides executives with an accurate picture of planned versus actual financial and operational targets

Market trends and opportunities often require the business to adjust production dynamically to achieve financial and operational goals. Due to its flexibility, SaaS-based solution can be scaled dynamically to allow the business to optimize IT costs in tune with market requirements. Additionally, one-time IT setup costs can easily be converted into consumption-linked operational costs, which can be directly linked to business utilization.

Despite the potential benefits, transforming in-house IT applications into SaaS solutions is highly complex, which can be difficult to achieve under the rigid timeline of a divestiture. A strong business case addressing the key challenges can enable the executive leadership to make the strategic decision for the organization. Important components of such a business case is outlined in Fig. 27.1 and described in the next sections.

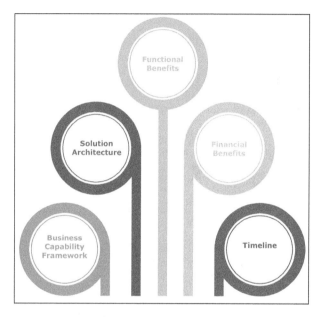

Fig. 27.1 Business Case Components

27.1 Business Capability Framework

Business capability framework, a blueprint which defines a transformational road map for industry-specific business/IT capabilities, must be developed to help identify a core set of minimum viable products (MVP) required to run the business.

MVP is a foundational set of enterprise capabilities which are core to the business; by assessing the MVP maturity, key architectural hotspots can be identified to improve the operational efficiency and lock down the scope of transformation for the on-time release of the overall solution.

The business capability framework should:

- Identify the scope of transformation across functions (e.g., sales, finance)
- Identify additional functionalities and efficiencies provided by the proposed solution
- Align with the divested entity's target state for business operations
- Define detailed business process and information flows aligned to specific activities
- Filter out non-core capabilities that are not relevant to the divested entity's business
- Address inefficiencies such as redundant processes and manual workarounds

The business capability framework can then be used to design future-state processes and identify opportunities for IT asset rationalization.

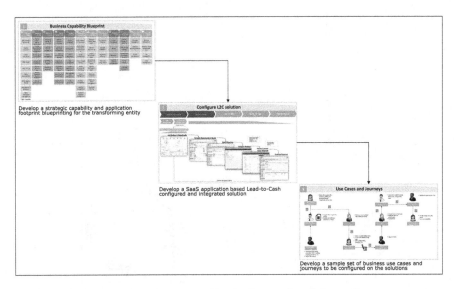

Fig. 27.2 Capability Scope Identification Process for a Software Company

27.2 Solution Architecture

Once the target state business blueprint and solution is defined, the next step is to finalize SaaS vendors that support the required functionality.

A vendor scorecard should be used to compare different SaaS vendors offering similar functionality with the following parameters:

- Maturity of the solution
- Functionality coverage
- Ease of implementation
- SME support availability
- Industry adoption rate
- Interoperability with other applications

Additionally, compiling market research and input from industry SMEs on proposed vendors is critical when finalizing the vendors and locking down the SaaS solution.

Some of the key challenges when selecting a vendor and SaaS solution include:

- Identifying the boundary functionality for applications that will not be covered by the SaaS solution
- Integrating the legacy functionality with the SaaS solution:

  - Ensure the integration itself does not lead to any significant custom development scope to perform a non-core functionality

- Identifying SaaS vendor licensing rules for the development, testing, and production environments

27.3 Functional Benefits

A key benefit of a SaaS solution is process standardization, which can improve time to market, reduce order processing time, and allow rapid adaptation to emerging business and monetization models and market demand.

An application landscape built with a SaaS solution based on an industry standard business capability framework can offer functionality covering a majority of core business capabilities such as sales, marketing, order management, and revenue recognition and allows for regional variations in the company's business model. Instead of attempting to customize a SaaS product solution to add a specific functionality, analysis should be done on why the business is deviating from an industry standard process supported by the product. Customizations should typically be less than 10%. The functional benefits that can be realized by SaaS solutions are summarized in the following sections.

27.3.1 Marketing and Sales

Business challenges

An M&A event brings to the forefront key business challenges across the organization ranging from marketing and sales to finance and procurement. These challenges should be addressed by an enterprise transformation to enable effective business operations post go-live. As an example, marketing functions may lack a 360 degree customer view or require long lead times to roll out marketing campaigns due to the manual configuration. Another common challenge is lack of a cross business unit bundling functionality.

Transformation benefits

SaaS-based solutions drive automation and self-service, which can enable rapid time to market of the company's product line, improve customer targeting, and lead to higher conversion rates. Automation also provides a 360 degree customer view (both pre- and post-sales nurture) and enhanced analytics capabilities that enable high return on investment (ROI) for the marketing function. Also, SaaS solutions can provide consistent configuration across the company's entire product catalog, enabling the sales function to generate and sell bundled product orders across business units and geographies.

27.3.2   Master Data Management

Business challenges

Product and customer master data are critical components of effective business operations. This data provides the company with a 360 degree customer view, as well as enables product life cycle management. But lack of data governance can lead to duplicate data sources that require manual reconciliation and reporting, which can generate inaccurate insights about customers, as well as disjointed customer account management and planning strategies. Limitations in centralized data governance also affect the time required to launch a new product and end-of-life product decommissioning.

Transformation benefits

SaaS-based solution can centralize data governance, simplify the customer and order management processes, and reduce manual reconciliations across systems. Due to its ubiquitous nature across geographies and business units, the solution can also uncover unforeseen gems in customer data that can be used for proactive account planning.

27.3.3   Finance

Business challenges

Business units often maintain their own customized systems to record and recognize revenue, which may result in multiple transactional and master data layers. Large organizations usually find it particularly challenging to reconcile financial numbers across multiple business units in time for periodic financial closing periods.

Transformation benefits

A central SaaS finance solution can enable all business units to report revenue using the same streamlined solution aligned with industry leading practices. The solution should be integrated across sales, order management, and reporting systems, thereby allowing all financial transactions to be recorded in real time. Additionally, many solutions provide built-in credit check services, giving account representative better visibility into customers' challenges, which in turn enables better account management.

27.4 Financial Benefits

SaaS-based solutions can provide a significant reduction in IT operational expenses in addition to dynamic scaling options. A subscription pricing model is often available for a SaaS solution that includes infrastructure hosting, support, maintenance, and licensing.

There are three major components to target-state IT operational costs for SaaS-based solutions:

- *Applications:* Costs for applications include licensing and annual maintenance (subscription) expenses. The licenses must include use in the development, testing, and production environments.
- *Infrastructure (Hosting and Support):* Infrastructure costs can be divided into server, storage, network, and end-user computing expenses. Server and storage expenses include the cost for on-premise applications that must be kept in check to realize the full cost benefits of SaaS solutions. To help reduce these expenses, on-premise, non-SaaS applications can be moved to a public cloud environment. Expenses for end-user computing devices such as laptops, desk phones, and video conferencing equipment, as well as network expenses, are also included in infrastructure costs. Network (i.e., LAN, WAN) expenses must be calculated based on the future-state real estate strategy.
- *People (IT Organization):* This includes the salary, benefits, bonus, and travel expenses for FTEs needed to help run business-as-usual operations on the new SaaS solution, as well as the costs for the IT helpdesk support teams.

27.5 Timeline

Timeline for transformation must be aligned with the M&A deal schedule to deliver maximum benefits. Historically, Day 1 timelines range from 10 to 12 months, and completion of the transformation before Day 1 is vital for realization of benefits. It allows the buyer company to leverage the divested entity's IT capabilities starting on Day 1.

When creating the transformation timeline, consider:

- *Stakeholder Alignment:* Alignment between business and IT stakeholders on critical phases of the timeline is important. If the major stakeholders are aligned, then top-down decision-making can be enforced to manage issues such as new business requirements, design changes, resource constraints, etc. across the phases.
- *Architecture Design:* The accuracy of the timeline is dependent on accurately mapping the current and target-state design. The system architecture, integration between systems, and data migrations between current and target-state systems should be carefully outlined and taken into account when creating the timeline.

- *Contract and License Procurement:* Contract signing and license procurement are long processes that can delay the availability of the development and testing environments required to stand up the solution; thus, they should be considered when creating the timeline.
- *Implementation Methodology:* Various teams involved in implementing multiple SaaS and legacy applications means each prefer to use a favorable implementation methodology. For example, finance and supply chain teams are usually more inclined to use waterfall approach, while CRM teams are inclined toward agile approach. Teams are bound to have integration and design dependencies with others and need to be managed to avoid major gaps and critical defects in later phase of the project. Locking down a common development approach at program level for the transformation before finalizing the timeline can help in aligning the dependencies.

27.6   Key Considerations for SaaS-Enabled Transformation

SaaS-enabled transformation for an M&A transaction significantly increases the complexity as there are challenges of SaaS transformation in addition to the regular M&A challenges such as Day 1 timeline, buyer-seller alignment issues, budget constraints, etc. Executing a SaaS-enabled transformation for M&A transaction successfully requires proper planning and a well-defined program setup. Also some key focus areas to be considered are the following.

27.6.1   Environment Strategy

Cost in a SaaS-enabled architecture varies dramatically based on the number of environments so optimization of SaaS application environments is required. Also procurement phase with new vendors generally undergoes multiple rounds of negotiations to get best discounts, and any delays due to procurement negotiations can lead to development delays, thereby putting the transformation program at risk.

The environment requirements of each SaaS application must be decided upon in the initial design phase in order to avoid any delays. When deciding upon the requirements of SaaS solutions environments, consider:

- Projected user base
- License type (e.g., administrative, reporting, read only)
- Application modules and packages
- Application criticality
- Data parameters (e.g., transaction per second, data volume, velocity)

Another important area for SaaS solutions is maintaining the environments. Provisioning SaaS solutions compared to on-premise solutions can be easier, but careful planning and centralized coordination with vendor teams is required to manage the differences in provisioning methodologies and limitations.

27.6.2   Security Architecture

Security and privacy concerns ranging from configuring virtual machines to managing user privileges are the main barriers to adoption of cloud technologies. Companies with multiple SaaS and on-premise solutions find it critical to develop a common security architecture that can handle the varied nuances of the different solutions.

Single sign-on (SSO) solutions are generally used for on-premise applications. For hybrid solutions with both SaaS and on-premise components, multiple configurations and customizations may be required. It is important to apply end-to-end transport-level encryption (i.e., IPSEC, TLS, SSL) to data transferred between applications within the hybrid solution. Access logs provided by SaaS vendors and on-premise solutions should be leveraged to monitor security controls.

27.6.3   Release Management

Code fixes and test execution across multiple SaaS applications can lead to a chaotic situation when development teams are performing in-house changes and SaaS vendors are performing global release cycle. Managing this chaos is possible if there is a robust release management process in place. The process should include a centralized release calendar, governance controls, common versioning mechanisms, and regular checkpoints. The release management process should be tested during the implementation phase to help ensure the smooth roll out of testing, simulation, and production environments.

27.6.4   Data Governance

Data governance is generally a major challenge in transformation projects, and it gets magnified when setting up a SaaS-enabled architecture for an organization. A detailed approach is required to maintain data integrity and data quality.

Some key elements of data governance include:

- Reference and master data management
- Data security management
- Data quality management
- Regulatory compliance
- Data warehouse

The cross-functional nature and scope of the enterprise transformation coupled with M&A transaction constraints make data dependencies complex to manage during the implementation and cutover phase. A well-defined data governance strategy created during the design phase and followed during the implementation and cutover phases can help significantly reduce the number of defects and change requests during the testing phase.

27.6.5   Integration Strategy

Interoperability and data integration across multiple disparate systems are critical to delivering the entire scope of business requirements, especially for an architecture made up of SaaS applications as well as on-premise applications. The integration strategy should ensure low latency and enable data security for the organization. Low latency of data is extremely important for business as organizations are moving large amount of data across their systems and doing so in an efficient manner is vital.

When planning the integration strategy, consider:

- Implementation complexity
- Licensing costs
- Scalability
- Security
- Performance

27.6.6   Change Management

A transformation event brings about a tremendous amount of change for employees of go-forward company. It essentially changes the way in which the employees use the IT systems to conduct business operations and leverage business services. For example, transformation of sales systems with a 360 degree customer view can completely change how a sales professional tracks customer activities from lead to order.

In order to ensure that the go-forward organization fully utilizes the potential of transformed systems, the employees and systems users need to be trained much before the systems go live.

Here are the key areas of focus for change management:

1. Leadership engagement—Engage the functional leads so that they can prepare their respective organizations for upcoming operational changes and provide their feedback on new processes.
2. Communication—Keep the go-forward organization informed about the transformed systems and resulting business benefits so that employees are aware of upcoming changes.

3. Training—Train the end users such as HR, sales, and marketing teams so that they are familiar with the new systems and can function effectively on Day 1.

Change management cannot be an afterthought in a transformation program and needs to be integrated into program execution from the beginning. In case of an end-to-end transformation, it takes some time for the go-forward employees to adapt to change and understand how they can execute their existing job better with the help of new IT systems.

27.7   Conclusion

Traditional M&A transactions require a long return on investment (ROI) period and a long lead time to realize the forecasted benefits. A SaaS-enabled transformation can reduce this timeframe by providing simplified and flexible SaaS solutions for standard business processes. The solutions can also provide effective integration and configuration of custom processes, if required, in case of future M&A events.

A SaaS-enabled transformation cannot only enable faster go-live for the divested entity vs. an on-premise systems transformation, but it can also reduce the go-live risks and IT operating costs. To deliver the projected benefits to the company, an end-to-end transformation requires detailed planning, risk assessment, and mitigation efforts to succeed within the targeted cost and schedule parameters.

As SaaS solutions mature and expand, more organizations may adopt them to increase their M&A flexibility across industries and their valuation to prospective strategic and financial buyers.

Case Study: 27

Background

The buyer acquired through one of its portfolio companies the seller's medical device business unit in 2015, which is a leading global manufacturer in its sector, and markets its products across 38 countries. With 2014 revenues of over €1B and over 14% share of the market globally, the buyer's portfolio company was engaged in a manufacturing and distribution alliance with the seller and helped to develop the seller's medical device products.

Challenges

The carve-out required separation of businesses across 38 countries in 3 waves, and Day 1 involved 24 Wave 1 countries in a highly compressed 6-month timeframe. A new tax and legal entity structure was required to be implemented in an accelerated manner to be ready for close. The carve-out from the seller, which was going through its own migration to a single global ERP, needed to be done with heavy dependence on the seller's supply chain, manufacturing and financial processes, and systems and resources in most of the countries. The seller's inability to continue supporting HR, financial consolidation, treasury, and legal and travel and expense processes and systems required the carve-out entity to identify, evaluate, and engage vendors to implement and integrate new systems for in-scope countries before close.

Approach

During pre-signing transaction period, an operational due diligence was conducted to develop carve-out and integration strategies for standing up a global IT environment leveraging SaaS- and cloud-based architectures enabled by a lean IT operating model. Diligence included estimating stand-alone run rate and one-time cost estimates. After assessing current IT capabilities, resources and services received from the seller, as well as investment required to stand up these functions in an independent entity during the post-signing period, the following activities were performed:

- Assigned disposition for ~500 applications currently being used. A detailed discovery process post-deal signing was conducted to validate the application list by functional area (sales, marketing, R&D, MFG, etc.).
- Identified and finalized TSAs for all IT assets providing services for all end-user devices and across 27 sites globally.
- Developed detailed Day 1 systems and integration architecture design against an end-state reference architecture model and supported the implementation of 31 new IT applications by transforming core processes and data and IT services to a lean IT services model on Day 1.

Impact/Results

- Stood up the carved-out legal entity for 24 Wave 1 countries and the buyer's global Day 1 IT infrastructure, enterprise applications, services, and a lean Day 1 IT management team
- On Day 1, list of application was rationalized to ~380 (25% rationalization of the enterprise application footprint in 6 months). The consolidation was done by standing up cloud-/SaaS-based platforms and rationalizing redundant applications prior to close
- Established end-state finance and controlling services operating model with back-office support, treasury services operating model, and human capital service delivery models that enable a global R&D, manufacturing, and supply chain network with 22 distribution centers
- Supported the development and implementation of organizational structure and HR processes for over 1500 employees.

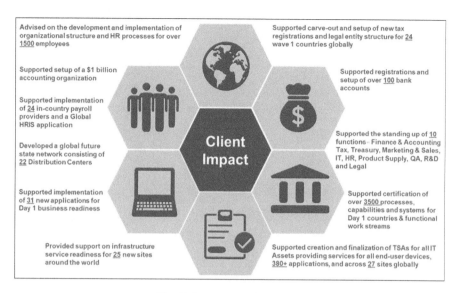

Fig. 27.3 Client Impact Metrics

Chapter 28
Managing Data Separation and Migration During a Divestiture

28.1 Overview

Although data separation and migration are among the most complex, riskiest, and critical activities involved in a divestiture, they are not typically considered during the initial planning and blueprinting phases. The quality of data migration and separation can significantly affect business operations and intelligence, as well as the overall transaction timeline. This chapter outlines key considerations and challenges encountered during data separation and migration and provides recommendations on how to manage these activities.

28.2 Typical Challenges and Considerations

Managing data during a divestiture is difficult due to the following challenges:

- Changing business processes
- Adapting different information technology (IT) landscapes
- Compliance with tax, legal, and security requirements
- Preventing the migration of unnecessary data
- Complex reporting requirements
- Managing structured versus unstructured data
- Infrastructure constraints
- Diverse resource requirements
- No interaction with buyer company prior to Day 1

© Deloitte Development LLC 2018   345
J. Joy, *Divestitures and Spin-Offs*, Management for Professionals,
https://doi.org/10.1007/978-1-4939-7662-1_28

28.2.1   Challenge 1: Changing Business Processes

The seller and buyer companies often follow significantly different business processes, and these differences can affect data separation and migration. For example, one company may engage in only domestic deals and, therefore, fulfills its reporting requirements using accounting principles generally accepted in the United States of America (US GAAP), while the other company may engage in only international deals and, thus, fulfills its reporting requirements using International Financial Reporting Standards (IFRS). The differences between US GAAP and IFRS can affect the underlying data structures used by each company. As a result, the buyer and seller companies must work together to optimize their business processes and resolve any gaps for the divested entity.

28.2.2   Challenge 2: Adapting Different Information Technology (IT) Landscapes

The seller and buyer companies also usually have very different IT landscapes that can further complicate data separation and migration. For example, in case of enterprise resource planning (ERP) systems, moving data between different ERP systems is difficult and requires significant effort. Often, the two companies do not even have the same number of applications to support business processes, which further complicates data migration.

28.2.3   Challenge 3: Compliance with Tax, Legal, and Security Requirements

In an attempt to maintain execution velocity, regulatory requirements (i.e., tax, legal, and security) that could have serious financial and legal implications may sometimes be overlooked. These regulatory requirements can significantly affect data migration. For example, to fulfill audit, legal, and compliance requirements as set by SEC and specific industry regulatory authorities such as FINRA, the seller company is usually required to archive 3–7 years of historical data for the buyer company.

28.2.4   Challenge 4: Preventing the Migration of Unnecessary Data

Information is a valuable asset, but not all of the seller company's information is required by the buyer company or divested entity; thus, unnecessary information should be carefully filtered out. Migrating unnecessary data increases the scope and complexity of the separation effort and can seriously affect IT processes and applications at both entities. Moreover, sometimes migrating data between systems is too costly and time intensive to complete before Day 1. In such cases, transition services agreements (TSAs) should be explored to enable a smooth transition.

28.2.5 Challenge 5: Complex Reporting Requirements

The reporting infrastructure is critical to the IT landscape and allows organizations at every level to manage their businesses effectively. In order to enable reporting, massive amounts of data must be collected and aggregated to derive at valuable business insights required to run the business post-Day 1. However, during divestitures, this essentially means the data migration team must:

1. Move large volumes of raw data from the seller company into the reporting infrastructure of the buyer company or divested entity, and the two systems are usually very different.
2. Ensure all aggregate data models constructed for the buyer company or divested entity are properly loaded with the required data from the seller company and that appropriate reports can be generated.
3. Create new data models and reports to account for the different processes and reporting infrastructures used by the seller and buyer companies.

Significant effort is required to migrate data across reporting infrastructures. If multiple reporting solutions exist at either entity, it further complicates the migration process.

28.2.6 Challenge 6: Managing Structured Versus Unstructured Data

Identifying the required structured (such as transactional and historical data stored in databases) and unstructured (such as files, images, etc.) data at the seller company that must be migrated to the divested entity or buyer company is a complex task. Not all applications are based on structured relational data in which inter-data relationships are formally defined. Unstructured data, such as images and web content, can be difficult to cleanse and migrate; thus, a well-planned data migration strategy (i.e., automated, manual, or semi-manual) is necessary. Identifying and delineating unstructured data from LAN systems and web portal sites are time-consuming and require the use of tools such as web crawlers.

Migrating structured and unstructured data requires an understanding of:

- Data structures at selling and buying entities
- Data mapping identifying how data at seller's side maps to the data at buyer's side
- Business rules required to convert seller's data as per buyer's requirements

28.2.7   Challenge 7: Infrastructure Constraints

The network limitations between data centers should be considered when migrating data from the seller company to the divested entity or buyer company. Migrating large volumes of data over the network can seriously affect the speed and success of the migration effort. The extent of the seller's, buyer's, or divested entity's network bandwidth will determine the data sets that can be migrated over the network, the sequence in which data migration scripts will be executed, and the volume of data that can be sent over network at one time. Maintaining the security of data while in transit is also an important consideration, and data transfer mechanisms should be carefully defined and leveraged while working with information security experts.

28.2.8   Challenge 8: Diverse Resource Requirements

The data migration effort requires a diverse set of resources, including business subject matter experts (SMEs), technical leads, data architects, job developers, and network IT personnel from both the buyer and seller companies. Engaging such a diverse set of resources is difficult during a divestiture, given the cost and time constraints involved.

28.2.9   Challenge 9: No Communication with Buyer Company Prior to Day 1

During divestitures, there are instances where there is no interaction with the buyer before Day 1 and seller is supposed to carve out the separate IT ecosystem on a leased or shared infrastructure. Such cases lead to additional complexities and effort around identifying the location of carved-out IT ecosystem, establishing service agreement for shared or leased infrastructure, determining all the applications and data that needs to be separated, and identifying all legal, tax, and compliance regulations for the divested entity. Also, such divestitures may require a different approach to migration, where applications are cloned on a separate infrastructure first and unrelated data is cleansed later.

28.3   Data Migration Approach for Divestitures

Data migration requires a business process-oriented approach. The data migration strategy should consist of three key phases with an overarching project management function, as outlined in Fig. 28.1.

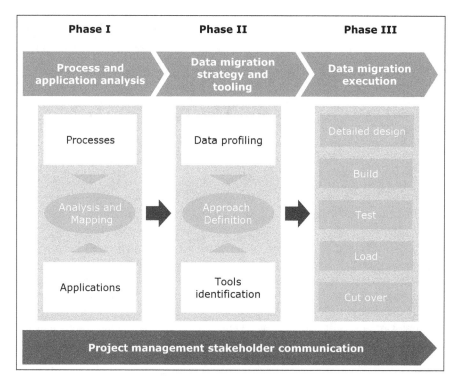

Fig. 28.1 Data Migration Phases

28.4   Phase 1: Process and Application Analysis

Analyzing processes and applications at the seller company, the divested entity, and the buyer company is essential to the data migration strategy. Detailed process analysis workshops should be held with business teams (such as sales, finance, tax, etc.) to:

- Identify key processes at the seller company and the buyer company.
- Define the key processes required by the divested entity.
- Identify gaps between these processes.

This detailed process analysis will help determine the conversions needed to migrate data from the seller company to the divested entity or buyer company.

Once the processes required by the divested entity or buyer company are clearly identified, these processes are mapped from the seller company's system to the requisite system at the divested entity or buyer company. Close collaboration between the business and IT functions at both the buyer and seller companies is essential.

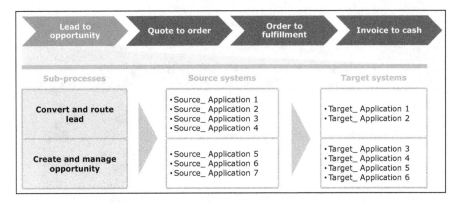

Fig. 28.2 Process-to-Application Mapping

When developing a process-oriented approach, using process-to-application mapping is essential to unravel complexities around differences in applications (such as count and type) catering to similar processes at seller and buyer companies. This mapping analysis provides critical insights needed to define and plan the data migration strategy.

Moreover, process-to-application mapping helps identify applications that are unavailable for key subprocesses either at the seller company or the divested or buyer entities, thereby alerting the data migration team that innovative solutions are required to manage the data. Mapping also helps ensure key processes are not missed during data conversion and migration.

Once the mapping is complete, the IT team should review the applications to understand:

- Underlying data types
- Differences between applications used by the seller company and the divested or buyer entities that require nontraditional data migration techniques
- Volume of data (at a high level) that must be migrated and how that data will be moved (e.g., over the network or via magnetic disk storage tapes)
- Data model differences that affect data migration scheduling and data cleansing
- Data extraction and loading methods that can be leveraged without customization
- Network constraints that should be considered for data migration
- Applications affected by legal, regulatory, security, and historical retention requirements

28.5 Phase 2: Data Migration Strategy Definition and Tool Setup

Once all the processes, applications, and underlying data in the IT landscape are uncovered, the next step is to define the approach for migrating the data. Data migration involves the following three-step extract, transform, and load (ETL) process:

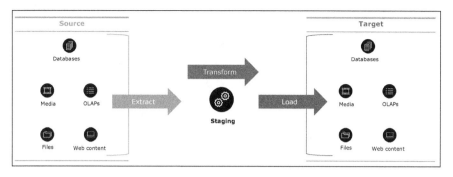

Fig. 28.3 Three-Step ETL Process for Data Migration

28.5.1   Extract

The extract process involves extracting data from the seller company's IT land-scape onto a staging area. Before extraction, the seller's data and systems must be prepared for migration. Such preparation provides a deeper view into applications at the seller company and the divested or buyer entity identified during Phase 1, allowing the team to understand the function of each application and structure of data within the same. The data migration team should consider modeling the seller's applications and underlying data structures to identify intersystem linkages. The team should also carefully assess whether all data sets within the seller's IT land-scape are captured and align with the overall business needs of the divested entity or buyer company. This assessment is called data assurance and includes:

- *Data Profiling.* Identifying data not fit for migration. Such data should be archived by the divested entity or buyer company for reference or tax purposes.
- *Data Quality.* Data properties and interrelationships required for successful data migration. Data quality rules are key inputs into the data profiling effort.
- *Data Cleansing.* Data cleansing identifies data that must be migrated manually versus via automation. Unstructured data is generally more difficult to cleanse.

The overall process of extraction depends on the applications and underlying data types that must be extracted. The approaches required to extract structured and unstructured data are significantly different.

Structured data

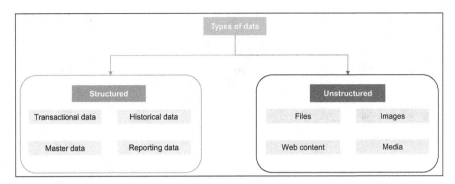

Fig. 28.4 Types of Data

Structured data such as reporting or transactional data has clear structures and relationships that are generally easy to analyze. Standard data modeling tools can be used to analyze structured data and are an important part of the overall data migration toolset. The data migration team should also work with the technical leaders to obtain production or production-like data stores to conduct the data analysis.

When planning how to extract structured data, the team should also consider the following:

- In certain cases, it may be easier to clone the entire database directly into the staging area, while other times it may be more prudent to copy only specific data sets (also called extracts) into the staging area.
- Some applications may not provide direct access to the data; in such instances, data may need to be pulled out as file extracts or via standard data retrieval services (such as API or web services).
- In certain cases, data (especially master data) may be tightly coupled with the application logic, making automated data extraction difficult.

Unstructured data

Unstructured data includes files, images, and web content that are difficult to analyze and extract. Both manual and automated techniques are used to analyze and extract unstructured data. The data migration team should standardize the extraction approach by data type, as follows:

- For files that end in ASN.1, DOC, DOCX, EML, OST, PST, PDF, RTF, PPT, PPTX, TXT, XML, XLS, and XLSX, extraction could simply involve reading the files from their respective folders. However, to read, analyze, and cleanse data, different techniques may be required. The XLS or XLSX files can be easily loaded into standard data modeler tools for analysis. Once loaded, the data can then be cleansed in the staging area and imported in XLS or XLSX format. Similarly, for PDF files, standard open source readers can be leveraged to extract key information and conduct analysis.
- For files on web portals, it is common to migrate all content first and then perform the cleanup and conversions, which is more like extract, load, and transform (ELT) rather than ETL.

Extraction tools

The type and volume of data and the nature of the IT landscape greatly affect the choice of extraction tools. Key considerations when choosing extraction tools include:

- Does it work with both structured and unstructured data?
- Does it have standard connectors to extract data from proprietary applications, on-premise applications, and software-as-a-service (SaaS) applications?
- Can it apply cleansing and transformation rules in real time during extraction?
- Does it not only support data extraction, but also data loading to minimize the number of tools required?
- Is it scalable to increase the speed of data extraction and loading when necessary?
- Is it easy to use?

28.5.2   Transform

Transformation is the phase in which business rules are applied to synchronize the seller's data with the data structures of the divested entity or buyer company. The raw (extracted) data is often loaded onto a staging area, and then data conversion rules are applied for consistency with the processes and data structures of the divested entity or buyer company.

Data conversion can include:

- Changing data formats
- Changing data attribute types or values
- Joining or splitting data from the seller company to align with data models for the divested entity or buyer company
- Calculating derived attributes or data values per the needs of the divested entity or buyer company
- Applying data quality and validation checks
- Applying required data security rules such as masking and encryption

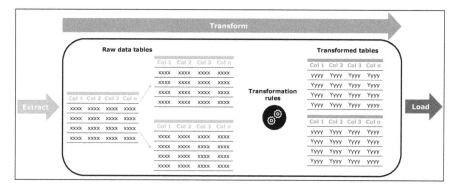

Fig. 28.5 Transformation Process

As shown in Fig. 28.5, a staging area is required to prepare data for eventual loading into the divested entity's or buyer company's systems. Depending on the types of systems and underlying data sets involved, the staging area could be a high-performance relational database or data warehouse for structured data or a file system for unstructured data. The toolset standardization is key as it can be extremely cumbersome to manage a large number of tools for data migration.

28.5.3   Load

In simple terms, loading is when transformed data is pushed into the divested entity's or buyer company's data stores. Loading techniques differ based on data type, application type, data volume, information security rules, and network capabilities. Loading considerations include:

- Transactional and relational data can be moved into target systems via scripts using tools such as Informatica™ or MuleSoft™ ETL platforms. Some SaaS systems, such as Salesforce™, provide web services that can be used to migrate data over the network.
- Structured or unstructured data can be migrated into target systems using magnetic disk storage tapes that can be shipped to the buyer allowing for quick migration without network bottlenecks at the end.
- Data extracts (i.e., files) can also be stored and migrated using Secure File Transfer Protocol (SFTP) batch transfers between the staging area and target systems.

Sequencing the data loads is essential when loading into the divested entity's or buyer company's systems. It is important to load the metadata or master data first before migrating transactional or operational data to allow for error-free data migration while maintaining referential integrity. Also, sequencing should account for data volumes, toolset constraints, and network bandwidth to ensure fast execution.

Once all data migration scripts are complete, validations are required to ensure all data extracts were migrated correctly and completely.

28.6   Phase 3: Data Migration Execution

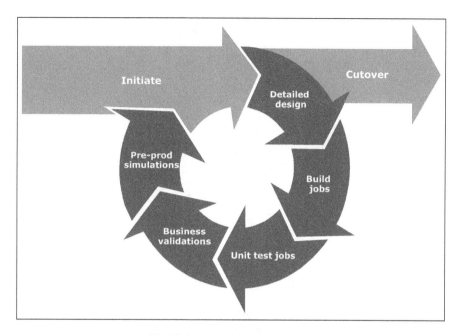

Fig. 28.6 Data Migration Execution

Divestitures are often bound by aggressive timelines that require business and technology changes to run in parallel, including data migration. Due to these time constraints and the vast scope of separation activities, data migration execution is often conducted in an iterative fashion.

The phases of data migration execution should align with the iterative delivery model, thereby enabling early issue detection and resolution. The key phases of data migration execution include:

1. *Plan the Execution.* An iterative delivery plan should be developed for data migration execution. The plan should deliver data migration scripts for processes and subprocesses to ensure the entire business flow such as sales order creation, customer invoicing, etc. can be tested with data migration. Appropriate resources should be engaged across the migration design, build, test, and delivery pipeline.
2. *Define the Design.* The data migration team should work with business teams and IT application owners at the seller, buyer, and divested entities to lay out the design for data migration scripts at the data element level. The design should be delivered to the development team, which will then generate data migration scripts.

Table 28.1 Data Migration Execution

Source table	Source attribute			Target table	Target attribute			Transformation rules
	Attribute name	Type	Value rules		Attribute name	Type	Value rules	
<Table name>	<Attribute name>	<Data type>	Potential values Derived value Derivation logic	<Table name>	<Attribute name>	<Data type>	Potential values Derived value Derivation logic	Any transformation required such as data type changes, value derivation etc.

The design should include detailed process flows, data extraction criteria, data cleansing and validation rules, and volume and performance considerations at the seller company, the divested entity, and the buyer company. The design should also consider security, audit, and control requirements for data encryption, archiving, exceptions, errors, rollback, and recovery processes.

3. *Build Data Migration Scripts and Procedures.* The design should be converted into data migration scripts and procedures. If the migration is manual or semimanual, this phase also serves as a training ground for the data migration team to practice the migration processes. The team must be provided with the appropriate tools to build the data migration scripts and procedures.

4. *Conduct Unit Tests.* Unit tests validate that the scripts are performing as designed. The tests should focus on three key areas:

   - *Validate Target Data Stores and Data.* Validate the integrity of target data stores by confirming the migration of all test data from the seller company to the divested entity or buyer company. Error logs should be carefully examined and appropriate changes made to the data migration scripts to help ensure that future jobs can be performed without errors.
   - *Test Security.* Confirm the security of the seller, buyer, and divested entities is not compromised, appropriate access controls are in place, and agreed-upon security and encryption rules are applied during data migration.
   - *Test Performance.* Ensure that jobs do not create unnecessary performance bottlenecks that could lead to eventual data migration disruptions.

5. *Business Validations.* The data migration team should work with business SMEs to validate that business processes can function without interruption following the data migration. Business SMEs for both the buyer and seller entities must clearly define the criteria for success and detailed process validation procedures for the data migration effort. This phase is critical to ensuring business continuity post-Day 1.

6. *Preproduction Validations.* Data migration scripts and procedures should be thoroughly tested in a production-like environment to help ensure:

   - Data migration scripts scale to production loads.
   - All business and data scenarios are tested with production-like data.
   - The data migration team practices dry runs prior to final cutover for Day 1.

7. *Cutover.* Data migration is an integral part of overall cutover, and the data migration team should work with the deployment and cutover teams to help ensure that appropriate procedures and time windows are in place for data migration. Also, cutover window could be large and may require data loads in two stages. The first stage is called the "initial load" where data is migrated for the first time into different target systems. The initial load can last few days to a couple of weeks. The second stage is called the "incremental loads" where all residual data that was generated since the initial loads is migrated.

28.7   Governance and Organizational Implications

The importance of data to an organization and the impact data loss and corruption can have on the business point to the need for stringent data governance and stewardship standards. The following resources should be assigned ownership for each data type:

- Business

  - *Data Stewards.* These resources understand the operational and strategic requirements of the data, as well as the business rules that govern data quality and accuracy.
  - *Executive Business Leader.* The executive business leader prioritizes and drives cross-functional data governance and engages with executive engagement.

- IT

  - *Data Architects.* These resources drive an end-to-end enterprise-wide view of master and transactional data, as well as define how data flows and interacts across business processes and systems.
  - *Application Data SMEs.* These resources have a deep understanding of the data models, structures, and relationships in the seller's IT landscape. They define the data structures, relationships between data elements, and data formats and map the data from the seller company's system to the divested entity's system or buyer company's system.

- Security

  - *Data Security Experts.* These critical resources support the IT team in delineating security, legal, and regulatory requirements for data migration.

Given the cross-functional nature of data, it is important to establish an enterprise-wide data governance, management, and protection team to clearly own the data needs across functional domains.

28.8   Conclusion

Data management and separation are key challenges during a divestiture. Structured versus unstructured data requires different migration strategies between the IT landscapes of the seller company, the divested entity, and the buyer company. Critical success factors include:

- Early planning to effectively account for time, effort, and skills required to effectively execute data migration
- Developing a process-driven approach to identify relevant IT assets at both the seller and buyer companies and corresponding application level data migration intricacies

- Effective data governance and stewardship in order to help ensure migrated data meets data quality standards and fulfill key processes at buyer's side effectively

Case Study: 28

Background

A large multinational high-tech company undergoing a divestiture wanted to carve out the IT application landscape as part of the deal. However, it had a bloated application landscape with 700+ legacy applications, not all of which were required to run the business of the divested entity. In order to decrease IT footprint, reduce IT operating costs, and enable future growth through acquisitions, the deal terms encapsulated the transformation of the IT ecosystem by significantly rationalizing legacy applications and incorporating 20+ SaaS application to support key lead-to-cash business processes. As part of the transformation, numerous legacy applications had to be retired, and data from these applications had to be migrated to SaaS applications, requiring an extensive data migration effort.

Challenges

Migration of data from large set of legacy applications into significantly smaller footprint of SaaS applications posed significant challenges for the team. These included:

- Significant effort in determining the source legacy applications for the data required to run the business post transformation.
- Differences in business process flows supported by legacy applications and processes offered out-of-the-box by SaaS applications.
- Significant differences in underlying data structures between legacy and transformed ecosystem.
- Data from multiple legacy systems—supporting the same business processes—had to be combined, converted, and loaded into target systems.
- Short duration of the project requiring process definition and implementation going on in parallel to the data migration requirements and design activities.
- Availability and active participation of IT and business experts from seller company across lead-to-cash process chain to support data migration activities.

In lieu of all these challenges, a structured approach and well-planned execution of data migration were essential.

Approach

A process-driven approach with a set of well-defined steps was leveraged to conduct data migration for the target state (transformed) IT ecosystem. These steps included:

- Target state business processes with SaaS applications were defined in detail for the divested entity. Data migration actively participated in business workshops conducted by functional teams to identify process and application relationships, identifying key data elements and data relationships in the lead-to-cash life cycle.

- Detailed interviews were conducted by the team with business and application experts to:
  - Identify the legacy and target-state SaaS applications' data stores
  - Assess quality of data in the legacy applications
  - Determine data mappings and transformation rules between legacy and SaaS applications' data stores
  - Define data extraction and loading mechanics
  - Understand additional constraints imposed due to legal and compliance requirements
- Detailed execution road map was developed and executed over a 9-month period that included:
  - Detailed design and development of automated data migration scripts
  - Iterative testing including multiple full data load (across all applications) simulated in nonproduction environments
  - Final cutover data migration as a part of go-live

Impact/Results

The divestiture transaction combined with big bang IT transformation in an aggressive timeline made the data migration effort extremely challenging. However, early planning and the structured approach adopted by the team allowed them to conduct the data migration successfully within the project timelines. As a part of the project:

- ~200 automated data migration scripts were designed and developed.
- Five full data load simulations or rehearsals were conducted prior to go-live.
- Data from more than 100 applications were extracted, converted, and loaded into 20 target-state SaaS applications.

Part IV
Focusing on RemainCo

Chapter 29
Real Estate and Site Separation

Every M&A deal has a significant real estate IT component that may be underestimated by even the most seasoned M&A practitioners. The complexities involved in dealing with hundreds of globally dispersed sites with a very significant IT footprint must be well understood before embarking on real estate-related M&A projects. Lack of proper knowledge of the company facilities and how these sites are equipped can have a significant impact on a transition program's scope and budget. This is an area that can certainly cause unanticipated project delays and cost overrun.

It is not unusual to see that many large multinational companies have global presence and use a myriad of nonstandard technologies deployed across the globe that makes M&A integration and separation efforts very challenging. When such companies go through acquisitions or divestitures, they are faced with a mammoth task of rationalizing hundreds of large and small offices. The challenge is exasperated in companies that have decentralized IT departments that are supported by local IT resources who are not fully aligned with the central team.

Companies going through a divestiture and dealing with site separations must consider conducting a thorough due diligence, considering factors like lease agreements, landlord approvals, IT readiness, vendors involved, new business requirements, etc. Upon completion of the due diligence exercise, the companies are likely in a better position to effectively execute changes before rendering the site ready for business operations.

Teams dealing with real estate separations should remain well versed with the technologies and the terminology involved when executing these projects. Unfamiliarity with the technical aspects of the facilities, like structured cabling, site floor plans, site wiring, IT room configurations, space and energy considerations, etc., can introduce unnecessary risks in the project, especially when dealing with vendors and landlords.

© Deloitte Development LLC 2018   363
J. Joy, *Divestitures and Spin-Offs*, Management for Professionals,
https://doi.org/10.1007/978-1-4939-7662-1_29

M&A Separation Management Office (SMO) teams involved on such projects can help in developing the right IT strategies and support in effectively tracking and monitoring site dispositions that allows for an optimized facilities portfolio that can help reduce project costs.

29.1   Understanding Site Dispositions

When companies go through acquisitions or separations, they are faced with numerous options to manage their real estate portfolio. Understanding these site dispositions can help decision-makers in developing effective strategies for the company and help project managers plan better.

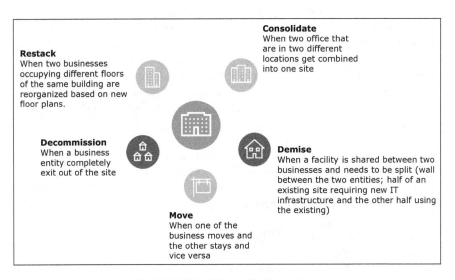

Restack
When two businesses occupying different floors of the same building are reorganized based on new floor plans.

Consolidate
When two office that are in two different locations get combined into one site

Decommission
When a business entity completely exit out of the site

Demise
When a facility is shared between two businesses and needs to be split (wall between the two entities; half of an existing site requiring new IT infrastructure and the other half using the existing)

Move
When one of the business moves and the other stays and vice versa

Fig. 29.1   IT Real Estate Site Dispositions

29.2   Understanding Site IT Footprint

Several IT components must be enabled at the sites before businesses can resume operations. There are various dependencies that the IT organization needs to track and manage to make a site operational. Detailed project plans should be developed listing all tasks required to enable the IT components required for a facility to be ready for business operations. Close coordination between the IT organization, facilities team, IT vendors, and local suppliers is important to help ensure that all the pieces come together smoothly.

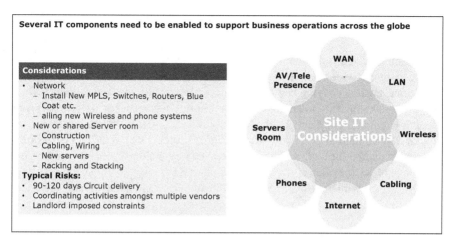

Fig. 29.2 Site IT Components

29.3   Site Readiness Due Diligence

Every site going through changes as a result of separation must consider some key project critical steps as it relates to IT. The facilities team along with the local suppliers supporting the site work must complete their due diligence to help ensure that all aspects of getting the site ready are tracked and evaluated. Local contractors who are expected to support the work in the absence of dedicated company resources must complete site surveys and share the results with the due diligence team to assess requirements.

The transaction team should ensure that key resources are onboarded to manage the project from an IT and facilities standpoint. Project managers must engage key stakeholders to understand site requirements and develop a site strategy before execution begins.

Figure 29.3 below highlights the steps that project managers should consider incorporating as key milestones in their project plans.

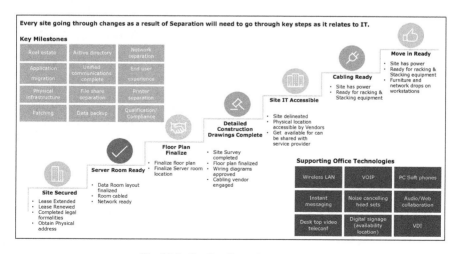

Fig. 29.3 Site Readiness Due Diligence

29.4   Managing Transition Risks Associated with Real Estate

Facilities-related issues can result in significant execution delays, which if not managed properly can cause business disruption and unanticipated incremental transitional costs. Engaging key stakeholders from IT, business, and supplier side in keeping a risk register and continuously monitoring risks is a key to the success of executing real estate projects. In the case of divestitures, spin and merge deals, it is critical to have both the RemainCo and SpinCo management agree on dispositions and timely communicate the strategies to all key stakeholders, considering the time to execute these transitions is typically very short. Moreover, facilities projects span various regions with dependencies on local resources, vendors, landlords, and local IT, HR, legal, security, and communications departments that impact execution).

Table 29.1   Risks of Not Completing Day 1 Site Separation on Time

Risk	Potential mitigation
Displaced organizational resources resulting in productivity loss	Locate swing space for employees or offer flexible working options
Increase in costs due to contract and lease extensions	Allow for provisions in the contracts to minimize the cost impact in case extensions are needed
Segregation of users due to lack of network connectivity	Provide alternative methods of interim connectivity (e.g., VPN) to ensure that users remain integrated
Cluttered workspace due to ongoing construction/renovation work, loose cables, unfinished workstations, etc.	Ensure contractors work during nonworking hours (nights) to complete the work, minimizing business disruption. Contractors should execute as per agreed-upon plan and secure the facility with proper barriers, interim workstations, phones, etc.
Security breaches	Secure the facility physically (security guard, locks, alarm systems, etc.) until more robust security measures are put in place
Low employee morale during transition	Providing leadership support and encouragement during the transition. Consider implementing flexible working options for employees
Cascading impacts of lease renewals, landlord approvals to access site, circuit installations, etc., resulting in potential business disruption	Develop a detailed plan that captures all the interdependencies and proactively engage with vendors and landlords to set expectations in case of anticipated delays
Potential extension of TSAs resulting in penalties and increased TSA costs	Have a mutual agreement in place between the two entities to account for such eventualities, so that budget impacts can be minimized
Inflexible landlords who pose constraints in terms of when and how tenants can access the sites to perform their IT activities prior to users moving in	Ensure that the landlords are made aware of the vendor visits to survey the site and identify demark locations, floor plans, etc. distribute the site visits schedule to the landlords to prepare them
Long lead times from hardware and telco vendors of typically over 120 days	Account for these lead times in the project plans and work backward to determine the site-ready date. Set early expectations with the user community on constraints

29.5   Key Takeaways

- Engage and communicate real estate strategy with key stakeholders (IT and business teams including executive leadership team) early during the planning cycles to set expectations and help ensure program level alignment.
- Real estate, business, and IT stakeholders are encouraged to partner and collaborate upfront in the project cycle to help ensure alignment on key priorities and better understanding of requirements. This helps in getting a better grasp of the IT landscape and improve understanding of various site dispositions at play.
- Clarity around real estate IT components, terminology, and key players in the space helps in managing facilities projects effectively, and the knowledge comes handy during crucial negotiations that frequently happen in this area.
- Remaining aware of all the moving parts associated with facilities projects helps M&A executives effectively manage the contractual and vendor dependencies before they start impacting the plans. Developing a comprehensive plan and having clearly defined activities and timelines is a key to project success.
- Project teams must keep equipment lead times in mind when planning such projects. The lead times to provision IT equipment, circuits, etc. typically can take up to 120 days to deliver. Accounting for these lead times is important before finalizing on a site-ready date and broadly communicating those dates to the stakeholders.
- In order to mitigate the risk of delays, project teams must engage with the telco provider like AT&T early on in the implementation cycle and establish stringent cadence with them regarding receiving status updates on circuit deliveries and site equipment. Project timelines are significantly dependent on AT&T circuit lead times, especially in countries outside of the United States and more so in remote cities across the globe.
- Project teams must develop robust contingency plans to prepare for uncertainties involving AT&T circuits. Few options to consider are as follows:

  - *Regus/Flex/Home.* Low telecom law risk. Labor law compliance issue in certain EMEA/complex countries, where work from home option is not permissible without employee consent and Regus option is not permissible unless location is reasonably close to employee's office.
  - *Tunnel Traffic on Shared Circuit.* High legal risk in sharing telecom links but it's a known and proven technology and AT&T-supported and WAN-based solution.
  - *Dedicate One Circuit to the RemainCo Site (Single or Dual Circuit Site).* High legal risk—business risk for both companies. If a dual circuit site, *both* are without redundancy for MC/EE.
  - *Point to Point.* No legal risk as it's just different WAN solution supported by AT&T. Only valid in India due to extended carrier implementation timelines elsewhere. Limited time and locations where this could be used.
  - *Local Carrier Broadband ISP to Houston Office Site.* Low legal risk AT&T-supported, WAN-based solution.

- Maintaining a site readiness tracker that is reviewed by all stakeholders on a frequent basis helps ensure timely execution of key activities.

- Early onboarding and engagement of critical resources such as facilities project managers, telecom engineers, IT infrastructure resources, site leads, etc. in the real estate planning brings ownership.
- Active early engagement of vendors in facilities planning and execution activities is critical.

29.6   Setting Up Entities for Success

Based on recent large M&A deals, it was observed that most organizations face similar challenges when it comes to understanding and solving the problems associated with IT real estate. The scope of work varies from one company to another, and the complexity increases with the increase in the number of site dispositions. The case study at the end of this chapter illustrated the complexity.

Based on a few large projects that had significant aspects of the separation activities related to real estate, it is evident that some guidance on the approach that project managers take on projects would be beneficial. A high-level facilities overview along with the terminology used on such projects is outlined in the section below. Project managers should follow basic guidelines before embarking on such efforts.

29.7   High-Level Facilities IT Overview

The core fundamentals of site infrastructure and site connectivity haven't changed in the last several years. However, the sophistication and the level of technologies that are used vary from country to country and site to site. Figure 29.4 provides a very high-level view that helps in visualizing the various IT components involved in making the business operational.

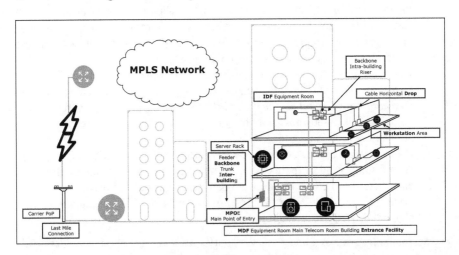

Fig. 29.4 Cross-Sectional View of an Office Facility

29.8   Site IT Terminology/Glossary of Terms

Table 29.2 Facilities Taxonomy

Facilities component	Description
MPLS	Multiprotocol label switching is a type of data-carrying technique for high-performance telecommunications networks that directs data from one network node to the other
Last mile	The *last mile* refers to the portion of the telecommunications network chain that physically reaches the end user's premises
PoP	Telco providers' point of presence
Inter-building (backbone, trunk, feeder)	Cable extending from the central office or from a main feeder cable and providing connections to one or more distribution cables
MPOE	Main point of entry
MDF	Main distribution frame
Riser cabling	Cable that extends vertically, one full story or more, to distribute data/voice service on different floors of a building. Has an intermediate fire protection rating
IDF (telco room, telco closet, equip. Room)	Intermediate distribution frame—Is a remote room or closet that interconnects and manages the telecommunications wiring between an MDF and workstations and devices. May hold switches and patch panels Provides network/data connectivity to and from workstations, copiers, and printers Provides voice services to and from workstations, fax machines, and modems
Horizontal work space cabling	Cable that extends connectivity within a workstation or office locations to end-user equipment (PC, laptop, network printer) Cable that extends connectivity to copiers, printers, fax machines, and modems. Different categories of the cabling are Cat3, Cat5e, Cat6, and Cat6a
Category 3	Industry standard for cable and connecting hardware products with transmission characteristics specified to 16Mhz, designed to support digital transmission of 10 Mb/s
Category 4	Industry standard for cable and connecting hardware products with transmission characteristics specified to 20Mhz, designed to support digital transmission of 16 Mb/s
Category 5	Industry standard for cable and connecting hardware products with transmission characteristics specified to 100Mhz, designed to support digital transmission of 100 Mb/s
Category 5e	Enhanced category specifications for cable and connecting hardware products with a transmission characteristic specified to 100Mhz for cable and connecting hardware products with transmission characteristics specified to 100Mhz, designed to support digital transmission of 100 Mb/s. Minimal compliant to support digital transmission of 1Gb/s
Category 6	Industry standard for cable and connecting hardware products with a transmission characteristic specified to 250Mhz, designed to support digital transmission of 1Gb/s

(continued)

Table 29.2 (continued)

Facilities component	Description
Category 6a(e)	Identified as augmented category 6 or new class E. Industry standard for cable and connecting hardware products with a transmission characteristic specified to 500Mhz, designed to support digital transmission of 10Gb/s over balanced pair UTP
t10BASE-T	10 Mb/s Ethernet using 2 pairs of category 3 cable
100BASE-T	100 Mb/s fast Ethernet using 2-pair category 5 cable
1000BASE-T	1000 Mb/s (1 Gb/s) Ethernet using 4 pairs of category 5e or category 6 cable
10GBASE-T	10Gb/s Ethernet using 4 pairs of category 6a cable
Access point (AP)	A wireless LAN base station that supports a wireless cell. APs are typically connected to the wired infrastructure
Ad hoc cabling	Cabling scheme where different types of cabling components from different vendors are linked together to form a cabling system
Bandwidth	The range of frequencies that can be used for transmitting information on a channel. Indicates the transmission carrying capacity of a channel. Thus, the larger the bandwidth, the greater the amount of information that can pass through the circuit
Cable fill	The ratio of cable installed into a conduit against the theoretical maximum capacity of the conduit
Cable routing diagram	A detailed drawing showing the layout of the cable routes
Horizontal cable	Cable connecting the floor distributor (IDF) to the telecommunications outlet(s)
Outlets	A term used to describe the sockets provided in the work location of a structured cabling system. These are usually 8 pin modular sockets which can support a variety of services
Patch cord	Flexible cable unit or Ethernet with connections, used to establish connections on a patch panel
Patch panel	Termination and administration hardware designed to accommodate the use of patch cords. It facilitates administration for moves and changes
Pathways	Pathways • Designated cable routes and/or support structures in a false ceiling or floor • Power over Ethernet (PoE) • A method of providing power to an end device via the date or spare pairs of the Ethernet cable
Riser	Term used to describe a space utilized by backbone cabling to house communications cabling and other building services. This space should preferably be specified, or allowed for, at the time of a building design
Power over Ethernet (PoE)	A method of providing power to an end device via the date or spare pairs of the Ethernet cable
Single mode fiber	Optical fiber with a small core diameter in which only a single mode of light is capable of propagation. 8.3 micron is the common standard core size
Work area	A building space where the occupants interact with telecommunications terminal equipment

Case Study: 29

Background

A large C&IP client with $6B in revenue was going through one of the biggest separation in the company's history. The company had a small IT staff and a corporate real estate group that was formed by pulling in resources from other departments. The company strongly relied on external vendors and contractors for getting facilities-related work done globally.

Challenge

The company had over 200 sites located worldwide that were to be either separated, consolidated, or decommissioned as a part of the divestiture. All the sites needed to be fully IT enabled and separated in a span of less than 6 months. The expectation was to set up all their global sites involving constructing new redesigned floors, building new server room, racking and stacking server equipment, and enabling connectivity to the floors. Majority of the remote sites did not have any local IT support available, which resulted in a lot of quality issues and deployment of nonstandard equipment in the server rooms and the execution of the separation strategy very challenging.

Approach

Developed a strategy and the process to track and manage vendors and IT components needed for all sites across the globe. To enable the execution of the real estate strategy, made facilities planning as an integral part of the IT project plans. All facilities and IT components were tracked using a city grid that captured site-specific IT requirements. This approach helped lay out the site readiness plan for each site, and the baseline information obtained from each site was used to explore and exploit opportunities for optimization and synergy realization for other sites. As a part of the site separation approach, introduced a travel team concept. The team was made up of facilities and IT experts who traveled to all the core business sites and engaged with the telecom providers and local contractors to operationalize the sites one at a time, executing on a detailed project plan.

Impact/Results

Migrated ~4900 users to the new company infrastructure and enabled IT infrastructure in over 200 new/demise sites and decommissioned 45 sites.

Planned and executed issue-free transition.

Received the "Fastest migration speed achieved by a company/team" award from Microsoft at the Metalogix Best of Breed Awards Program 2015.

Chapter 30
Transition Services Agreements (TSAs): Approach to De-risk Divestitures

30.1 TSAs: A Necessity or an Overhead?

The decision to divest a business unit is a key corporate strategy of many organizations. When a company announces a business divestiture, the information technology (IT) systems that support its business processes must be separated as well. Once the decision to divest is made, business and IT operational teams begin evaluating the path to separate the targeted business unit from the remaining organization (the "seller company"). IT starts to analyze the feasibility of completing certain separation activities before the deal is closed. Key challenges include separating systems, data, infrastructure (e.g., LAN, WAN, end-user computing, security), and people identified to go with the divested business. The difficulty to separate is surmountable considering many of the IT capabilities were designed and built to support a shared services structure, not rapid separation.

Once the deal is announced, there is great urgency to close the transaction so that gains from the sale can be quickly put to work by the seller company. When there is a conflict on how quickly the deal can close versus how quickly the organizations can separate, transition services agreements (TSAs) become a practical option. TSAs are service agreements between buyer and seller companies (or divested entities) in which one entity provides services and support (i.e., IT, finance, HR, real estate, payroll, etc.) to another after the closure of a divestiture to ensure business continuity. Often, TSAs serve as mechanisms to de-risk a transaction while enabling business continuity in the face of aggressive separation timelines.

In general, TSAs are viewed as a necessary overhead, and their use should be minimized. The seller company is usually not in the business of providing services to third-party organizations and would like to avoid becoming a service provider for the divested entity. Additionally, the strategic road maps of the seller company and the divested entity diverge rapidly post-transaction close, making long-term TSAs

© Deloitte Development LLC 2018
J. Joy, *Divestitures and Spin-Offs*, Management for Professionals,
https://doi.org/10.1007/978-1-4939-7662-1_30

problematic. Thus, it is in the best interest of both entities to minimize TSAs or clearly define the following objectives prior to deal close:

- Services the seller company and the divested entity require from each other to mitigate Day 1 business continuity, legal, and contractual risk
- Duration, service-level agreements (SLAs), and cost of services that are fair to all the internal and external parties involved
- Exit criteria and conditions that provide flexibility without being open ended
- The operating and governance model of how issues will be escalated and resolved

For IT teams, it can be a difficult task to price and execute a TSA due to the complexities inherent in a shared IT environment, including dependency on contracts with external parties, lack of a clear separation timeline, and inadequate baseline cost and consumption data for different IT components. Also systems are only one piece of the TSA puzzle, business user input is required to properly delineate where the system ends, and the associated business process takes over. When the line is blurred, the option remains to bundle business and IT services for a TSA. Where this option can simplify TSA costing, it may create complexities later if the buyer attempts to split the combined service for TSA exit (e.g. exit the business process prior to exiting the system).

30.2 De-risking Business Continuity Through TSAs

Although there are multiple reasons why TSAs are used in a divestiture, the primary reason is that a full separation is not achievable by Day 1; thus, the divested business unit may not be able to operate on Day 1 without ongoing support from the seller, who acts as a service provider, while the divested entity acts as a service receiver. Through TSAs, the seller ensures the buyer that underlying technology support will be available to maintain business continuity. This de-risking approach provides the buyer with breathing room, allowing time to evaluate IT options to absorb the acquired assets into its IT environment. TSAs also allow the seller a path to sell its business unit without immediately addressing the complexities of separating the IT environment (e.g., enterprise resource planning (ERP), human resources (HR), network, voice, data, end-user computing (EUC), and applications). TSAs also play a role when the divested business unit retains IT assets and services required by the seller. In such a scenario, a reverse TSA where the transitionary services are provided by the divested business is usually used to provide business continuity to the seller.

The goal of most sellers is to minimize or exclude TSAs from the transaction; thus, they become an afterthought until the criticality of closing the divestiture quickly makes TSAs indispensable. Regardless of the reason why TSAs are required, the service provider starts the TSA effort by scoping and costing of services under the TSA agreement. Challenges abound when developing, pricing, and executing on TSAs. These challenges range from identifying the right scope to managing TSA contract schedules and sign-off timelines.

Addressing these challenges early, before they become real issues, supports the close of the deal and prepares the service provider's IT team for the journey ahead. Smooth service delivery and TSA execution also set the stage for both the buyer and the seller IT teams to work collaboratively toward the TSA exit effort. As mentioned before, early exits are generally preferred both by the service provider and the receiver to achieve stand-alone business and IT operations with no interdependencies.

TSA development and execution are complex processes involving various internal and external factors that drive the seller's ability to define and execute services. With upfront planning and careful consideration, an IT organization can successfully navigate the TSA development process and execute TSA services. Leading practices to address the key roadblocks faced by buyers and sellers during the TSA development and execution process are the focus of this chapter.

30.3 Common Pitfalls During TSA Scoping and Documentation

Scoping and documenting TSAs consume significant attention and effort from both the buyer and the seller companies as each attempts to meet its short-term post-close objectives. Since their objectives are typically at odds with each other, the number of divestitures that adequately address the needs of both organizations through proper TSA documentation is far and few between. Knowing and avoiding some common pitfalls for TSA scoping and documentation can go a long way in driving more consensus and trust between the companies involved in the transaction during deal negotiations and delivery of transition services. Consider the following frequent, high-impact pitfalls and how to avoid them.

30.3.1 Day 1 Continuity Risk

Starting TSA scoping and documentation close to Day 1 leaves insufficient time to gain alignment between the service provider and the service receiver. This usually results in a hastily pulled together TSA that lacks the necessary details about the in-scope services the buyer and/or seller needs on Day 1 to ensure business continuity. Identifying the scope of TSA(s) as soon as IT blueprint for separation is completed can provide sufficient time to address the following:

- For the buyer stand-up of IT capabilities that are not available to the buyer through the TSA.
- Expedite Day 1 separation projects that can help avoid increases in TSA scope.
- Drive alignment on cost based on IT baseline data collected.

As with any balancing act, there is a bit of a catch-22 in the timeline between IT blueprint for separation and TSA development. Application and infrastructure blueprinting must be completed before gaining a good understanding of the TSA requirements. But in some cases, evaluating the separation options for landing IT applications and infrastructure at the divested entity may take considerable time, which could delay application blueprinting. Nevertheless, spinning up the TSA development effort as early as possible in the strategy and planning stage will help lead to better alignment and less strain in the post-close operational cycle.

30.3.2   Regulatory and Compliance Risk

In large divestitures involving multiple countries, the regulatory environment in each country becomes a critical factor in determining the scope and duration of TSA services. Lack of country-specific legal guidance during the scoping of TSAs can lead to regulatory risk exposure post-Day 1. Embedding legal counsel with business and IT teams driving the TSA effort will help avoid this risk before it is too late. Additionally, the legal team can help evaluate the impact of regulatory influences on the TSA strategy. In the United States, the Securities and Exchange Commission (SEC), the Committee on Foreign Investment in the United States (CFIUS), or other federal regulators may have country-specific separation requirements or limit what TSA services are allowed.

Legal counsel also plays a critical role in helping draft the master TSA governing document. This document establishes the overall ground rules related to TSA duration, exits, extensions, and standard costing elements. The TSA governing document drives consensus between all entities involved in the transaction and completion of underlying TSA schedules.

30.3.3   Risk from Third-Party IT Vendors

Typically, third-party IT vendors may have little to no incentive to support provisioning of transition services for the service provider. Lack of explicit rights secured from vendors in support of TSA services may result in contractual risk for the service provider. Both the buyer and seller organizations should review their contractual obligations and put the wheels in motion to negotiate and obtain sufficient TSA rights from third-party IT vendors early on in the TSA documentation process.

30.3.4   Risk from Uncovered Service Costs

TSA service costs are often a source of disagreement and dispute between the buyer and seller organizations during the TSA planning phase and TSA execution. Understanding of the service costs and cost drivers is not trivial and requires significant data, time, and diligence from the entities involved in the transaction. Usage of ambiguous cost metrics or lack of knowledge about the cost components and assumptions used to compute cost estimates may lead to poorly defined service costs.

Key cost elements often missed during TSA cost estimation include:

- One-time costs to stand-up TSA services
- One-time costs to exit from or retire TSA services
- Stranded costs post exit from TSA services
- Markup costs for TSA extensions

In some cases, there is no easy way to determine the baseline costs for services that will fall under the scope of a TSA. Without clear baseline costs, determining the costs of TSA services becomes a nonstarter. For such scenarios, the TSA documentation should include a detailed costing methodology that identifies key metrics, benchmarks, and calculations used to identify actual service costs during service execution.

The seller's and buyer's IT organizations typically assume a fixed or variable cost framework or approach that will be sufficient for TSA costing. Keeping a fixed cost for the duration of the TSA may result in low overhead, but it does not account for cost variables (e.g., variations in usage or variations due to currency fluctuations). In such situations, the service provider must absorb any additional costs. On the other hand, maintaining a variable cost framework helps ensure the service provider is paid based on actual costs incurred, although this framework also creates billing and invoicing overhead along with audit requirements. Based on the type of services provided in each TSA, the service provider and receiver may need to employ either or both fixed or variable cost frameworks.

30.3.5 Risk Related to Insufficient Exit Incentives

If a TSA does not explicitly limit the number and duration of allowable extensions, it may inadvertently lock the service provider into the agreement indefinitely. Also, if the TSA extension costs are based on actual costs incurred, the receiver may not be incentivized to exit the TSA any time soon. To build in a strong exit incentive, the TSA should include a costing approach that scales up significantly with time after the initial term of the agreement (i.e., during extensions to the agreement).

30.3.6 Stakeholder Involvement

Since there are multiple IT disciplines across an IT organization, not engaging applicable subject matter experts (SMEs) from both the seller company and the divested business unit in the TSA effort may compromise proper identification of IT services for consumption. By engaging applicable SMEs, the team managing the TSA effort can identify TSA services, associated costs, and TSA exit solutions during the early stages of TSA development. In addition to SMEs for different IT areas, other stakeholders critical to TSA documentation and execution should be engaged early in the TSA development process, including the legal team, IT finance team, vendor management, and procurement.

30.3.7   Governance During TSA Execution

TSA documentation acts as a key reference document for the buyer and seller organizations during TSA execution, which extends long after the team documenting the TSAs has been dismantled. As a result, ambiguous and loosely defined content within the TSA documentation may lead to escalations and disputes in the delivery and/or billing of TSA services. The following mechanisms can help prepare for and manage these disputes:

- Establish a robust post-close TSA governance process with representatives from all entities involved in the transaction (i.e., the seller and buyer companies, as well as the divested entity, if applicable). The TSA governance process should outline change management, oversight, and dispute escalation procedures. Either the master governing document or each TSA schedule should specify a dispute resolution mechanism to help resolve any disputes that surface during TSA execution. A clear owner should be assigned from each entity as the first point of contact to help resolve concerns or disputes, and an escalation path to higher management should be defined, if needed.
- Beyond clearly describing the in-scope services, sometimes it is helpful to explicitly specify the services that are out of scope for the TSA in order to avoid any disputes caused by assumptions made by any of the entities involved in the transaction.
- Include flexibility within each TSA for the receiver to renew the terms of the agreement. This will help preserve business continuity for the receiver in the event that a planned TSA exit project is delayed. At the same time, it is important to ensure that extensions are capped (e.g., only two extensions are allowed— each for a 6-month duration) so the service provider is not locked into providing the services for an indefinite period.
- A detailed billing and invoice management process and a proper reporting structure will help avoid confusion and conflicts during the monthly billing process. The TSA must define what services will be charged and how the charges will be calculated. Additionally, a monthly true-up process aligned with service ramp-down should be included to avoid conflicts and disputes between the entities involved in the transaction during the TSA execution period.

30.4 Features of an Effective TSA Document

Like any other critical commercial agreements, TSAs have major operational, legal, and financial implications for both the seller and the buyer companies involved in a divestiture. Setting up effective TSAs could prove to be highly complex and time-consuming with multiple stakeholders from both business and IT involved. Special emphasis should be given to documenting these agreements with a high degree of accuracy and quality in order to help ensure clear understanding by all entities involved in the transaction. Since IT is always central to continuity of business activities, the finalization of TSAs demands time and data from personnel across all areas of IT. The task becomes even more complex and time-consuming when third-party software or hardware vendors are required to provide transitionary support for functions such as telecommunications and licensing.

Based on experience from big and small divestitures, a list of key features for effective TSA documentation is provided in this section. This list should help TSA documentation teams optimize and focus their efforts to achieve quick sign-off from IT and business teams, while minimizing any legal or financial risks.

30.4.1 Necessary and Sufficient Scope

To provide a clear understanding of the IT services to be delivered under a TSA, the service description section in the TSA document should not only specify the services that are in scope but also any services that are not in scope. This also helps minimize assumptions the service provider or receiver may make about the coverage provided under the TSA. The scope of a TSA should be constructed based on individual service elements that may get phased out at different milestones over the course of the TSA duration. This allows TSA service costs to ramp down for the receiver as certain services are exited before others. The TSA should also list discrete services (e.g., infrastructure and application support) and their costs, as well as the SLA requirements for each of the identified service elements.

30.4.2 Unambiguous and Simple Service Descriptions

Lack of clarity on the details of services or broad, general, and ambiguous language to describe them may result in confusion regarding the responsibilities of both the service provider and receiver. No matter how complex the services are, TSAs should be written with simple language that reduces the complexity of service descriptions. In the interest of transparency for all entities involved in the transaction, the services should be defined at the appropriate level of detail and should be included as a baseline for all schedules. Not agreeing upon and documenting appropriate key performance metrics (KPIs) to measure service levels may allow the service provider to technically abide by the TSA, but not provide the service level actually needed by the receiver. Using terms such as "reasonable," "commercially reasonable," or "best commercial efforts" can lead to such scenarios.

30.4.3 Measurable and Auditable Service Levels

Clearly documented SLAs help mitigate a common root cause of discord between service providers and receivers regarding the quality of services delivered. Adequate metrics and a practical measurement approach should be specified to help ensure the appropriate expectations are set prior to service commencement, as well as enable transparency in audit and reporting of service performance during the TSA period.

30.4.4 Time-Bound and Finite Services

As TSAs are critical to ensuring post-close business continuity, their primary objective is to enable the provision of transitory services to the divested entity until it ends its reliance on the seller company's IT landscape. To align with this key objective, both the divested entity and the seller company should establish a limit for TSA duration as a key governing mandate. Allowances for limited term request-based extensions may be added to provide flexibility for continuity of a small subset of transitionary services for a longer duration than others. Documenting TSA services without an overall mandate limiting TSA duration typically leads to lack of a well-thought-out strategy for exiting the TSA or consumes additional time and resources to determine service duration for each individual service.

Beyond the predefined duration, TSAs should also include clauses that allow the service provider or receiver to terminate the contract before term by mutual agreement. This incentivizes the entities involved in the transaction to quickly plan for and execute projects that aim to eliminate the need for TSA services beyond what is absolutely required.

30.4.5 Comprehensive TSA Documentation

TSA documentation should be standardized and provide comprehensive details on every aspect of the services to be provided. Tiering the documentation into a master TSA document with multiple TSA schedules for different IT services is a tested way of avoiding documentation creep and redundancy while achieving the desired goal. The master TSA document should cover all terms and conditions common to the schedules, and the schedules should help IT organizations understand specific details that matter in delivery, invoicing, and management of the services on an ongoing basis. The next section provides details of what an effective TSA schedule should contain.

30.5   Sections in a Typical TSA Document

TSAs should be clear about the scope, type, level of performance, and duration of each IT service to be provided. The following are the important sections of a TSA document:

30.5.1   Description of Services

TSAs provide a complete list of all transition-related services to be provided by the service provider, plus a range of optional services the service provider is willing to offer that are beyond the scope of the transition. These optional services must be agreed upon on a case-by-case basis. Essentially, the description of services should cover the following:

- *Why Is the Service Required?*: This helps establish the context of TSA requirements and the core purpose of standing up the agreement.
- *What Services and Associated Assets Will Be Delivered?*: This clearly articulates the set of services the receiver will obtain from the service provider.
- *Who Are the Service Provider and Receiver?*: This clearly identifies the legal entities that will provide and receive services. These legal entities may be country or region specific and need clear mention in the document.
- *How Long Is the Service Going to Be Provided For?*: The duration of each service element along with allowed extensions should be made transparent to both the service provider and receiver.
- *Service Provider and Receiver Obligations?*: Delineates key aspects of the service that are dependent on key activities performed by the service provider or receiver to trigger, set up, and deliver the service.

An example of how the service description would look like is presented below:

TSA Service Description:			
Provider will share and support existing WAN circuits on a cost pass-through basis with Receiver at pre-defined 'Shared' site locations, until new WAN network is provisioned and activated by Receiver at these sites.			
Providing entity: ABC organization	Receiving entity: XYZ organization	Service duration: 12 months	Service start date: 01/01/2017
Asset definition: 1. Site A, Chicago, IL, USA 2. Site B, San Francisco, CA, USA 3. Site C, Bangalore, INDIA			
Service provider responsibilities: 1. Services and support (such as monitoring, provisioning, architecture, design, performance, capacity)	Service receiver responsibilities: 1. Administer directory services (AD)		

30.5.2   Service Performance Standards and Levels

TSA documentation should provide a detailed description of service performance levels for all service elements, as well as specifications for all measures to be adopted for service-level monitoring and the agreed-upon frequency for measurement and reporting activities. Broadly, the SLA should cover:

- Services subject to the SLA
- Metrics (e.g., 99% availability of mission critical systems)
- Measurement approach
- Financial impact (e.g., financial credits for deficient performance)

30.5.3   Service Costs and Payment Terms

A clear definition of all service costs, costing methodologies, and invoicing procedures should be documented in the TSA as follows:

- Service costs broken down by service elements.
- Costing methodology that depicts how the costs will be determined if they are based on post-close measurements.
- Unit charges, rate cards, and volume metrics that may be used for cost methodology.
- Adjustments (i.e., true up or true down) in costs that align with changes in scope during the TSA duration.
- Payment terms should cover frequency of invoicing, incremental costs added during invoicing, local or regional invoicing components, and payment due dates.

30.5.4   Communication and Reporting

Each TSA in-scope service is operationally managed and delivered by a TSA owner from the service provider. The TSA owner is also responsible for providing regular reports on service performance to the receiver. A list of such reports, including audit reports, reporting frequency, and a recipient list, should be clearly articulated in the TSA document. An outline of the procedures to report and escalate problems must also be defined and documented to support the overall governance model during TSA execution.

30.5.5 Audit Obligations

Though sometimes not explicitly discussed, the receiver must be provided with IT service audit rights and data protection rights to meet the requirements of internal audit teams and external regulators.

30.5.6 Umbrella Terms and Conditions

Several TSAs should be grouped under a single umbrella agreement to provide a central repository for all legal and financial terms and conditions shared among the individual TSAs. This umbrella agreement will help prevent contradictory definitions across TSA documents, along with related disputes.

Capturing all the details in the TSA document typically requires multiple iterations by TSA owners from both the buyer and seller companies. Once the IT service details are captured in a TSA document, all entities involved in the transaction should set up discussions to negotiate and finalize key terms and service details.

30.6 TSA Negotiation

The TSA should be negotiated based on a balanced perspective of the buyer's and seller's interests. Regardless of who the service provider or receiver is, typical factors that surface during TSA negotiations are not limited to service costing and duration, but also include exit strategies, service levels, third-party contracts and licenses, service audit rights, data protection obligations, and post-close governance. Details about some of the most important factors that should be negotiated by all transaction-related entities before they will sign off on TSAs include the following:

- *Service Cost*: The TSA should clearly define the charges for the services to be delivered under the agreement, along with guiding principles, components, and assumptions that will be used to calculate the charges together, as well as a mechanism for dispute resolution. The aggregate cost of all the TSAs may be subject to a TSA price protection clause under the deal. Clearly documenting the pricing and the cost rationale will assist with negotiations between the service provider and receiver. Cost step-downs or step-ups may help mitigate the service provider's risk of incurring stranded costs, while addressing the receiver's demands for service extension or expansion.
- *Service Levels*: Service levels typically follow the as-is principle such that the receiver consumes TSA services that are not degraded from the service levels the divested business unit received before the split. A rationale for the service levels should be clearly documented to expedite TSA negotiations.

- *Exit Plans*: Successful TSAs are based on service provider and receiver readiness to exit the service agreement within an agreed-upon timeframe and under agreed-upon terms and conditions. The details around one-time separation projects that will enable an exit from the TSA should be documented in a formal exit plan that includes dates, tasks, and responsibilities to the extent possible. Preparing a detailed exit plan gives confidence to the service provider and the service receiver that the duration of the TSA is realistic, and the exit is attainable without unreasonable extensions.
- *Third-Party Service Arrangements*: The TSA should specify how third-party service arrangements, contracts, and licenses will be handled during the transition period. Providing a view into third-party service arrangements facilitates TSA negotiations since it calls attention to all the external vendor dependencies, which can then be discussed and agreed upon by the entities involved in the transaction.

While negotiating, it is important for the buyer and seller to adhere to a timeline to achieve readiness by Day 1. Once the negotiations are completed, the TSA management team from both the buyer and the seller should plan and set up an effective change management and governance process.

30.7   TSA Governance

TSA owners are responsible for documenting the TSAs. They are an integral part of the go-forward TSA governance model to manage day-to-day delivery and receipt of services. To maintain continuity of TSA services and address any requirements and issues that arise down the line, TSA owners should work closely with stakeholders in different roles. The most critical roles required as part of the governance model include:

- *Executive Management*: This is the highest level of decision-making authority within the governance model. Executive management handles issue escalation, mitigation, and dispute management.
- *TSA Managers*: They define and refine TSA management processes, identify and mitigate TSA delivery risks, and help manage financial commitments and exits. Additionally, the managers work closely with TSA owners to report execution status and escalate issues through the right channels.
- *TSA Billing*: This group is responsible for compiling monthly status updates from TSA owners, coordinating with billing teams for invoicing and collections, and tracking and reporting progress toward TSA exits.
- *Need-Based Support*: These are specialized teams that support TSA execution on an as-needed basis and include representatives from:
  - *Legal*: Legal support for TSA interpretation and issue resolution
  - *IT Finance*: Support for TSA payments and collections
  - *Tax*: Advisory support on tax implications of TSA terms

30.7.1   Billing Management

A mandatory step in operationalizing the TSA governance model is setting up billing for TSA services among identified entities. This billing setup will enable effective delivery of financial commitments between the service provider and receiver. The process to set up billing involves identifying the cost centers that will be used to bill for each TSA service (by cost element) at an appropriate level of aggregation (i.e., local, regional, global). Billing threshold criteria appropriate for the billing frequency (e.g., quarterly billing for more than $5000) should be defined in the TSA invoicing and payment terms and agreed upon by both the service provider and receiver. Timeframes required for filing and resolving billing disputes should also be defined in the TSA invoicing and payment terms.

30.7.2   Change Management

Robust change management procedures provide the service provider and receiver with a process to address unforeseen circumstances that may come up during TSA execution. These circumstances may range from adding services to TSAs that were not identified before deal close to TSA extension scenarios driven by delays with TSA exit projects. A change request form supported by an easy-to-use workflow and decision-making approval framework involving the governance team is a tried and tested approach to effectively change management during the post-close period.

30.7.3   Communication

Effective and timely communication is a key pillar of the overall governance model. Sharing status reports with governance stakeholders helps ensure the transparency of the ongoing service agreements. Additionally, periodic status conference calls can bring all stakeholders up to date on the status of TSAs and encourage discussions related to mitigating risks, issues, and disputes.

30.8   Conclusion

Strategic value creation is the main driver of a divestiture deal, and a well-planned TSA strategy with meticulous TSA operation and governance brings the deal closer to its objectives. TSAs provide the divested business unit with the transition services and support it needs to maintain business continuity post-Day 1. Unfortunately, many divestitures end up being messy operational affairs with high transaction risks because transition services were not adequately planned or executed.

Key insights gathered from the trenches over multiple divestitures and shared in this chapter can help the buyer and seller develop an effective strategy for planning and executing TSAs to avoid last-minute surprises and minimize the operational risks involved with a divestiture.

Case Study: 30

Background

The client, a leading bank in the business of commercial and consumer banking services, primarily engaged in banking and financial activities, insurance activities, and pension and severance fund segments. It operates a network of 30+ branches, few loan centers, and business centers. The bank decided to divest its multi-billion dollar credit card portfolio business.

Challenges

The credit card portfolio business was heavily integrated with the seller's IT systems and call centers. A "transition services agreement" was part of the initial sale document, outlining at a high level—services that could be provided—those that were excluded and the principles for defining, pricing, and managing the TSA. Few of the services that were included both from business and IT perspective are as follows:

1. Card issuance
2. Payment servicing
3. Account management
4. Treasury operations
5. Financial reporting
6. Proprietary systems and software
7. Facility services
8. Information security

Given the duration of transition, some TSAs were exited before they were ever delivered, as the buyer was able to stand up a replacement solution. Example of these services included facility services in some of the countries. Also, in certain cases, the business requirements of the buyer changed, and a process had to be set up for the services to be adapted to accommodate this change (within reason).

As the transition period neared completion, the seller turned their attention to planning for the elimination of stranded costs (costs associated with providing service to the divested business which would no longer be required).

Some challenges experienced:

- The schedule of services was hundreds of lines long, and interdependencies between services needed to be carefully delineated so that exit of one service did not make delivery of another impossible.

- Some services were provided by staff conveying from seller to buyer; managing the conflict of accountability to the company that currently employs you vs. the one that will employ you in a few weeks was difficult for staff.

Approach

Leading up to Day 1—200+ detailed TSAs were developed across 10+ work-streams with the following details:

- Detailed descriptions of services, pricing metrics, durations
- Service-level agreements
- Preliminary exit conditions (i.e., for this TSA to be exited, what must occur)
- Reverse TSAs where the buyer would provide services to the seller (staff conveyed to the buyer but were still required post-sale to support some of the seller's business)

Transition Period—It was ensured that:

- A robust, jointly overseen, management process supported disciplined exits and changes to the services.
- Invoicing and billing process is defined and operationalized to handle accuracy of month-to-month charges between the two parties.
- As both parties agreed for individual services that the exit conditions had been met, the service was ceased, and the buyer was no longer billed.

Impact/Results

The successful creation of a new IT organization was achieved within the stipulated time of 6–8 months:

- Day 1 operations for both the buyer and seller were seamless.
- Buyer and seller were able to work within the framework to jointly arrive at an accelerated solution for transition.

Both parties felt they had "fair" levels of leverage over the outcome.

Chapter 31
Contract Separation: Early Identification and Negotiations

In any divestiture, the chief information officer (CIO) is under pressure to prevent negative operational and financial outcomes. While segregating corporate systems, untangling infrastructure and applications, and reorganizing operations may provide cost reduction opportunities, third-party information technology (IT) contracts comprise a significant part of cost outlay, and managing them is a critical priority.

Third-party IT contracts are among the largest, most costly, and complex contractual arrangements to separate. These contracts often encompass both software licenses and physical assets, such as servers and telecommunications equipment. A divestiture presents an opportunity for both the parent company and the to-be-divested entity to reduce their vendor base and rationalize third-party spending. However, it can also result in stranded costs that remain after the transaction is complete.

Benjamin Franklin said, "An ounce of prevention is worth a pound of cure." This adage certainly applies to IT contract separation. Without sufficient preparation and a strategic approach, CIOs run the risk of incurring substantial costs due to vendor lawsuits or expensive contract renegotiations.

31.1 Threat to Business Continuity

In general, companies buy licenses to use products and services. However, these licenses may not carry over to the divested entity in a divestiture. The parent company must secure transition licensing rights or right-to-use licenses to support the divestiture; otherwise, early termination of contracts may be necessary.

If the required licensing rights are not secured at the time of an M&A transaction, it can lead to significant business continuity risks on Day 1. Companies are often unaware of these contract licensing constraints; however, most vendors are

© Deloitte Development LLC 2018
J. Joy, *Divestitures and Spin-Offs*, Management for Professionals,
https://doi.org/10.1007/978-1-4939-7662-1_31

very familiar with them, and some may see M&A transactions as opportunities to gain the upper hand in contract renegotiations which may include:

- Charging exorbitant fees for assignment or transition rights
- Mandating the company upgrade to newer product versions or buy additional licenses
- Using the deal as an opportunity to initiate an audit
- Assessing punitive termination penalties
- Discontinuing support and service on Day 1

Given the power vendors can wield during a divestiture, the CIO must proactively address third-party IT contracts prior to engaging in the transaction. The complicated nature of contracts makes it important that one pays close attention to the details in order to avoid surprises that could result in costly mistakes.

31.2 IT Contract Separation: Current Realities

There are many challenges to successful IT contract separation during a divestiture, including the following:

- Large and complex contract inventory
- Evolving future state
- Huge separation costs
- Regional differences
- Segmented vendor list

31.2.1 Large and Complex Contract Inventory

Large companies often have several third-party IT contracts that hold inventories of 2000 or more documents, which makes the assessment of contracts for divestiture impact an enormous task. In addition to the sheer number of documents, the following factors add significant complexity to the assessment exercise:

- Typically, a vendor contract involves a master services agreement (MSA), along with multiple addendums and amendments signed over the course of the contract. For example, a contract with a software vendor may include an MSA signed 5 years ago, intermittent addendums for product additions, and various amendments to alter terms and conditions such as minimum revenue commitments.
- Often, companies do not have a centralized procurement team that owns all contracts; instead, contracts are owned by individual business groups, which can lead to the existence of multiple MSAs with the same vendor. For example, the IT group at a company may have a contract with leading IT solution provider for

its project management suite, while the sales group may have a separate contract with the same company for a different software.

- Contracts are usually spread across multiple systems and geographies. Due to the decentralized nature of some companies or past serial acquisitions, business units may have multiple procurement applications to organize their contracts. Some contract management systems are not robust enough to prevent human error from deleting documents, and in such instances, the company may need to contact the vendor to obtain copies. Additionally, many business units only have physical copies of contracts, some of which are lost over time due to negligence. As a result, many companies lack a unified repository to store all of their contracts.
- Contracts are not standardized, which leads to huge heterogeneity in contract specifications. A contract signed 10 years ago may be significantly different from a contract signed 2 years ago, with different terminology used to describe the same specifications. For example, a contract with a software vendor may use "right to use" to refer to transition services, while a contract with a telecommunications provider may use "transition services" to refer to the same thing.

Organizing such a landscape of contracts into a single inventory and then extracting data relevant to the M&A transaction from that inventory are challenging tasks, and companies undergoing M&A transactions tend to underestimate the effort required.

31.2.2 Evolving Future State

Both the seller and buyer companies must determine their future-state landscape. Prior to the divestiture, both companies likely had multiple IT initiatives in progress involving third-party products and services. As part of divestiture planning, they must analyze these IT initiatives to determine which ones to continue post-divestiture. Contracts with third parties may need to be renegotiated to accommodate changes that result from the divestiture. For instance, due to lower supply chain requirements or reduced headcount, the seller company may need to negotiate a decrease in the quantity of products or software user licenses it will purchase from a third party, whereas due to higher supply chain requirements or increased headcount, the buyer company may need to negotiate an increase in the quantity of products or software user licenses it will purchase, and this increased volume may allow the buyer company to negotiate better pricing with the third party. For the buyer company, increased supply chain requirements may require the addition of a new module and additional software user licenses not covered in the existing contract, whereas the seller company may require a reduction of the same.

Many companies are not proactive at incorporating contingencies related to divestitures into their third-party IT contracts.

31.2.3 Huge Separation Costs

Contract transfer and separation involves high costs. Third-party vendor costs associated with separations are classified into the following four categories:

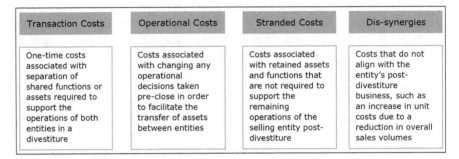

Transaction Costs	Operational Costs	Stranded Costs	Dis-synergies
One-time costs associated with separation of shared functions or assets required to support the operations of both entities in a divestiture	Costs associated with changing any operational decisions taken pre-close in order to facilitate the transfer of assets between entities	Costs associated with retained assets and functions that are not required to support the remaining operations of the selling entity post-divestiture	Costs that do not align with the entity's post-divestiture business, such as an increase in unit costs due to a reduction in overall sales volumes

Fig. 31.1 Separation Costs

It is possible to contain or even eliminate such costs by addressing them early in the post-announcement phase of a divestiture.

31.2.4 Regional Differences

When separation involves companies with operations across the globe, the interpretation of contractual terms per local laws becomes critical. For example, a silent clause within a contract related to third-party use may be treated differently across various jurisdictions. Countries such as the United Kingdom and many US states interpret a silent clause as implicit approval for third-party use, whereas some countries and US states interpret it as implicit disapproval.

During divestitures, many companies tend to overlook such contract nuances, which may lead to legal complications in the future. Coordination with local legal counsel in the applicable jurisdiction (or foreign counsel) can help define the scope, structure, and planning of contract transfers and separation.

31.2.5 Segmented Vendor List

Based on spend and size, a company should segment vendors into high-, medium-, and low-priority tiers. The CIO could then use different strategies to address each segment.

But this segmentation exercise is more difficult than it appears. Typically, a company has contracts with multiple vendors, with each vendor providing several products and services. While a company may have a few priority vendors it uses more than most, approximately 80 percent of vendors usually represent a small spend, making it difficult to establish a segmented vendor list.

31.2.6 IT Contract Separation: Call for a Systematic Approach

Most IT contracts limit the use of products and services to the original licensee and its affiliates. Therefore, when designing an approach to contract separation, the first priority is to determine whether the existing contracts are even valid for the carve-out entity and not subjected to any penalties beyond Day 1.

By working proactively and fostering a collaborative approach, both the third-party vendor and the company can renegotiate contract terms that are beneficial to all. The following key considerations can help the CIO execute an effective IT contract separation:

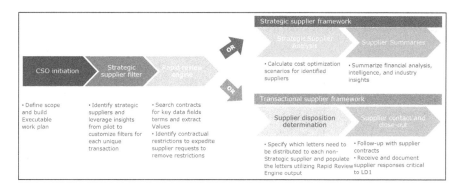

Fig. 31.2 Contract Separation Systematic Approach

31.2.7 Setting Up a Contract Separation Office (CSO)

A CSO can help manage the daunting task of IT contract separation during an M&A transaction. The CSO works with internal and external partners to separate IT applications and infrastructure for the new stand-alone divested entity. Setting up a CSO can help in:

- Identifying the business intent early
- Performing contract assessment
- Evaluating critical vendors
- Negotiating and communication with vendors

Getting external vendors involved in the separation process is essential, as it will allow the internal IT group to focus on business-as-usual (BAU) activities and other critical separation planning efforts.

31.2.8 Identifying Business Intent Early

Business intent, as it relates to IT contract separation, addresses how the company wants to receive a product or service provided by a third-party vendor. The three most important reasons to identify business intent early in a divestiture include:

- To provide continuity of business operations on Day 1
- To request rights from vendors to help ensure contractual compliance on Day 1
- To minimize the cost impact associated with third-party products and services

Business intent drives procurement activities and contract management processes. During a divestiture, it is essential to maintain wide-ranging awareness of the vendor landscape, distinguish vendors from resellers, and consider small vendors for specific uses.

31.2.9 Performing Contract Assessment

It is necessary to review and assess each contract during a divestiture. However, since many companies have huge contract inventories, this can be an enormous task. The first step is to segment vendor contracts into critical and transactional agreements:

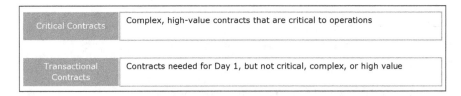

Fig. 31.3 Performing Contract Assessment

To perform the assessment, search the contracts for key terms, extract values, and identify contractual restrictions. This will help reduce the time required to review contracts and allow the company to focus on other key priorities.

31.2.10   *Evaluating Critical Vendors*

Certain vendor relationships require an in-depth analysis in order to secure all Day 1 rights and minimize stranded costs. A scenario-based analysis of all vendors will allow the CSO to identify critical vendors and cost reduction opportunities, review and assess contracts, and recommend detailed negotiating strategies.

31.2.11   *Negotiating and Communication with Vendors*

Vendors often have service-level agreements (SLAs) that require the company to notify them of any changes in contractual terms. A delay in notification could result in issues with contractual modifications or terminations. Thus, communicating and information sharing with vendors must be carefully managed. The CSO should set up a communication channel with vendors to plan and document the contractual negotiations that are critical for Day 1.

31.3   Conclusion

The separation of IT contracts by the seller company to ensure both the buyer company and the divested entity have the necessary contracts on Day 1 is a daunting and complex task. Separating contracts based on business intent should start soon after the divestiture is announced. Few companies proactively manage third-party IT contract risks; instead, most companies focus on the aspects of M&A transactions that drive growth and revenue. But third-party IT contract risks, if not mitigated, can lead to huge costs for all the entities involved in the deal due to legal noncompliance and lost operational efficiencies. These costs may be immediate, punitive, and negate synergies. However, the separation of IT contracts also presents opportunities to renegotiate long-term contracts with vendors. By effectively analyzing contracts to determine what to cut and what to add, all entities involved in the deal will be empowered to develop clear and focused renegotiation strategies for third-party IT contracts that, ultimately, enable them to realize significant value.

To proactively manage the separation of IT contracts in an M&A transaction, companies should:

- Understand the current IT contract landscape.
- Carefully plan for the post-divestiture, future-state landscape.
- Involve the CIO to deal with third-party IT contracts and maintain deal value.
- Be prepared to deal with vendors by developing:
    - Knowledgeable resources
    - Clear communication strategies

- ○ A deep understanding of business intent
- ○ A deep understanding of vendors' intent
- Ensure compliance with third-party IT contracts by securing the necessary assignment or transition rights.
- Leverage the separation of IT contracts resulting from the M&A transaction to the company's advantage.

Vendors can exert far more control over the fate of a divestiture than many companies realize, but proactively managing IT contract separation can help reduce their influence.

Case Study: 31

Background

A large software company announced that it entered into a definitive agreement to sell a part of its business to an investment firm. The buyer planned to operate the carved-out entity as a stand-alone company. Upon completion of the sale, the divested entity became a privately held company. This development gave both the seller and the divested entity the financial wherewithal to accelerate the execution of their respective strategies.

Challenges

The IT separation management office of seller company was tasked with forming and operating a CSO to ensure the divested entity had all the necessary third-party vendor contracts on Day 1. The seller company had more than 800+ third-party IT contracts with 200+ IT vendors at the local, regional, and global levels. An important priority for the CSO was to minimize the seller company's stranded costs by assigning an appropriate number of licenses and other third-party vendor contracts to the divested entity.

Approach

In order to achieve the desired outcome, the CSO drafted the following plan:

Fig. 31.4 Approach

In the first step, "establish governance and project management," the CSO defined the overall program scope and built an executable work plan to undertake vendor communications and contract collection, as well as the setup of a data room and vendor-tracking database.

In the second step, "review contracts," all vendor contracts were reviewed, segmented, and prioritized. Vendor tier groups were identified by value, utilization, and business continuity risk in conjunction with licensing dispositions.

In the third step, "initiate, track, and monitor supplier communications," initial vendor communications were sent out, with 3–7-day follow-ups, and a process to report and track vendor responses was implemented.

In the fourth step, "negotiate and execute," a strategy to deal with vendors who push back on contract renegotiations was developed. As pushbacks from vendors started trickling in, negotiation and escalation mechanisms were implemented. Contract addendums with all the necessary divestiture rights were finalized and signed a month before Day 1.

In the final step, "close out and hand over"—the final report—a consolidated view of contracts and negotiation analysis was presented to the seller company, along with a repository containing all applicable contracts and agreements.

Impact/Results

The above established approach streamlined the contract separation process and led to significant business impact:

- Rapidly reviewed 800+ contracts with 200+ suppliers
- Determined and managed Legal Day 1 (LD1) communications with supplier to achieve the desired separation rights
- Identified 3-year cost avoidance of $30 + M across 20+ critical suppliers

Chapter 32
Expediting TSA Exits to Enable Strategic Transformation

32.1 Transition Services Agreements (TSAs): A Complex Challenge

Transition services agreements or TSAs are seen as paths to post-divestiture business continuity. They can support the smooth separation of two independent entities. However, TSAs may also have a downside. They can lock up assets and contribute to stranded cost. With growing pressure on IT departments to reduce stranded costs, some chief information officers (CIOs) are exiting TSAs to preempt their negative operational and financial impacts. Despite their utility in ensuring business continuity, TSAs are binding agreements that prevent both the third-party vendor and the contracting entity from making changes to IT applications and infrastructure covered under the agreements.

> *TSA exits are strategic: A Fortune 50 Technology Company underwent a recent separation and was planning for a series of M&A activities. However, as a result of its earlier separation, the entity had several operational TSAs. A key challenge for the chief operating officer (COO) and CIO was to exit all TSAs before initiating any new divestiture or separation. This led the entity to create a strategic initiative called the "TSA Exit Program" to ensure all TSAs were exited before any new deals were announced.*

32.1.1 TSAs: A Quick Recap

TSAs are service agreements between buyer and seller companies (or divested entities) in which one entity provides (TSA provider) services and support (i.e., infrastructure, applications, or services) to another (TSA receiver) after the closure of an M&A transaction to ensure business continuity.

© Deloitte Development LLC 2018

J. Joy, *Divestitures and Spin-Offs*, Management for Professionals,
https://doi.org/10.1007/978-1-4939-7662-1_32

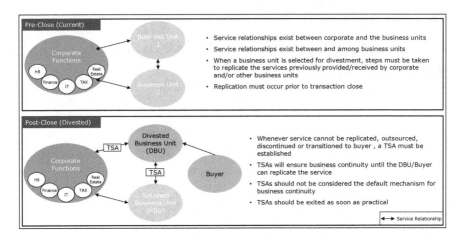

Fig. 32.1 TSA Relationship

TSA formalization usually starts during the initial phase of divestiture planning and includes:

- Capturing key data points and information
- Identifying required services, duration, provider, and recipient
- Determining optimum pricing for the duration of the TSAs
- Identifying TSA owners at both the buyer and seller companies

Following the successful execution of the divestiture, the buyer and seller companies:

- Ensure all services are provided and received as prescribed by the TSAs.
- Track any service-related issues.
- Bill and collect TSA fees.

32.1.2   Why TSA Exits Should Be Expedited

An early exit from a TSA can not only eliminate dependency on another entity, it may also provide an opportunity for CIOs at both the buyer and seller companies to unlock resources and focus on strategic priorities. Both companies can realize the following potential benefits by expediting TSA exits:

Overall buyer and seller company benefits: By exiting TSAs early, the seller company can minimize post-Day 1 support for the buyer company, allowing the seller more flexibility to focus on business alignment priorities, reduce stranded costs, and improve IT efficiency and effectiveness. Similarly, exiting TSAs early can be positive for the buyer company too. Early TSA exit provides the buyer with an opportunity to maximize revenue and cost synergies achieved by integrating the carved-out entity with existing business.

Focus on IT investments to drive business value: TSAs will generally lock up the seller company's capital and IT infrastructure for several years. An early TSA exit will free up multiyear TSA budgets and contingencies, thereby allowing the CIO to make forward-looking steps toward transformation and growth. Early TSA exits can act as strategic enablers to help executives align the IT organization with the strategic business needs of the separated entities.

Need for a well-defined IT road map: Immediately after a divestiture, the buyer and seller companies must finalize their strategic IT road maps and execution plans. As CIOs define their respective company's IT and business enablement strategies, a parallel focus to expedite TSA exits can help them to remove the constraints related to locking up capital and infrastructure in ongoing TSAs.

Preempting risks to future M&A transactions: It is not uncommon for companies to have multiple M&A activities going on simultaneously. Existing TSAs from earlier M&A transactions can jeopardize new M&A transactions by restricting the company's flexibility with respect to IT infrastructure and applications. Hence, it is critical for companies to exit TSAs early to free up the resources needed to execute new M&A transactions.

32.2   Approach to Expediting TSA Exits

In order to expedite TSA exits, it is important to have a well-defined approach. Below activities are essential to streamlining and expediting TSA exits:

- Develop a TSA exit schedule.
- Map interdependencies for a successful exit.
- Determine the post-TSA IT landscape.
- Reuse IT hardware and infrastructure to reduce costs.
- Establish TSA exit governance.
- Develop an actionable TSA exit road map.

What is TSA exit schedule: A TSA exit schedule is a list of IT applications and services to be delivered that includes the following information:

- *Service name and description*
- *Service provider and recipient*
- *Service period*
- *Pricing of services*
- *Service managers*
- *Third-party licenses*
- *Exit plans (i.e., exit dates, exit strategy, pricing)*

A TSA exit schedule should be used to track the status of closed and pending TSA exits.

To help ensure a smooth TSA exit, it is imperative to perform these actions at the appropriate stage in the separation timeline. Figure 32.2 illustrates the steps involved in a typical separation timeline.

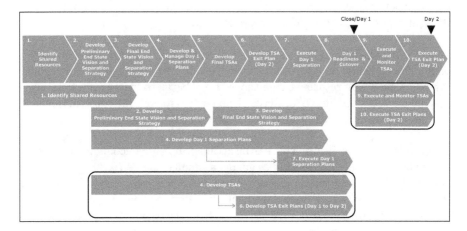

Fig. 32.2 Key Steps in Separation Timeline

32.2.1 Develop a TSA Exit Schedule

TSA exit plans should be completed prior to transaction close. Early planning will allow sufficient time to validate the exit plans of different business units and accurately determine TSA duration and cost. To prevent slippage and help manage risks, TSA exit plans should include descriptive milestones, well-defined roles, and responsibilities for each stakeholder in the process, schedules, and accountable leadership.

32.2.2 Map Interdependencies for a Successful Exit

TSAs are not limited to IT applications and services, but they may also include licenses, staff, and knowledge transfer. Therefore, it is imperative to consider upstream and downstream interdependencies when devising TSA exit plans. Efficient TSA planning involves bundling-dependent IT applications, services, and licenses and staggering their exits to help ensure optimal resource allocation and cost minimization. Key factors to consider when planning TSA exits include:

- Early identification of resources
- Prioritizing conflicts between running the business, exiting TSAs, and executing future-state initiatives

- Exit planning coordinated across different functions
- Early identification of interdependencies to streamline the exit

32.2.3 Determine the Post-TSA IT Landscape

It is important to define a clear future-state IT landscape and transition initiatives. Often, these initiatives may involve transitioning to a more effective future-state solution rather than an interim TSA solution, which may in turn change the TSA exit strategy for particular IT applications and services.

32.2.4 Reuse IT Hardware and Infrastructure to Reduce Costs

IT hardware and infrastructure are significant contributors to exit costs. Application teams should perform proactive due diligence to determine areas where it may be possible to redistribute underutilized infrastructure capacity to meet new demands. Application teams should also evaluate alternative options such as cloud-based solutions for meeting infrastructure demands.

32.2.5 Establish TSA Exit Governance

A dedicated execution team is necessary to manage the TSA exit process and ensure adherence to timelines. This team will serve as a critical decision-making body for change requests, early exits, and major risks and issues. An IT transition service management office (TSMO), which is discussed later in the chapter, is established for governance of the overall TSA exit program. An IT TSA lead should be appointed to oversee the TSA exit strategy, ensure activities are performed on schedule, and provide updates to the CIO.

32.2.6 Develop an Actionable TSA Exit Road Map

During an M&A transaction, the companies involved often have shifting priorities and may lose their focus in the absence of a clear actionable road map. Developing a TSA exit road map with key milestones, responsibilities, resource requirements, and interdependencies is critical for effective tracking against plan.

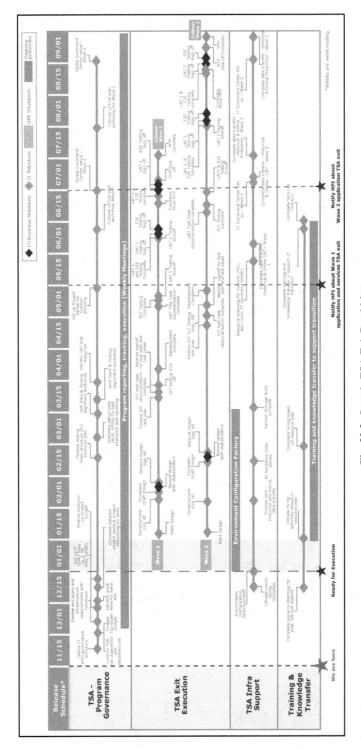

Fig. 32.3 Sample TSA Exit Road Map

32.3   Operationalize the TSA Exit

The purpose of TSA exit planning exercise (or Day 2 planning) is to develop solutions to enable the exit strategy, as well as finalize exit costs. The key steps to operationalize the TSA exit under a TSA exit program include:

- Finalize Day 2 blueprint and strategy.
- Develop exit cost estimate.
- Develop and finalize exit work plans.
- Engage execution team and manage milestones.

32.3.1   Finalize Day 2 Blueprint and Strategy

TSA exit plans should be developed as part of the TSA development process. These exit plans should include projects that will enable the buyer and seller companies (or divested entity) to become independent at the conclusion of the TSAs.

Exit planning is a cross-functional exercise. Due to their own priorities, business functions may not want to exit a TSA for an application or service that may impact them. Hence, finalizing the Day 2 blueprint (i.e., final exit strategy, scope, and road map) and engaging all stakeholders for exit planning are imperative. Key steps involved in finalizing the Day 2 blueprint include:

- TSA exit program kickoff
- Establishing TSA exit program management guidelines
- Reviewing Day 2 blueprints with business units and discussing future-state solutions
- Defining the Day 2 migration plan
- Defining the scope of handover (e.g., applications) to the buyer company

32.3.2   Develop Exit Cost Estimate

Developing an exit cost estimate is essential to finalizing the scope and timeline of the TSA exit strategy. Key activities involved in developing an exit cost estimate include:

- Reviewing the scope and work requirements of the exit strategy
- Estimating resource requirements for the TSA exit
- Aligning the cost estimate across all business units
- Establishing project and hour tracking mechanisms

"Deal Name" Cost Estimation Critical Program Activities								
Day 2 Planning Date Assumption								
Note: Each workstream must have a detailed workplan in Microsoft Project								
Activity #	Activity	Resource (Name or Expenditure)	Estimated Hours	Rate	Estimated Cost	3rd Party Costs	Other Spend	Total Spend
	Activity #1							
		Team Member #1						
		Team Member #2						
		External Support						
		Server Purchase						
	Activity #2							
	Totals							

Fig. 32.4 Sample Exit Cost Estimate

32.3.3 Develop and Finalize Exit Work Plans

Work plans are necessary to organize the work required for TSA exit. Primarily, work plans should be based on the exit strategy. Due to the different nature of activities involved, an application with an exit strategy that requires cloning and cleansing may have a different work plan than an application with an exit strategy that requires transformation. Work plans help ensure all activities required to exit a TSA are identified in advance, as well as help capture cross-functional interdependencies that pose risks to exit execution.

32.3.4 Engage Execution Team and Manage Milestones

Once the exit plans are finalized and the TSA exit program has kicked off, key activities must be performed in each phase of the software development life cycle (SDLC). Figure 32.5 illustrates that the majority of these activities are performed during the planning stage, including establishing TSA exit governance, as well as finalizing disposition, resource requirements, and infrastructure requirements.

	Planning	Requirements & Design	Development	Testing	Cutover
Key Activities	•Define IT TSMO governance structure including roles, responsibilities and communication •Finalize TSA exit disposition and dependencies •Finalize top-down and bottoms-up budget •Create detailed project plans with significant milestones •Finalize resource requirements and onboard team resources •Conduct infrastructure requirements session with application teams •Create infrastructure demand forecast and action plan for capacity gaps •Finalize Infrastructure demand package	•Draft and review project requirements •Complete TSA exit design •Place all new hardware orders •Track program progress, issues and risks •Complete server and storage build using build factory model for Dev/Test	•Track program progress, issues & risks •Perform development tests •Track individual project progress against plan •Complete server and storage build for Staging/Prod	•Create test strategy and test plans •Conduct Business and IT joint data and testing alignment workshop •Execute SIT, UAT & E2E test cases and close defects •Get testing signoffs •Perform historical and live data transfers for production •Track individual project's testing progress against plan	•Modify project plans to incorporate detailed cutover tasks •Conduct cutover resources planning and setup IT and Global Command Center •Conduct mock cutovers •Get business alignment on blackout window •Run Global Command Center •Perform Move To Production (MTP) and cutover •Monitor and track progress for cutover
Key Deliverables	•Project Plan •Finalized resource plan and budget •Application and service inventory •Infrastructure Demand Plan •Security Intake	•Design principles & specs •Integration Solution Map	•Development Plan •Risk Mitigation Plan •Security Remediation Form	•Test Strategy Plan •End of Acceptance Test Sign off •Security Signoff	•Cutover Verification/Data cleanse/migration verification
Reporting Tools & Templates	•TSA Exit Program Progress Report •Project Planning Gap Report	•App. Status report •Issues/Risks Report •Delinquency Report •Server Build Command Center Reporting	•Issues/Risks Report	•SIT and UAT Execution Dashboard •SIT and UAT Executive Reporting Dashboard	•MTP/Cutover Planning Dashboard •Cutover Critical Tasks & Issue Tracking Dashboard
Workshops				•Data and Testing Workshop	•Cutover Critical Plan Workshop

Fig. 32.5 Key Activities and Deliverables During Each SDLC Phase

32.3.5 TSA Exit Governance

A comprehensive TSA exit governance is critical for successful execution of the TSA exit. A governing body, spearheaded by the CIO, should be created to support the monitoring and tracking of TSA exit activities, as well as make decisions to ensure the successful TSA exit. An IT transition service management office (TSMO) should be established to govern the TSA exit. Figure 32.6 outlines the structure of the TSMO and Table 32.1 documents responsibilities of each stakeholder involved in the TSA exit program.

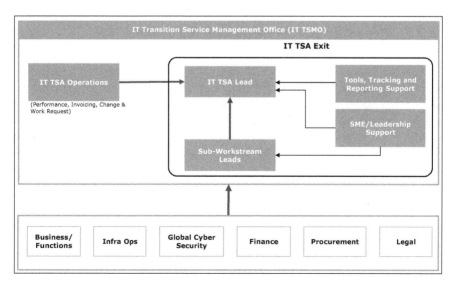

Fig. 32.6 Structure of IT Transfer Management Office

Table 32.1

Role	Responsibilities
IT TSA lead	○ Responsible for the overall success of the TSA exit program ○ Oversees IT TSA exit and operations and reports progress to CIO ○ Ensures IT TSA exit activities are on track as per the TSA exit plan ○ Ensures required support is available from the TSA provider
IT TSA operations	○ Manages all change requests from business unit leaders ○ Incorporates changes into the TSA exit plan and revises timelines ○ Ensures that performance service-level agreements (SLAs) are met ○ Escalates issues as appropriate
SME/leadership support	○ Drives the TSA exit program, including executive-level tracking ○ Provides structure and defines cross-functional approaches ○ Engages resources to expedite the resolution of issues
Functional leads	○ Responsible for all applications within their business units ○ Coordinates with other teams to ensure TSA exit occurs as planned ○ Reports any delays or additional support needs to TSA lead
Tools, tracking, and reporting support	○ Creates and manages tools and templates ○ Automates program reporting, including executive-level reporting

32.3.6   Reporting and Meetings with Stakeholders

After the TSA exit program kickoff, it is critical to track progress. It is important to set up regularly scheduled meetings with all program stakeholders, supplemented by program status reports. The following table discusses the different types of reports required, along with their recipients and frequency. Figure 32.7 provides a sample TSA exit program meeting schedule. The meeting agenda should include discussion of program status, key issues and risks, and any dependencies or escalations.

Please note: Frequency and report types may differ from program to program.

Table 32.2

Report	Description	Report recipients	Frequency of report
TSA exit program status report	○ Critical path status update ○ Program-level issues and risks ○ Resource status report ○ Budget status update ○ Upcoming milestones	CIO, other senior leadership	Weekly
Application TSA exit online dashboard	○ Red-amber-green (RAG) status at the application level to indicate the level of risk associated with the application ○ Execution-level milestone completion percentage per application ○ Risks, issues, and associated mitigation strategies per application	IT TSMO stakeholders	On demand
Services TSA exit online dashboard	○ RAG status at the service level ○ Execution-level milestone completion percentage per service ○ Risks, issues, and associated mitigation strategies per service	IT TSMO stakeholders	On demand

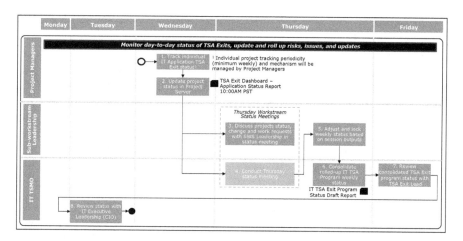

Fig. 32.7 Sample of TSA Exit Program Meeting Schedule

32.4   Conclusion

Divestitures and separations require setting a path for the future-state landscape. Post-divestiture, the CIO has the opportunity to transform the IT organization and make it more efficient and responsive to the needs of the business.

When creating this new IT organization, the CIO should attempt to get rid of long-running projects and historical practices that no longer hold value. Expediting TSA exits will help the CIO to focus on organizational initiatives and free up resources to make the new technology investments required to stay competitive in these evolving times.

Case Study: 32

Background

A leading global provider of enterprise solutions in the IT industry went through a divestiture, and the two new entities created as a result of the separation required each other's services for business continuity. This resulted in TSAs between them.

One of the separated entities was scheduled to receive 50 TSAs over a two-year period starting on Day 1 that comprised 85 applications and 80 services.

However, soon after separation, there was a change in the corporate strategy of the separated entity. In order to further growth and align with corporate goals, the chief executive officer (CEO) planned a series of immediate spin-offs. Since the entity was bound by TSA liabilities to the other separated entity, it was difficult to execute the new strategy. The only solution was to expedite the TSAs and reach an exit quickly, before the planned 2-year period expired.

Challenges

Because the TSAs were to remain in effect for 2 years, the bandwidth of application teams was locked up for the 2-year duration.

The lack of a well-defined transformation road map prevented a direct path to achieve the future-state landscape architecture. Based on initial analysis for Day 2, 75 percent of TSA applications were planned to be cloned, thus minimizing the opportunity to eliminate applications.

Also, long-running TSA exits meant there were more monthly payments to the TSA provider (approximately $23 million), and there was a higher TSA exit cost (approximately $50 million).

Approach

A TSA exit strategy was developed based on detailed analysis of applications and services. A complexity framework was used to determine the exit disposition, application complexity, and comparison with similar applications transformed or cloned during Day 1 execution.

Day 1 program governance was implemented in order to enforce the rigor and focus required to achieve an aggressive timeline. A TSMO was set up to diligently follow the progress and report to senior management.

The plan was to expedite the TSA exits to an interim state for applications with planned transformations in the future, as well as finalize the entity's transformation strategy in order to enable teams to focus on critical transformations immediately after the exits, which resulted in:

- Exit for cloned applications: 7 months
- Exit for transformed applications: 9 months
- Exit for service TSAs: 7 months

Impact/Results

The entity's CIO procured advice on the TSA exit strategy and, as a result, expedited the exit timeline by 15 months and saved approximately $18 million in monthly payments and TSA exit costs.

The early TSA exits enabled the entity to gain early independence following the original divestiture and focus on its stand-alone transformation, including the execution of a series of spin-offs. The early TSA exits had minimal or no impact on the spin-offs.

Chapter 33
Managing Separation Costs, Stranded Costs, and Dis-synergies

33.1 Show Me the Money

Four fundamental questions help determine the business case of a divestiture:

- Why is the divestiture required?
- What is the potential benefit for the seller?
- What is the one-time and ongoing cost to the seller?
- What is required to attract the best possible valuation from a buyer?

While the first two questions are dependent on market conditions and seller's business strategy, the last two questions are the ones that may keep the CFO and COO awake at night. These two questions are the focus of this chapter.

The one-time costs of a divestiture for the seller are primarily associated with separating people, processes, and technology for the divested entity so that it can operate independently of the seller. These are typically referred to as separation costs. Sometimes one-time separation costs can far outweigh the value from the divestiture.

The valuation for a divested entity is governed largely by the product of operating profit (measured in terms of EBITDA) and the EBITDA multiplier. While the multiplier is a function of comparable deals in the recent past or valuation of comparable companies in the market, the operating profit (EBITDA) is inversely proportional to the operating cost, also referred to as the cost envelope of the divested entity. The cost envelope can be controlled by the seller through a sound divestiture strategy and can significantly impact deal valuation positively. On the other hand, if it is not managed properly, it may introduce significant financial and legal risks, potentially even putting the deal itself in jeopardy.

© Deloitte Development LLC 2018
J. Joy, *Divestitures and Spin-Offs*, Management for Professionals,
https://doi.org/10.1007/978-1-4939-7662-1_33

The ongoing cost impacts of a divestiture to the seller or the buyer have two dimensions, both of which may adversely impact the ongoing profitability of the seller:

(a) Dis-synergies: Cost increases due to duplication of common resources between the seller and the divested entity or reduction in economies of scale
(b) Stranded Costs: Costs associated with the divested entity that are left behind with the seller

Overall, cost impacts of a divestiture can be significant enough to necessitate disclosure as part of the deal announcement as well as updates as part of quarterly earnings reports (for public companies).

33.2   Separation Costs

Separation costs or the one-time costs to enable the divested entity to operate on a stand-alone basis can be significant. Separation costs typically include internal labor, external labor, technology, legal fees, third-party supplier fees, etc. to enable, plan, and execute separation projects.

Cost drivers vary by functions and businesses. Key separation efforts that drive costs for major functions are outlined in Table 33.1.

Table 33.1 Separation Costs

Function	Cost drivers
Finance	Carve-out financials—Historical and pro forma
	Special regulatory filings for divestiture
	Asset separation
	Setting up bank accounts and tax structures
	Costs for complying with international accounting standards such as GAAP, IFRS, etc.
Human resources	Organization design and location strategy for seller company and divested entity
	Employee retention and relocation
	Employee severance
	Accelerated equity
Supply chain	Carve-out of distribution centers
	Carve-out of logistics
	Carve-out of distribution channels
Real estate	Lease termination
	New leases
	Separation of existing sites
	New land and building purchases
	Site closures and sale
Information technology	Carve-out of infrastructure at data centers and sites
	Carve-out of systems, including hardware, software, and labor
Marketing and sales	Carve-out of marketing, branding, and sales channels
	Change management for external partners
Legal	Setting up new legal entities
	Divestiture legal documentation
	Separation of pending litigation
Procurement	Securing TSA rights
	Additional one-time purchases to support divestiture
	Assigning or cloning contracts
Divestiture management office	External and internal support for program enablement, planning, and execution
	Change management
	Communications with buyer

The magnitude of separation costs is governed primarily by the approach selected to carve out the divested entity from the seller company. Separation costs will be lower for a logical separation/transition services agreement (TSA) approach, higher for a clone/replication approach, and highest for a transformation approach. The nature of the costs also depends on the approach, as outlined in Table 33.2.

Table 33.2 Nature of Costs Based on Carve-Out Approach

#	Carve-out approach	Nature of separation costs
1	Logical separation/TSA	• Internal and external labor for program management and development of logically separate processes and supporting systems • Third-party supplier right-to-use fee to allow seller company to provide services to divested entity • Hiring costs for additional labor required to support logically separated processes and systems
2	Clone/replication	• Internal and external labor for program management and replication of processes and systems • Technology purchases including hardware, software, support contracts, etc. for replicated systems • Hiring costs for additional labor required to support the replicated processes and systems
3	Transformation	• Significantly higher internal and external labor to plan and execute transformation of operating model and processes • Significantly higher technology purchases including net new software, hardware, support contracts, etc. • Internal and external labor to develop net new systems to support the transformed processes • Reorganization costs associated with hiring and reduction of labor to align with transformed processes

33.3 Leading Practices for Managing Separation Costs

There are some key factors and practices to manage separation costs during a divestiture:

- Estimate functional separation costs early during diligence as this can impact deal economics significantly.
- Internal labor may not be considered under one-time costs in regulatory filings.
- Factor costs for post-Day 1 activities.
- Leverage existing systems and processes to track actuals.
- Factor in write-offs and duplicative costs (also known as double bubble) during the separation.
- Clearly define who bears the costs—buyer or seller.
- Look at project portfolio rationalization to mitigate separation costs.

33.3.1 Cost Envelope of a Divested Entity

In general, when a divestiture deal is signed, the agreement includes defined upper boundaries for the overall cost envelope as well as individual cost envelopes of functions and business units of the divested entity. Inability to maintain these cost envelopes on Day 1 may invoke clauses in the divestiture agreement that negatively impact the deal valuation or, in the worst case, result in deal termination. It becomes imperative therefore that the cost envelope is managed closely throughout the deal cycle.

Typical cost envelopes of functions as a percentage of operating expenses are exhibited in Table 33.3. These cost envelopes may vary by industry and size of the company. A few consulting and professional services firms offer benchmarking analyses based on company revenue, sector, and industry. Such analyses can be leveraged to arrive at more precise estimates.

Table 33.3 Cost Envelopes of Functions as Percentage of Operating Expenses

#	Function	Cost envelope
1	Information technology	34–38%
2	Marketing	18–21%
3	Real estate	11–15%
4	Finance	11–12%
5	Legal	5–6%
6	Human resources	5–6%
7	Supply chain	2.5–3.5%
8	Procurement	1.5–2.0%
9	Executive management	1.5–2.0%
10	Cybersecurity	1.0–1.5%

33.4 Developing Cost Envelope for a Divested Entity

Developing cost envelope of a divested entity can be a complex exercise, especially if the divested entity is tightly integrated with the rest of the company's operations. Although many companies track financials by business unit and geography, costs associated with functions may be allocated to business units and geographical units based on factors such as revenue, headcount, etc. However, such allocated costs may vary significantly from the real costs incurred by the functions for various business units and geographical units. Cost envelopes based on allocations may differ significantly from reality and impact deal execution and valuation. It is therefore critical to carefully estimate the cost envelope of the entities identified for divesture.

Developing cost envelope for a divested entity involves the activities described below.

- Evaluate available financials of the divested entity from the company's financial systems.
- By function, identify costs of dedicated people, processes, and technology associated with the divested entity.
- By function, identify costs of shared people, processes, and technology that will transfer as part of the divested entity. The portion of these costs that was not allocated to the divested entity comprises *stranded costs*.
- By function, identify costs of shared people, processes, and technology that will not transfer as part of the divested entity. Run-rate costs associated with standing up replacements for these comprise *dis-synergies*. Any such costs that can be avoided by leveraging the equivalent elements of the buyer comprises *synergies*, a key element associated with value generation from an acquisition

33.4.1 Reducing Cost Envelope

Cost envelope assessed using the above approach may not be attractive enough to get expected valuations for the divestiture. Some strategies that can be leveraged to help reduce the cost envelope are outlined below.

- Evaluate potential for an overall transformation of the divested entity for functions or processes that cost significantly higher than the benchmarks.
- Identify costs of standard processes and technology used by the divested entity as synergies that can temporarily be provided through transition services agreements (TSAs) by the buyer to the seller and can be provided by the buyer's existing processes and technology.
- Outsource inefficient functions of the divested entity where possible.

33.4.2 Ongoing Costs: Stranded Costs and Dis-synergies

Divestitures generally result in an increased cost envelope for the seller company arising from two cost buckets outlined below.

(a) Dis-synergies: Cost increases due to duplication of common resources between the seller and the divested entity or reduction in economies of scale
(b) Stranded Costs: Costs associated with the divested entity that are left behind with the seller

The ongoing cost impacts of a divestiture have two dimensions, both of which may adversely impact the ongoing profitability of the seller. These costs may be associated with shared infrastructure, IT systems, real estate, headcount, third-party licensing/services, etc. It is critical to manage stranded costs and dis-synergies actively during execution. Stranded costs and dis-synergies, if left unchecked or undetected, can significantly hinder achieving the goals from a divestiture. The increased costs may negatively impact future earnings and market value.

33.5 Sources of Stranded Costs and Dis-synergies

Some of the principal sources of stranded costs and dis-synergies are outlined below.

- Loss of scale due to divestitures may result in an increase in unit pricing for products and services, resulting in dis-synergies.
- Tightly integrated shared services for functions such as IT, finance, HR, legal, sales, marketing, etc. when separated may result in both stranded costs and dis-synergies.
- Shared infrastructure with the divested entity including real estate, IT data centers and systems, etc.
- Long-term vendor contracts supporting multiple business units with early termination costs, minimum revenue commitments, etc.
- Costs of unused portion of third-party products/services due to contractual obligations like maintenance which might not be prorated. For example, enterprise software licenses that may not be separated during the divesture.
- Leverage provided by accelerated divestiture timelines to third-party suppliers to ink long-term high-pricing contracts to provide contractual rights for supporting divestitures.

Understanding the sources of stranded costs and dis-synergies before finalizing the deal can significantly structure the divestiture transaction efficiently and can also help eliminate these costs at the earliest, thus maximizing the potential value of the divesture.

33.6 Focus Areas for Managing Stranded Costs and Dis-synergies

Stranded costs and dis-synergies reduction should follow a strategy centered on prioritization, detailed analysis, and close coordination. Stranded cost reduction opportunities should be identified for each function and line of business, with emphasis on the focus areas outlined below.

Information Technology

- Redundant IT infrastructure
- Software consolidation
- Outsourced services optimization

Real Estate

• Space adjustments to align with decreased headcount
• Cost assessment of occupancy, repair, and maintenance
• Location and market analysis

Operations

• Project prioritization
• Help desk and support functions
• Maintenance activities
• Call center staffing and processes

Human Resources

• Current and target state organizational structure
• Workload analysis and staffing levels
• Span of control analysis
• Benefit plans—structure and pricing
• HR operations
• Payroll
• Management incentive plan

Procurement

• Vendor consolidation
• Vendor pricing—leverage existing agreements/contracts
• Payment terms
• Standardization of materials

Finance

• Expense payable processing
• Receivables management
• Federal tax strategic review
• Property, sales, and use review
• International and multistate analysis

Shared Services

• Duplicate shared services across functions and line of business
• Duplicate shared services across geographies

33.6.1   *Leading Practices to Manage Stranded Costs and Dis-synergies*

• Identify and develop plan to minimize stranded costs and dis-synergies in parallel with divestiture planning, well in advance of Day 1.

- Determine, validate, and communicate the current cost baseline so that functional and line-of-business leaders have sufficient clarity on cost goals.
- Drive functional and line-of-business leads to clearly articulate and quantify cost reduction initiatives so that they can be incorporated into divestiture work plans and/or road map.
- Set cost reduction targets based on the decrease in relative size/volume resulting from the divestiture.
- Use cost reduction targets to challenge functional and line-of-business teams to meet and exceed overall cost reduction goals for the divestiture.
- Plan for longer cost reduction lead times in some functional and line-of-business areas to reduce risk of cost overhang (e.g., sale of real estate).
- Centrally manage organizational design cost reduction initiatives to help ensure alignment with overall divestiture plan, comply with legal requirements, and provide consistency in timing and messaging.
- Manage the impact of change through communications and stakeholder management.
- Track any transition services related to the divestiture, which may impact the timing of some cost reduction initiatives (e.g., headcount reduction).
- Leverage momentum from the divestiture to identify further cost reduction initiatives for transformation opportunities beyond targets.

33.6.2 Common Challenges Faced

- *Change Management*: Mitigating the "double dose" of change that employees must digest, due to the divestiture and the resulting downsizing of functions and lines of business
- *Operational Focus*: Ensuring that business is uninterrupted and remains consistent (business as usual) despite the focus on cost reduction initiatives
- *Clear Ownership*: Establishing clear ownership of activities/tasks to maintain focus on achieving the overall cost reduction
- *TSA Contract Compliance*: Ensuring coordination with and adherence to any master services and service-level agreements with buyer

33.6.3 Framework to Reduce Stranded Costs and Dis-synergies in Information Technology

Information technology (IT) is typically the biggest source of stranded costs and dis-synergies during divestitures. A framework to identify and prioritize stranded costs and dis-synergies in IT and maximize value from a divestiture is outlined below.

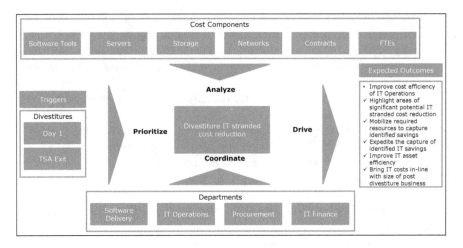

Fig. 33.1 Stranded Cost Reduction Approach

- *Analyze costs*: Collect cost information for all functions and identify cost allocations prior to divestiture to analyze costs of divested portion.
- *Determine cost reduction targets*: Identify cost reduction targets for each function and assign responsibility to the functions to define stranded costs and develop cost reduction strategies.
- *Develop implementation plans*: Develop detailed implementation plan for each opportunity, including actions necessary to implement, dates of important milestones, responsibilities, and dependencies.
- *Track progress in eliminating stranded cost*: Ensure alignment between evolving TSA exit plans and stranded cost reduction plans and track cost reduction progress for each function, and ensure tie-in to planning/budgeting process.

33.7 Conclusion

Estimating and managing divestiture-related costs—separation costs, cost envelope of divested entity, stranded costs, and dis-synergies—tightly are critical not only to the success of a divestiture transaction but for the future market value of the seller as well. Therefore, these cost impacts should be evaluated and tracked very closely right from the divestiture deal strategy to the TSA exits, with a sustained visibility for executive management and the board of directors.

Case Study: 33

Background

As one of the global leaders in aluminum mining and production, Client X specialized across the complete metal value chain from mining and refining of natural resources like aluminum and bauxite to producing finished rolled and engineered aluminum products and solutions for some of the largest OEMs in the world. Following increasing market pressures along with agitation of activist investors, management concluded in late 2015 to separate into two distinct organizations—an Upstream Co. focusing on mining and refining natural resources at competitive costs and a Value-Add Co. focusing on growth in the industrials and lightweight aluminum manufacturing.

Challenges

The cost team was assembled to support the analysis and development of separation cost models (including one-time, stranded, and dis-synergy costs). As with many large manufacturing spin-offs, the scale and complexity of operations (including the expansive shared service, real estate, and technology footprint) had an observable effect on one-time, stranded, and dis-synergy costs. Upon analysis, the team was tasked with working cross-functionally to minimize both stranded costs and dis-synergies with an ultimate cost savings target of *$127 M*.

Approach

In order to complete a full separation cost analysis, the team worked first to establish top-down overhead baselines, perform functional cost benchmarking, and develop bottom-up labor costs. An *overhead cost model, top-down baseline*, provided visibility into the amount of costs to be allocated across the business units and workstreams and assisted leadership with the preliminary planning for the future state organization. *Functional cost benchmarking* leveraged existing functional cost data in order to compare current company performance against competitors and was used to help determine post-divestiture cost targets for each corporate function. An *overhead cost model, bottom-up labor costs*, using fully loaded labor cost and job band assumptions was not only used to inform key stakeholders of the cost implications of the bottom-up org structure developed by functional leaders and org design team but also to compare cost implications of bottom-up org design with top-down estimates to ensure accuracy and/or magnify large variances.

Finally, the team worked to rapidly define, identify, and track stranded, dis-synergy, and one-time costs. Though related, these costs are distinctly different and setting/aligning on clear definitions was key to correctly allocating costs to ensure proper impact assessments were made and mitigation strategies could be developed. No/few dis-synergies or stranded costs within a function may have indicated that functional leadership had not fully thought through the cost impact of the separation, whereas numerous dis-synergies within a function presented an opportunity to mitigate. Lastly, the team analyzed one-time costs of separating the business, closely tracking variances between expected and actual spend across cost categories; under-expected spend may have indicated delay in crucial separation activities, whereas over-expected spend may have indicated unexpected costs being incurred. Throughout the entirety of the separation, both one-time costs and stranded/dis-synergy cost estimates were routinely monitored and refined to ensure cost targets were achieved.

Impact/Results

Set up and transitioned tools that provided management with high visibility into current and future overhead costs, dis-synergies, and integration costs. Built cost model to manage over $500 M in one-time separation costs and worked with functional teams to capture and track costs over time. Leveraged past experience and expertise to help the client identify and quantify incremental sources of dis-synergies and stranded costs, mitigating over 50% of stranded costs. Additional support through benchmarking and headcount costing exercises helped validate/track savings commitments and unearth additional savings opportunities.

Chapter 34
Cost Reduction Through Outsourcing

34.1 Outsourcing: An Enabler for M&A

Some key concerns for C-suite executives who are considering a divestiture include the operational and financial impacts of separating people, processes, and technology between the seller company and the divested entity. The financial impact of the separation is a key driver of deal valuation, while the operational impact is a key driver of deal probability and the deal timeline. Financial and operational impacts manifest themselves as both one-time events occurring at deal execution and ongoing effects such as stranded costs and dis-synergies between the entities involved in the deal.

Outsourcing can be highly effective at minimizing the operational and financial impacts of a divestiture across multiple functional areas, including information technology (IT), finance, and human resources (HR). Outsourcing minimizes the replication of people, processes, and technology across the common functions of the separated entities during a divestiture.

Outsourcing is generally most beneficial when the people, process, and technology of the divested entity are tightly integrated with those of the seller company, which usually increases the time and cost to structurally separate the divested entity from the seller company. By outsourcing processes and/or technology for both the seller company and the divested entity to an agreed-upon third party, the time and cost associated with the separation can be significantly reduced.

34.2 What Is Outsourcing?

There are numerous definitions of "outsourcing" based on the context, scope, and need for services. However, the most holistic and accurate definition describes outsourcing as "a process whereby an organization decides to contract out or sell its

© Deloitte Development LLC 2018

J. Joy, *Divestitures and Spin-Offs*, Management for Professionals,
https://doi.org/10.1007/978-1-4939-7662-1_34

assets, people, and/or activities to a third-party supplier, who in exchange provides and manages these assets and services for an agreed fee over an agreed time period,"[1] as defined by information management scholars Kern and Willcocks.

Although this overarching definition of outsourcing is universal, there are also regional models referred to as offshore, nearshore, and onshore outsourcing. There are many different types of outsourcing, but those particularly important to a divestiture are IT outsourcing and business process outsourcing. IT outsourcing relates to the types of components being outsourced, such as application maintenance, network management, infrastructure as a service, platform as a service, and software as a service. Business process outsourcing relates to the processes being outsourced, such as customer service, accounts receivables, account payables, HR, payroll, contract management, procurement, and legal services.

The fundamental benefit of outsourcing is the ability to hand over services for common functions to a third party who, due to economies of scale, can more efficiently deliver them. Outsourcing can enable the company to focus on activities that provide strategic and competitive advantages.

But outsourcing has its challenges. Although it offers advantages in terms of cost savings, outsourcing requires a company to provide its proprietary assets and knowledge base to third-party vendors, which generates significant risk. The matrix in Fig. 34.1 serves as a basic tool to help a company decide if a particular activity in their organization should be outsourced or insourced.

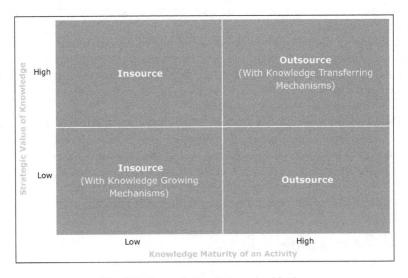

Fig. 34.1 Insourcing vs. Outsourcing Matrix

---

[1] "Exploring relationships in information technology outsourcing: The interaction approach," T. Kern and L.P. Willcocks, *European Journal of Information Systems* (11), pp. 3–19, 2002.

Back-office functions such as IT, finance, and HR are often the most effective candidates for outsourcing. If a company's products and services are commoditized or homogenous, then manufacturing and customer service may also be good candidates for outsourcing. Processes that provide the company with a competitive or strategic advantage are typically not outsourced, including product design, quality assurance, and strategic procurement.

34.3 Potential Benefits of Outsourcing to Support an M&A Transaction

When a company is divesting one or more business units, its common functions (i.e., IT, finance, HR, and procurement) must be separated for the divested entity. The seller company often chooses to replicate its common functions for the divested entity, which results in significant one-time costs for the seller and creates incongruity for both entities in terms of people, processes, and technology. Transition services agreements (TSAs) are often implemented to bridge any gaps in services for the divested entity on Day 1. TSAs allow the seller to provide temporary services to the divested entity on Day 1 and thereafter (until the end date stated in the TSA). Although TSAs are helpful to the divested entity, they are a burden to the seller as they consume the seller's resources while providing zero or insignificant returns. TSAs also introduce inflexibility into the separation process, making it difficult for the buyer, seller, or divested entity to make changes without affecting one or more of the other entities involved in the deal. Ultimately, the divested entity must entirely replace the services provided by the seller under TSAs before these agreements expire.

Outsourcing these common functions to a third party can help reduce costs and alleviate some of the pressure involved in separating services for the divested entity by Day 1. Outsourcing can also provide a higher degree of flexibility than TSAs. The potential benefits of using outsourcing to support an M&A transaction include the following.

Table 34.1 Potential Benefits of Outsourcing to Support an M&A Transaction

#	Potential benefit	Description
1	Deal value uplift	Reduces incongruity between the separating entities, which results in higher earnings before interest, taxes, depreciation, and amortization (EBITDA) for the divested entity
2	Improved deal probability	Improves the likelihood of deal finalization by reducing the risks associated with separating the divested entity from the seller company
3	Improved ability to meet deal timeline	Reduces the risk of missing deal execution milestones, especially day 1, since the outsourced third-party vendor owns the logical separation of services between the seller company and divested entity
4	Reduction in incongruity	Reduces incongruity between the seller company and the divested entity since the outsourced third-party vendor does not replicate the seller's people, processes, and technology for the divested entity
5	One-time cost reduction	Reduces the one-time costs associated with hiring additional personnel and buying new assets to support separation activities between the seller company and the divested entity
6	Stranded cost reduction	Reduces stranded costs for the seller company since it is not saddled with partial assets left behind by the divested entity as these are transferred over to the outsourced third-party vendor
7	TSA operation overhead reduction	Eliminates most of the operational overhead associated with managing TSAs for the divested entity since the outsourced third-party vendor manages the TSAs

The potential benefits outlined in Table 34.1 are in addition to the potential benefits related to outsourcing in general, including the following.

Table 34.2 Potential Benefits of Outsourcing

#	Potential benefit	Description
1	Operating cost reduction	Due to economies of scale, third-party vendors usually incur lower costs for labor, equipment, and management than the companies that outsource to them. To stay competitive, third-party vendors pass some of these lower costs on to their customers—The companies that outsource to them
2	Operational flexibility	Outsourcing provides an effective pathway for a company to scale or reduce capacity in order to adjust to fluctuating market demands and avoid high fixed costs related to labor, equipment, and management
3	Increased quality	Outsourced third-party vendors are specialists in the services they provide, and to stay competitive, they are incentivized to adopt the latest innovations to enhance service delivery
4	Reduced risks	To stay competitive, outsourced third-party vendors must remain informed about the regulations associated with the services they provide. Additionally, the cost of breaking contractual service-level agreements (SLAs) with outsourced third-party vendors is low in comparison to the costs related to the operational and regulatory risks that outsourcing can prevent
5	Focus on core competencies	By outsourcing services for common functions and realizing cost savings, the company can focus its attention and capital on building its core functions and facilitating a better customer experience. In some scenarios, outsourcing triggers the need for a restructuring of related functions for better strategic alignment

34.4 When Is Outsourcing Relevant for M&A?

Outsourcing may not be relevant for every M&A transaction. It is generally the most useful in the following divestiture scenarios.

(a) *Divested Entity's Processes Are Tightly Integrated with the Seller Company*: The level of integration between the seller company and divested entity is directly related to the benefit of outsourcing. If a process or service is tightly integrated between the entities, then the value of outsourcing that process or service is high.

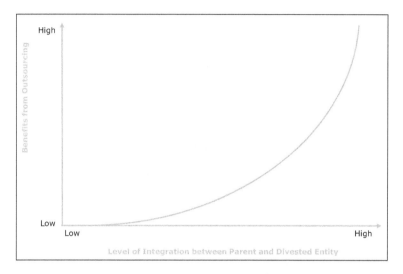

Fig. 34.2 Marginal Potential Benefit Curve of Outsourcing for Divestitures

When a divested entity is tightly integrated with the seller company, separating people, processes, and technology for most common functions (i.e., IT, finance, HR, procurement, legal services, real estate) can be very time and resource intensive due to the high degree of replication (also known as cloning) and TSAs involved. In such a scenario, outsourcing may result in one-time and ongoing cost savings.

However, in some cases, the separated entities may have their own separate IT, finance, HR, and procurement functions before separation. In such instances, it can be easier and inexpensive to separate these functions between the seller company and the divested entity without outsourcing.

(b) *Buyer Wishes to Keep the Divested Entity Relatively Independent*: If the buyer is a financial buyer or a company with a completely different business model than the seller, the buyer may want to keep the newly acquired entity relatively independent. In such cases, outsourcing common functions may be a viable option for a divested entity with a moderate level of integration with the seller company.

(c) *Buyer Requires Long-Term TSAs, but Seller Is Not Inclined*: Sometimes the buyer does not have the time and resources to integrate the divested entity with its own business and may need TSAs for more than 2 years to cover the divested entity's common functions. However, most sellers are unlikely to extend TSAs for more than 1–2 years because TSAs do not provide a healthy rate of return, if any. In such instances, outsourcing these common functions may be a viable option for the seller in order to keep the one-time costs of the separation to a minimum. Outsourcing also allows a path for the buyer to eventually merge these common functions for the divested entity with its own common functions over time, while allowing flexibility to change processes whenever necessary.

34.5   Orchestrating Outsourcing for M&A

Outsourcing a function during an M&A transaction is different from outsourcing that same function during a non-M&A scenario in two key ways.

Table 34.3 Outsourcing Differentiators During an M&A Transaction vs. Non-M&A Scenario

#	Differentiator	Description
1	Time to execute	During a non-M&A scenario, the time to execute available for such an outsourcing deal could be between 9 and 24 months. However, during an M&A transaction, the time to execute spans between the deal announcement date and the execution date (day 1) of a transaction, which is typically between 6 and 15 months
2	Two versus three (or more) stakeholders	During a non-M&A scenario, only one outsourcing agreement must be negotiated between the company and the outsourced third-party vendor for a particular service. However, during an M&A transaction, two outsourcing agreements must be negotiated with the outsourced third-party vendor—One agreement between the vendor and the seller company and another agreement between the vendor and the divested entity

34.5.1   Setting Up an Outsourcing Agreement

Every outsourcing agreement is unique; however, the implementation methodology is fairly consistent across organizations. Figure 34.3 illustrates the workstreams and phases involved in implementing an outsourcing agreement.

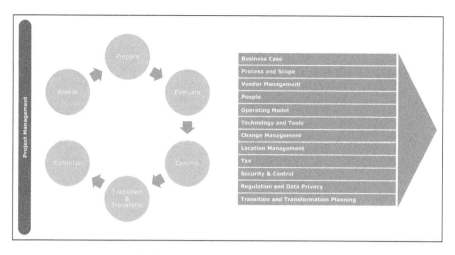

Fig. 34.3 Outsourcing Life Cycle

34.5.2 Nuances of Setting Up an Outsourcing Agreement for an M&A Transaction

Setting up an outsourcing agreement in the context of a divestiture requires a specific approach, as outlined in Table 34.4.

Table 34.4 Nuances of Outsourcing for an M&A Transaction

#	Phase	Activities	
1	Assess	Define objectives, assess capacity, and assess third-party vendors	
		General activities: • Develop business case • Determine scope • Evaluate baseline spend • Develop guiding principles • Assess third-party vendors	*Additional activities for M&A*: • Evaluate the business case based on the level of integration between the seller and the divested entity, TSA duration, and deal terms • Define the scope of outsourcing in consideration of regulatory requirements for shared services (i.e., data and voice circuits cannot be outsourced and shared) • Create a baseline spend for the seller company and the divested entity

(continued)

Table 34.4 (continued)

#	Phase	Activities
2	Prepare	Define services with levels, create requests for proposals (RFPs) for the outsourcing agreement, develop a list of third-party vendors
		General activities: • Define operating model requirements • Design new organizational structure for the outsourced activity • Define and structure outsourcing agreement • Initiate vendor due diligence and engagement approach • Develop and issue RFPs for the outsourcing agreement	*Additional activities for M&A*: • Define requirements to limit exposure to additional costs when either entity exits shared applications in the RFP
3	Evaluate	Evaluate the responses of third-party vendors and select the final vendor
		General activities: • Monitor risks, issue budgets, create detailed plans • Manage vendor evaluations • Refine structure of outsourcing agreement based on vendor proposal • Conduct vendor question and answer (Q&A) session • Evaluate proposal • Conduct initial negotiations	*Additional activities for M&A*: • Consider any buyer constraints when selecting a vendor • Ensure outsourcing proposal is comprehensive and splits costs between the seller company and divested entity based on respective volumes of work
4	Commit	Develop and finalize the outsourcing agreement
		General activities: • Monitor business case • Finalize organizational design of outsourced functions • Develop transition plan for seller company personnel • Develop pricing model for the outsourcing agreement • Define services along with terms and conditions • Select vendor, negotiate outsourcing agreement, sign deal • Finalize outsourcing agreement	*Additional activities for M&A*: • Include stranded cost management in the vendor's scope • Build two separate outsourcing agreements for the seller company and the divested entity • Include terms for potential future M&A transactions in the outsourcing agreement

(continued)

Table 34.4   (continued)

#	Phase	Activities	
5	Transition and transform	Implement the outsourcing model with the outsourced third-party vendor	
		General activities: • Measure and track the value of the outsourcing agreement • Set up team to manage the outsourcing agreement, including the relationship with the vendor • Monitor vendor transition • Monitor vendor dispute resolution	*Additional activities for M&A*: • Plan transition of divested entity contract to the buyer • Set up joint governance structure between outsourcing vendor, the seller company, and the divested entity to address mutual freeze periods, disruptions to common systems, etc.
6	Optimize	Stabilize governance with outsourced third-party vendors	
		General activities: • Monitor value to company from outsourcing • Ongoing tracking of outcomes against business case • Plan for end of contract term • Assess vendor performance • Improve governance	*Additional activities for M&A*: • Track invoices and underlying work volumes for both entities • Ensure costs do not increase for either of the two entities due to one of them exiting shared applications or infrastructure

34.6   Risks of Outsourcing

Outsourcing has its share of risks and may not be ideal for companies unable to manage these risks. Five key outsourcing risks include:

1. *Quality Issues*: When large IT functions are outsourced, vendor quality assurance teams often lack the ability to track and validate the deliverables. However, most outsourcing agreements include service-level agreements (SLAs) that mandate a minimum quality standard that must be delivered by the vendor to avoid loss of the contract.

2. *Loss of Direct Control*: When the services of a function are delivered by a third-party vendor, an inherent lack of insight into the day-to-day operations of the third-party vendor creates risks that may lead to issues, such as an inability to meet timelines. Additionally, the company is dependent on the third-party vendor to deliver as contracted, especially for functions in which the company lacks the specialized skills or knowledge to perform. To mitigate such risks, the company should create a robust governing structure with key stakeholders who must sign off on any major changes to the contract.

3. *Increased Security Risk*: Large volumes of sensitive data may be shared between the company and the outsourced third-party vendor in an outsourcing

arrangement, which may put the company at risk of losing control over sensitive information. This may lead to a loss of confidentiality for the company's customers, which could damage the company's image and reputation. A high degree of data encryption, utilization of virtual private networks, and usage of secure sharing portals are some of the methods being used to help prevent such breaches.

4. *Different Time Zones, Languages, and Other Barriers*: According to the recent analysis published by A.T. Kearney to identify the global services location index, India was identified as the number one company for outsourcing, followed by China and Malaysia. Through creation of such operational models, companies may face language and cultural barriers. In addition, if the time zones are completely different, it can be difficult for the company to effectively collaborate and communicate with the outsourced third-party vendor, which could lead to increased turnaround times and potentially create processing delays.

5. *Future Conflicts Between the Seller Company and Divested Entity*: Until the shared processes or functions between the seller company and the divested entity are completely separated, changes to such functions may become more time-consuming for both entities due to conflicting business freeze periods.

34.7   Key Outsourcing Considerations for an M&A Transaction

Table 34.5 outlines some key considerations when establishing an outsourcing deal for an M&A transaction.

Table 34.5 Key Outsourcing Considerations for an M&A Transaction

#	Consideration	Description
1	Exhaust quick wins (easily attainable objectives) before signatures	*Challenge* • Functions may not be able execute quick wins for cost reduction or architecture changes due to other high priorities • The outsourced third-party vendor may reduce costs, but not to pass those cost savings on to the seller company *Mitigation* • Quick wins before outsourcing should be prioritized and resourced with leadership support
2	Beware of scope/cost creep	*Challenge* • Costs may increase just before deal sign-off due to dis-synergies involved with the separation effort • May lead to financial surprises in the future *Mitigation* • Incongruities should be evaluated and proactively added to the outsourcing agreement
3	Address communication gaps	*Challenge* • Interpretation of terms during outsourcing negotiations may vary and may result in unpleasant surprises *Mitigation* • Define terms clearly in the agreement to avoid future conflicts arising from subjective interpretation of terms
4	Misalignment of interests	*Challenge* • The outsourced third-party vendor's interests may not align with the interests of the functions for which processes are being outsourced • Contract terms may not align with the long-term interests of the corresponding functions *Mitigation* • Functions should play leading roles in the outsourcing negotiations

34.8 Conclusion

When considering a divestiture, outsourcing can be a game changer for deal value and the likelihood of deal success. The challenges posed by the separation of highly integrated common functions such as IT, finance, and HR can be mitigated to a large extent through outsourcing, which can minimize the replication of people, processes, and technology. However, it is critical for both the seller company and the divested entity to each have a clear strategic business case for the outsourcing relationship, along with skilled resources to manage the outsourcing relationship.

Case Study: 34

Background

A large Fortune 50 multinational enterprise IT company with more than 190,000 employees worldwide, generating more than $50 billion in revenue. The company decided to spin off one of core business units to another large technology services conglomerate based in the United States. The divested entity comprised more than 100,000 employees and about 35% of the company's overall revenue. The IT functions of the seller company and divested entity were highly integrated and managed by the divested entity. The seller company decided to outsource most of the IT function to the buyer.

Challenges

The complexity of spinning off, transitioning, and transferring most IT assets and labor to the divested entity, along with the execution of related outsourcing agreements, posed the following challenges:

Scope

- Migration of more than 100,000 employees across 5 continents and more than 40 countries worldwide.
- More than 100 employees dedicated to delivering the separation of the divested entity and outsourcing program.
- The outsourcing contract included more than 1000 applications; more than 30,000 servers, storage, and network devices; more than 200 sites and facilities; and more than 50 shared service applications.

Timeline

- Day 1 was 12 months post-deal announcement.
- Outsourcing contracts were scheduled to start on Day 1.
- There was a 3–6-month stabilization phase post-separation covered under a TSA to ensure smooth conduct of activities covered in the outsourcing contracts.

Other complexities

- Highly integrated environment across multiple business units with little to no logical separation of IT applications and the underlying IT infrastructure.
- Acquisitions of other companies during the time of separation and transition to the outsourced model would need additional diligence on integration planning and ensuring business continuity.

Approach

The IT outsourcing agreement primarily covered IT applications and IT infrastructure. The first step involved agreeing on the scope of services the company needed as a service from the third-party vendor. An elaborate exercise was undertaken to understand the baseline costs for the seller company, the divested entity, and the third-party vendor. Many workshops were held between teams representing the three entities to align on the scope and the cost drivers across IT applications, IT infrastructure, and other components, including incongruities and stranded costs.

The primary factors that contributed to the success of the IT outsourcing program include:

Leadership team

- Key stakeholders from the company were identified to lead the negotiations with the third-party vendor's pricing team.
- Senior IT and business leaders accurately estimated the scope and costs of the outsourced services, which helped align scope, pricing, and issue resolution in the final agreement.

Governance

- Periodic workshops were held to bring together key stakeholders from the seller company, the divested entity, and the third-party vendor.
- A well-defined plan and meeting cadence for the steering committee and working committee were critical to monitoring progress and timelines.

Impact/Results

Within 10 months, the IT outsourcing agreement was successfully negotiated and signed for a 5-year term. Highlights include the following:

- Successful separation of more than 750 applications and their underlying infrastructure and transition to the outsourcing company.
- Robust implementation of the location strategy for all sites shared or transitioned through the separation for management under the outsourcing contracts.
- Successful transition of more than 100,000 employees across 5 continents through the establishment of new roles and responsibilities at the divested entity, including the outsourcing unit.
- Identification and execution of an infrastructure optimization strategy by the outsourcing vendor that consolidated IT servers and storage components, resulting in efficiency gains.
- A 60% reduction in retained fixed costs as a result of the outsourcing agreement.
- Transformation of the operating model to align with the retained entities business goals.
- Outsourced operating model facilitated volume-based usage and reduced operating expenses.
- Increased flexibility achieved through transfer of large fixed assets enabling ability to transform from legacy environment.

Part V
Conclusion

Chapter 35
Separation Management Office:
Leading Practices

35.1 Overview

Separations are lengthy, operationally taxing, costly, one-time events with the opportunity to generate enormous value for companies on both sides. If done right, it can result in a seller who is cost and operationally efficient, focused and nimble with accretive partnerships and fit-for-purpose in the right size. Done right, the buyer will acquire a viable organization and hit the ground running to enable an effective integration with partnerships in place to drive immediate revenue momentum starting Day 1. Done wrong, it can result in higher cost and operational inefficiencies that will rob value from both parties.

It is imperative to get the strategy and approach right and drive these through effective execution. In this chapter we'll discuss leading practices that are essential to driving successful separations.

- Start with the end in mind.
- Build a master narrative.
- Simplified governance and decision rights.
- Major decisions front-loaded.
- Robust execution plan, anchored on dependencies.
- Capture the hearts and minds.

35.2 Start with the End in Mind

When a $110B technology company decided to split into two Fortune 50 Companies, the first step was establishing the strategy: What was the strategic focus of each company? How would they operate independently, and what did the split mean for shared resources and infrastructure? The company then translated this overarching strategic vision into specific business and functional blueprints which

© Deloitte Development LLC 2018
J. Joy, *Divestitures and Spin-Offs*, Management for Professionals,
https://doi.org/10.1007/978-1-4939-7662-1_35

articulated how the business operated today and how that would change over key moments in time. This ultimately translated into execution plans. Starting with the end in mind helped the organization anchor on a shared vision of the future and focus organizational energy toward achieving that common vision.

Starting with the end in mind involves two elements:

1. Aligning on a broad strategic direction
2. Translating this into blueprints

The strategic direction is the cornerstone of any separation or transformation and should involve components, like which solutions to focus on, what business capabilities are essential for the future, how these translate into an operating model, and which cost envelope to operate in. Driving alignment at the strategic level on these decisions can be extremely challenging. It's usually more efficient to go faster with a smaller group of executives empowered with decision rights. In the case of the $110B technology company mentioned above, the broad strategic direction was set by the CEO and the COO and adopted, enabled, and supported by the rest of the organization.

The next step is translating this broad strategic direction into blueprints. Blueprints capture details on process, people, technology, and assets to guide Day 1 planning efforts and cost reduction opportunities. In order to document the "end," business and functions must document how they operate today and how they will operate in the future, including any interim or transitionary phases.

The most critical aspect of creating blueprints, however, is not each individual blueprint, but how these blueprints come together into a unifying organizational framework. This blends top-down strategic direction (e.g., the skeleton of an operating model) with the detailed bottom-up operating knowledge that sits within the functions and business units.

For example, during a large and complex separation which spanned 150 K global employees and a significant shared services organization, the operating model was changed drastically to move from a global shared services model to a disaggregated model where relevant services were embedded into each of the business and functional areas. Where the rubber hit the road, however, was when each team developed their blueprints and sized the number of resources, systems, and other capabilities needed to support the model, in addition to when the hand-offs between functions took place. In some cases, these created synergies, while in others, it created dissynergies. Either way, the organization aligned on a common operating framework and recognized the trade-offs associated.

35.3   Build a Master Narrative

M&A and speed are two sides of the same coin. But in the need for speed, M&A executives often make suboptimal decisions that can plague the company for years to come and even dilute deal value. Instead, a more measured approach is to go slow when making critical decisions upfront and accelerate once decisions have been made.

Divestitures also bring tremendous amount of uncertainty to the ordinary course of business—What happens when? How will day jobs be impacted? When will the organization know their future role and vision? In order to synchronize organizational momentum with the transaction focus, it is imperative to get to a common master narrative or program road map on how the organization and the transaction team will operate from start to finish. This should lay out the road map of what happens when and how the organization and the transaction team will go from start of transaction to completing the separation.

In the case of the $110B separation, this master narrative was developed and communicated within the first 2 months and was shared as part of the transaction kick-off. As a result, 200 VPs and SVPs across the organization understood how the next 11 months leading to close would unravel and how this overlapped with run the business operations. They were ready for the journey ahead.

35.4 Simplified Governance and Decision Rights

Setting up the right governance model is the foundation for success in any large M&A or transformational program. In large complex and matrixed organizations, it is particularly difficult to establish the right balance between decision-makers, accountable owners, and broader group of stakeholders whose buy-in is essential for longer-term success. It is imperative to develop a model that balances the need for organizational involvement with the need to condense decision control and program stewardship within the hands of a few critical individuals.

In order to do this, it is important to empower and hold a few key leaders accountable for overall strategic decisions, buyer coordination, execution success, and success of the program, while simultaneously empowering and holding functional leaders accountable for the scope of functional work. Ensure visibility on progress with executive teams, business teams, board of directors, and the buyer. Also, have a single source of truth for all parties concerned to help ensure crystal clear visibility into program status and the big rocks.

A disciplined program management office, process, and cadence are essential to support the above goals. Running a disciplined program spans bottom-up and requires detailed tracking, supported by a structured cadence. As a result, it is necessary to (1) track workstream-level execution progress; (2) establish an effective cadence, which will typically involve weekly workstream-Separation Management Office (SMO) meetings, status reports, buyer and seller functional line, and business meetings; and (3) instill a regular cadence of management targets and reviews to drive accountability and business momentum. This cadence will accelerate tracking work-plan progress, escalate issues, and help ensure consistent communication between the buyer, seller teams, program executives, and project leadership teams. It will also help ensure risks are tracked and remedial actions are taken.

It is critical for the workstreams and SMO to be transparent. For instance, if milestones have not been met on time or issues come up that threaten a successful

Day 1, it is imperative that the executives are informed. Although the preferred method and style of executive-level status updates will vary, most executives find weekly emails that summarize project developments to be effective. These weekly emails should focus on the high-level status of separation activities.

The SMO plays a key role as neutral arbiter between the seller company, the divested entity, the buyer company, and any other relevant parties interested in the deal. The SMO team is responsible for escalating and resolving relevant issues within a short timeframe. It is a leading practice to implement a "12 h to escalate, 24 h to resolve" rule. Designate a point of contact (POC) within the SMO team to work with individual teams to ensure clear two-way communication between the SMO team and workstreams.

The SMO should also enable workstream leaders to make decisions specific to their workstream, such as team structure, site strategy alignment (for real estate), benefits readiness (for HR), minor timeline changes, etc., without unnecessary oversight to help ensure issues are resolved quickly and effectively.

Finally, issue resolution is also affected by the size of the deal and the separation management philosophy. Determining whether the deal will require a joint decision-making structure, in which buyer and seller workstream leaders agree upon and resolve issues together, or a more formal command structure is entirely dependent on the size of the deal.

35.5 Major Decisions Front-Loaded

The first few months of a separation are critical as most significant decisions are made during that time. Decisions such as operating model, organization and talent split, cost envelops to transfer, legal entity structure, country and go-to-market presence, and IT and operational separation strategy are key examples. Front-loading these decisions enables speed and focus and minimizes debate during detailed planning which could derail the timeline. It also helps ensure that the buyer is aligned on the overarching approach before resources are assigned and dollars are spent on execution. Lastly, it aids in integration planning for the buyer, as they have a clear vision of what to expect when the newly separated entity comes over the fence.

35.5.1 Organizational and Talent Decisions

Talent decisions are critical to separations—how much headcount is going over, the makeup of that headcount (geographical footprint, spans, layers), and the mechanics to ensure an equitable talent split are key issues that need to be addressed. While actual talent selection decisions will occur over time, early agreement on the principles of talent selection and separation can aid the process enormously.

For example, some of the dimensions that can be agreed upon early are as follows:

- How much headcount cost should transition over?
- What is the breakdown of total headcount cost by functions?
- Is the headcount being sent over adequate to run the newly created entity independently, or does it need to operate in conjunction with the buyer's organization?
- What is the approach to talent selection? How much is interview and selection based, versus assigned in a top-down carve-out fashion?
- What is the timing of the talent selection process?
- What decision rights does each entity have in the talent selection process?
- How can and should employees operate in the interim execution period? What should their priorities and focus be? How do you prevent talent poaching during that period to respect the agreed-upon approach?

Aligning on these decisions upfront can greatly accelerate the overall execution process.

35.5.2 Go-to-Market Strategy

Another important decision is customer and partner separation approach, strategy, and timing, as well as approach to overall partner relationships. This is discussed in detail in Chapter 19 (Managing Customer and Partner Transitions During a Separation).

35.5.3 IT Divestiture Planning

The SMO must establish how and when IT infrastructure will be transferred, as well as how IT resources will be allocated among the entities involved post-Day 1. In addition to separating current resources, a divestiture provides an opportunity for the seller company to adjust its technology strategy, rationalize applications, and adopt more efficient systems. The following approach can be used to kick-start IT divestiture planning:

- Map the usage of applications, servers, and networks to business processes.
- Establish end-state blueprints for the IT systems of the divested entity and the seller company that provide the appropriate mix of functional support and cost efficiency.
- Use the blueprints to define who will assume ownership of each existing application or asset, and develop a strategy for the buyer to fill in the gaps.

35.5.4 Cost Envelopes

Another critical decision is on managing costs as follows: (1) aligning on the total cost of functions and business that will remain with the seller, costs that are transitioned to the buyer, or those that remain with the seller but are "stranded" as they have no economic value to the seller and (2) aligning on a one-time separation cost budget, the allocation of that cost across functions, and the mechanics and governance of that budget.

Cost envelopes should be managed at the workstream level to avoid cost overruns. Start by focusing on initiatives that do not result in significant disruptions to existing processes. This can be facilitated by establishing workstream-level cost centers and assigning resources to accurately report costs incurred for separation activities.

At a minimum, stranded costs should be estimated and monitored. Stranded costs are costs that were previously shared with the divested entity but remain with the seller company post-divestiture. Costs arising from the partial use of resources should be analyzed to determine if innovative methods can be used to deploy underutilized resources in other areas. Stranded costs should be tracked according to the divestiture timeline to avoid delays and slippages from targets. Examples of common stranded costs include building or office space left unutilized following the separation. These stranded costs may cause the company's new cost structure to be disproportionate relative to its new size.

For the one-time separation budget, companies should considered what costs are internal or non-GAAP costs and what costs are external costs and would add incremental net new costs to the company. Companies will provide guidance during quarterly earnings calls to the investor community on net new costs expected to be incurred to separate the company and categorize the same as "restructuring" costs. The investor community expects these to be "one time" and is typically more forgiving of these costs as it relates to the overall valuation of the company. Examples of one-time costs include severance, lease terminations, real estate costs to separate facilities, or costs to procure technology infrastructure to separate systems.

35.5.5 Legal Entity Structure

Significant amount of value is locked within legal entity structure which controls country presence and tax structure and liabilities. Aligning early on country presence and legal entity strategy then translates into a detailed tactical execution plan that takes several months to execute.

35.6 Robust Execution Plan Anchored on Dependencies

Detailed and robust execution plans that are aligned for dependencies and account for the long poles in the tent are critical to drive program management success. A great way to achieve this degree of granularity in work plans and to drive cross-functional alignment is by hosting a "Walk-the-Walls" workshop in which the functional teams work together to determine major milestones that must be tracked to ensure timely project completion before the teams dive into execution. This workshop also helps identify dependencies between milestones and workstreams. For example, a major responsibility of the treasury function is to set up new and separate bank accounts for the divested entity. These timelines must match with IT testing timelines in order for the end-to-end process to be tested and operational. The cross-functional Walk-the-Wall sessions is a great forum to drive alignment between the execution plans of both teams and help de-risk execution.

Splitting companies with hundreds of employees, interconnected systems, and applications can be extremely complex, and there may be a bias to transform while separating or to develop a new and industry leading solution that may drive cost, complexity, and execution time. In developing the detailed execution approach and plans, the SMO should ensure the workstreams involved maintain a balance between speed and perfection and are solving for what has been agreed upon between the executives of both companies and is legally required. It's essential to pressure test these plans to help ensure that the teams are not adding undue risk and complexity in order to develop a solution that is beyond the immediate call of duty. The goal should be to separate first and optimize later unless the deal terms require different outcomes.

"Understanding what the big rocks were and focusing on those helped provide clarity on priorities." — *Fortune 50 Tech Giant*

35.7 Capture the Hearts and Minds

Last, but not the least, separations are gut-wrenchingly difficult experiences for the organization. The uncertainty, the division of teams, and the extra workload can significantly impact motivation and engagements of staff and leaders alike, especially when multiple separations or transformations have occurred sequentially.

When a $110B organization split into two Fortune 50 companies, it used the separation as an opportunity to rebuild culture and to drive employee motivation and engagement. As the stock market responded and rewarded the separation efforts, and as the organization rewarded those who enabled a successful separation, employee engagement improved. In parallel, the company unveiled its vision of the future driving increased levels of motivation and excitement.

The mantra to effectively addressing the emotions of internal and external stakeholders is to engage them frequently and communicate successes early and often. Articulate the vision and strategy clearly, and share success stories and execution wins, as well as wins in the marketplace to connect with both internal and external stakeholders and bring them along for the journey.

35.8   Conclusion

The strong governance and structure and breadth and depth of skill allowed one of the most complex and largest divestitures to complete on time with no issues. Operational separation was achieved in 10 months, 3 months ahead of schedule.

Case Study: 35

Background

A Fortune 10 diversified technology company, with over $110B in annual revenues, found itself in multiple markets with multiple product lines after years of acquisitions, several of which were not yielding growth. Differences in the business model across these product lines and business units meant dis-synergies and complexity. In parallel, several segments were declining in growth due to industry headwinds and the company was losing revenue and margin, while losing ground to competitors.

Challenge

The company made a strategic decision to split into two—both firms would have yearly revenues exceeding $55B, across 115+ countries, making it the largest and one of the most complex corporate divestitures in history. The divestiture involved multiple functions working under tight timelines to execute the transaction. There were many interdependencies between the functions, which added to the complexity of the divestiture. The company had less than 1 year to complete two operational cutovers, before completing its legal separation.

Approach

Three Separation Management Offices (SMOs) were established, one for SpinCo, one for RemainCo, and one to manage core functions that were common across both pillars, to centrally drive the program and to ensure leadership alignment and issue resolution. Governance was simple and effective—with decision-making power resting with a few critical individuals and a broader inform-and-consult approach with other important executives. The approach centered on separating effectively, while creating an efficient organization in parallel.

Impact/Results

A structured programmatic cadence and process was established to drive clear visibility into status, issues, and risks. A clear master narrative was established to drive clarity on the 11-month journey from start to finish and to focus organizational energy toward that road map. The strategic direction was issued by the CEO in very clear and unambiguous terms; the Separation Management Office then translated that into strategic decisions that governed the separation journey. Operating model decisions were made early and were adopted within functional blueprinting. These blueprints then became the basis of the execution plan.

The SMOs monitored cross-functional activities, held weekly status check-ins with workstreams, managed executive reporting, and escalated and resolved issues. They held a kick-off workshop to establish guiding principles that would govern the project and develop cross-functional Day 1 plans. Fifteen functional workstreams were identified and responsible for executing Day 1 plans.

Cross-functional dependencies were identified and tracked shortly after the kick-off in a Walk-the-Walls™ workshop. Cutover was managed by the SMO, a "transaction execution" team, and the functional workstreams. The transaction execution team oversaw country/regional execution and legal execution.

Teams were led through a variety of exercises to identify and confirm the milestones necessary for a successful Day 1. To facilitate the workshops, all initial timelines were printed and placed on the walls of a room so that the seller company's executive leadership and workstream leadership could visualize the necessary processes and requirements to achieve a successful Day 1.

Global command centers were established to triage and resolve risks and issues. The command centers utilized a "follow the sun" model, where multiple teams throughout Europe, Asia, and the Americas took shifts managing the command center to help ensure continuous coverage. The IT teams tested applications and systems to ensure cutover readiness and managed multiple blackouts.

Chapter 36
Summing It All Up

Companies are under constant pressure to increase shareholder value, and management can boost that value by divesting noncore businesses. Key to enhancing the deal value is by ensuring that the planned timeline and allocated budget to separate the divested entity from the seller company remain on target. This generally leads to a positive perception of the transaction by shareholders and may increase the seller company's stock price in the long term. On the contrary, execution delays and spiraling costs can quickly erode shareholders' perceptions about the value of the divestiture. Thus, it is essential to plan and execute an effective and realistic divestiture strategy that keeps the timeline and costs for the separation on target. A poorly planned divestiture strategy can not only erode shareholder value but also lead to the loss of customers and employees.

Some major challenges that can hinder an effective separation include:

- Complex and comingled assets that need to be separated
- Extraordinary speed of execution to meet the Day 1 timeline
- Governance and resource issues
- Executing normal business activities during the separation
- Adherence to country-specific regulations
- Regulatory and legal scrutiny of the divestiture

Deft planning, governance, and management of the divestiture throughout the deal execution life cycle can not only address the above challenges but also unlock additional value drivers for both the seller company and the divested entity.

36.1 Planning for the Divestiture

It is important to underpin the divestiture with an appropriate buyer-seller fit, a strong divestiture strategy, and a plan to address conflicting priorities.

© Deloitte Development LLC 2018
J. Joy, *Divestitures and Spin-Offs*, Management for Professionals,
https://doi.org/10.1007/978-1-4939-7662-1_36

36.1.1 Identifying the Appropriate Buyer

In order to identify the right buyer, the companies should document their strategic priorities and develop evaluation criteria for profiling potential buyers:

- Identify buyers with capabilities of their own that are a good fit to the purchase of the assets. Such buyers can make the best use of the capabilities (processes, governance, skills and technology, etc.) associated with the assets being divested.
- It is important to select a buyer that has the commitment to effectively execute the divestiture.
- Coordination between the seller company, the buyer company, and the divested entity is a critical aspect of identifying a buyer so identify a buyer that shares the values followed by the seller.

36.1.2 Defining the Divestiture Strategy

In a divestiture, some capabilities owned by the seller company must be transitioned out to the divested entity. As a result, it is essential to develop a comprehensive list of separation activities, a strategy to perform those activities, as well as a plan for how to operate the entities post-Day 1.

- Design a high-level operating model for the separation that contains the processes needed to perform the separation activities without disrupting the processes needed to perform business as usual during the separation.
- Develop a divestiture road map to complete all divestiture activities based on the operating model and processes.
- Establish functional and line-of-business teams.
- Establish a Separation Management Office (SMO) with defined roles and responsibilities for the separation.
- Create high-level documentation of the transition services that will be needed by the divested entity post-Day 1.

36.1.3 Addressing Legal, Finance, Human Resources, and Information Technology Considerations

A critical success factor for deal execution is coordination of separation activities across core functions affected by the divestiture, including legal, finance, human resources (HR), and information technology (IT). Key considerations across these functions are:

- *Legal:* For each country in which the divested entity will operate, a legal entity must be established to represent the divested entity. As a result, the IT team must grapple with diverse entity names, tax IDs, and banking and employee information.

- *HR:* It is important to develop an organizational structure with roles and responsibilities for the seller company and the divested entity in which HR function plays a critical role. Additionally, the HR and legal teams must work together to ensure adherence to country-specific labor laws for employee transitions to the divested entity or terminations from the seller company.
- *Finance:* Carve-out financial statements must be generated for the divested entity, and the time required for regulators to analyze these carve-out financial statements, as well as the time required to submit specific forms (e.g., Form 10-K), must be factored into the separation timeline.
- *IT:* A plan must be developed to separate IT applications and infrastructure between the seller company and the divested entity, including messaging capabilities, enterprise directories, data centers, networks, business applications, and unstructured data segregation.

36.2 Executing the Divestiture

Each of the following elements helps balance the risks and demands of a multi-faceted separation, while also creating a value (cost reduction or increased revenue) opportunity in the divestiture.

36.2.1 Dealing with the Financial Impacts of a Divestiture

Identifying and prioritizing Cost Reduction Opportunities (CROs) Following a divestiture, companies are frequently left with a disproportionately larger cost structure relative to their new size. The divestiture process provides the remaining company an opportunity to evaluate the overall cost structure and delivery of shared services. Due to a typical integration and proliferation of shared services, most companies need to formally baseline their current cost, identify areas where they can reduce cost, and pursue those opportunities with a disciplined focus.

These leading practices can help achieve cost reduction through divestitures:

- Identify and document CROs for application and infrastructure rationalization.
- Prioritize CROs.
- Assign accountability for addressing CROs.
- Develop CRO implementation plans.
- Document and track progress against CRO targets.
- Map CROs to the operating budget.

Stranded costs A divestiture transaction can leave the seller company burdened with a large portfolio that is disproportionate to its new and smaller size, thereby resulting in stranded costs. Stranded costs are costs that are "left behind" after the divestiture is complete like fixed IT cost, real estate, administrative and legal costs, etc. To minimize the stranded costs, extra resources must be divested or reabsorbed elsewhere. Stranded costs impact the divestiture in several different ways:

- Negatively affect the value of the divestiture
- Obscure business objectives
- Lead to decreased operational efficiency and reduced synergies
- Lead to inequality in supplier-buyer relationships because of an increase in supplier power

To avoid potential material stranded costs which may not be discovered until after the transaction, it is essential to analyze the costs, determine cost reduction targets, develop implementation plans, and continuously track progress in eliminating stranded costs.

36.2.2 Managing Confidentiality and Restrained Information Disclosure

Maintaining the confidentiality of the deal is critical to ensuring a successful divestiture. Information-sharing guidelines should be developed by the legal team and shared with the divestiture planning team. The flow of information during various phases of the divestiture life cycle can be controlled as follows:

- Due diligence phase (pre-deal announcement)
  - The seller company, potential buyer company, and third-party consultants must sign nondisclosure agreements (NDAs).
  - Use clean teams in a clean room to perform due diligence.
- From deal announcement to Day 1
  - Information disclosure should be followed with caution through risk assessment behind every information exchange between the buyer and the seller.
  - Legal- and technology-related controls should be applied for information exchange channels like legal review and approval before any material information can be exchanged.
  - Maintaining technology-based audit trail for every information exchange through document management systems.
- Post-Day 1
  - This is generally the least risky stage for information exchange since the legal entities have been separated. Protocol to exchange new and archived information between the two businesses should be established and followed post-close interaction.

36.2.3   Protecting the Value of the Divestiture

An extended period of uncertainty resulting from the divestiture can jeopardize ongoing operations and customer service.

Employee Retention Programs: Since employees may be unsure about their future roles as well as the future of the new company, critical talent may jump ship to more stable competitors. Thus, developing an effective retention awards program for employees who remain with the company through the divestiture is essential. The retention awards program should:

- Define appropriate retention awards not only for key employees, but all personnel.
- Execute retention awards and manage effective change communications.
- Establish an ongoing governance structure for the retention awards program.

Develop Transition Services Agreements (TSAs): TSAs are needed to help ensure the business continuity of the buyer, seller, and divested entities post-Day 1. TSAs allow the receivers of transition services to develop their own capabilities or find new third-party providers to perform the required services. To develop effective TSAs, companies should:

- Explain the structure of TSAs and their role in the divestiture process.
- Engage all functions and lines of business to identify shared services requiring TSAs.
- Negotiate TSAs with service receivers (i.e., divested entity, buyer company).
- Develop and agree upon TSA exit plans, TSA management, and TSA governance.

Monitoring, Reporting, and Governance: Developing separation work plans, monitoring and tracking the progress of separation activities against milestones, and actively addressing separation issues as they arise are critical to achieving an efficient and effective separation on Day 1. Some key tips include:

- Use reporting cadence and governance processes established during the initial divestiture planning phases to communicate progress.
- Use divestiture work plans to develop functional and line-of-business status reports.
- Use a divestiture dashboard to manage and track the status of separation activities.
- Use weekly divestiture management meetings as forums to discuss cross-functional issues, and escalate any risks to leadership.

Day 1 Testing and Cutover Readiness: To help ensure separation readiness and effective cutover execution, the key business and IT processes separation should be tested:

- Determine areas and processes to pressure test including customer and partner linkages.

- Develop a detailed cutover plan.
- Perform a mock cutover.
- Establish a command center to manage cutover issues and execute the cutover.
- Identify the resources needed to perform cutover activities.
- Ramp up needed resources prior to cutover execution, and then reduce these resource levels post-Day 1, as the divested entity transitions to a steady state.

Execute and Monitor TSAs: Effectively executing and monitoring TSAs, including tracking the delivery of services, help manage the financial commitments involved in a divestiture:

- Implement TSA status reports to track the delivery of TSA services (and service levels, if applicable).
- Manage the overall status of TSA-related commitments, including timely invoicing for services rendered, invoice receipt and payment, and payment collection.
- Confirm details related to the termination of each TSA and ensure they are met prior to the related TSA exit.
- Refine TSA exit plans with updated timing and costs (including one-time project and exit costs) to ensure timely TSA exits.
- Facilitate the timely TSA exits by tracking exit plan progress.

Astute TSA management includes timely TSA exit that helps the buyer and the seller minimize the length of the entanglement.

36.3   Continuing with the Wins

A successfully executed divestiture often results in positive stock market sentiments for the seller company. Investors expect the seller company to be more efficient and nimble post-divestiture, as well as more capable of responding to changing market dynamics, since the seller company focuses only on its core businesses post-divestiture.

However, shareholder value creation is only a short-term gain. A divestiture, in essence, is only one step in the long journey toward sustainable value creation. Once the entire divestiture transaction has been successfully closed, the financial gains from the divestiture should be realized by the remaining company and laying the foundation for longer term wins. The seller company should refocus the overall organizational strategy to address the growth objectives of the remaining business. The following four approaches can help executives drive these growth objectives:

- *Clean-Sheet Approach*: The seller company's IT landscape, go-to-market strategy, and operating model often radically change as a result of a divestiture, which presents a unique opportunity to redefine business goals from a refreshed state, without any of the constraints or mistakes from the past. This refreshed state is referred to as a clean sheet. The clean-sheet approach enables the seller company to implement leading practices from the industry and proactively build capabilities to leverage market dynamics instead of merely responding to market trends.

- *Enterprise Transformation:* The divestiture of a business unit and its associated employees and IT infrastructure provides an opportunity for the seller company to transform the business by rationalizing legacy assets and processes, adopting new technologies and alliances that enable rapid growth. Particularly, the divestiture affords the seller company the opportunity to develop a new technology strategy that leads to better user experience and lower operational costs (e.g., moving to cloud-based solutions). Hence, divestitures can lead to a more nimble target state for the seller company that can respond more quickly to market trends.
- *Outsourcing:* Outsourcing processes or technology to third-party providers can help reduce the time and cost associated with separation. Some divestiture scenarios in which outsourcing can be most beneficial include:
  - The divested or carved-out entity's processes are tightly integrated with the seller company.
  - The buyer company wishes to keep the divested entity relatively independent.
  - The buyer company or divested entity requires long-term TSAs, but the seller company is not inclined to provide such TSAs.

However, outsourcing also comes with control, quality, and conflict-of-interest risks that must be managed.

- *Deploying Cash Proceeds for Growth:* Divestures generally lead to an increase in working capital for the seller company. These newly available funds can be used to invest in areas that support the seller company's future growth. Typically areas of investment include IT assets and human capital resources. Research and development (R&D) capabilities are often overlooked, but R&D can often lead to a substantial return on investment (ROI). Thus, the seller company should consider boosting its R&D budget, along with new IT systems, processes and clean-sheeting the business and functions.

36.4   Conclusion

Divestitures are complex endeavors. A divestiture permeates virtually all functions of a company. Although a divestiture can offer tremendous opportunities to transform the business, it also creates its own perils. Without expertise in divestiture planning, companies may find it difficult to execute divestitures effectively enough to grow and generate positive enterprise value. By applying leading divestiture management practices, companies can divest rapidly, perform serial divestitures, transform the business, and enhance business efficacy. The companies that can trim down to their core businesses through divestitures are likely in the best position to command their market segments and grow rapidly, while generating the greatest shareholder value.

Appendix A: Divestiture Playbook Overview

Given the complexity that divestitures entail, as well as the multiple interdependencies and coordination required across all areas of the organization, it is a good practice to develop a divestiture playbook. A divestiture playbook will provide guidelines and define ground rules for all relevant parties to understand their roles within the transaction and march toward the same goals.

A divestiture playbook is a prescriptive guide that documents the steps and considerations required for a successful transaction from due diligence to Day 1. No company and no transaction are the same, which is why the playbook is tailored for the peculiarities of the organization, and it should be flexible to allow for fine-tuning throughout execution.

Scope of the Playbook

The breadth and depth of themes to be covered in a divestiture playbook will vary depending on specific aspects of the organization and the divestiture itself. Sometimes the playbook is a compilation of individual playbooks that as a whole provide a complete and detailed view of the phases or components of the divestiture. The following themes are typically covered in playbooks:

- Governance structure: The playbook should address clearly the hierarchical structure, levels of reporting, and escalation points across all the participating groups and individuals. It should also define the organizational structure of the Divestiture Management Office (DMO) or Separation Management Office (SMO) that centrally drives and orchestrates all workstreams across the transaction.
- Processes and methodologies: In order to successfully execute the divestiture, the standard process, methodologies, and tools should be leveraged including

© Deloitte Development LLC 2018

J. Joy, *Divestitures and Spin-Offs*, Management for Professionals,
https://doi.org/10.1007/978-1-4939-7662-1

project management tools, budget and resourcing allocation procedures, and software development life cycle methodology.

- Business processes blueprinting: It is recommended that the process and timeline to create the blueprints of the future state is clearly documented, identifying dependencies and owners
- Organizational design: Given the relevance, sensitivity of the information managed, and complexity of this thread, the organizational design of the divested and remaining entities can constitute a playbook by itself. The organizational design playbook outlines the road map to setting up the new organizations from roles and positions definition to training and change management.
- Risk management: Continual and consistent assessment of risk from early phases of the transaction throughout execution until Day 1 is a key component to be addressed as part of the divestiture playbook to help ensure compliance and appropriate management of the risks that the divestiture entails.
- Information technology: This can be one of the most extensive playbooks with a variety of themes to cover from software design to deployment. Given the criticality and almost surgical detail that requires the deployment of the changes in the IT landscape to support the business operations for all entities, it is common to have deployment or cutover playbooks that provide ample guidance on all the necessary steps to develop and execute the deployment or cutover plans.
- Infrastructure: The strategies to disposition hardware and data centers and separate the network (including voice and data), end-user computing, and active directory migration should be addressed in the playbook. The approach for standing up the infrastructure of the separated entities is also in scope of the playbook.
- Security and compliance: Privacy and data segregation are always a top concern for executives when undergoing a divestiture. The security and access policies and controls that are required to help ensure the confidentiality of information when divesting are of topmost relevance and need to be defined in the early stages of planning, since that will drive the design and development of solutions, such as logical and physical segregation of data in system (if they will be shared) or redefining access levels to employees of the separated entities.
- Communications model: Outline the communications strategy for the different audiences, including employees, customers, partners, vendors, and the buyer or divested entity (if applicable) for the different phases of the transaction. Clearly outline what is considered classified information and who is responsible for sharing what information at particular points in time.

The divestiture playbook should be a live document that evolves with the company's experience on M&A transactions and corporate directions. As a set of guidelines, the playbook should remain relevant, incorporating learnings, trends, and leading practices. It might also become part of an M&A playbook, as companies typically go through different growth and diversification cycles, and make acquisitions after a divestiture.

Sample Table of Contents

Following is a sample table of context for a divestiture playbook:

7. Organizational Design

   7.1. Organizational Structure Definition
   7.2. Employee Communications and Training
   7.3. Change Management

8. Post-Day 1 Planning

   8.1. Transition Services Agreements (TSA) costs and operations
   8.2. Post-TSA plans
   8.3. Stranded Cost planning

9. Appendix

   9.1. Templates
   9.2. Tools and Accelerators
   9.3. Glossary

Tools and Templates

An important value add of a well-built divestiture playbook is the inclusion of tools and templates that can help save executors valuable time, while also enforcing homogeneity across different teams and business units. The tools and templates should be flexible enough to be adapted to different teams and phases of the transaction. For the tools and templates to be easily leveraged, there should be a common set of definitions and internal jargon that is understood and adopted by all workstreams. For example, having a common definition of a project's health, where there is a single connotation for green, yellow, and red across different teams, is a critical component for tools to be collectively utilized and for information retrieved from the tools to be standard. The following is a non-exhaustive list of typical tools and templates in a divestiture:

- Program/project welcome pack (includes program overview, logistics information, points of contact, FAQ's)
- Generic project plans/work plans
- Project status reporting templates
- Budget request forms
- Program roster/contacts
- Meeting minutes and action items templates
- IT project plans by application disposition
- Security requirements forms
- Transition services agreements checklist
- Day 1 readiness checklist
- Go/no-go checklist

It is also a good practice to keep the project tools stored in a central location organized and controlled in such a way that only people that require them have access. This shared location should have a logical structure that the teams can easily follow so they can rapidly find the most current versions of the materials they are looking for.

Corporations that have gone through previous M&A experiences can also include sample deliverables that can help as a point of reference and include lessons learned from previous deals. A few examples of such sample deliverables are:

- Sample current state assessment report
- Sample future state infrastructure blueprint
- Sample program dependency matrix
- Sample testing plan
- Sample go-live simulation plan
- Sample cutover plan

Conclusion

No company is the same, even when comparing to the very same corporation from a few years earlier. Despite the uniqueness of each deal, there are always common principles and basics that can be applied, along with learnings from previous experience that provide a solid foundation for future transaction executions. An organization that dedicates the resources and effort into building a divestiture playbook can better manage the complexities of such changes to the business that are native to a divestiture. It is also worth highlighting that, as good as a handbook can be, the playbook's goal is to provide structure and direction, but it does not replace the strategic thinking, problem-solving, and critical decision-making required from all levels of the organization involved in the execution for a successful divestiture.

Appendix B: Glossary

Key term	Abbreviation	Definition
Cutover	None	Focuses on executing the plans required for day 1 readiness, including but not limited to • Separation of people, processes, and systems • Provision of transition services agreements (TSAs) • Ensuring the separation does not negatively affect customers, suppliers, or employees
Defense readiness condition	DEFCON	The defense readiness condition (DEFCON) is an alert state used by the United States Armed Forces. It prescribes five graduated levels of readiness (or states of alert) for the US military. It increases in severity from DEFCON 5 (least severe) to DEFCON 1 (most severe) to match varying military situations
Integrated cutover plan	ICP	ICP is a sequenced plan for the completion of all critical path business and IT cutover tasks, and it includes detailed timing and duration estimates to migrate functionality into production
Letter of intent	LOI	Letter of intent outlines the terms of a deal and serves as an "agreement to agree" between two parties
Memorandum of understanding	MoU	Memorandum of understanding is a nonbinding agreement between two or more parties outlining the terms and details of an understanding, including each parties' requirements and responsibilities
Nondisclosure agreement	NDA	A nondisclosure agreement (NDA) is a legal contract between two or more parties that signifies a confidential relationship exists between the parties involved
Software as a service	SaaS	Software as a service is a software licensing and delivery model in which software is licensed on a subscription basis and is centrally hosted
Accounts payable	AP	N/A

(continued)

© Deloitte Development LLC 2018
J. Joy, *Divestitures and Spin-Offs*, Management for Professionals,
https://doi.org/10.1007/978-1-4939-7662-1

Key term	Abbreviation	Definition
Accounts receivable	AR	N/A
Application separation life cycle	ASLC	N/A
Asset deal	None	In an asset deal, the seller retains possession of the legal entity and sells the individual assets of the business
Big bang (cutover)	None	All day 1 cutover activities are executed in one stretch, including implementation of all cutover-related code changes and the simultaneous migration of employees and customers from RemainCo to their respective information technology (IT) landscapes
Data room	None	A virtual online data room will be set up and hosted by one of the few recognized professional data room providers. Physical data rooms are no longer standard but may be used in specific situations
De minimis provision	None	This is an agreement according to which only claims exceeding a certain amount per each single claim will be considered
Enterprise resource planning	ERP	N/A
HR business partners	HRBP	N/A
Key performance indicators	KPI	N/A
Information and consultation process	(I&C process)	Information and consultation process (I&C process) is an HR activity related to employee information including consultation with established works councils and/or unions
Most favored	MFN	N/A
Nondisclosure agreement	NDA	N/A
Organization resign and structure	ODS	This is an organizational development technique for identifying organization roles and responsibilities and align them in a structure
Share deal	None	Share deal—In a share deal, the seller sells the shares in the entity itself. Refer to asset deal
Software development life cycle	SDLC	N/A
Service-level agreement	SLA	N/A
Secure file transfer protocol	SFTP	N/A

(continued)

Key term	Abbreviation	Definition
Stock sale	None	In the context of a stock sale, seller will recognize a tax gain or loss based on the difference between the consideration received and the tax basis in the target shares
Target	None	Refers to the distributed corporation
Tax and legal step plan	TLSP	N/A
Treasury management system	TMS	N/A
Transition services agreement	TSA	N/A
User acceptance testing	UAT	N/A
Vendor setup	None	Setting up the new entities in their systems
Works council	None	Works councils are organizations that represent employees at the local level in many countries outside the United States—Majority of these are located in the EMEA region (Europe, Middle East, and Africa)
Command center	None	A central coordination unit that oversees cutover activities, facilitates coordination across teams, and resolves issues through effective decision-making
CAIRO matrix	None	Consulted, accountable, informed, responsible, and omitted—Provides a clearly defined roles and responsibilities matrix
Extract, transform, and load	ETL	Extract, transform, and load is a process that pertains to data and is generally followed while migrating data from one environment to another
RACI matrix	None	Responsible, accountable, consulted, and informed—Provides a clearly defined roles and responsibilities matrix
Red, amber, green status	RAG status	Red, amber, and green status is the mechanism for reflecting progress of a project or a program usually against the planned schedule
Risk and issue identification	RAID	N/A
Subject matter expert	SME	Subject matter experts come from various business units and have expertise and knowledge of the business processes, applications, and data needed by the business unit
Security operations center	SOC	A security operations center is a centralized unit that deals with security issues on an organizational and technical level
Secure file transfer protocol	SFTP	A standard protocol used for the transfer of data from one location to another in a secured manner
Wide area network	WAN	A telecommunications network or computer network that extends over a large geographical distance
Questions and answers	Q&A	N/A
War room	None	Establishment of a strong governance model to manage cross collaboration and appropriate escalation when required

Index

A

Accounts payable (AP), 172
Accounts receivable (AR), 172
Aligning partnerships, 215, 218, 219
Anti-money laundering (AML), 178
Antitrust requirements, 13
Application blueprinting
    blueprint interlock sessions, 234
    business processes, 234
    develop execution plans, 235
    document business processes, 232
    sub-phases, 232
Application disposition
    decision tree, 230
    definition, 228, 229
    high-level application categorization, 228
Application rebranding, 208–210
Application separation life cycle
        (ASLC), 221, 223, 224
    activities, 224
    application inventory collection, 226
    application profile creation, 226, 227
    baselining application landscape, 225–227
    cutover, 238
    deal governance structure, 227
    design and development, 236
    requirements analysis, 235
    testing, 236, 237
Approaches to divestiture, 37
Asia-Pacific (APJ), 297
Asset allocation in divestiture
    categorize, 49
    considerations, 48
    criteria, 50
    distribution, 53
    separation, 52
Asset deal divestiture, 185, 186
Asset inventory, 49
Asset trades, 14

B

Balance sheet, 73
Balanced portfolio during divestiture, 213, 218
Banking connectivity, 178
Banking implication of divestiture
    company's treasury function, 169
    primary objective, 170
    purchasing company, 170
Benefits of outsourcing during
        divestiture, 426–428
Big bang cutover, 276
Business (B2B) companies, 204
Business continuity plan (BCP), 284, 389
Business engagement, 215, 216
Business intent, 394
Business to consumer (B2C), 204
Business unit (BU) level, 301
Business-as-usual (BAU), 314, 394
Buyers
    alignment, 126, 127
    conduct due diligence, 27
    deliberations and analyses, 26
    management presentation, 26
    preliminary due diligence, 28
    requests, 27
    and seller companies, 3, 14
    treasury system, 175

CPSIA information can be obtained
at www.ICGtesting.com
Printed in the USA
LVHW060730240619
622154LV00001B/45/P